JN412047

제8판

재무관리

김 남 곤

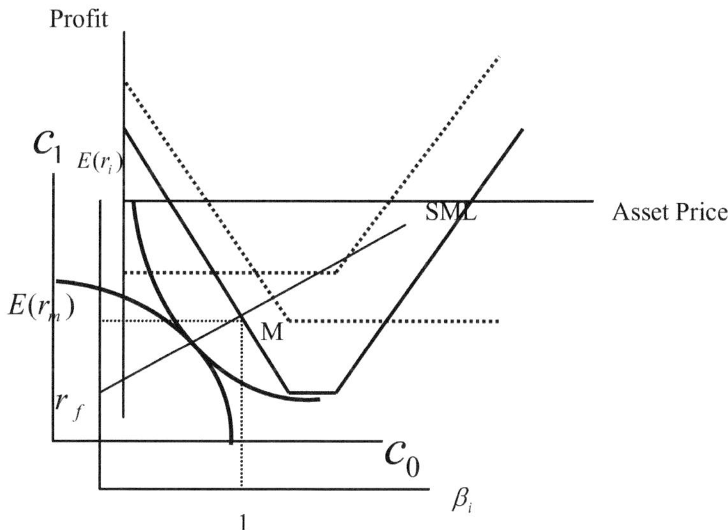

經 文 社

〈Essence, Easy, Example, English, Effective〉

Globalization으로 세계 사회가 정치적, 경제적, 문화적으로 더욱 밀접하게 연결되고 있고, 영어가 Global language로서 사용되고 있으며, 경영학이나 재무관리에서는 특히 영어가 중요하게 사용되고 있다. 재무관리를 공부하는 학생들은 재무관리 이론에 대해 정확하게 잘 이해하고, 재무관리 분야에 대한 깊이 있는 지식을 학습하기 위해 영어 실력을 향상시킬 필요가 있으며, 재무관리에서 사용되는 영어 표현에 익숙해지는 기회를 통하여 재무분야에 대한 향후의 심화학습으로 쉽게 발전시켜 나갈 수 있다.

이 책은 다양한 Numerical Example과 재무관리 분야의 English Expression을 통하여, 재무관리의 핵심적이고 기본적인 내용을 학생들이 쉽게, 그리고 효과적으로 이해할 수 있게 하는 데 중점을 두고 작성하였다. 자본조달과 투자결정에 관한 의사결정 문제를 다루는 재무관리의 핵심적 내용(Essence)을 쉽게(Easy) 전달하기 위해 예제(Example) 중심으로 설명하였으며, 영어(English) 표현에 익숙할 수 있는 기회를 제공하여 재무관리를 효과적(Effective)으로 이해할 수 있도록 하였다.

2026년 2월

김남곤

Contents

chapter

1

Introduction to Finance

What is Corporate Finance?

Two Key Result Areas in Corporate Finance

Investment Decisions

What projects to invest in.

Financing Decisions

How to pay for the projects.

The two key result areas in corporate finance are investment decisions, which involve choosing projects to invest in, and financing decisions, which involve determining how to pay for those projects.

The Financial Manager's Role

1) Raise funds from investors
2) Invest funds in value-enhancing projects
3) Manage funds generated by operations
4) Return funds to investors
5) Reinvest funds in new projects

The financial manager's role encompasses raising funds from investors, investing those funds in value-enhancing projects, managing funds generated by operations, returning funds to investors, and reinvesting funds in new projects to optimize financial resources and maximize shareholder value.
재무 담당자는 기업의 자금수요를 예측하고(anticipating), 예상되는 필요자금을 조달하고 (acquiring), 조달된 자금을 기업내의 자산에 배분하는(allocating) 종합적 기능을 수행한다.

The financial manager must find answers to three kinds of important questions.
What long-term investments should the firm take on?
How can cash be raised for the required investments?
How will the firm manage its day-to-day cash and financial affairs?

What are the two components of financial strategy?
The two components of financial strategy are:
Raising the funds needed by a firm in the most appropriate manner.
Managing the employment of those funds within the firm.

The four decisions in financial strategy
The four decisions in financial strategy encompass:
How large should the asset base be, and in what assets?
How much of the finance should be debt, and how much in equity?
How much profit should be paid out in dividend, and how much retained?
Should new equity be issued?

What is the difference between capital market theories and financial strategies?

Capital market theories are mainly concerned with the macro economic level, whereas financial strategies are specific and tailored to the needs of the individual company.

The two-stage investment process

Investors choose the companies in which they want to invest, and the companies choose how to apply those funds to their activities.

Two different types of investments are:

Investment in Business:

Investment in business refers to the process by which companies acquire or develop assets or facilities to improve productivity.

Such investments are typically used to support and enhance the production and operations processes of a company, leading to improved business performance.

For example, purchasing new production equipment, upgrading existing facilities, or conducting research and development activities are examples of investment in business.

Investment in business refers to allocating funds or resources to acquire assets, improve operations, or expand activities within a business entity. It involves investing in tangible or intangible assets such as machinery, equipment, research and development, marketing, or infrastructure to enhance productivity, efficiency, and growth prospects.

"Investment in business" involves allocating funds to acquire assets or improve operations within a company, aiming to enhance productivity and generate long-term returns through improved business performance. This may include investments in tangible assets like machinery or equipment, as well as intangible assets like research and development or marketing efforts.

Investment in Stocks:

Investment in stocks involves purchasing and holding shares in the stock market.

Stock investors hold a portion of ownership in a company and can profit or incur losses based on changes in the stock price in the market.

Such investments are typically made with the goal of pursuing long-term investment returns or for short-term trading purposes.

Investment in business involves acquiring or developing assets to improve productivity and operations, while investment in stocks involves purchasing shares in the stock market with the aim of making profits from changes in stock prices.

Investment in business focuses on enhancing the operations and productivity of a company, while investment in stocks involves participating in the ownership and financial performance of publicly traded companies.

Types of business organization

Proprietorships

A proprietorship is a form of business organization with a single owner who has unlimited liability for the firm's debts and other legal obligations.

Advantages: Easy to establish, simple decision making process, and profits are only taxed once.

Partnerships

A partnership is a form of business organization involves two or more owners who both unlimited liability for the debts and other legal obligations of the partnership.

Advantages: Easy to establish, decision making is diversified among partners, and profits are only taxed once.

Corporations

A corporation is owned by its stockholders, and their liability is legally limited to the amount of money they have invested in the firm. The firm is a legal entity that pays corporate income taxes.

Advantages: Owners have limited liability, large amounts of relatively inexpensive capital are available, and management expertise is not limited to that of the owners.

Disadvantages: Relatively complex management structure may make the decision-making process slow and costly, and double taxation — corporate earnings are taxed when earned and again when distributed to owners as dividends.

Example

Company X announced a total dividend of $500,000 paid to shareholders in the upcoming quarter. Currently, there are 1 million shares outstanding.
Calculate DPS.

Solution

The dividend per share would simply be the total dividend divided by the shares outstanding. In this case, it is $500,000 / 1,000,000 = $0.50 dividend per share.

DPR

DPR = Total Dividends / Net Income

DPR = Dividends Per Share / Earnings Per Share

The Dividend Payout Ratio is the amount of dividends paid to shareholders in relation to the total amount of net income the company generates. In other words, the dividend payout ratio measures the percentage of net income that is distributed to shareholders in the form of dividends.

To calculate the dividend payout ratio, the formula divides the dividend amount distributed in the period by the net income in the same period.

For example, if a company issued $20 million in dividends in the current period with $100 million in net income, the payout ratio would be 20%.

For example, let's assume Company ABC has earnings per share of $1 and pays dividends per share of $0.60. In this scenario, the payout ratio would be 60%. Let's further assume that Company XYZ has earnings per share of $2 and dividends per share of $1.50. In this scenario, the payout ratio is 75%.

Retained earnings

Retained earnings represent the accumulated profits of the company that have not been distributed as dividends.

Retained earnings represent the cumulative net income of a company that has been retained within the business rather than distributed to shareholders as dividends. It reflects the portion of profits that a company keeps and reinvests in its operations or uses to pay off debt rather than distributing them to its shareholders.

Example

ABC Corporation has a beginning retained earnings balance of $200,000 for the year. During the year, the company generates a net income of $50,000 and pays out dividends totaling $20,000 to its shareholders. What is ABC Corporation's retained earnings at the end of the year?

Solution

$230,000

RR

Retention Ratio

Retention Ratio = 1 − Payout Ratio

The Retention Ratio is the portion of net earnings that are retained by a company rather than being paid out as dividends to shareholders.

Example

Company ABC reported a net income of $20,000 for the year. In the same time period, Company ABC declared and issued $5,000 of dividends to its shareholders. Calculate DPR.

Solution

The DPR calculation is as follows:

$$DPR = \frac{5,000}{20,000} = 25\%$$

Therefore, a 25% dividend payout ratio shows that Company ABC is paying out 25% of its net income to shareholders. The remaining 75% of net income that is kept by the company for growth is called retained earnings.

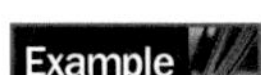

XYZ Inc. has reported a dividend per share of \$5 per share and an earning per share of \$20 per share. Calculate the Dividend Payout Ratio.

Solution

25%

Example

For instance, let's say a company has reported a net income of \$100,000 in 2024 and paid \$40,000 of annual dividends. Calculate the retention ratio.

Solution

60%

After-tax dividend

The term "after-tax dividend" refers to the amount of dividend income an investor receives after accounting for taxes.

After-tax dividends are dividends paid to shareholders after taxes have been deducted. When a company pays out dividends to its shareholders, those dividends are typically subject to taxation based on the investor's applicable tax rate.

Example

What is the after-tax dividend an investor would receive if a company declares a dividend of \$5 per share and the investor's tax rate on dividends is 15%?

Solution

$5(1-0.15)=\$4.25$

Example

What is the after-tax amount an individual would receive from a dividend payment if the total dividend per share is \$5 and the individual's tax rate on dividends is 15%?

Solution

$5(1-0.15)=\$4.25$

Example

You are a shareholder in a corporation. The corporation announces a profit of \$6 per share, of which it retains \$1 for reinvestment and distributes the rest as dividend payments. The corporate tax rate is 39%, the personal tax rate on dividends is 15%, and the personal tax rate on non-dividend income is 36%. What is the after-tax amount an individual would receive from the dividend?

Solution

$5(1-0.15)=\$4.25$

Example

A corporation earns \$8.30 per share before taxes and the company pays a dividend of \$4.00 per share. The corporate tax rate is 39%, the personal tax rate on dividends is 15%, and the personal tax rate on non-dividend income is 36%. What is the after-tax amount an individual would receive from the dividend?

Solution

$4(1-0.15)=\$3.4$

The ownership cycle

The ownership cycle includes some or all of the following steps:

1) Sole trader

2) Partnership

3) Company with equity funding from the management

4) Company with equity funding from close associates

5) Company with funding from private equity

6) Company with funding from the public

The ownership cycle for business includes sole trader, partnership, company funded by management, close associates, private equity, or the public through stock offerings.

Stocks

기업이 주식을 발행하여 조달한 자금은 대차대조표에 자기자본으로 계상된다. 기업이 발행한 채권은 은행으로부터 빌린 차입금과 마찬가지로 기업의 부채로 계상된다. 주식은 채권과 달리 만기가 없으며, 기업이 청산하는 경우를 제외하고는 기업으로부터 원금을 상환받지 못한다. 주주는 기업으로부터 배당금(dividends)을 받는데, 배당금은 그때그때 기업의 경영성과에 따라 달라질 수 있다. 배당과 달리, 채권에 대한 이자는 액면가의 일정한 비율로서, 채권을 발행할 때 정해진다.

기업이 청산할 때 채권자는 주주에 우선하여 자기 몫을 찾아갈 수 있다. 기업 자산에 대한 청구권자는 세무당국, 노동자, 원료공급자, 채권자, 주주 등이 있다. 기업이 청산할 때의 청구권 우선순위에서 주주의 순서는 맨 나중이다. 즉 여러 청구권자들에게 지불한 후 남는 금액이 주주의 몫이다. 만일 남는 금액이 없다면 주주는 아무 것도 가져갈 수 없게 된다. 그러므로 주주를 잔여청구권자(residual claimants)라고 부르기도 한다. 주주는 유한책임(limited liability)을 진다. 즉 기업이 청산할 경우 주주는 자기가 투자한 금액 이상의 부담을 지지 않는다.

Example

다음 진술이 맞으면 T, 틀리면 F

1) 채권자를 잔여청구권자(residual claimants)라고 부르기도 한다.
2) 회사가 영업을 잘 해서 발생한 이익을 주주들에게 나누어 주는 것을 이자라고 한다.
3) 기업의 자본금을 늘리는 방법으로 필요한 자금을 조달하는 것을 투자라 한다.

Solution

1) F, 주주를 잔여청구권자(residual claimants)라고 부르기도 한다.
2) F, 이익을 주주들에게 나누어 주는 것을 배당금이라고 한다.
3) F, 기업의 자본금을 늘리는 방법으로 필요한 자금을 조달하는 것을 증자라 한다.

Example

다음 진술 중 틀린 것은?

1) 채권은 회사의 해산시 주식에 우선하여 원리금을 지급받을 권리가 있다.

2) 채권자에게는 경영참가권이 있다.

3) 채권은 만기가 정해져 있는 반면, 주식은 만기가 없다.

4) 주식의 발행은 자본금의 증가를 수반하지만, 채권은 부채의 증가를 수반한다.

Solution

2)

주식 샘플

채권 샘플

일백만
三星電子株式會社 第80回社債券
金壹百萬원整
₩ 1,000,000
제 80 회
다 000000 호
발행일 1991년 11월 26일
상환일 1995년 11월 26일
이 채권은 삼성전자주식회사가 1991년 11월 4일 개최한 이사회 결의에 의하여
478조의 규정에 따라 이면에 기재한 조건으로 발행합니다.
見 樣
1991년 11월 26일
三星電子株式會社
代表理事 강 진 구
무보증
Ⅱ00720861Ⅱ

三星電子株式會社
제 80 회사채권
다 000000 호
이자지급교부표 ⑧
지급일 1993년 11월 26일

三星電子株式會社
제 80 회사채권
다 000000 호
이자지급교부표 ⑦
지급일 1993년 8월 26일

三星電子株式會社
제 80 회사채권
다 000000 호
이자지급교부표 ⑥
지급일 1993년 5월 26일

三星電子株式會社
제 80 회사채권
다 000000 호
이자지급교부표 ⑤
지급일 1993년 2월 26일

이자지급교부표 ④
지급일 1992년 11월 26일

이자지급교부표 ③
지급일 1992년 8월 26일

이자지급교부표 ②
지급일 1992년 5월 26일

이자지급교부표 ①
지급일 1992년 2월 26일

Characteristics of debt and equity

Debt is money borrowed by one party from another.

The borrower promises to repay the money in the future, usually with interest.

Principal: The original amount borrowed.

Maturity: The date by which the debt must be repaid.

Debt financing is generally considered low-risk due to fixed repayment terms and priority claims, while equity financing is high-risk with uncertain returns and lower priority in financial difficulties.

Debt financing typically does not offer potential upside beyond the fixed returns specified in the terms of the debt agreement. Lenders receive interest payments and principal repayment but do not participate in the company's profits or growth.

Equity financing offers the potential for high upside as investors share in the company's profits and growth. If the company performs well, shareholders can benefit from increasing stock prices and dividends.

	Debt	Equity
Risk to the investor	Low, protected by security and covenants	High
Yield	Interest, normally contractually agreed	Dividends, at the discretion of the directors
Potential upside to the investor	None	Very high

Debt is a low risk instrument from the lender's point of view. A contract is entered into which specifies how long the monies will be outstanding, and schedules their repayments; legally, the lender is a creditor of the company. The agreement also states what interest is to be paid, and how.

Equity is permanent capital for the company. The investor puts money into the company with no guarantee of any return at all. The yield comes, if it comes at all, at the directors' discretion, dependent on the levels of cash and profit, and the company's future investment needs.

Upside potential

The amount by which analysts or investors expect the price of a security may increase.

Interest Income vs Dividend Income

Interest income is money earned from lending money to someone else. When you lend money, the borrower pays you interest for the use of your money. The amount of interest you earn is determined by the interest rate and the amount of money you lend. For example, if you lend $100 at a 5% interest rate, you will earn $5 in interest income.

Dividend income is money earned from owning shares of stock in a company. When a company makes a profit, they can choose to either reinvest that money back into the business or pay it out to shareholders in the form of dividends. If you own shares of stock in a company that pays dividends, you will receive a portion of those dividends based on the number of shares you own.

The amount of dividend income you earn is determined by the dividend yield, which is the percentage of the stock price that is paid out in dividends. For example, if a stock is trading for $100 per share and has a dividend yield of 2%, you will earn $2 in dividend income for every share you own.

After-tax interest

"After-tax interest" refers to interest income that has been taxed. It represents the net interest remaining after taxes have been deducted from interest earned on deposits, investments, etc. The after-tax interest income is the amount of interest earned on an investment after accounting for taxes.

Example

How much would an individual's savings account balance be at the end of the year if they deposited $1,000 into an account with a 1% annual interest rate, considering a 20% tax rate on interest income?

Solution

After-tax interest income $= 10(1-0.2) = 8$

The individual's savings account balance at the end of the year would be $1,008.

Risk from different perspectives

	Debt	Equity
Features for issuer	Interest must be paid Repayments must be made The lender may have the right to repossess assets	Can choose whether to pay dividends No repayment obligation
Features for investor	Interest is contractual Repayment is contractual The lender may obtain security	Dividends are at the discretion of the company No right to receive capital back

Balance sheet

Example

A balance sheet example for XYZ Bakery

Cash: 10,000 Accounts Receivable: 5,000 Inventory: 15,000 Equipment: 30,000	Accounts Payable: 5,000 Long-term Debt: 15,000 Equity 40,000

V = 60,000

B = 20,000, S = 40,000

Accounts Receivable: This represents the amount of money owed to XYZ Bakery by its customers for goods or services that have been sold on credit.

Inventory: This is the value of the bakery's raw materials, work-in-progress, and finished goods that are ready for sale.

Equipment: This represents the value of the bakery's machinery, ovens, mixers, refrigerators, and other equipment used in production.

Accounts Payable: These are amounts the bakery owes to its suppliers or vendors for goods or services purchased on credit.

Long-term Debt: This represents debt that is due to be repaid over a period longer than one year.

The owner has contributed $40,000 of their own funds to finance the bakery's operations.

Income Statement

An income statement, also known as a profit and loss statement, is a financial statement that summarizes a company's revenues, expenses, and profits over a specific period of time. It provides valuable insights into a company's financial performance during the stated period. Here's a basic format and explanation of the components typically found in an income statement:

Revenue: This represents the total amount of money generated from the sale of goods or services during the specified period.

Cost of Goods Sold: This includes the direct costs associated with producing or purchasing the goods that were sold during the period.

Gross Profit: Gross profit is calculated by subtracting the COGS from the revenue.

Operating Income: It reflects the profit generated from a company's normal business operations.

Net Income: Net income, also known as net profit or the bottom line, is the final figure after deducting taxes from the income before taxes. It represents the company's overall profitability for the period.

The income statement provides valuable information to investors, creditors, and other stakeholders about a company's ability to generate profits, manage expenses, and sustain its operations over time. It is typically prepared on a quarterly and annual basis and is one of the key financial statements used in financial analysis and reporting.

FINANCIAL MANAGEMENT

chapter

2

Financial Analysis

The Balance sheet

대차대조표

The balance sheet states what the firm owns and how it is financed.

Assets = Liabilities + Stockholders' equity

대차대조표란 일정시점에서의 기업의 재무상태 즉 자산, 부채 및 자본의 내용을 수록한 표이다.
대차대조표는 자산과 이를 구입하기 위해 투입한 자본 및 부채를 좌우로 나눠 표로 정리한 것이다.
자본과 부채는 대차대조표의 오른쪽인 대변에 기록되어 자금의 조달원천을 나타내고 자산은 대차대조표의 왼쪽인 차변에 기록되어 조달된 자금의 운용상태를 나타낸다.

An asset is a resource controlled by the enterprise as a result of past events and from which future economic benefits are expected to flow to the enterprise.

Financial statements are the medium by which a company discloses information concerning its financial performance. The balance sheet represents a record of a company's assets, liabilities, and equity at a particular point in time.
Assets represent the resources that the business owns or controls at a given point in time. This includes items such as cash, inventory, machinery, and buildings. The other side of the equation represents the total value of the financing the company has used to acquire those assets.

The Income statement

손익계산서

The income statement measures performance over a specific period of time.

Net income is calculated as:

Total Revenue－Total Expenses=Net income

The first component in an income statement is Revenue.

The final component of an income statement is Net Income.

Revenue is the total amount of money a business earns from its activities, usually from the sale of goods or services. It's commonly referred to as "sales" or "top line" because it represents the starting point before any expenses are subtracted.

The formula:

Revenue=Price per Unit×Number of Units Sold

Example

ABC Company has total revenue of $500,000 and total expenses of $400,000. How much is its net income?

Solution

ABC Company's net income is $100,000.

손익계산서는 일정기간의 기업 경영성과를 나타내는 표이다.
생산이나 판매 등 기업의 고유한 영업활동의 결과로 발생한 손익은 영업손익이라 하고 이자의 수입과 지급 등 영업외적인 활동의 결과로 발생한 손익은 영업외손익으로 각각 구분하고 이들 활동과는 관계없이 발생한 손익을 특별손익, 기업이 얻은 모든 수익에서 기업이 지출한 모든 비용을 차감하여 순수하게 기업에 이익으로 남은 몫을 당기순이익이라 한다.

While the balance sheet takes a snapshot approach in examining a business, the income statement measures a company’s performance over a specific time frame.

GAAP

Generally Accepted Accounting Principles

Matching principle

GAAP says to show revenue when it accrues and match the expenses required to generate the revenue.

CFS

A statement reporting the impact of a firm's operating, investing and financing activities on cash flows over an accounting period.
The cash flow statement measures how well a company manages its cash position, meaning how well the company generates cash to pay its debt obligations and fund its operating expenses.

현금흐름표는 일정기간 동안 기업이 조달한 현금 내역과 조달된 현금이 어떻게 이용되었는가 하는 운용내역을 영업활동, 투자활동 및 재무활동으로 나누어 정리한 표이다.
현금은 기업이 경영활동을 수행하는 데 있어서 가장 중요한 재원일 것이다. 사람에게는 체내의 혈액순환이 건강을 유지하는데 중요하듯이 기업의 경우는 현금의 흐름이 중요하다.

The statement of cash flows represents a record of a business' cash inflows and outflows over a period of time.

CFFA
Cash Flow From Assets

CFFA = CF to creditors + CF to stockholders

The cash flow of a firm which is available for distribution to the firm's creditors and stockholders.

Interest rate

If you had invested the $10,000 in a savings account with a 5% annual interest rate, the interest earned over the year would be $500.

Growth rate

The growth rate typically refers to the rate at which a quantity increases over time. It is commonly used to describe the increase in the value of investments, revenues, earnings, or other financial metrics over a specific period.

The interest rate represents the cost of borrowing money or the return on investment for lending money. It is expressed as a percentage and is used to calculate the amount of interest charged or earned over a certain period of time. Interest rates can be fixed or variable and can vary depending on factors such as inflation, economic conditions, and central bank policies.

The growth rate measures the increase in value over time, while the interest rate represents the cost of borrowing or the return on investment. While they are both expressed as percentages, they are used in different contexts and calculations within finance.

Timeline

A timeline is a visual representation of events or data points arranged chronologically along a line. In finance, timelines are often used to illustrate the timing of cash flows, investments, or other financial events over a period of time.

Example

Translate the sentence into an equation.

The growth rate refers to the rate at which a quantity increases over time.

Solution

$$g = \frac{x_t - x_{t-1}}{x_{t-1}}$$

Growth rate

The growth rate refers to the rate at which a quantity increases over time.

$$g = \frac{x_t - x_{t-1}}{x_{t-1}}$$

$$g = \frac{x_t}{x_{t-1}} - 1$$

$$x_t = x_{t-1}(1+g)$$

For example, if a company's revenue increases from $100,000 last year to $120,000 this year, the growth rate would be 20%.

COGS (Cost of Goods Sold)

COGS is the total cost a company incurs to produce or purchase the goods it sells during a period.

It includes direct costs only, such as:

Cost of raw materials

Direct labor

Factory or production costs directly tied to the product

Freight-in (shipping cost to acquire inventory)

Cost of purchasing finished goods for resale

It does NOT include:

Selling expenses

Administrative expenses

Marketing

Freight-out (shipping to customers)

Basic Formula

COGS=Beginning Inventory+Purchases−Ending Inventory

Example

A company has:

Beginning inventory: $20,000

Purchases during the year: $50,000

Ending inventory: $15,000

COGS=20,000+50,000−15,000=55,000

So COGS = $55,000.

COGS in Income Statement

Sales−COGS=Gross Profit

A company reports the following information for the year:

Beginning Inventory: $30,000

Purchases: $85,000

Ending Inventory: $25,000

Calculate the Cost of Goods Sold (COGS).

Determine the company's gross profit if sales revenue was $150,000.

Calculate COGS

COGS

=Beginning Inventory

+Purchases

−Ending Inventory

COGS=Beginning Inventory+Purchases−Ending Inventory

COGS=30,000+85,000−25,000=90,000

So, COGS = $90,000.

Gross Profit

Gross Profit=Sales−COGS

Gross Profit

Gross Profit=150,000−90,000=60,000

So, gross profit = $60,000.

Depreciation is the accounting process of spreading the cost of a long-term asset (equipment, buildings, vehicles, etc.) over the years the asset is used.

Why do we depreciate?

Assets lose value as they are used.

Companies should match the cost of the asset to the revenue it helps generate each year.

Depreciation is a non-cash expense (no cash goes out, but it reduces taxable income).

Example

Cost = $100,000

Salvage value = $10,000

Useful life = 5 years

Depreciation expense = $18,000 per year

Example

A company purchases a machine for $100,000.

The machine has an estimated salvage value of $10,000 and a useful life of 5 years.

Using the straight-line depreciation method,

Calculate the annual depreciation expense.

Solution

The annual depreciation expense is $18,000 per year.

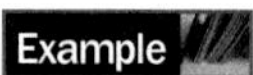

A company purchases a machine for $100,000.

The machine has an estimated salvage value of $10,000 and a useful life of 5 years.

Using the straight-line depreciation method,

Determine the book value at the end of Year 3.

Solution

The annual depreciation expense is $18,000 per year.

Year	Book Value
0	100,000
1	82,000
2	64,000
3	46,000
4	28,000
5	10,000

The book value at the end of Year 3 is $46,000.

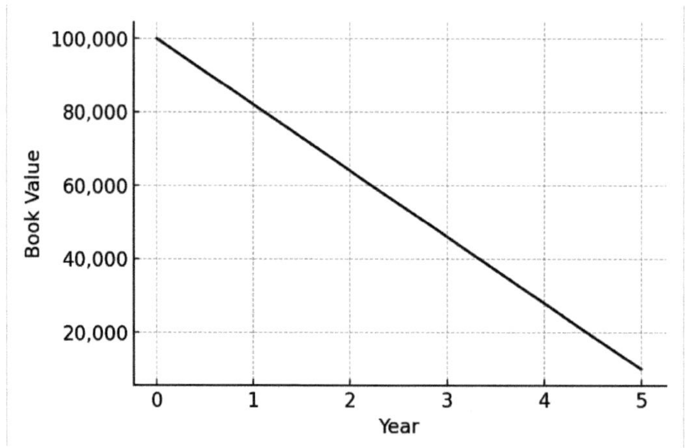

A company reports the following information for the year:

Beginning Inventory: $30,000

Purchases: $85,000

Ending Inventory: $25,000

Depreciation Expense: $12,000

Sales Revenue: $150,000

Calculate COGS.

Calculate Gross Profit.

Calculate Operating Income after deducting depreciation.

COGS

COGS=30,000+85,000−25,000=90,000

So COGS = $90,000.

Gross Profit

Gross Profit=150,000−90,000=60,000

So Gross Profit = $60,000.

Operating Income (after depreciation)

Operating Income

Operating Income=Gross Profit−Operating Expenses

Here, depreciation is the only operating expense given.

60,000−12,000–48,000

So Operating Income = $48,000.

Net income, also known as net profit or earnings, is a company's total revenue minus its total expenses. It's a key indicator of a company's profitability and is often reported on the income statement.

Mathematically, net income can be calculated as:

Net income=Total revenue−Total expenses

For example, if a company has total revenue of $500,000 and total expenses of $400,000, the net income would be $100,000.

For example, if a company's net income was $200,000 last year and $250,000 this year, the growth rate of net income would be 25%.

For example, if a company's total assets were $1,000,000 last year and $1,200,000 this year, the growth rate of assets would be 20%.

Net Cash Flow

The actual net cash, as opposed to accounting net income, that a firm generates during some specified period.

Net cash flow = Net income + Depreciation

The primary example of a noncash charge is depreciation. This item reduces net income but is not paid out in cash, so we add it back to net income when calculating net cash flow. Likewise, some taxes may be deferred and some revenues may not be collected in cash during the year, and these items must be subtracted from net income when calculating net cash flow. Typically, though, depreciation is by far the largest noncash item, and the other items often roughly net out to zero. Therefore, unless otherwise indicated, we will assume that noncash items other than depreciation sum to zero. Given the assumption, net cash flow equals net income plus depreciation.

Example

Write T for True and F for False statement. If the statement is false, correct the statement. The primary example of a noncash charge is depreciation. This item increases net income but is not paid out in cash, so we add it back to net income when calculating net cash flow.

Solution

F; The primary example of a noncash charge is depreciation. This item reduces net income but is not paid out in cash, so we add it back to net income when calculating net cash flow.

Depreciation

감가상각

Depreciation refers to two very different but related concepts:

1. the decline in value of assets, and
2. the allocation of the cost of assets to periods in which the assets are used.

The former affects values of businesses. The latter affects net income.

Depreciation is an annual charge against income which reflects the estimated dollar cost of the capital equipment used up in the production process.

유형자산은 용역잠재력이라는 물적 속성과 원가라는 가격속성을 갖고 있으며, 자산의 취득시에는 두 속성이 일치하였으나 시간이 지나고 사용함에 따라 용역잠재력이 감소하는 감가현상이 나타난다. 이러한 용역잠재력의 감소를 원가에 일치시키기 위하여 일정한 원가배분절차를 사용하며 이것이 감가상각이고 원가배분액이 감가상각비이다.
이것은 결국 상각자산이 수익을 획득하기 위하여 공헌한 가액을 평가하여 수익과 대응시키고 그 장부가치를 결정하는 것이다.
감가상각은 유형자산의 사용에 따른 수익과 비용의 적절한 대응을 위하여 유형자산의 원가를 효익이 실현되는 기간에 체계적이고 합리적인 방법으로 배분하는 원가배분의 과정이다.

감가상각비는 현금유출이 아닌 비용으로 이익을 감소시키는 효과가 있기 때문에 현금흐름에 영향을 주게 된다.
감가상각비의 감세효과는 [법인세율 × 감가상각비] 만큼의 현금유입으로 나타난다.

Straight-line Method

$$Depreciation\ \mathrm{Expense} = \frac{Acquisition\ \mathrm{cost} - Salvage\ value}{The\ Life\ of\ a\ machine}$$

정액법(straight-line method)은 자산의 내용년수 동안 매년 같은 금액의 감가상각비를 인식하는 방법이다.

In straight line depreciation method, depreciation is charged uniformly over the life of the asset. In this method, residual value of an asset is subtracted from its cost to get the depreciable amount. The depreciable amount is then divided by the useful life of the asset in number of periods to get the depreciation expense per period.

Salvage value

The estimated value of an asset at the end of its useful life.

Example

Write T for True and F for False statement. If the statement is false, correct the statement. In constant percentage depreciation method, depreciation is charged uniformly over the life of the asset.

Solution

F; In straight line depreciation method, depreciation is charged uniformly over the life of the asset.

Constant percentage Method

In this method, it is assumed that the property will lose its value by a constant percentage of its value at the beginning of every year.
For the constant percentage method over 2 years, the depreciation percentage is derived so that the asset goes from its initial value to a given final value in 2 years.

$$P = 1 - \sqrt{\frac{S}{A}}$$

P is the percentage.
S is the salvage value.
A is the acquisition cost.

$$Percentage = 1 - \sqrt[n]{\frac{Salvage\ Value}{Acquisition\ Cost}}$$

$$P = 1 - \sqrt[n]{\frac{S}{A}}$$

P is the percentage.
S is the salvage value.
A is the acquisition cost.
n is the number of periods.

정률법(constant percentage method)은 내용년수 말의 자산의 장부가치가 잔존가치와 일치하도록 매년 사용할 일정한 상각률을 계산한 후 특정년도의 감가상각비를 [기초장부가치×감가상각률]로 계산하는 방법이다.

Example

Suppose an asset with a two year life.

Show $Percentage = 1 - \sqrt{\frac{Salvage\ Value}{Acquisition\ Cost}}$ in Constant percentage method.

Solution

0	1	2
A	$A(1-P)$	$A(1-P)^2$
	$A \cdot P$	$A(1-P)P$

$$A(1-P)^2 = S$$

$$(1-P)^2 = \frac{S}{A}$$

$$1-P = \sqrt{\frac{S}{A}}$$

$$P = 1 - \sqrt{\frac{S}{A}}$$

Example

Suppose an asset with a two year life.

Using the constant percentage method, the expense is (　　) in the first year and (　　) in the second year.

Solution

0	1	2
A	$A(1-P)$	$A(1-P)^2$
	$A \cdot P$	$A(1-P)P$

Using the constant percentage method, the expense is AP in the first year and A(1−P)P in the second year.

Example

Suppose an asset with a three year life.

Using the constant percentage method, the depreciation expense is (   ) in the third year.

Solution

0	1	2	3
A	$A(1-P)$	$A(1-P)^2$	$A(1-P)^3$
	$A \cdot P$	$A(1-P)P$	$A(1-P)^2P$

Using the constant percentage method, the depreciation expense is $A(1-P)^2P$ in the third year.

Example

Suppose an asset with a three year life.

Show $Percentage = 1 - \sqrt[3]{\frac{Salvage\ Value}{Acquisition\ Cost}}$ in Constant percentage method.

Solution

0	1	2	3
A	$A(1-P)$	$A(1-P)^2$	$A(1-P)^3$
	$A \cdot P$	$A(1-P)P$	$A(1-P)^2P$

$$A(1-P)^3 = S$$

$$(1-P)^3 = \frac{S}{A}$$

$$1-P = \sqrt[3]{\frac{S}{A}}$$

$$P = 1 - \sqrt[3]{\frac{S}{A}}$$

A company purchases a machine for 1,500,000 won with an estimated salvage value of 300,000 won at the end of its two-year useful life.

What is the annual depreciation expense for this machine using the straight-line method?

What is the book value of the machine at the end of the first year?

What is the book value of the machine at the end of the second year?

Solution

$$Depreciation\ Expense = \frac{Acquisition\ cost - Salvage\ value}{The\ Life\ of\ a\ machine} = 600,000$$

At the end of the first year, the book value of the machine is calculated by subtracting the accumulated depreciation for the first year from the original cost. In this case, the original cost of the machine is 1,500,000 won, and the depreciation expense for the first year, as calculated earlier, is 600,000 won. Therefore, the book value at the end of the first year is 900,000 won.

Moving to the end of the second year, we need to consider the total accumulated depreciation up to that point. By the end of the second year, the machine will have been depreciated by 600,000 won for the first year and an additional 600,000 won for the second year, totaling 1,200,000 won in accumulated depreciation. Subtracting this total accumulated depreciation from the original cost gives us the book value at the end of the second year, which is 300,000 won.

Thus, the book value of the machine gradually decreases from 900,000 won at the end of the first year to 300,000 won at the end of the second year, reflecting the portion of its cost that has been allocated as depreciation expense over the two-year period.

Year	0	1	2
Book Value	1,500,000	900,000	300,000
Depreciation		600,000	600,000

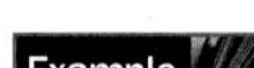

Assume that a company buys a machine at a cost of 1,500,000 won. The company decides on a salvage value of 300,000 won and a useful life of two years. Using the constant percentage method, the expense is (   ) in the first year and (   ) in the second year.

Solution

$$Percentage = 1 - \sqrt{\frac{S}{A}} = 1 - \sqrt{\frac{300{,}000}{1{,}500{,}000}} = 1 - \sqrt{0.2} = 55.3\%$$

Year	0	1	2
Book Value	1,500,000	670,500	300,000
Depreciation		829,500	370,787

Using the constant percentage method, the expense is 829,500 won in the first year and 370,787 won in the second year.

Example

수정이는 1,500,000원짜리 컴퓨터를 샀는데, 앞으로 2년 동안 사용한 후에 300,000원에 중고품으로 팔 예정이다. 정액법과 정률법에 따라 년도별 감가상각비와 장부가치를 구하라.

Solution

Straight-line Method

$$Depreciation\ \ Expense = \frac{Acquisition\ \text{cos}t - Salvage\ value}{The\ Life\ of\ \ a\ machine} = 600{,}000$$

Year	0	1	2
Book Value	1,500,000	900,000	300,000
Depreciation		600,000	600,000

Constant percentage Method

$$Percentage = 1 - \sqrt{\frac{S}{A}} = 1 - \sqrt{\frac{300,000}{1,500,000}} = 1 - \sqrt{0.2} = 55.3\%$$

Year	0	1	2
Book Value	1,500,000	670,500	300,000
Depreciation		829,500	370,787

Example

Assume that a company buys a machine at a cost of 1,000,000 won. The company decides on a salvage value of 400,000 won and a useful life of two years. The depreciable amount is (   ) and the annual depreciation using the straight-line method is (   ).

Solution

Year	0	1	2
Book Value	1,000,000	700,000	400,000
Depreciation		300,000	300,000

The depreciable amount is 600,000 won and the annual depreciation using the straight-line method is 300,000 won.

Example

Assume that a company buys a machine at a cost of 1,000,000 won. The company decides on a salvage value of 400,000 won and a useful life of two years. Using the constant percentage method, the expense is (   ) in the first year and (   ) in the second year.

Solution

$$Percentage = 1 - \sqrt{\frac{S}{A}} = 1 - \sqrt{\frac{400,000}{1,000,000}} = 1 - \sqrt{0.4} = 36.8\%$$

Year	0	1	2
Book Value	1,000,000	632,000	400,000
Depreciation		368,000	232,576

Using the constant percentage method, the expense is 368,000 won in the first year and 232,576 won in the second year.

Example

Assume that a company buys a machine at a cost of 2,000,000 won. The company decides on a salvage value of 500,000 won and a useful life of two years. The depreciable amount is (   ) and the annual depreciation using the straight-line method is (   ).

Solution

Year	0	1	2
Book Value	2,000,000	1,250,000	500,000
Depreciation		750,000	750,000

The depreciable amount is 1,500,000 won and the annual depreciation using the straight-line method is 750,000 won.

Assume that a company buys a machine at a cost of 800,000 won. The company decides on a salvage value of 200,000 won and a useful life of two years. The depreciable amount is (   ) and the annual depreciation using the straight-line method is (   ).

Solution

Year	0	1	2
Book Value	800,000	500,000	200,000
Depreciation		300,000	300,000

The depreciable amount is 600,000 won and the annual depreciation using the straight-line method is 300,000 won.

Example

Assume that a company buys a machine at a cost of 800,000 won. The company decides on a salvage value of 200,000 won and a useful life of two years. Using the constant percentage method, the expense is (   ) in the first year and (   ) in the second year.

Solution

$$Percentage = 1 - \sqrt{\frac{S}{A}} = 1 - \sqrt{\frac{200{,}000}{800{,}000}} = 1 - \sqrt{0.25} = 50\%$$

Year	0	1	2
Book Value	800,000	400,000	200,000
Depreciation		400,000	200,000

Using the constant percentage method, the expense is 400,000 won in the first year and 200,000 won in the second year.

Example

A company purchases a machine for $2,000,000 with an estimated salvage value of $500,000 at the end of its two-year useful life.

Using the constant percentage method:

What is the depreciation expense recorded in Year 1?

What is the book value of the machine at the end of the first year?

What is the book value of the machine at the end of the second year?

Solution

$$Percentage = 1 - \sqrt{\frac{S}{A}}$$

A = 2,000,000

S = 500,000

Plug these values into the formula.

$$Percentage = 1 - \sqrt{\frac{S}{A}} = 1 - \sqrt{\frac{500{,}000}{2{,}000{,}000}} = 1 - \sqrt{0.25} = 50\%$$

Using the constant percentage method, the expense is 1,000,000 won in the first year and 500,000 won in the second year.

Year	0	1	2
Book Value	2,000,000	1,000,000	500,000
Depreciation		1,000,000	500,000

What is “n” in this equation?

$\sqrt[n]{625} = 5$

Solution

The 4th root of 625 must be 5.

Example

대한기업은 내용년수가 5년인 기계를 구입하려고 한다. 이 기계의 구입원가는 10,000만원이며 5년 후의 잔존가치는 2,000만원이 될 것이라고 예상하고 있다. 이 회사의 법인세율이 30%일 때, 감가상각 방법으로 정액법을 이용하는 경우에 감가상각비와 감가상각비의 감세효과를 계산하면?

Solution

	1	2	3	4	5
감가상각비	1,600	1,600	1,600	1,600	1,600
감세효과	480	480	480	480	480

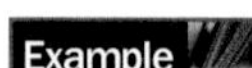

Assume that a company buys a machine at a cost of $10,000. The company decides on a salvage value of $2,000 and a useful life of five years. Using the constant percentage method, the expense is (   ) in the first year and (   ) in the second year. The 5th root of 0.2 is 72.48%.

Solution

$$Percentage = 1 - \sqrt[5]{\frac{2,000}{10,000}} = 27.52\%$$

	1	2	3	4	5
Book Value	7,248				2,000
Depreciation	2,752	1,995			

Using the constant percentage method, the expense is $2,752 in the first year and $1,995 in the second year.

Example

대한기업은 내용년수가 5년인 기계를 구입하려고 한다. 이 기계의 구입원가는 10,000만원이며 5년 후의 잔존가치는 2,000만원이 될 것이라고 예상하고 있다. 이 회사의 법인세율이 30%일 때, 감가상각방법으로 정률법을 이용하는 경우에 감가상각비와 감가상각비의 감세효과를 계산하면?

Solution

$$Percentage = 1 - \sqrt[5]{\frac{2,000}{10,000}} = 27.52\%$$

	1	2	3	4	5
장부가치	7,248	5,253	3,808	2,760	2,000
감가상각비	2,752	1,995	1,446	1,048	759
감세효과	826	598	434	314	228

Depreciation tax shield

A depreciation tax shield is a tax reduction technique under which depreciation expense is subtracted from taxable income.

$$Tax = t \times EBT$$

$$\begin{aligned} Tax &= t(Rev - COGS - Dep - Int) \\ &= t(Rev - COGS - Int) - tDep \end{aligned}$$

Example

If the applicable tax rate is 30% and the amount of depreciation that can be deducted is \$1,600, then the depreciation tax shield is (   ).

Solution

\$480

Example

If a company has an annual depreciation of \$2,000 and the rate of tax is set at 10%, the tax savings for the period is (   ).

Solution

\$200

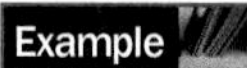

A company carries a debt balance of \$8,000,000 with a 10% cost of debt and a 20% tax rate. This company's tax savings is equivalent to the interest payment multiplied by the tax rate. The shield is (   ).

Solution

The shield is $8,000,000 \times 10\% \times 20\%$ = \$160,000. This is equivalent to the \$800,000 interest expense multiplied by 20%.

Example

A company carries a debt balance of \$8,000,000 with a 10% cost of debt and a 35% tax rate. This company's tax savings is equivalent to the interest payment multiplied by the tax rate. The shield is (   ).

Solution

The shield is $8,000,000 \times 10\% \times 35\%$ = \$280,000. This is equivalent to the \$800,000 interest expense multiplied by 35%.

Tax Shield

A tax shield is the reduction in income taxes that results from taking an allowable deduction from taxable income.

A tax shield is an allowable deduction from taxable income that results in a reduction of taxes owed.

Interest Tax Shield

The interest tax shield refers to the tax savings a company enjoys as a result of the tax-deductible nature of interest payments on debt. It represents the reduction in taxable income due to the interest expense.

Example

What amount of tax savings does a company with $2,500,000 in debt, a 6% annual interest rate, and subject to a 30% corporate tax rate, achieve due to the deductibility of interest payments?

Solution

Interest expense = Debt amount * Interest rate

= $2,500,000 * 6%

= $150,000

Interest tax shield = Interest expense * Tax rate

= $150,000 * 30%

= $45,000

Therefore, the interest tax shield for the company is $45,000. This represents the tax savings due to the deductibility of interest payments.

Noncash Items

Noncash items refer to expenses which do not directly affect cash flows.

The most important of these is depreciation.

Another noncash expense is deferred taxes.

Example

Suppose an asset with a five year life and no resale value is purchased for 2,500,000 won. According to accountants, the 2,500,000 won cost must be expensed over the useful life of the asset. From a finance perspective, the cost of the asset is the actual negative cash flow incurred when the asset is acquired.

	0	1	2	3	4	5
Book Value	2,500,000	2,000,000	1,500,000	1,000,000	500,000	0
Dep		500,000	500,000	500,000	500,000	500,000
Cash Flow	−2,500,000					

Example

On July 1, 2023, a company purchases a computer for $2,500 with cash. The computer is estimated to have a useful life of five years, so an annual depreciation expense of $500 is created for the next five years.

Operating Cash Flow

That cash flow which arises from normal operations

Operating cash flow = (Operating income)(1 − Tax rate) + Depreciation

After-tax Operating Income = Operating Income × (1 − Tax Rate)

After-tax operating income is determined by multiplying the operating income by one minus the tax rate, providing a measure of the profit generated by a company's core operations after accounting for taxes.

NOPLAT

NOPLAT is a financial term that stands for Net Operating Profit Less Adjusted Taxes. EBIT(1 − t) provides the after-tax operating income, adjusting Earnings Before Interest and Taxes for the impact of taxes.

Some alternative equations for calculating net income

$$\begin{aligned} Net\ Income &= EBT - Tax = EBT - t \times EBT = EBT(1-t) \\ &= (EBIT - Interest\ Expense) - t \times EBT \\ &= (EBIT - Interest\ Expense) - t(EBIT - Interest\ Expense) \\ &= (EBIT - Interest\ Expense)(1-t) \\ &= (Operating\ income - Interest\ Expense)(1-t) \end{aligned}$$

EAT = EBT(1 − t)

EAT is calculated by multiplying EBT by one minus the tax rate.

Write T for True and F for False equation. If the equation is false, correct the equation.

Net Income = EAT(1−t)

Solution

F,

Net Income = EBT(1−t)

EBIT

Earning Before Interest & Tax

Operating Income

The amount of profit realized from a business's operations after taking out operating expenses. A company's operating income is calculated by subtracting operating costs from revenue, and these values are shown on its income statement.

Revenue

The amount of money that a company actually receives during a specific period. Revenue is calculated by multiplying the price at which goods or services are sold by the number of units or amount sold.

Raw materials are the input goods or inventory that a company needs to manufacture its products.

COGS

An income statement figure which reflects the cost of obtaining raw materials and producing finished goods that are sold to consumers.

Cost of goods sold is an expense incurred from directly creating a product, including the raw materials and labor costs applied to it. However, in a merchandising business, the cost incurred is usually the actual amount of the finished product paid for by a merchandiser from a manufacturer or supplier.

Cost of goods sold is also referred to as “cost of sales”.

Example

Let's say we have a clothing store that sells various types of clothing items. Here are the relevant details for the fiscal year:

Beginning Inventory of Clothing: $50,000

Purchases Costs of Clothing: $200,000

Ending Inventory of Clothing: $70,000

Calculate COGS.

Solution

COGS = Beginning Inventory + Purchases Costs - Ending Inventory

Substituting the values:

COGS = $50,000 + $200,000 - $70,000

COGS = $180,000

So, the Cost of Goods Sold would be $180,000.

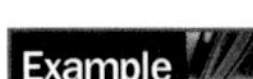

The cost of goods sold for a bakery typically includes expenses related to the ingredients used in baking, such as flour, sugar, yeast, eggs, butter, and flavorings. It may also encompass costs associated with packaging materials for finished products, as well as direct labor costs for bakery staff involved in production. Additionally, expenses related to utilities, equipment maintenance, and other overhead costs directly attributable to the production process may be factored into COGS calculations for a bakery.

Example

Last year K Inc. reported the following income statement:

Sales	2,000,000
Cost of goods sold	1,200,000
Depreciation	500,000
Operating income(EBIT)	300,000
Interest expense	100,000
EBT	200,000
Taxes (40%)	80,000
Net income	120,000

Assume that K's only noncash item was depreciation.

1) What was the company's net cash flow?

2) What was the company's operating cash flow?

Solution

1) Net cash flow = Net income + Depreciation

$$= \$120,000 + \$500,000 = \$620,000$$

2) Operating cash flow = (Operating income)(1 − Tax rate) + Depreciation

$$= \$300,000(1-0.4) + \$500,000$$

$$= \$680,000$$

Suppose you are given the following information for K company: Sales=$2,000,000; COGS=$1,200,000; Depreciation=$500,000; Interest expense=$100,000; tax rate=40%. What is the company's net cash flow?

Solution

Sales	2,000,000
Cost of goods sold	1,200,000
Depreciation	500,000
Operating income(EBIT)	300,000
Interest expense	100,000
EBT	200,000
Taxes (40%)	80,000
Net income	120,000

Net cash flow = Net income + Depreciation

= $120,000 + $500,000 = $620,000

Example

Last year J Inc. had $5,000,000 in operating income(EBIT). The company had an interest expense of $1,000,000; its corporate tax rate was 40 percent.

What was the company's net income for the year?

Solution

EBIT	5,000,000
Interest	1,000,000
EBT	4,000,000
Taxes (40%)	1,600,000
Net income	2,400,000

Example

Last year J Inc. had $5,000,000 in operating income(EBIT). The company had a depreciation expense of $1,000,000 and an interest expense of $1,000,000; its corporate tax rate was 40 percent. Assume that J's only noncash item was depreciation.

1. What was the company's net income for the year?
2. What was the company's net cash flow?
3. What was the company's operating cash flow?

Solution

1.

EBIT	5,000,000
Interest	1,000,000
EBT	4,000,000
Taxes (40%)	1,600,000
Net income	2,400,000

2. Net cash flow = Net income + Depreciation

= $2,400,000 + $1,000,000 = $3,400,000

3. Operating cash flow = (Operating income)(1 − Tax rate) + Depreciation

= $5,000,000(1 − 0.4) + $1,000,000

= $4,000,000

Operating Expenses

Operating expenses, operating expenditures, or "opex," refers to the costs incurred by a business for its operational activities. In other words, operating expenses are the costs that a company must make to perform its operational activities.

Operating expenses are essential for analyzing a company's operational performance. It is therefore important for both internal and external analysts to identify a company's opex, to understand its primary cost drivers, and assess management efficiency.

Before calculating a company's operational expenses, it is essential to identify the operational activities or the primary revenue-producing activities of the business and other activities that are not financing or investing activities.

The operating activities primarily cover the commercial activities of the company. For example, the main operating activity for a manufacturing company is to produce the product from raw materials, while for a trading company, it is to buy products from the supplier and sell them to the end-users.

For businesses, operating expenses may typically include advertising expenses, administration fees, wages, rent, and utility costs.
Capital expenditures are assets that are purchased and have a multiyear life, and are used in the operations of the business. Purchasing machinery, for example, is considered a capital expenditure, whereas, repair and maintenance of the machinery is considered an operating expense.

COGS vs. Operating Expenses comes down to how COGS are the direct cost of selling products/services while OpEx is the indirect costs not tied to revenue production.
Part of running a company properly is recording operating costs, which comprises two categories:

1. COGS
2. OpEx

COGS and operating expenses each represent costs incurred by the daily operations of a business.

COGS and OpEx are both considered "operating costs," which means that the expenses are related to the company's core operations.

The cost of goods sold line item represents the direct cost of selling products/services to customers.

Operating expenses, on the other hand, refer to the costs related to the core operations but NOT directly tied to revenue production.

The operating cost is deducted from revenue to arrive at operating income and is reflected on a company's income statement.

Operating costs are the ongoing expenses incurred from the normal day-to-day of running a business.
Operating costs include both costs of goods sold and other operating expenses—often called selling, general, and administrative expenses.
Common operating costs in addition to COGS may include rent, equipment, inventory costs, marketing, payroll, insurance, and funds allocated for research and development.

Operating cost = COGS + Operating expenses

Operating costs are made up of the COGS and operating expenses.

An operating expense is any expense incurred as part of normal business operations. Depreciation represents the periodic, scheduled conversion of a fixed asset into an expense as the asset is used during normal business operations. Since the asset is part of normal business operations, depreciation is considered an operating expense.

Let us take an example of an income statement of a company named XYZ Ltd.

Net Sales	125
Raw Material Cost	50
Labor Cost	20
Rent	5
Utilities	5
Depreciation	8
Interest Expense	7
Tax Paid	6

Calculate COGS.

Calculate OPEX.

Calculate Operating income.

Calculate Net profit.

Solution

COGS =70

Operating Expense = Rent + Utilities + Depreciation

= 18

Operating income = 37

Net profit = 24

Profit percentage

Profit as percentage of cost price

Where:

Profit is the difference between the selling price and the cost price.

Cost Price is the price at which an item was purchased.

Example

Suppose you bought a product for $500 and sold it for $700. Find the profit percentage.

Solution

Given:

Cost Price = $500

Selling Price = $700

The profit percentage in this example is 40%.

Example

What is the profit percentage if an item was bought for $800 and sold for $1000?

Solution

Given:

Cost Price = $800

Selling Price = $1000

The profit percentage in this example is 25%.

Profit margin

Profit as percentage of selling price

Example

Suppose that something is bought for $100 and sold for $150.

Profit percentage? Profit margin?

Solution

cost price: $100

selling price (revenue): $150

$profit = 50$

$profit\ percentage = \frac{50}{100} = 50\%$

$profit\ margin = \frac{50}{150} = 33.3\%$

Example

Tom bought a product for $100 and sold it for $130.

What is Profit Percentage?

Solution

$profit = 30$

$profit\ percentage = \frac{30}{100} = 30\%$

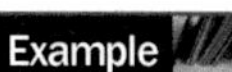

cost price: \$100

selling price: \$130

Profit percentage?

Solution

$profit = 30$

$profit\ percentage = \frac{30}{100} = 30\%$

Example

cost price: \$4,000

selling price: \$5,200

Profit percentage?

Solution

$profit = 1{,}200$

$profit\ percentage = \frac{1{,}200}{4{,}000} = 30\%$

Example

Suppose that something is sold for \$5,000 and $profit\ percentage = 30\%$.

Cost price?

Solution

$\frac{5{,}000 - x}{x} = 0.3$

$x = 3{,}846.2$

Example

A company with $2,000 in debt at 10% interest has (   ) in annual interest expense.

Solution

A company with $2,000 in debt at 10% interest has $200 in annual interest expense.

Example

Last year G Inc. reported the following income statement:

Sales	5,000
Cost of goods sold	3,846
Depreciation	800
EBIT	354
Interest expense	200
EBT	154
Taxes	31
Net income	123

1) What was the company's net cash flow?

2) What was the company's operating cash flow?

Solution

Net cashflow = 923

Operating cashflow $= 354(1-0.2)+800=1{,}083$

Example

수정이는 그동안 저축한 돈 1억원과 은행에서 10%로 대출받은 2,000만원을 합쳐, 학교앞에 옷가게를 하나 차렸다. 옷가게는 동대문에서 여성의류를 가져다가 판매를 하는데, 동대문 가격에 30%를 붙여 옷가게에서 판매한다. 1년 동안 5,000만원의 매출을 기록하였고, 옷가게 인테리어 관련 감가상각비는 800만원이다. 세율 20%일 때, 수정이네 옷가게의 대차대조표와 손익계산서를 작성하고, 순현금흐름과 영업현금흐름을 계산하시오.

Solution

Asset 12,000	Debt 2,000
	Equity 10,000

$x \times 1.3 = 5,000$

$x = 3,846$

Sales	5,000
Cost of goods sold	3,846
Depreciation	800
EBIT	354
Interest expense	200
EBT	154
Taxes	31
Net income	123

Net cashflow = 923

Operating cashflow $= 354(1-0.2)+800=1,083$

K company paid $75 in dividends and $511 in interest expense. The addition to retained earnings is $418. The tax rate is 35 percent. Sales are $15,900 and depreciation is $680. What are the earnings before interest and taxes?

Solution

Net income = $75 + $418 = $493

Taxable income = $493/(1 − 0.35) = $758.46

Earnings before interest and taxes = $758.46 + $511 = $1,269.46

Example

ABC company had sales of $843,800 and costs of $609,900. The firm paid $38,200 in interest and $18,000 in dividends. It also increased retained earnings by $62,138 for the year. The depreciation was $76,400. What is the average tax rate?

Solution

Earnings before taxes = $843,800 − $609,900 − $76,400 − $38,200 = $119,300

Net income = $18,000 + $62,138 = $80,138

Taxes = $119,300 − $80,138 = $39,162

Tax rate = $39,162/$119,300 = 32.83 percent

Example

The percentage of the next dollar you earn that must be paid in taxes is referred to as the _____ tax rate.

Solution

marginal

Example

The _____ tax rate is equal to total taxes divided by total taxable income.

Solution

average

Marginal tax rate

The marginal tax rate refers to the percentage of tax that will be applied to your next dollar of income. In other words, it's the tax rate you'll pay on your last dollar of income earned. It's essential in progressive tax systems where tax rates increase as income rises.

For example, in a progressive tax system, you might have different tax brackets with increasing rates as income increases. Your marginal tax rate would be the rate applied to the highest income bracket you're in.

Example

For instance, if you earn $80,000 and the tax rates are 15% for the first $50,000, 25% for the next $25,000, and 34% for income from $75,000 to $100,000, then your marginal tax rate would be ( ) because that's the rate applied to your next dollar of income beyond $75,000.

Solution

Tax liability: $50{,}000 \times 0.15 + 25{,}000 \times 0.25 + 5{,}000 \times 0.34 = 15{,}450$

34%

Corporate Progressive Taxes

Taxable Income	Tax Rate
0~50,000	15%
50,000~75,000	25%
75,000~100,000	34%
100,000~335,000	39%

Corporate progressive tax is a tax system in which the tax rate increases as the taxable income of a corporation increases.

In a corporate progressive tax system, different tax rates are applied to different income brackets.

Example

Suppose there are tax brackets of 15%, 25%, 34%, and 39%, where the 15% rate applies to income from $0 to $50,000; the 25% rate applies to income from $50,000 to $75,000; the 34% applies to income from $75,000 to $100,000; and the rate 39% applies to income from $100,000 to $335,000.

Suppose your firm earns $80,000 in taxable income.

What is the firm's tax liability?

What is the average tax rate?

What is the marginal tax rate?

Solution

Tax liability: $50,000 \times 0.15 + 25,000 \times 0.25 + 5,000 \times 0.34 = 15,450$

Average tax rate: $\frac{15,450}{80,000} = 19.3\%$

Marginal tax rate: 34%

Example

Suppose there are tax brackets of 15%, 25%, 34%, and 39%, where the 15% rate applies to income from $0 to $50,000; the 25% rate applies to income from $50,000 to $75,000; the 34% applies to income from $75,000 to $100,000; and the rate 39% applies to income from $100,000 to $335,000.

Suppose your firm earns $70,000 in taxable income.

What is the average tax rate?

Solution

Tax liability: $50{,}000 \times 0.15 + 20{,}000 \times 0.25 = 12{,}500$

Average tax rate: $\frac{12{,}500}{70{,}000} = 17.9\%$

Understanding Inventory

Inventory is a very important asset for any company. It is defined as the array of goods used in production or finished goods held by a company during its normal course of business. There are three general categories of inventory, including raw materials, work-in-progress, and finished goods or those that are ready for sale.

Raw materials are unprocessed materials used to produce a good. Examples of raw materials include:

Aluminum and steel for the manufacture of cars

Flour for bakeries that produce bread

Crude oil held by refineries

Work-in-progress inventory is the partially finished goods waiting for completion and resale. WIP inventory is also known as inventory on the production floor. A half-assembled airliner or a partially completed yacht is often considered to be work-in-process inventory.

Finished goods are products that go through the production process, and are completed and ready for sale. Retailers typically refer to this inventory as merchandise. Common examples of merchandise include electronics, clothes, and cars held by retailers.

An example of inventory

Consider a fashion retailer such as Zara, which operates on a seasonal schedule. Because of the fast fashion nature of turnover, Zara, like other fashion retailers is under pressure to sell inventory rapidly. Zara's merchandise is an example of inventory in the finished product stage. On the other hand, the fabric and other production materials are considered a raw material form of inventory.

Merchandise specifically refers to goods that are bought and sold in a retail setting. It is often used to describe products that are available for sale in stores, both physical and online. The term emphasizes the commercial aspect of the goods, including their marketing, display, and sales.

Example

A store started the week with 144 boxes of chocolate candy in its inventory, and it sells 44 of those boxes by the end of the week. Calculate the percent change in its chocolate candy inventory.

Solution

Percentage change $= \frac{-44}{144} = -30.56\%$

Paid-in surplus

A paid-in surplus is the incremental amount paid by an investor for a company's shares that exceeds the par value of the shares.

APIC

Additional Paid In Capital is the value of share capital above its stated par value.

Example

A company's common shares have a par value of $1. The company prices these shares at $10 on the IPO. The paid-in surplus is the difference between the par value and the price, or $9. If the company sells one million shares, they put (   ) in the paid in surplus section on the balance sheet.

Solution

A company's common shares have a par value of $1. The company prices these shares at $10 on the IPO. The paid-in surplus is the difference between the par value and the price, or $9. If the company sells one million shares, they put $9 million in the paid in surplus section on the balance sheet.

The major components of stockholders' equity are common stock, paid-in surplus, and retained earnings.

Sample Balance Sheet

Cash	20	A/P	10
A/R	10	N/P	10
Inventory	20	Total Current liabilities	20
Total Current assets	50	LT Debt	30
FA	30	Common stock and paid-in surplus	20
Total Assets	80	RE	10

Calculate stockholders' equity.

Solution

30

Example

Suppose you are given the following information for ABC company: Common stock and paid-in surplus = \$600; Retained earnings = \$1,320. Calculate stockholders' equity.

Solution

\$1,920

Retained earnings

Once your business begins to earn a profit, you'll need to reinvest some of those earnings. This will help your business grow and gain more profit. Any additional funds that aren't distributed to shareholders and investors are referred to as retained earnings.

What can you do with these leftover funds? Businesses often reinvest in things like new equipment, repaying debt, product development, or marketing.

Retained earnings are the part of a business' profit that's reinvested in the business, rather than being distributed to investors and shareholders as dividends. They are reported on the balance sheet for each accounting period.

The leftover funds from a business' profit that aren't given to investors and shareholders are known as retained earnings. And these funds are often reinvested into the business. The goal of reinvesting this additional profit is to grow your business and increase earnings over time.

Retained earnings are calculated by starting with the previous accounting period's retained earnings balance, adding the net income, and subtracting dividends paid to shareholders. The formula for calculating retained earnings is as follows:

Ending RE = Beginning RE + NI − Dividend

Retained Earnings (End of Period) = Retained Earnings (Beginning of Period) + Net Income − Dividends

Retained earnings at the beginning of the period.

Plus: Net income or profit earned during the current accounting period.

Minus: Any dividends declared or paid to shareholders during the period.

Equals: Retained earnings at the end of the period.

Change in retained earnings

Addition to retained earnings

ΔRE = Ending RE − Beginning RE = NI − Dividend

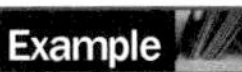

BCD company has sales of \$546,000, costs of \$295,000, depreciation expense of \$37,000, interest expense of \$15,000, and a tax rate of 32 percent. The firm paid \$59,000 in cash dividends. What is the addition to retained earnings?

Solution

Net income = (\$546,000 − \$295,000 − \$37,000 − \$15,000) (1 − .32) = \$135,320

Addition to retained earnings = \$135,320 − \$59,000 = \$76,320

Example

BCD company has net income of \$135,320. The firm paid \$59,000 in cash dividends. What is the addition to retained earnings?

Solution

Net income = \$135,320

Addition to retained earnings = \$135,320 − \$59,000 = \$76,320

Example

A firm has common stock of \$6,200, paid-in surplus of \$9,100, total liabilities of \$8,400, current assets of \$5,900, and fixed assets of \$21,200. What is the amount of the shareholders' equity?

Solution

Shareholders' equity = \$5,900 + \$21,200 − \$8,400 = \$18,700

Example

Four years ago, V company purchased a mailing machine at a cost of $176,000. This equipment is currently valued at $64,500 on today's balance sheet but could actually be sold for $58,900. This is the only fixed asset the firm owns. Net working capital is $57,200 and long-term debt is $111,300. What is the book value of shareholders' equity?

Solution

Book value of shareholders' equity = $64,500 + $57,200 − $111,300 = $10,400

Example

Suppose you are given the following information for BCD company: sales = $30,000; costs = $15,000; addition to retained earnings = $4,221; dividends paid = $469; interest expense = $1,300; tax rate = 30 percent. What is the amount of the depreciation expense?

Solution

Net income = $469 + $4,221 = $4,690

Earnings before taxes = $4,690/(1 − .30) = $6,700

Earnings before interest and taxes = $6,700 + $1,300 = $8,000

Depreciation = $30,000 − $15,000 − $8,000 = $7,000

Example

Suppose you are given the following information for K company: Change in retained earnings = $631; dividends paid = $420; tax rate = 34 percent. What is the amount of the taxable income?

Solution

Net income = 420 + 631 = 1,051

$$\text{Taxable income} = \frac{1{,}051}{1-0.34} = 1{,}592.42$$

J company paid \$1,300 in dividends and \$920 in interest this past year. Common stock increased by \$1,200 and retained earnings increased by \$310. What is the net income for the year?

Solution

Net income = \$1,300 + \$310 = \$1,610

Example

J company paid \$1,300 in dividends and \$920 in interest this past year. Common stock increased by \$1,200 and retained earnings decreased by \$310. What is the net income for the year?

Solution

Net income = \$1,300 + (−\$310) = \$990

Example

Suppose the beginning RE of the Company is \$ 150,000, the Company had earned a profit of \$ 10,000, and the Board of the Company decides to pay \$ 1,500 in the form of a dividend. Now, the RE calculation at the end of the financial year will be (   ).

Solution

Ending RE = Beginning RE + NI − Dividend = \$158,500.

Example

If a company had \$10,000 in retained earnings last year and shows \$19,000 in retained earnings this year with (   ) in dividends paid, the net income is \$16,000.

Solution

\$7,000

For example, say a company earned $100 million in a given year. It started with $50 million in retained earnings and ended the year with $70 million. The increase in retained earnings was $70 million minus $50 million, or (   ).

Solution

$20 million

Example

Jenny owns a small bookstore and wants to bring on an investor to help expand the shop to multiple locations. The investor wants to know what retained earnings look like to date. Financials for the most recent quarter look like this:

Beginning retained earnings: $100,000

Net income: $15,000

Dividends paid: $10,000

Calculate the retained earnings.

Solution

The retained earnings: $100,000 + $15,000 − $10,000 = $105,000

Tom is the owner of ABC Robotics, a startup that sells robot cats, and he wants to hire new developers. Before he can hire any new employees, Tom needs to know how much money he has on hand to invest.

This is ABC Robotics's information for the year:

Beginning retained earnings: $93,000

Net income for the year: $14,000

Dividends paid: $22,000

Calculate the retained earnings.

Solution

The retained earnings formula: $93,000 + $14,000 − $22,000 = $85,000

The Purpose of Retained Earnings

Retained earnings represent a useful link between the income statement and the balance sheet, as they are recorded under shareholders' equity, which connects the two statements. The purpose of retaining these earnings can be varied and includes buying new equipment and machines, spending on research and development, or other activities that could potentially generate growth for the company. This reinvestment into the company aims to achieve even more earnings in the future.

Financial Analysis

Financial ratios are useful byproducts of financial statements and provide standardized measures of a firm's profitability and riskiness.

Liquidity Ratios

Liquidity Ratios are used to examine the firm's ability to meet short-term cash outflow needs.

Current Ratio

$$Current\ Ratio = \frac{Current\ Assets}{Current\ Liabilities}$$

The current ratio compares all of a company's current assets to its current liabilities.
Indicator of company's ability to pay it's short term liabilities
The current ratio is a liquidity ratio that measures a company's ability to pay short-term obligations or those due within one year. It tells investors and analysts how a company can maximize the current assets on its balance sheet to satisfy its current debt and other payables.

A current ratio that is in line with the industry average or slightly higher is generally considered acceptable. A current ratio that is lower than the industry average may indicate a higher risk of distress or default. Similarly, if a company has a very high current ratio compared with its peer group, it indicates that management may not be using its assets efficiently. The current ratio helps investors understand more about a company's ability to cover its short-term debt with its current assets and make apples-to-apples comparisons with its competitors and peers.

유동비율(current ratio)은 대차대조표상에 있는 유동자산을 유동부채로 나눈 것이다. 유동자산에는 현금·시장성이 있는 유가증권·외상매출금과 재고자산 등이 포함되며, 유동부채에는 장기부채 중 1년내에 만기가 되는 부분과 외상매입금 등 단기부채, 그 밖에 미지급비용(accrued expenses) 등이 포함된다.

Quick Ratio

$$Quick\,Ratio = \frac{Current\,Assets - Inventories}{Current\,Liabilities}$$

Quick Ratio measures ability to pay off short term obligations excluding inventory.

The quick ratio measures a company's capacity to pay its current liabilities without needing to sell its inventory or obtain additional financing.

The quick ratio is considered a more conservative measure than the current ratio, which includes all current assets as coverage for current liabilities.

당좌비율(quick ratio)은 산성시험비율(acid test ratio)이라고도 하는 것으로, 유동자산 중에서 재고자산을 뺀 부분을 유동부채로 나눈 것이다. 유동자산 중에서 재고자산은 유동성이 가장 낮은 항목일 뿐만 아니라 처분할 때에도 손실을 입을 위험이 크다. 그러므로 기업이 재고자산을 처분하지 않고서도 단기부채를 갚을 수 있는가가 중요하다. 이런 의미에서 당좌비율은 유동비율보다 더 엄격히 유동성을 측정하는 비율이다.

NWC to total assets

$$\frac{NWC}{TA}$$

Interval Measure

$$\frac{CA}{average\ daily\ operating\ \text{costs}}$$

Average Daily Expenditures

=(Cost of Goods Sold + Annual operating expenses − Noncash charges)/365

Example

Calculate Average Daily Expenditure using the given information.

Details	Amount
COGS	3,000,000
Operating expenses for the year	900,000
Depreciation	100,000

Solution

$$\frac{3,800,000}{365} = 10,411$$

Example

Suppose Company A has $50,000 cash, $25,000 marketable securities, and $25,000 accounts receivables. The daily operating expenses for Company A are $2,000.

Calculate Interval Measure.

Solution

Thus, the total liquid assets for Company A is $100,000.

The interval measure in this case is 50 days ($100,000 / $2,000).

Notes Payable

Notes payable are written agreements in which one party agrees to pay the other party a certain amount of cash.

Notes payable appear as liabilities on a balance sheet. Additionally, they are classified as current liabilities when the amounts are due within a year.

These are written agreements in which the borrower obtains a specific amount of money from the lender and promises to pay back the amount owed, with interest, over or within a specified time period.

Example

John borrowed $100,000 from Michelle on January 1, 2025. John signs the note and agrees to pay Michelle $100,000 six months later. Additionally, John also agrees to pay Michelle a 15% interest rate every 2 months.

Accounts Payable

Accounts payable is an obligation that a business owes to creditors for buying goods or services. Accounts payable do not involve a promissory note, usually do not carry interest, and are a short-term liability.

When a company purchases goods or services on credit from a supplier or vendor, the transaction is recorded in the accounts payable account. This means that the company receives the goods or services immediately but agrees to pay for them at a later date, typically within a specified period, such as 30 days or 60 days.

Leverage Ratios

Leverage Ratios assess the ability of the firm to cover long-term debt obligations.

Debt-to-asset ratio

$$\frac{Total\ Debt}{Total\ Assets}$$

Debt-to-asset ratio measures extent to which borrowed funds have been used to finance the firm's operations. Includes long term, short term debt.

The total-debt-to-total-assets ratio is calculated by dividing a company's total amount of debt by the company's total amount of assets.

Example

ABC Company has total liabilities of $500,000 and total assets of $1,000,000. Its debt to assets ratio is ( ).

Solution

ABC Company has total liabilities of $500,000 and total assets of $1,000,000. Its debt to assets ratio is:

$500,000 ÷ $1,000,000

= 0.5

Debt-to-equity ratio

$$\frac{Total\ Debt}{Total\ stockholder's\ equity}$$

Debt-to-equity ratio provides another measure of the funds provided by creditors vs. funds provided by owners.

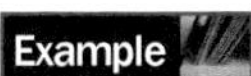

Company XYZ has total debt of $750,000 and total equity of $1,500,000. Calculate the debt-to-equity ratio for Company XYZ.

Solution

0.5

TIE

Times Interest Earned Ratio

$$Times\,Interest\,Earned = \frac{EBIT}{Interest\,Expense}$$

이자보상비율(times interest earned 또는 interest coverage ratio)은 타인자본의 사용으로 발생하는 금융비용 즉, 이자가 기업에 어느 정도의 압박을 가져오는가를 보기 위한 것이다. 기업의 영업이익(이자 및 납세전이익)이 매년 지급해야 할 금융비용의 몇 배에 해당하는가를 나타내는 비율이다.

A ratio that measures the firm's ability to meet its annual interest obligations, calculated by dividing earnings before interest and taxes by interest charges.

A higher ratio indicates that a company has a better capacity to cover its interest expense.

TIE is also referred to as the interest coverage ratio.

Example

Assume, for example, that XYZ Company has $10 million in 4% debt outstanding.

The company's EBIT is $2 million.

This means that the TIE ratio for XYZ Company is (   ).

Solution

5

Cash Coverage

$$Cash\ Coverage = \frac{EBIT + Dep}{Interest\ Expense}$$

EM

Equity multiplier is a measure of the firm's financial leverage.

$$EM = \frac{TA}{TE}$$

An equity multiplier is a measure of the portion of the company's assets that is financed by stock rather than debt.

The Equity Multiplier measures the proportion of a company's assets funded by its equity shareholders as opposed to debt providers.

The Equity Multiplier is the proportion of a company's assets financed by equity.

It established the proportion between the total assets of a company and its equity financing.

Example

Let's say that Company Z has total assets of $100,000. Its total equity is $20,000. Calculate equity multiplier.

Solution

Multiplier = $100,000 / $20,000 = 5.

The multiplier is 5 means that total assets are financed by 20% of equity and the rest is financed through debt.

Profitability Ratios

Profitability Ratios are ratios used to measure the profitability of the firm.

NPM

Net Profit Margin

$$\frac{Net\ profit\ after\ taxes}{net\ sales}$$

Net Profit Margin shows how much after tax profits are generated by each dollar of sales. Net profit margin is a financial ratio that measures the profitability of a company by expressing its net profit as a percentage of its total revenue. It indicates how much of each dollar of revenue is converted into profit after all expenses have been deducted.

A higher net profit margin indicates that a company is more efficient at converting revenue into profit, while a lower net profit margin suggests lower profitability or higher expenses relative to revenue.

Example

Suppose Company XYZ reported the following financial information for the year:

Net Income: $50,000

Revenue: $500,000

Calculate NPM.

Solution

The net profit margin for Company XYZ is 10%.

GPM

Gross Profit Margin

$$\frac{Sales - Cost\,of\,goods\,sold}{Sales}$$

Gross Profit = Sales − COGS

Gross profit margin is a financial metric that indicates the percentage of revenue retained by a company after deducting the cost of goods sold. It measures how efficiently a company is producing its goods or services.

Gross Profit Margin indicates the total margin available to cover other expenses beyond cost of goods sold, and still yield a profit.

The ratio indicates the percentage of each dollar of revenue that the company retains as gross profit.

For example, if the ratio is calculated to be 20%, that means for every dollar of revenue generated, $0.2 is retained while $0.8 is attributed to the cost of goods sold.

Example

Tina's T-Shirts is a small business that has been open for about a year.

Her total revenue from sales is $400,000 for the year.

Her cost of goods sold is $325,000.

Calculate Gross Profit Margin.

Solution

To calculate gross profit in dollars, she would do the following calculation:

$400,000 - $325,000 = $75,000

This means Tina has generated $75,000 in gross profit.

The gross margin calculation is:

75,000 ÷ 400,000 = 18.75%

Gross profit margin is 18.75%.

ROI

$$\frac{Net\ profit\ after\ taxes}{Total\ assets}$$

Return on Investment : a measure of a company's efficiency, it shows the return on all assets under it's control.

The term return on assets refers to a financial ratio that indicates how profitable a company is in relation to its total assets. Corporate management, analysts, and investors can use ROA to determine how efficiently a company uses its assets to generate a profit.
The metric is commonly expressed as a percentage by using a company's net income and its average assets. A higher ROA means a company is more efficient and productive at managing its balance sheet to generate profits while a lower ROA indicates there is room for improvement.

Return on assets is a metric that indicates a company's profitability in relation to its total assets.
ROA can be used by management, analysts, and investors to determine whether a company uses its assets efficiently to generate a profit.
You can calculate a company's ROA by dividing its net income by its total assets.
It's always best to compare the ROA of companies within the same industry because they'll share the same asset base.
Return on assets is a profitability ratio that provides how much profit a company is able to generate from its assets.
Return on assets measures how efficient a company's management is in generating profit from their total assets on their balance sheet.
ROA is shown as a percentage, and the higher the number, the more efficient a company's management is at managing its balance sheet to generate profits.
Companies with a low ROA usually have more assets involved in generating profit, while companies with a high ROA have fewer assets.

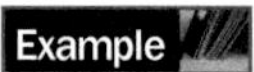

If a business posts a net income of $10 million in current operations, and owns $50 million worth of assets as per the balance sheet, what is its return on assets?

Solution

$10 million divided by $50 million is 0.2, therefore the business's ROA is 20%. For every dollar of assets the company invests in, it returns 20 cents in net profit per year.

Example

ABC company has annual sales of $687,400, total debt of $210,000, total equity of $365,000, and a profit margin of 4.8 percent. What is the return on assets?

Solution

NI = 0.048 × 687,400 = 32,995

Return on assets = 32,995/(210,000 + 365,000) = 5.74 percent

ROE

$$\frac{Net\ profit\ after\ taxes}{Shareholder's\ eqity}$$

Return on Equity measures rate of return on the book value of shareholder's total investment in the company.

Return on equity is the measure of a company's net income divided by its shareholders' equity.

ROE is a gauge of a corporation's profitability and how efficiently it generates those profits.

The higher the ROE, the better a company is at converting its equity financing into profits.

To calculate ROE, divide net income by the value of shareholders' equity.

ROEs will vary based on the industry or sector in which the company operates.

Example

For example, imagine a company with an annual income of $1,800,000 and average shareholders' equity of $12,000,000. This company's ROE would be (   ), or $1.8 million divided by $12 million.

Solution

15%

Return on Equity is a financial ratio that measures a company's profitability relative to the equity shareholders have invested in it. It's calculated by dividing net income by shareholders' equity. ROE indicates how effectively a company is utilizing its equity to generate profits for its shareholders.

Example

For example, if a company has a net income of $1,000,000 and shareholders' equity of $5,000,000, the ROE would be 20%. This means that for every dollar of equity invested by shareholders, the company generates (   ) of profit.

Solution

20 cents

Profit Margin = Net Income / Sales

Profit margin is a measure of the firm's operating efficiency - how well it controls costs.

ROA = Net Income / Total Assets

ROE = Net income / Total Equity

DuPont Analysis

DuPont analysis is a useful technique used to decompose the different drivers of ROE. Dupont analysis breaks ROE into its constituent components to determine which of these factors are most responsible for changes in ROE.

The DuPont Identity

ROE = (NI/Sales)(Sales/TA)(TA/TE)

ROE = PM × TAT × EM

What is the DuPont Identity?

The Dupont identity decomposes return on equity into three parts: profitability, efficiency, and financial leverage.

The DuPont identity is an expression that shows a company's return on equity can be represented as a product of three other ratios: the profit margin, the total asset turnover, and the equity multiplier.

DuPont identity tells us that ROE is affected by three things:

1. Operating efficiency, which is measured by profit margin;
2. Asset use efficiency, which is measured by total asset turnover; and
3. Financial leverage, which is measured by the equity multiplier.

The formula for the DuPont identity is:

ROE = profit margin × asset turnover × equity multiplier

Activity Ratios

활동성 비율

Activity Ratios measure the efficiency with which the firm conducts its business.

Inventory turnover

Inventory turnover = COGS / Average Inventory

The equation for inventory turnover equals the cost of goods sold divided by the average inventory.

Inventory turnover is a financial ratio that measures how efficiently a company manages its inventory. It indicates how many times a company's inventory is sold and replaced over a certain period, typically a year.

Inventory turnover, or the inventory turnover ratio, is the number of times a business sells and replaces its stock of goods during a given period. It considers the cost of goods sold, relative to its average inventory for a year or in any a set period of time.

A high inventory turnover ratio generally indicates that a company is selling its inventory quickly and efficiently, which can be a sign of effective inventory management.

A high inventory turnover generally means that goods are sold faster and a low turnover rate indicates weak sales and excess inventories, which may be challenging for a business.

Inventory turnover is a ratio showing how many times a company has sold and replaced inventory during a given period.

Average inventory is the average cost of a set of goods during two or more specified time periods. It takes into account the beginning inventory balance at the start of the fiscal year plus the ending inventory balance of the same year.

These two account balances are then divided in half to obtain the average cost of goods resulting in sales.

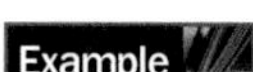

Let's say Company XYZ had a Cost of Goods Sold (COGS) of $500,000 over the past year, and its average inventory value during the same period was $100,000.
Calculate Inventory Turnover.

Solution

Inventory Turnover = 5
This means that Company XYZ's inventory turned over 5 times during the year. In other words, on average, its entire inventory was sold and replaced 5 times within the year. A high inventory turnover ratio like this suggests that Company XYZ is efficiently managing its inventory, quickly converting it into sales and minimizing holding costs.

Example

With the given beginning inventory of $80,000 and ending inventory of $120,000, we can calculate the average inventory by adding the beginning and ending inventories together and then dividing by 2:
Average Inventory = (Beginning Inventory + Ending Inventory) / 2
Average Inventory = $100,000
So, the average inventory for this period is $100,000.

Average inventory

Average inventory represents the mean value of a company's inventory over a specific period. It's often calculated by adding the beginning inventory to the ending inventory for a given period and dividing the sum by two.

Example

Let's say a company's beginning inventory for the year was $50,000, and its ending inventory was $70,000. To find the average inventory for the year, you would add the beginning and ending inventory together and then divide by two. Therefore, the average inventory for the year would be ( ).

Solution

$60,000

Inventory turnover is a financial ratio that measures how many times a company's inventory is sold and replaced over a certain period, typically a year. It's calculated by dividing the cost of goods sold by the average inventory for the period. A higher inventory turnover ratio indicates that a company is selling its inventory quickly and efficiently, while a lower ratio suggests slower sales or excess inventory.

Example

Let's say a company had a cost of goods sold (COGS) of $500,000 and an average inventory of $100,000 during a year. To calculate the inventory turnover ratio, you would divide the COGS by the average inventory:

Solution

Inventory Turnover Ratio = COGS / Average Inventory

Inventory Turnover Ratio = $500,000 / $100,000

Inventory Turnover Ratio = 5

So, in this example, the company's inventory turnover ratio is 5, meaning its inventory is being sold and replaced 5 times within the year.

Inventory period

The length of time that elapses between the day a firm purchases an inventory item and the day that item sells is called the inventory period.

Example

D company, has sales of $836,000 and cost of goods sold of $601,000. The firm had a beginning inventory of $36,000 and an ending inventory of $47,000. What is the length of the inventory period?

Solution

Inventory turnover = $601,000/[($36,000 + $47,000)/2] = 14.48

Inventory period = 365/14.48 = 25.20 days

Example

A firm has sales of $729,000 and cost of goods sold of $478,000. At the beginning of the year, the inventory was $37,000. At the end of the year, the inventory balance was $41,000. What is the inventory turnover rate?

Solution

Inventory turnover = $478,000/[($37,000 + $41,000)/2] = 12.26 times

Example

K Co. has a cost of goods sold of $5M for the current year. The company's cost of beginning inventory was $600,000 and the cost of ending inventory was $400,000. Given the inventory balances, the average cost of inventory during the year is calculated at $500,000. As a result, inventory turnover is rated at ( ) times a year.

Solution

10

The formular for inventory turnover

Inventory turnover = COGS / Average Inventory

or Inventory turnover = $\frac{Sales}{Inventory}$

or Inventory Turnover = Net Sales / Average Inventory at Selling Price

재고자산회전율(inventory turnover)은 매출액을 재고자산으로 나눈 값으로, 재고자산이 한 회계연도 즉, 1년 동안에 몇 번이나 당좌자산(현금 또는 매출채권)으로 전환되었는가를 측정하는 것이다. 재고자산회전율이 낮다는 것은 매출액에 비하여 과다한 재고를 소유하고 있다는 것이며, 높다는 것은 적은 재고자산으로 생산과 판매활동을 효율적으로 수행하고 있다는 뜻이다.

Operating cycle

The length of time between the purchase of inventory and the receipt of cash from the sale of that inventory is called the operating cycle.

Receivables turnover

Accounts Receivable Period = 365/Receivables Turnover

Receivables turnover = $\frac{Sales}{Average\ Acconts\ Receivable}$

Days'Sales in Receivables = 365/Receivables Turnover

매출채권회전율(receivables turnover)은 매출액을 외상매출금으로 나눈 값이다. 같은 매출액에 비하여 외상매출금이 적을수록 매출채권관리를 잘하고 있다고 볼 수 있으므로, 매출채권회전율은 클수록 좋다.

Example

BCD company has sales of $811,000. The cost of goods sold is equal to 63 percent of sales. The beginning accounts receivable balance is $41,000 and the ending accounts receivable balance is $38,000. How long on average does it take the firm to collect its receivables?

Solution

Average Accounts Receivable = 39,500

Receivables turnover = 811,000/39,500 = 20.53

Receivables period = 365/20.53 = 17.78 Days

Operating Cycle = Inventory Period + Accounts Receivable Period

Example

On average, A company is able to sell its inventory in 27 days. Its average customer pays with a credit card which allows the firm to collect its receivables in 4 days. Given this information, what is the length of operating cycle?

Solution

31 days

TAT

$$TAT = \frac{Sales}{TA}$$

Total assets turnover is a measure of the firm's asset use efficiency – how well does it manage its assets.

The asset turnover ratio analyzes how well a company uses its assets to drive sales.

The ratio is calculated by dividing a company's net sales for a specific period by the average total assets the company held over the same period.

The asset turnover ratio compares performance from the income statement with the company's financial health on the balance sheet.

The formula is:

Asset Turnover Ratio = Net Sales / Average Total Assets

Net sales is the total amount of revenue retained by a company. It is the gross sales from a specific period less returns, allowances, or discounts taken by customers.

Average total assets are found by taking the average of the beginning and ending assets of the period being analyzed.

Companies with a higher asset turnover ratio are more effective in using company assets to generate revenue.

The asset turnover ratio is highly industry-specific. Sectors like retail and food & beverage have high ratios, while sectors like real estate have lower ratios.

The asset turnover ratio measures how effectively a company uses its assets to generate revenue. The ratio compares the dollar amount of sales to the company's total assets to measure the efficiency of the company's operations.

A higher ratio is generally favored as there is the implication that the company is more efficient in generating sales. A lower ratio illustrates that a company may not be using its assets as efficiently. Asset turnover ratios vary throughout different sectors, so only the ratios of companies that are in the same sector should be compared. The ratio is typically calculated on an annual basis.

Example

Suppose company ABC had total revenue of $12 billion at the end of its fiscal year. Its total assets were $3 billion at the beginning of the fiscal year and $5 billion at the end. Calculate TAT.

Solution

Suppose company ABC had total revenue of $12 billion at the end of its fiscal year. Its total assets were $3 billion at the beginning of the fiscal year and $5 billion at the end. Assuming the company had no returns for the year, its net sales for the year was $12 billion. The company's average total assets for the year was $4 billion.

TAT = 3

Every $1 in total assets generates $3 in sales.

Example

What is the total asset turnover ratio for ABC Corporation if its ending total assets are $2,000,000 and the company reported total sales of $5,000,000?

Solution

If the beginning total assets are not provided, we can use the ending total assets to calculate the total asset turnover ratio.

Since we don't have the beginning total assets, we'll use the ending total assets as the average total assets.

Average Total Assets = Beginning Total Assets = Ending Total Assets = $2,000,000

The total asset turnover ratio for ABC Corporation is 2.5.

Suppose company ABC had total revenue of $10 billion at the end of its fiscal year. Its total assets were $3 billion at the beginning of the fiscal year and $5 billion at the end. Assuming the company had no returns for the year, its net sales for the year was $10 billion. The company's average total assets for the year was $4 billion.

ABC Company's Asset Turnover Ratio = $10 billion / $4 billion = 2.5

On the other hand, company XYZ – a competitor of ABC in the same sector – had total revenue of $8 billion at the end of the same fiscal year. Its total assets were $1 billion at the beginning of the year and $2 billion at the end.

XYZ Company's Asset Turnover Ratio = $8 billion / $1.5 billion = 5.33

Though ABC has generated more revenue for the year, XYZ is more efficient in using its assets to generate income as its asset turnover ratio is higher.

The asset turnover ratio is most useful when compared across similar companies. Due to the varying nature of different industries, it is most valuable when compared across companies within the same sector.

Total asset turnover is a management profitability ratio that measures how effectively a company turns its assets into sales. It is calculated by dividing the sales by the total assets of a company.

What is Total Asset Turnover?

Total asset turnover is a financial metric that measures a company's efficiency in using its assets to generate sales. TAT is calculated by dividing a company's total sales by its average total assets. The higher the TAT, the more efficient a company is in using its assets to generate sales.

A company that is able to generate a high TAT is likely to be more profitable than one with a lower TAT. This is because a high TAT indicates that the company is able to generate sales with fewer assets. This allows the company to keep more of its profits, which can be reinvested or distributed to shareholders.

There are a few things that investors can look at to get a sense of a company's TAT. These include the company's income statement, balance sheet, and cash flow statement.

The income statement can give investors a sense of how much revenue the company is generating. The balance sheet can give investors a sense of how much debt the company has and how much equity it has. The cash flow statement can give investors a sense of how much cash the company has generated and how much it has spent.
Investors can use all of this information to get a sense of a company's TAT and how it has changed over time. They can also use it to compare companies within an industry.

What Does Total Asset Turnover Tell You?
Total asset turnover is a measure of a company's ability to generate sales from its assets. It is calculated by dividing total sales by total assets. TAT can be used to indicate how efficiently a company is using its assets to generate sales. A high TAT indicates that a company is using its assets efficiently, while a low TAT indicates that a company could be using its assets more efficiently. TAT can be used to compare companies within an industry or to compare a company's performance over time.

How Do You Calculate Total Asset Turnover?
Asset turnover is a financial metric that measures a company's efficiency in using its assets to generate sales. It is calculated by dividing a company's total sales by its total assets.

Total asset turnover can be used to measure a company's performance over time or compare it to its competitors. A high total asset turnover ratio means that the company is using its assets more efficiently to generate sales. This may be due to a variety of factors, such as a strong sales force or efficient production process.

A low total asset turnover ratio may be due to a number of factors, such as a weak sales force or inefficient production process. It can also be due to the company having a large amount of excess assets, which is not generating any sales.

There are a few different ways to improve a company's total asset turnover ratio. One way is to improve the efficiency of the company's production process. Another way is to improve the sales force by increasing its size or its effectiveness.

The most basic measure of efficiency for a company is its total asset turnover. This ratio is computed by dividing a company's total sales by its total assets. This measures how efficiently a company is using its assets to generate sales. A high total asset turnover means that a company is using its assets very efficiently.

How Could You Use Total Asset Turnover to Make Better Decisions?
Total asset turnover is a ratio that measures a company's efficiency in using its assets to generate sales. The higher the TAT, the more efficient the company is in its use of assets. This is important to investors because a company with a high TAT is likely more efficient and profitable than a company with a low TAT.

There are a few ways investors can use TAT to make better decisions. First, TAT can be used to compare a company's performance to its peers. If a company has a high TAT, it is likely more efficient and profitable than its peers. Second, TAT can be used to identify companies that are under-utilizing their assets. A company with a low TAT may be an attractive investment because it has room for improvement. Finally, TAT can be used to predict a company's future performance. A high TAT is typically a sign of a healthy, growing company, while a low TAT may be a sign of a company in decline.

The asset turnover ratio measures the value of a company's sales or revenues relative to the value of its assets. The asset turnover ratio can be used as an indicator of the efficiency with which a company is using its assets to generate revenue.

The higher the asset turnover ratio, the more efficient a company is at generating revenue from its assets. Conversely, if a company has a low asset turnover ratio, it indicates it is not efficiently using its assets to generate sales.

Asset turnover is the ratio of total sales or revenue to average assets.
This metric helps investors understand how effectively companies are using their assets to generate sales.
Investors use the asset turnover ratio to compare similar companies in the same sector or group.

The asset turnover ratio uses the value of a company's assets in the denominator of the formula. To determine the value of a company's assets, the average value of the assets for the year needs to first be calculated.
Add the beginning asset value to the ending value and divide the sum by two, which will provide an average value of the assets for the year.
Divide revenue by the average value of the assets for the year.

Typically, the asset turnover ratio is calculated on an annual basis. The higher the asset turnover ratio, the better the company is performing, since higher ratios imply that the company is generating more revenue per dollar of assets.

Since this ratio can vary widely from one industry to the next, comparing the asset turnover ratios of a retail company and a telecommunications company would not be very productive. Comparisons are only meaningful when they are made for different companies within the same sector.

A key component of DuPont analysis is the asset turnover ratio. A system that began being used during the 1920s to evaluate divisional performance across a corporation, DuPont analysis calculates a company's return on equity. It breaks down ROE into three components, one of which is asset turnover.

총자산회전율(total assets turnover)은 매출액을 총자산으로 나눈 것이다. 총자본은 자기자본과 타인자본을 합한 것으로 총자산과 같은 크기를 가지므로 총자산회전율은 총자본회전율이라고도 한다. 이 비율은 기업의 총자본(또는 총자산)이 1년에 몇 번이나 회전하였는가를 나타내므로 기업이 사용한 총자산의 효율적인 이용도를 종합적으로 표시하는 것이다.
총자산회전율이 높으면 유동자산·고정자산 등이 효율적으로 이용되고 있다는 것을 뜻하며, 이 회전율이 낮으면 과잉투자와 같은 비효율적인 투자를 하고 있다는 것을 의미한다.

Fixed asset turnover

$$FAT = \frac{Sales}{Fixed\,Assets}$$

고정자산회전율
매출액을 고정자산으로 나눈 값이다. 고정자산이 얼마만큼 효율적으로 이용되었는가를 측정한다.

Tangible fixed assets turnover

$$\frac{Sales}{tangible\ fixed\ assets}$$

유형자산회전율 = 매출액 / 유형자산
유형자산회전율이 높을수록 유형자산을 효율적으로 활용하고 있음을 나타내고, 낮으면 유형자산에 대한 과도한 투자를 의미한다.

NWC Turnover
Sales/NWC

Example

Suppose you are given the following information for K company: Cash = $20; Accounts receivable = $10; Inventory = $20; Fixed Assets = $30; Notes payable = $10; Accounts payable = $10; Long-term Debt = $30; Total equity = $30.
Compute Current Ratio.

Solution

Current Ratio = Current Assets / Current Liabilities = 250%

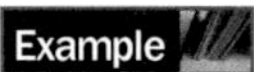

A firm has $20 in inventory, $30 in fixed assets, $10 in accounts receivables, $10 in accounts payable, and $20 in cash. What is the amount of the current assets?

Solution

Current assets = $20 + $10 + $20 = $50

Example

Sample Balance Sheet

Cash	20	A/P	10
A/R	10	N/P	10
Inventory	20	Total Current liabilities	20
Total Current assets	50	LT Debt	30
FA	30	SE	30
Total Assets	80	Total Liab. & Equity	80

What is the amount of the current assets?

Solution

Current assets = $20 + $10 + $20 = $50

Example

Sample Balance Sheet

Cash	20	Notes payable	10
Accounts receivable	10	Accounts payable	10
Inventory	20	Total Current liabilities	20
Total Current assets	50	Long-term Debt	30
Fixed Assets	30	Total equity	30
Total Assets	80	Total Liab. & Equity	80

Sample Income Statement

Revenues	500
Cost of Goods Sold	300
Operating Expenses	130
EBIT	70
Interest Expense	20
Taxable Income	50
Taxes	20
Net Income	30

1) Compute Current Ratio.

2) Compute Quick Ratio.

3) Compute Debt-to-equity Ratio.

4) Compute Net Profit Margin.

5) Compute ROI.

6) Compute ROE.

Solution

1) $Current\ Ratio = \frac{Current\ Assets}{Current\ Liabilities} = 250\%$

2) $Quick\ Ratio = \frac{Current\ Assets - Inventories}{Current\ Liabilities} = 150\%$

3) Debt-to-equity Ratio $= \frac{Total\ Debt}{Total\ stockholder's\ equity} = 167\%$

4) $Net\ Profit\ Margin = \frac{Net\ profit\ after\ taxes}{Net\ sales} = 6\%$

5) $ROI = \frac{Net\ profit\ after\ taxes}{Total\ assets} = 37.5\%$

6) $ROE = \frac{Net\ profit\ after\ taxes}{Shareholder's\ equity} = 100\%$

Suppose you are given the following information for K company: Cash = $20; Accounts receivable = $10; Inventory = $20; Fixed Assets = $30; Notes payable = $10; Accounts payable = $10; Long-term Debt = $30; Total equity = $30; Revenues = $500; COGS = $300; Operating Expenses = $130; Interest Expense = $15; Tax Rate = 40%.
Compute Net Profit Margin.

Solution

Sample Balance Sheet

Cash	20	Notes payable	10
Accounts receivable	10	Accounts payable	10
Inventory	20	Total Current liabilities	20
Total Current assets	50	Long-term Debt	30
Fixed Assets	30	Total equity	30
Total Assets	80	Total Liab. & Equity	80

Sample Income Statement

Revenues	500
Cost of Goods Sold	300
Operating expenses	130
EBIT	70
Interest Expense	15
Taxable Income	55
Taxes	22
Net Income	33

$$Net\ Profit\ Margin = \frac{Net\ profit\ after\ taxes}{Net\ sales} = 6.6\%$$

Example

Suppose you are given the following information for K company: Cash = \$20; Accounts receivable = \$10; Inventory = \$20; Fixed Assets = \$30; Notes payable = \$10; Accounts payable = \$10; Long-term Debt = \$30; Total equity = \$30; Revenues = \$500; COGS = \$300; Operating Expenses = \$130; Interest Expense = \$15; Tax Rate = 40%.
Compute ROI.

Solution

Sample Balance Sheet

Cash	20	Notes payable	10
Accounts receivable	10	Accounts payable	10
Inventory	20	Total Current liabilities	20
Total Current assets	50	Long-term Debt	30
Fixed Assets	30	Total equity	30
Total Assets	80	Total Liab. & Equity	80

Sample Income Statement

Revenues	500
Cost of Goods Sold	300
Operating expenses	130
EBIT	70
Interest Expense	15
Taxable Income	55
Taxes	22
Net Income	33

$$\text{ROI} = \frac{33}{80} = 41.3\%$$

Suppose you are given the following information for K company: Cash = \$20; Accounts receivable = \$10; Inventory = \$20; Fixed Assets = \$30; Notes payable = \$10; Accounts payable = \$10; Long-term Debt = \$30; Total equity = \$30; Revenues = \$500; COGS = \$300; Operating Expenses = \$130; Interest Expense = \$15; Tax Rate = 40%.
Compute ROE.

Solution

Sample Balance Sheet

Cash	20	Notes payable	10
Accounts receivable	10	Accounts payable	10
Inventory	20	Total Current liabilities	20
Total Current assets	50	Long-term Debt	30
Fixed Assets	30	Total equity	30
Total Assets	80	Total Liab. & Equity	80

Sample Income Statement

Revenues	500
Cost of Goods Sold	300
Operating expenses	130
EBIT	70
Interest Expense	15
Taxable Income	55
Taxes	22
Net Income	33

ROE = 110%

Example

Sample Balance Sheet

Cash	20	Notes payable	10
Accounts receivable	10	Accounts payable	10
Inventory	20	Total Current liabilities	20
Total Current assets	50	Long-term Debt	30
Fixed Assets	30	Total equity	30
Total Assets	80	Total Liab. & Equity	80

Sample Income Statement

Revenues	500
Cost of Goods Sold	300
Operating expenses	130
EBIT	70
Interest Expense	15
Taxable Income	55
Taxes	22
Net Income	33

1) Compute Net Profit Margin.

2) Compute ROI.

3) Compute ROE.

Solution

1) $Net\ Profit\ Margin = \dfrac{Net\ profit\ after\ taxes}{Net\ sales} = 6.6\%$

2) $ROI = \dfrac{Net\ profit\ after\ taxes}{Total\ assets} = 41.3\%$

3) $ROE = \dfrac{Net\ profit\ after\ taxes}{Shareholder's\ equity} = 110\%$

Example

한국기업 (단위: 백만원)

현금	20	지급어음	10
외상매출금	10	외상매입금	10
재고자산	20	유동부채 합계	20
유동자산 합계	50	사채	30
고정자산	30	자본금	30
계	80	계	80

한국기업 (단위: 백만원)

매출액	500
매출원가	300
영업비용	130
영업이익	70
이자	20
세전이익	50
세금	20
당기순이익	30

한국기업의 Current Ratio는 (a), Quick Ratio는 (b), Debt-to-equity Ratio는 (c)이다. 한국기업의 이자 20 백만원을 25% 감소시키면, Net Profit Margin은 (d)에서 (e)로 증가하고, ROI는 (f)에서 (g)로 증가하며, ROE는 (h)에서 (i)로 증가한다.
괄호(a~i)에 적당한 값을 계산하라.

Solution

(a) $Current\ Ratio = \dfrac{Current\ Assets}{Current\ Liabilities} = 250\%$

(b) $Quick\ Ratio = \dfrac{Current\ Assets - Inventories}{Current\ Liabilities} = 150\%$

(c) Debt-to-equity Ratio$= \dfrac{Total\ Debt}{Total\ stockholder's\ equity} = 167\%$

$$Net\ Profit\ Margin = \frac{Net\ profit\ after\ taxes}{Net\ sales}$$

(d) 6% (e) 6.6% $ROI = \dfrac{Net\ profit\ after\ taxes}{Total\ assets}$

(f) 37.5% (g) 41.3% $ROE = \dfrac{Net\ profit\ after\ taxes}{Shareholder's\ equity}$

(h) 100% (i) 110%

Example

Sample Balance Sheet

Cash	30	Notes payable	10
Accounts receivable	20	Accounts payable	20
Inventory	20	Total Current liabilities	30
Total Current assets	70	Long-term Debt	30
Fixed Assets	30	Total equity	40
Total Assets	100	Total Liab. & Equity	100

Sample Income Statement

Revenues	700
Cost of Goods Sold	500
SG&A expense	120
EBIT	80
Interest Expense	10
Taxable Income	70
Taxes	14
Net Income	56

1) Compute Current Ratio.

2) Compute Quick Ratio.

3) Compute Debt-to-equity Ratio.

4) Compute Times Interest Earned Ratio.

5) Compute ROI.

6) Compute Fixed asset turnover.

7) Compute Gross Profit Margin.

8) Compute Net Profit Margin.

Solution

(1) Current Ratio: $\frac{70}{30} = 233\%$,

(2) $\frac{50}{30} = 167\%$, (3) $\frac{60}{40} = 150\%$, (4) $\frac{80}{10} = 8$

(5) $\frac{56}{100} = 56\%$, (6) $\frac{700}{30} = 23.3$, (7) $\frac{200}{700} = 28.6\%$, (8) $\frac{56}{700} = 8\%$

Example

Suppose you are given the following information for K company: Revenues = \$700; COGS = \$500; Operating Expenses = \$120; Interest Expense = \$8; Tax Rate = 20%. Compute Net Profit Margin.

Solution

Sample Income Statement

Revenues	700
Cost of Goods Sold	500
Operating expenses	120
EBIT	80
Interest Expense	8
Taxable Income	72
Taxes	14.4
Net Income	57.6

net profit margin: $\frac{57.6}{700} = 8.2\%$

Example

Sample Income Statement

Revenues	700
Cost of Goods Sold	500
Operating expenses	120
EBIT	80
Interest Expense	8
Taxable Income	72
Taxes	14.4
Net Income	57.6

Compute Net Profit Margin.

Solution

net profit margin: $\frac{57.6}{700} = 8.2\%$

Example

Suppose you are given the following information for K company: Cash = \$30; Accounts receivable = \$20; Inventory = \$20; Fixed Assets = \$30; Notes payable = \$10; Accounts payable = \$20; Long-term Debt = \$30; Total equity = \$40; Revenues = \$700; COGS = \$500; Operating Expenses = \$120; Interest Expense = \$8; Tax Rate = 20%.

Compute ROI.

Solution

Sample Balance Sheet

Cash	30	Notes payable	10
Accounts receivable	20	Accounts payable	20
Inventory	20	Total Current liabilities	30
Total Current assets	70	Long-term Debt	30
Fixed Assets	30	Total equity	40
Total Assets	100	Total Liab. & Equity	100

Sample Income Statement

Revenues	700
Cost of Goods Sold	500
Operating expenses	120
EBIT	80
Interest Expense	8
Taxable Income	72
Taxes	14.4
Net Income	57.6

ROI = 57.6%

Example

서울기업 (단위: 백만원)

현금	30	지급어음	10
외상매출금	20	외상매입금	20
재고자산	20	유동부채 합계	30
유동자산 합계	70	사채	30
고정자산	30	자본금	40
계	100	계	100

서울기업 (단위: 백만원)

매출액	700
매출원가	500
영업비용	120
영업이익	80
이자	10
세전이익	70
세금	14
당기순이익	56

서울기업의 Current Ratio는 (1), Quick Ratio는 (2), Debt-to-equity Ratio는 (3)이다. Times Interest Earned Ratio는 (4), ROI는 (5), Fixed asset turnover는 (6)이다. Gross Profit Margin은 (7)이다.
서울기업의 이자 10백만원을 20% 감소시키면,
Net Profit Margin은 (8)에서 (9)로 증가한다.

Solution

(1) Current Ratio: $\frac{70}{30} = 233\%$,

(2) $\frac{50}{30} = 167\%$, (3) $\frac{60}{40} = 150\%$, (4) $\frac{80}{10} = 8$

(5) $\frac{56}{100} = 56\%$, (6) $\frac{700}{30} = 23.3$, (7) $\frac{200}{700} = 28.6\%$, (8) $\frac{56}{700} = 8\%$

(9) 세전이익: 72, 세금: 14.4, 순이익: 57.6, net profit margin: $\frac{57.6}{700} = 8.2\%$

A firm has net working capital of $2,715, net fixed assets of $22,407, sales of $31,350, and current liabilities of $3,908. How many dollars worth of sales are generated from every $1 in total assets?

Solution

Total asset turnover = $31,350/($2,715 + $22,407 + $3,908) = 1.08

Every $1 in total assets generates $1.08 in sales.

Example

A firm has net working capital of $2,000, net fixed assets of $22,000, sales of $35,000, and current liabilities of $4,000. How many dollars worth of sales are generated from every $1 in total assets?

Solution

Total asset turnover = $35,000/($2,000 + $22,000 + $4,000) = 1.25

Every $1 in total assets generates $1.25 in sales.

The Point of Intersection of Two Lines

The point of intersection of two distinct, nonparallel lines is the single point where they meet or cross.

It is the ordered pair of the values of x and y where the lines meet on the graph and that satisfies the equations of both lines.

Distinct, parallel lines are lines in a plane that are always the same distance apart. They will have no points of intersection.

An intersection point between two functions is a point where the graphs of the functions meet each other. You find intersections by solving the system of equations consisting of the two functions.

Example

Find out the point of intersection of two lines $y = x+1$ and $y + 2x = 4$.

Solution

$(x, y) = (1, 2)$

Example

Find out the point of intersection of two lines $x + 2y + 1 = 0$ and $2x + 3y + 5 = 0$.

Solution

$(x,y) = (-7, 3)$

Example

Find out the point of intersection of two lines $2x + 4y + 6 = 0$ and $6x + 9y + 12 = 0$.

Solution

$(x,y) = (1, -2)$

Break-even analysis

손익분기점 분석

BEP is the point at which total cost and total revenue are equal, i.e."even". All costs that must be paid are paid, and there is neither profit nor loss.

Break-even analysis refers to the point at which total costs and total revenue are equal. A break-even point analysis is used to determine the number of units or dollars of revenue needed to cover total costs.

The Break Even Point is the necessary level of output for a company's revenue to be equal to its total costs – or said differently, the inflection point at which a company begins to generate a profit.

손익분기점(break-even point)은 기업의 판매 또는 생산활동에서 총수입과 총비용이 같아지는 점이다. CVP analysis 이라고도 한다.

원가(cost), 판매액(volume), 이익(profit)

$(p-v)$: 공헌이익

p: 단위당 판매가격, v: 단위당 변동비

Contribution Margin

The contribution margin is computed as the selling price per unit, minus the variable cost per unit.

$(p-v)$: contribution margin

p: Selling price per unit

v: Variable cost per unit

Example

The contribution margin is the excess between the selling price of the product and the total variable costs. For example, if an item sells for $100, the total fixed costs are $25 per unit, and the total variable costs are $60 per unit, the contribution margin of the product is (   ).

Solution

$40

$\frac{p-v}{p}$: contribution margin ratio

$\frac{p-v}{p}$: 공헌이익률

$TR = p \cdot Q$

$TC = FC + VC = FC + v \cdot Q$

FC: 고정비, VC: 변동비

생산량의 손익분기점

$p \cdot Q^* = FC + v \cdot Q^*$

$Q^* = \frac{FC}{p-v}$

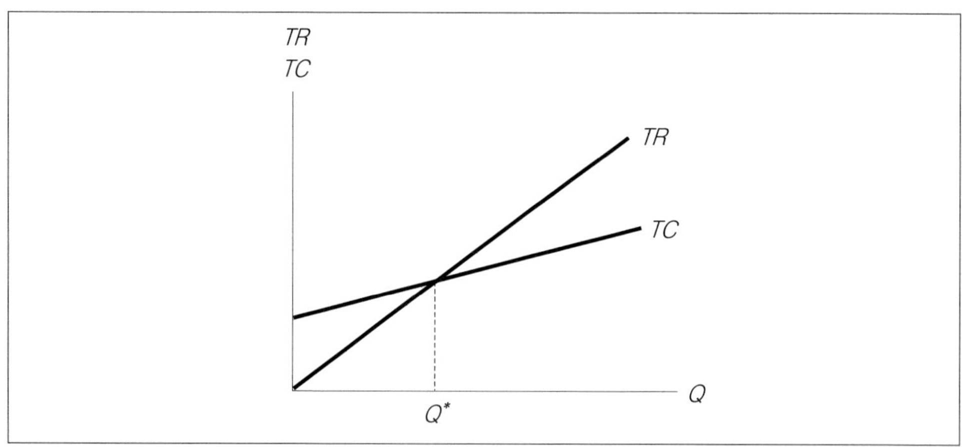

Total Cost

The total cost of production, which includes both fixed costs and variable costs, can be expressed mathematically as the sum of fixed costs and variable costs:

TC = FC + VC

Fixed costs and variable costs are two types of expenses that businesses incur in their operations:

Fixed Costs

Fixed costs are expenses that remain the same regardless of production output.

Fixed costs are expenses that remain constant regardless of the level of production or sales volume.

These costs do not vary with the quantity of goods or services produced.

Examples of fixed costs are rent, employee salaries, and office supplies.

Variable Costs

Variable costs are dependent on production output.

Variable costs are expenses that change proportionally with the level of production or sales volume.

These costs fluctuate based on the quantity of goods or services produced.

Examples of variable costs are cost of raw materials used in production and utility costs.

Utilities expense is the cost - during a given time period - of using things such as electricity, water, and heating.

고정비는 매출액의 크기가 변하더라도 영향을 받지 않고 일정하게 발생하는 비용이다. 고정비의 성격을 갖는 비용으로는 감가상각비, 이자비용 등을 들 수 있다.

변동비는 매출액이 변할 때 매출액의 크기에 따라 일정 비율로 같이 변하는 비용이다. 변동비로 분류될 수 있는 비용항목으로는 재료비, 노무비 등을 들 수 있다.

Example

Find BEP from the following price and cost data.

Sale price per unit: 1,000 won

Variable cost per unit: 600 won

Rent: 60,000 won

Depreciation: 20,000 won

Solution

$$Q^* = \frac{FC}{p-v} = \frac{80,000}{1,000-600} = 200$$

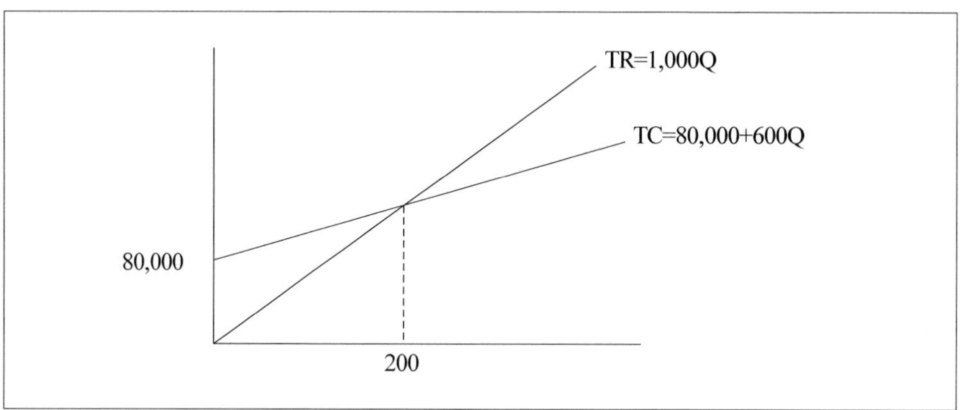

Example

If a company has $10,000 in fixed costs per month, and their product has an average selling price of $100, and the variable cost is $20 for each product.

Find BEP.

Solution

Fixed Costs = $10,000 Average Selling Price (ASP) = $100

Variable Cost per Unit = $20 Contribution Margin = $80

Then, by dividing $10,000 in fixed costs by the $80 contribution margin, you'll end up with 125 units as the break-even point.

BEP = 125 Units

Example

지은이는 학교 앞에서 액세서리 가게를 운영하는데, 남대문에서 600원에 사다가 1,000원에 판매한다. 점포를 빌리는데 한 달에 6만원이 들고, 감가상각비로 2만원이 드는 경우, 한 달에 몇 개를 팔아야 영업손실을 면할 수 있을까?

Solution

$$Q^* = \frac{FC}{p-v} = \frac{80,000}{1,000-600} = 200$$

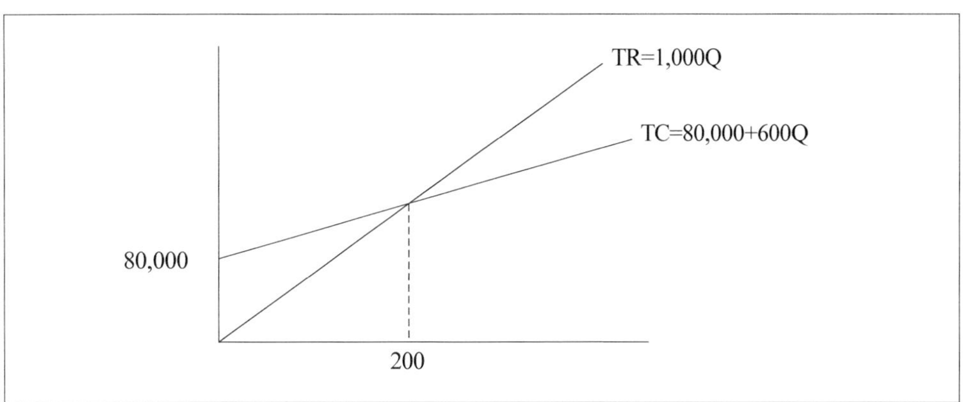

Example

Find BEP from the following price and cost data.

Sale price per unit: 100 won

Variable cost per unit: 50 won

Fixed cost: 350,000 won

Solution

$$Q^* = \frac{FC}{p-v} = \frac{350,000}{100-50} = 7,000$$

Example

판매가격은 100원이고, 고정비는 350,000원, 단위당 변동비는 50원인 경우, 손익분기점의 매출량은?

Solution

$$Q^* = \frac{FC}{p-v} = \frac{350,000}{100-50} = 7,000$$

영업레버리지

Operating leverage refers to the phenomenon whereby a small change in sales triggers a relatively large change in operating income.

매출액의 변화율보다 영업이익의 변화율이 더 크게 나타나는 현상을 영업레버리지효과(operating leverage effect)라고 한다.

Example

Revenues	1,000
Fixed Costs	300
Variable Costs	500
EBIT	200

A 10% revenue increase should result in a (　　　) increase in operating income.

Solution

Revenues	1,000	1,100
Fixed Costs	300	300
Variable Costs	500	550
EBIT	200	250

$$\frac{\Delta Rev}{Rev} = 10\%$$

$$\frac{\Delta EBIT}{EBIT} = 25\%$$

A 10% revenue increase should result in a 25% increase in operating income.

Example

Revenues: $1,000

Fixed Costs: $300

Variable Costs: $500

EBIT: $200

A 10% revenue increase should result in a (   ) increase in operating income.

Solution

Revenues	1,000	1,100
Fixed Costs	300	300
Variable Costs	500	550
EBIT	200	250

$$\frac{\Delta Rev}{Rev} = 10\%$$

$$\frac{\Delta EBIT}{EBIT} = 25\%$$

A 10% revenue increase should result in a 25% increase in operating income.

Example

매출액	1,000	1,100
고정비	300	300
변동비	500	550
영업이익	200	250

매출액이 1,000만원에서 1,100만원으로 10% 증가한 경우, 영업이익은 25% 증가한다.

영업레버리지도

DOL (degree of operating leverage)

DOL is the percentage change in EBIT divided by the percentage change in sales.
영업레버리지도는 매출액이 1% 증가할 때 영업이익이 몇 % 증가하는지를 나타내는 지표이다.

$$DOL = \frac{\frac{\triangle EBIT}{EBIT}}{\frac{\triangle Q}{Q}}$$

$$\frac{\Delta Rev}{Rev} = \frac{p(\Delta Q)}{pQ} = \frac{\Delta Q}{Q}$$

$$EBIT = Q(p-v) - FC$$

$$\triangle EBIT = \triangle Q(p-v)$$

$$DOL = \frac{Q(p-v)}{EBIT}$$

Example

Given $y = 3x - 2$, find Δy.

Example

Given $y = 3x - 2$, find change in y.

Example

Given $y = (a-b)x - c$, find Δy.

Example

Company K sells 500 products for a unit price of 100 won each. The company's fixed costs are 28,000 won. It costs 30 won in variable costs per unit to make each product. Calculate company K's degree of operating leverage.

Solution

$$EBIT = Q(p-v) - FC = 500 \times 70 - 28{,}000 = 7{,}000$$

$$DOL = \frac{Q(p-v)}{EBIT} = \frac{35{,}000}{7{,}000} = 5$$

Example

Calculate DOL from the following price and cost data.

Sale price per unit: 100 won

Variable cost per unit: 30 won

Fixed cost: 28,000 won

Sales units: 500

Solution

$$EBIT = Q(p-v) - FC = 500 \times 70 - 28{,}000 = 7{,}000$$

$$DOL = \frac{Q(p-v)}{EBIT} = \frac{35{,}000}{7{,}000} = 5$$

Example

매출단가: 100원, 고정비: 28,000원, 단위당 변동비: 30원인 경우, 매출량이 500개일 때, 영업레버리지도를 구하면?

Solution

$$EBIT = Q(p-v) - FC = 500 \times 70 - 28{,}000 = 7{,}000$$

$$DOL = \frac{Q(p-v)}{EBIT} = \frac{35{,}000}{7{,}000} = 5$$

Example

Sale price per unit: 100 won

Variable cost per unit: 30 won

Fixed cost: 28,000 won

Sales units: 500

10 percent change in sales results in (   ) percent change in EBIT.

Solution

$$EBIT = Q(p-v) - FC = 500 \times 70 - 28{,}000 = 7{,}000$$

$$DOL = \frac{Q(p-v)}{EBIT} = \frac{35{,}000}{7{,}000} = 5$$

10 percent change in sales results in 50 percent change in EBIT.

Example

매출단가: 100원, 고정비: 28,000원, 단위당 변동비: 30원인 경우, 매출량이 500개일 때, 매출량이 10% 증가하면 영업이익은 몇 % 증가하는가?

Solution

매출량이 500개일 때, 영업이익은 다음과 같다.

$$EBIT = Q(p-v) - FC = 500 \times 70 - 28{,}000 = 7{,}000$$

매출량이 550개일 때, 영업이익은 다음과 같다.

$$EBIT = Q(p-v) - FC = 550 \times 70 - 28{,}000 = 10{,}500$$

영업이익은 50% 증가한다.

Example

Find BEP from the following price and cost data.

Sale price per unit: 900 won

Variable cost per unit: 400 won

Rent: 50,000 won

Depreciation: 10,000 won

Solution

$$Q^* = \frac{FC}{p-v} = \frac{60,000}{900-400} = 120$$

Example

Calculate DOL from the following price and cost data.

Sale price per unit: 900 won

Variable cost per unit: 400 won

Rent: 50,000 won

Depreciation: 10,000 won

Sales units: 200

Solution

$$EBIT = Q(p-v) - FC = 200 \times 500 - 60,000 = 40,000$$

$$DOL = \frac{Q(p-v)}{EBIT} = \frac{100,000}{40,000} = 2.5$$

Example

The interpretation of DOL of 2.5 is that 1 percent change in sales results in (   ) percent change in EBIT.

Solution

The interpretation of DOL of 2.5 is that 1 percent change in sales results in 2.5 percent change in EBIT.

Example

수진이는 학교 앞에서 액세서리 가게를 운영하는데, 남대문에서 400원에 사다가 900원에 판매한다. 점포를 빌리는데 한 달에 5만원이 들고, 감가상각비로 1만원이 드는 경우,

1) 한 달에 몇 개를 팔아야 영업손실을 면할 수 있을까?

2) 판매량이 200개일 때, 영업레버리지도는?

Solution

1) $Q^* = \dfrac{FC}{p-v} = \dfrac{60,000}{900-400} = 120$

2) $EBIT = Q(p-v) - FC = 200 \times 500 - 60,000 = 40,000$

$$DOL = \frac{Q(p-v)}{EBIT} = \frac{100,000}{40,000} = 2.5$$

Example

Calculate DOL from the following price and cost data.

Sale price per unit: $30

Variable cost per unit: $6

Fixed cost: $80,000

Sales units: 5,000

Solution

$$EBIT = Q(p-v) - FC = 5{,}000 \times 24 - 80{,}000 = 40{,}000$$

$$DOL = \frac{Q(p-v)}{EBIT} = \frac{120{,}000}{40{,}000} = 3$$

Example

매출단가: $30, 단위당 변동비: $6, 고정비: $80,000인 경우, 판매량이 5,000일 때 영업레버리지도는?

Solution

$$EBIT = Q(p-v) - FC = 5{,}000 \times 24 - 80{,}000 = 40{,}000$$

$$DOL = \frac{Q(p-v)}{EBIT} = \frac{120{,}000}{40{,}000} = 3$$

The operating leverage and DOL

The higher DOL, the more sensitive a company's earnings before interest and taxes are to changes in sales.

EPS

Earnings per share is a financial metric that represents the portion of a company's profit allocated to each outstanding share of common stock. It's calculated by dividing the company's net income by the number of outstanding shares.

Example

Let's consider a fictional company, ABC Inc., which has a net income of $1,000,000 for the year and has 500,000 outstanding shares of common stock.
Find EPS.

Solution

EPS = Net Income / Number of Outstanding Shares
The earnings per share for ABC Inc. for the year is $2. This means that for each share of common stock, the company earned $2 in profit.

Example

Translate the sentence into an equation: The market value of equity can be calculated by multiplying the price per share by the number of shares outstanding.

Solution

$S = np$

if we denote:

Equity as S

Number of shares as n

Price per share as p.

This formula calculates the total market value of the company's equity based on the current price per share and the number of shares outstanding.

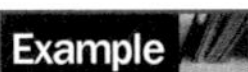

If the common stock for Company XYZ is $600,000, then the total equity for Company XYZ would also be $600,000, assuming there are no additional components contributing to equity such as retained earnings or additional paid-in capital.

Financial leverage effect

재무레버리지효과

영업이익의 변화율보다 세후 순이익의 변화율이 크게 나타나는 현상

$\frac{\Delta EBIT}{EBIT}$: Percentage change in EBIT

$\frac{\Delta NI}{NI}$: Percentage change in Net Income

$$\frac{\Delta EBIT}{EBIT} < \frac{\Delta NI}{NI}$$

Financial leverage is an investment strategy where businesses borrow money to buy assets and increase capital to expand their venture. The firms opt for this option only when they know that their investment has the potential to generate profits that could easily help them pay back their debt.

When a company is highly leveraged, it indicates that it has more debt than equity. In the process, companies borrow finances instead of issuing stocks to investors to raise capital. Though companies can also use equity to build assets, they prefer taking debts as the cost of borrowing is less than the cost of equity.

Example

Given the following information:

EBIT: $10,000

Interest Expense: $2,000

Tax Rate: 50%

Operating income increases by 40%

What is the percentage increase in net income as a result of this 40% increase in operating income?

Solution

EBIT	10,000	14,000
Interest	2,000	2,000
EBT	8,000	12,000
Taxes	4,000	6,000
Net income	4,000	6,000

$$\frac{\Delta EBIT}{EBIT} = 40\%$$

$$\frac{\Delta NI}{NI} = 50\%$$

A 40% operating income increase should result in a 50% increase in net income.

Example

관악기업의 영업이익이 1억원이며, 매년 지불해야 하는 이자는 2,000만원이다. 법인세율을 50%라고 가정하면, 세후 순이익은 4,000만원이다. 만약 영업이익이 40% 증가하면, 세후 순이익은 50% 증가하게 된다.

영업이익	10,000	14,000
이자	2,000	2,000
세전이익	8,000	12,000
법인세	4,000	6,000
세후 순이익	4,000	6,000

자본조달분기점

Financial break-even point

주당 이익을 같게 하는 점

$$EPS_1 = EPS_2$$

$$\frac{NI_1}{n_1} = \frac{NI_2}{n_2}$$

$$\frac{(EBIT - I_1)(1-t)}{n_1} = \frac{(EBIT - I_2)(1-t)}{n_2}$$

Example

K company is considering two financing plans. The key information is as follows:

(a) Total funds to be raised, $10,000.

(b) Financing plans

Plans	Equity	Debt
A	$5,000	$5,000
B	$2,000	$8,000

(c) Cost of debt: 10%

(d) Tax rate: 50%

(e) Stock price: $100

Find financial break-even point.

Solution

$$\frac{(EBIT-I_1)(1-t)}{n_1}=\frac{(EBIT-I_2)(1-t)}{n_2}$$

$$\frac{(EBIT-500)(1-0.5)}{50}=\frac{(EBIT-800)(1-0.5)}{20}$$

$$\frac{(EBIT-500)}{100}=\frac{(EBIT-800)}{40}$$

$$EBIT=1,000$$

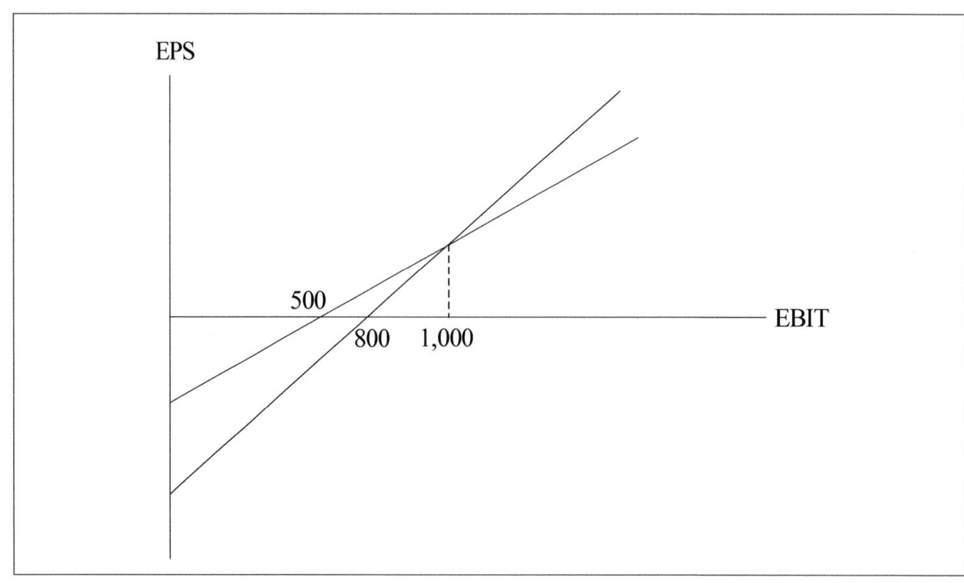

Example

K company is considering two financing plans: 50 percent equity and 50 percent debt; and 20 percent equity and 80 percent debt.

Total funds to be raised, $10,000.

Cost of debt: 10%

Tax rate: 50%

Stock price: $100

Find financial break-even point.

Solution

$$\frac{(EBIT-I_1)(1-t)}{n_1}=\frac{(EBIT-I_2)(1-t)}{n_2}$$

$$\frac{(EBIT-500)(1-0.5)}{50}=\frac{(EBIT-800)(1-0.5)}{20}$$

$$\frac{(EBIT-500)}{100}=\frac{(EBIT-800)}{40}$$

$$EBIT=1,000$$

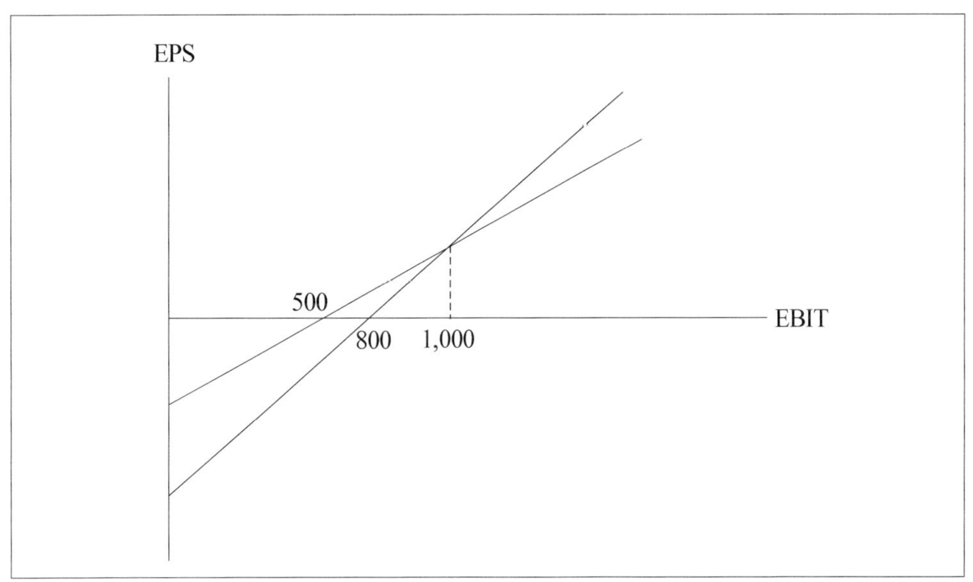

Example

관악기업은 10,000만원의 자금을 조달하는 방법으로 다음과 같은 2가지 안을 가지고 있다.
제 1안은 5,000만원은 부채로, 5,000만원은 자기자본으로 조달하는 경우
제 2안은 8,000만원은 부채로, 2,000만원은 자기자본으로 조달하는 경우
이자율은 10%, 세율은 50%, 주당 가격은 100원인 경우, 자본조달분기점에서의 영업이익은?

Solution

$$\frac{(EBIT - I_1)(1-t)}{n_1} = \frac{(EBIT - I_2)(1-t)}{n_2}$$

$$\frac{(EBIT - 500)(1-0.5)}{50} = \frac{(EBIT - 800)(1-0.5)}{20}$$

$$\frac{(EBIT - 500)}{100} = \frac{(EBIT - 800)}{40}$$

$$EBIT = 1,000$$

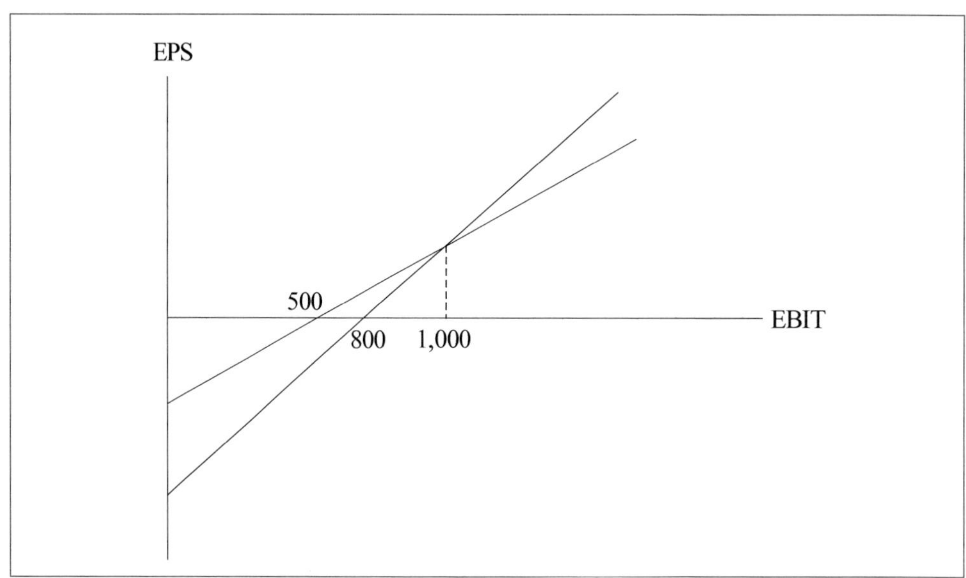

Example

서울기업은 400,000원의 자금을 조달하는 방법으로 다음과 같은 2가지 안을 가지고 있다.

	자본	부채
1안	20%	80%
2안	40%	60%

이자율은 5%, 세율은 20%, 주당 가격은 500원인 경우, 자본조달분기점을 구하라.

Solution

Plans	Equity	Debt
A	$80,000	$320,000
B	$160,000	$240,000

$$\frac{(EBIT - I_1)(1-t)}{n_1} = \frac{(EBIT - I_2)(1-t)}{n_2}$$

$$\frac{(EBIT - 16,000)(1-0.2)}{160} = \frac{(EBIT - 12,000)(1-0.2)}{320}$$

$$\frac{(EBIT - 16,000)}{160} = \frac{(EBIT - 12,000)}{320}$$

EBIT: 20,000

Financial break-even point

$$\frac{(EBIT-I_1)(1-t)}{n_1}=\frac{(EBIT-I_2)(1-t)}{n_2}$$

$$\frac{(EBIT-I_1)}{n_1}=\frac{(EBIT-I_2)}{n_2}$$

$$\frac{(EBIT-r_B B_1)}{n_1}=\frac{(EBIT-r_B B_2)}{n_2}$$

$$n_2(EBIT-r_B B_1)=n_1(EBIT-r_B B_2)$$

$$S=np$$

$$S_2(EBIT-r_B B_1)=S_1(EBIT-r_B B_2)$$

$$(S_2-S_1)EBIT=r_B(S_2 B_1-S_1 B_2)$$

B=V−S

$$(S_2-S_1)EBIT=r_B S_2(V-S_1)-r_B S_1(V-S_2)$$

$$EBIT=r_B V$$

where:

V: Total funds to be raised

B: Amount of debt

S: Amount of equity

n: Number of Outstanding Shares

p: Stock price

Example

Write T for True and F for False for the following equation. If the equation is false, correct the equation.

$$n_1(EBIT-r_B B_1)=n_2(EBIT-r_B B_2)$$

Solution

F,

$$n_2(EBIT-r_B B_1)=n_1(EBIT-r_B B_2)$$

Example

Write T or F for the equation. If the equation is false, correct the equation.

$$S_1(EBIT - r_B B_1) = S_2(EBIT - r_B B_2)$$

Solution

F,

$$S_2(EBIT - r_B B_1) = S_1(EBIT - r_B B_2)$$

Example

K company is considering two financing plans: 60 percent equity and 40 percent debt; and 40 percent equity and 60 percent debt.

V: $2,000,000

r_B: 8%

Tax rate: 20%

Stock price: $5,000

V: Total funds to be raised

Find financial break-even point.

Solution

Plans	Equity	Debt
A	$1,200,000	$800,000
B	$800,000	$1,200,000

$$\frac{(EBIT - I_1)(1-t)}{n_1} = \frac{(EBIT - I_2)(1-t)}{n_2}$$

$$\frac{(EBIT - 64{,}000)(1-0.2)}{240} = \frac{(EBIT - 96{,}000)(1-0.2)}{160}$$

$$\frac{(EBIT - 64{,}000)}{240} = \frac{(EBIT - 96{,}000)}{160}$$

$$2(EBIT - 64{,}000) = 3(EBIT - 96{,}000)$$

EBIT: 160,000

DFL

DFL measures the percentage in EPS for a unit change in EBIT.

The DFL is calculated by dividing the percentage change of a company's earnings per share by the percentage change in its earnings before interest and taxes over a period.

재무레버리지도(degree of financial leverage)

영업이익이 1% 증가할 때 당기순이익이 몇 % 증가하는지를 나타내는 지표

$$DFL = \frac{\frac{\Delta EPS}{EPS}}{\frac{\Delta EBIT}{EBIT}}$$

$$\frac{\Delta EPS}{EPS} = \frac{\frac{\Delta EBIT(1-t)}{n}}{\frac{(EBIT-I)(1-t)}{n}} = \frac{\Delta EBIT}{EBIT-I}$$

$$DFL = \frac{\frac{\Delta EPS}{EPS}}{\frac{\Delta EBIT}{EBIT}} = \frac{EBIT}{EBIT-I}$$

Example

Given $y = \frac{5(x-3)}{2}$, find Δy.

Example

Given $y = \frac{5(x-3)}{2}$, find change in y.

Example

Given $y = \frac{(x-a)(1-b)}{c}$, find Δy.

Example

Given $y = \dfrac{(x-a)(1-b)}{c}$, find change in y.

Example

Given y=a(x−b)(1−c), find change in y.

Example

Calculate DFL from the following data.

Debt: $5,000

Equity: $5,000

Cost of debt: 10%

EBIT: 1,000

Solution

$$DFL = \frac{1,000}{1,000-500} = 2$$

Example

Company K has EBIT of $1,000 million with interest expense of $500 million. Calculate DFL.

Solution

$$DFL = \frac{1,000}{1,000-500} = 2$$

Example

A company has debt of $5,000 and pays an annual interest rate of 10% on it. Currently, its EBIT (operating income) is $1,000.

If the company's EBIT (operating income) increased by 3% in the last fiscal year, what was the resulting percentage increase in its net income for that same period?

Solution

$$DFL = \frac{1,000}{1,000 - 500} = 2$$

If the company's EBIT increased by 3%, its net income would increase by 6%.

Example

Calculate DFL from the following data.

Debt: $8,000

Equity: $2,000

Cost of debt: 10%

EBIT: 1,000

Solution

$$DFL = \frac{1,000}{1,000 - 800} = 5$$

Example

관악기업은 10,000만원의 자금을 조달하는 방법으로 다음과 같은 2가지 안을 가지고 있다.
제 1안은 5,000만원은 부채로, 5,000만원은 자기자본으로 조달하는 경우
제2안은 8,000만원은 부채로, 2,000만원은 자기자본으로 조달하는 경우
이자율은 10%이고 영업이익은 1,000만원일 때, 재무레버리지도는?

Solution

제1안: $DFL = \frac{1,000}{1,000 - 500} = 2$

제2안: $DFL = \frac{1,000}{1,000 - 800} = 5$

Example

K Company is debating between a leveraged and an unleveraged capital structure. The all equity capital structure would consist of 40,000 shares of stock. The debt and equity option would consist of 25,000 shares of stock plus $280,000 of debt with an interest rate of 7 percent. What is the break-even level of earnings before interest and taxes between these two options?

Solution

All-equity option (Unleveraged):
Number of shares = 40,000
Debt and equity option (Leveraged):
Number of shares = 25,000
Debt = $280,000
Interest rate = 7%
Interest expense = $19,600

$$\frac{EBIT}{40,000} = \frac{(EBIT - 19,600)}{25,000}$$

EBIT=52,267

Example

ABC Company is debating between a leveraged and an unleveraged capital structure. The all equity capital structure would consist of 40,000 shares of stock. The debt and equity option would consist of 25,000 shares of stock plus $270,000 of debt with an interest rate of 7 percent. What is the break-even level of earnings before interest and taxes between these two options?

Solution

Interest expense = $18,900

$$\frac{EBIT}{40,000} = \frac{EBIT - 18,900}{25,000}$$

EBIT=50,400

Least Squares Principle

Determining a regression equation by minimizing the sum of the squares of the vertical distances between the actual Y values and the predicted values of Y.

Regression Line

The regression line is the line that minimizes the squared deviations between the line and the actual data points.

Residual: vertical distance between observed value and predicted value

RESIDUAL = OBSERVED − PREDICTED

$$\epsilon_i = y_i - \hat{y_i}$$

$|\epsilon_i|$ is a vertical distance.

the square of the residual: ϵ_i^2

RSS, SSR, or SSE

the residual sum of squares

the sum of squared residuals

the sum of squared estimate of errors

Example

Find the vertical distance between y=2x+1 and (1,5).

Solution

$\epsilon_i = 2$

Example

Calculate RSS.

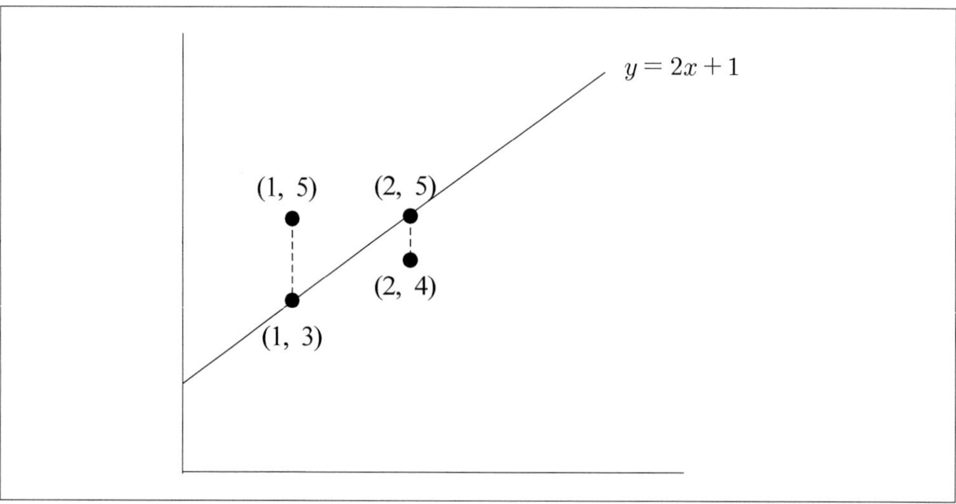

Solution

$\epsilon_i = Y_i - \widehat{Y_i}$

Regression Line: $y = 2x + 1$

i	Y_i	X_i	$\widehat{Y_i}$	e_i	e_i^2
1	5	1	3	2	4
2	4	2	5	−1	1
Sums	9	3	8	1	5

$$RSS = \sum_{i=1}^{2} \epsilon_i^2 = (5-3)^2 + (4-5)^2$$

$RSS = 5$

점(1,5)와 점(1,3)의 선분의 길이 제곱은 $(5-3)^2$ 이다.

점(2,4)와 점(2,5)의 선분의 길이 제곱은 $(4-5)^2$ 이다.

회귀분석법에 의한 소요자금예측

회귀분석에 의한 소요자금예측은 소요자금과 상관관계가 가장 큰 항목이 매출액이라는 가정에서 출발한다. 즉, 과거의 매출액 변화와 소요자금 변화와의 상관관계로부터 미래매출액 증가에 따른 소요자금을 예측하는 방법이다.

Linear Regression

Linear regression attempts to model the relationship between two variables by fitting a linear equation to observed data.

Example

Last year K Inc. reported the following income statement:

Sales	$2,000,000
Cost of goods sold	1,200,000
Depreciation	500,000
Operating income(EBIT)	300,000
Interest expense	100,000
EBT	200,000
Taxes (40%)	80,000
Net income	120,000

The company's CEO was unhappy with the firm's performance. This year, he would like to see net income doubled to $240,000. Depreciation, interest expense, and tax rate will all remain constant, and the cost of goods will also remain at 60 percent of sales. How much sales must the company generate to achieve the CEO's net income target?

Solution

$(X-0.6X-500{,}000-100{,}000)(1-0.4)=240{,}000$

X=$2,500,000

Example

Suppose we choose to consider sales as the explanatory variable, and funds required as the dependent variable.

x: sales

y: funds required

Below is table of data.

Year	x	y
2020	24	17
2021	26	18
2022	29	21
2023	33	24
2024	36	27

We got the equation as $y = -3.51 + 0.84x$.

Calculate the predictor of y for $x = 40$.

Solution

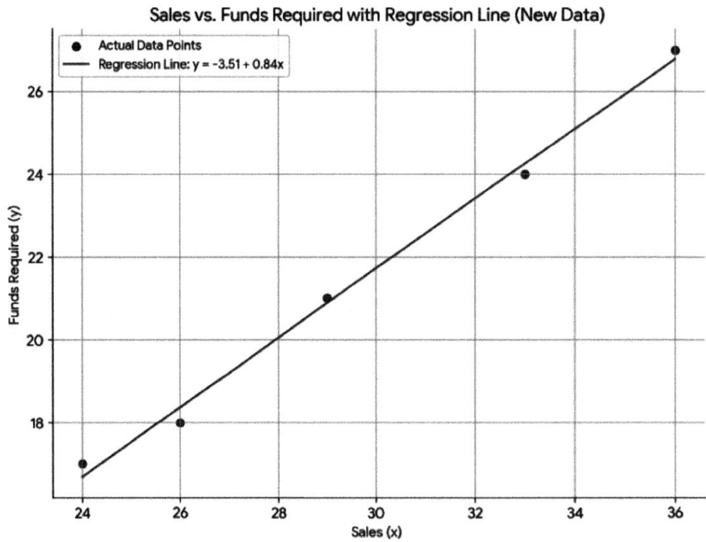

$y = -3.51 + 0.84 \times 40 = 30.09$

Example

Last year K Inc. reported the following income statement:

Sales: $2,000,000

COGS: 1,400,000

Depreciation: 200,000

EBIT: 400,000

Interest expense: 100,000

EBT; 300,000

Taxes: 120,000

Net income: 180,000

The company's CEO was unhappy with the firm's performance. This year, he would like to see net income doubled to $360,000. Depreciation, interest expense, and tax rate will all remain constant, and the cost of goods will also remain at 70 percent of sales. How much sales must the company generate to achieve the CEO's net income target?

Solution

X=3,000,000

Example

Last year K company had sales of $2,000,000, costs of $1,400,000, depreciation expense of $200,000, interest expense of $100,000, and a tax rate of 40 percent.

The company's CEO was unhappy with the firm's performance. This year, he would like to see net income doubled to $360,000. Depreciation, interest expense, and tax rate will all remain constant, and the cost of goods will also remain at 70 percent of sales. How much sales must the company generate to achieve the CEO's net income target?

Solution

X=3,000,000

Example

Last year K Inc. reported the following income statement:

Sales: $2,500,000

COGS: 1,750,000

Depreciation: 200,000

EBIT: 550,000

Interest expense: 100,000

EBT; 450,000

Taxes: 180,000

Net income: 270,000

The company's CEO was unhappy with the firm's performance. This year, he would like to see net income doubled to $540,000. Depreciation, interest expense, and tax rate will all remain constant, and the cost of goods will also remain at 70 percent of sales. How much sales must the company generate to achieve the CEO's net income target?

Solution

X=4,000,000

질적 분석

질적 분석이란 기업마다 가지고 있는 질적인 특성, 즉 기업의 연혁, 경영자의 능력, 기업고유의 경영전략, 다른 기업이 흉내 낼 수 없는 노하우, 회사의 존속기간 등을 분석하는 것을 말한다.

Interest on interest

Interest-on-interest, also referred to as 'compound interest', is the interest that is earned when interest payments are reinvested.

Simple interest, on the other hand, is only charged on the original principal amount.

화폐의 시간가치

화폐의 시간가치는 소비자들이 미래의 소비보다는 현재의 소비를 선호하는 유동성 선호(liquidity preference)에 그 기반을 두고 있다.

Future Value

Value of a sum after investing it over one or more periods.

The amount to which a cash flow will grow over a given period of time when compounded at a given interest rate.

Compounding

The arithmetic process of determining the final value of a cash flow when compound interest is applied.

Savings account

A savings account is a type of deposit account offered by banks and financial institutions that allows individuals to deposit money and earn interest on their savings.

Example

Suppose you deposit 100 thousand won in an account. If the account earns 10%, how much will be in the account after one year?

Solution

$100(1+0.1)=110$ thousand won.

Example

Suppose you deposit 100 thousand won in an account. If the account earns 10%, how much will be in the account after two years?

Solution

$100(1+0.1)^2 = 121$ thousand won.

Example

You deposit $100 in a bank for 2 years at 10% per year compounded annually. What will be the value of the money at the end of 2 years?

Solution

$100(1+0.1)^2 = 121$

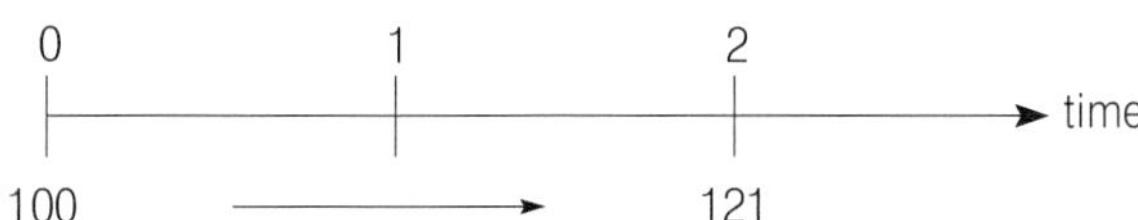

Example

Suppose you deposit 10,000 won in an account. If the account earns 20%, how much will be in the account after two years?

Solution

$10,000(1+0.2)^2 = 14,400$

Example

Suppose you deposit 300,000 won in an account. If the account earns 5%, how much will be in the account after three years?

Solution

$300,000(1+0.05)^3 = 347,288$ won

Example

Tom invested $5,600 in an account that pays 5 percent simple interest. How much money will he have at the end of ten years?

Solution

Ending value = \$5,600 + (\$5,600 × .05 × 10) = \$8,400

Example

Calculate the compound interest on a $100 deposit after two years. The principal is compounded annually at a rate of 10%.

Solution

$100(1+0.1)^2 = 121$

21

Example

Calculate the compound interest on a $1 million deposit after five years. The principal is compounded annually at a rate of 5%.

Solution

$1,000,000 \times 1.05^5 = 1,276,282$

276,282

Example

John invests $10,000 in an account with a bank that offers a 5% annual simple interest rate. If John keeps his money in the account for 3 years, how much interest will he earn in total?

Solution

John would earn $1,500 in total interest over 3 years with a simple interest rate of 5%.

Example

How is the future value of an investment calculated in the nth year, incorporating compound interest?

Solution

The future value of an investment in the nth year, considering compound interest, can be calculated using the formula:

$A(1+r)^n$

CAGR

CAGR stands for Compound Annual Growth Rate. It's a measure of the mean annual growth rate of an investment over a specified time period, assuming that the investment has been compounding over that period.

CAGR is a useful measure to understand the mean annual growth rate of an investment, revenue, or other metrics over a specified period. It smooths out the volatility over the period to provide a consistent growth rate.

CAGR is a valuable metric for evaluating the average annual growth of revenues, investments, or other financial metrics over a period, smoothing out the effects of volatility to provide a clearer picture of performance.

Example

Let's assume a company's revenue was $100,000 in 2021 and grew to $130,000 in 2023. Calculate the CAGR.

Solution

$100(1+r)^2 = 130$

CAGR = 14%

Example

Imagine you invest $1,000 in a real estate property. Over a period of 2 years, the value of the property appreciates to $1,300. Calculate the CAGR.

Solution

The compound annual growth rate (CAGR) of your investment over those 2 years would be approximately 14.0%.

Let's say you invested $1,000 in a stock, and after 2 years, it grew to $1,300. Calculate the CAGR.

Solution

The compound annual growth rate (CAGR) of your investment over those 2 years would be approximately 14.0%.

Present Value

The value of a future cash stream discounted at the appropriate market interest rate.

The value today of a future cash flow.

현재가치는 미래에 발생하게 될 현금흐름을 현재 시점의 가치로 환산한 금액을 말한다.

Discounting

The process of finding the present value of a cash flow; discounting is the reverse of compounding.

Example

Calculate the present value of the following cash flows discounted at 10%.

1) 100 thousand won received one year from today.

2) 100 thousand won received two years from today.

Solution

1) $\frac{100}{(1+0.1)}=90.91$ thousand won.

0 1 time

90.91 ← 100

2) $\frac{100}{(1+0.1)^2}=82.64$ thousand won.

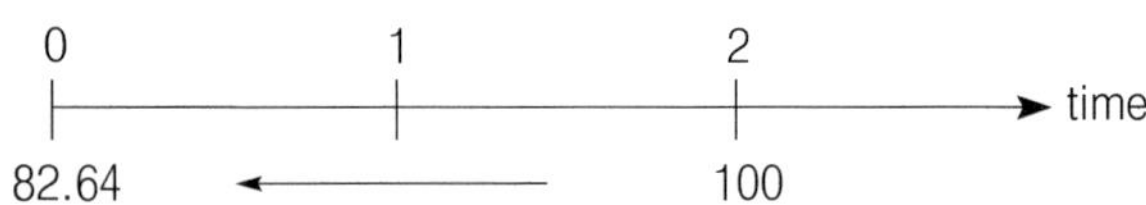

Example

Calculate the present value of 10,000 won discounted back for 2 years at 20 percent.

Solution

$$PV=\frac{10,000}{1.2^2}=6,944$$

Annuity

a sequence of equal cash flows, occurring at the end of each period.

equal cash flows at equal intervals of time for a specific period of time.

An annuity is a series of payments of fixed amount.

Normal annuity: This type of cash flow is received at the end of each period.

Annuity due: When you get a cash flow periodically at the beginning of each period.

Example

Payments of $1,000 each are made at the beginning of each year for 3 years with interest at 5% compounded annually.

Find the FV at the end of last payment period.

Solution

$1{,}000 \times 1.05^3 + 1{,}000 \times 1.05^2 + 1{,}000 \times 1.05 = 3310.125$

Cost of Capital

기업에서는 새로운 투자를 위해서나 원활한 경영을 위해서 자금이 필요하다. 기업이 자금을 조달하는 데는 그 대가를 지불하여야 한다. 은행으로부터 자금을 차입했을 때는 대출이자를 지급하여야 하며, 주주로부터 자금을 조달한 경우에는 투자수익을 지급하여야 한다. 이처럼 기업이 자금을 조달할 때에는 타인자본뿐만 아니라 자기자본에서도 비용이 수반되는 것이다.

Firms need to acquire capital from others to operate and grow. Individuals who are willing to provide their funds to others desire to be rewarded. Capital providers seek returns on their funds, which must be commensurate with the risk undertaken.
Firms obtain capital from two kinds of sources: lenders and equity investors. From the perspective of capital providers, lenders seek to be rewarded with interest and equity investors seek dividends and appreciation in the value of their investment. From a firm's perspective, they must pay for the capital it obtains from others.

수익률은 자금의 공급자인 투자자의 관점에서 볼 때 투자한 자금에 대한 보상의 결과로 주어지는 이익률을 의미한다.
자본비용은 자금의 수요자인 기업의 관점에서 볼 때 조달된 자금에 대한 사용의 대가로 지불해야 하는 비용을 의미한다.

Appreciation

Appreciation in stocks typically refers to the increase in value of a stock over time.

Example

Let's say you buy shares of a company for $50 each. Over the next year, due to strong financial performance and positive market sentiment, the price of the stock increases to $70 per share. This increase in price from $50 to $70 represents appreciation in the value of your investment. If you were to sell the shares at $70 each, you would realize a gain of $20 per share.

Example

K company is investing in a new project. The minimum rate of return the firm requires on this project is referred to as the cost of capital.

Cost of Debt

The cost of debt is the firm's borrowing rate.
타인자본비용(cost of debt)은 기업이 타인자본 즉, 부채를 사용할 때 지급하여야 하는 대가이다.

After-tax cost of debt

The after-tax cost of debt is the effective interest rate a company pays on its debt after accounting for the tax benefits of interest payments.

Example

Let's say a company has a pre-tax cost of debt of 6% and a marginal tax rate of 25%. Find the after-tax cost of debt.

Solution

After-tax cost of debt = Pre-tax cost of debt * (1 - tax rate)

= 6% * (1 - 0.25)

= 4.5%

So, the after-tax cost of debt for this company would be 4.5%.

Cost of Equity

자기자본비용(cost of equity)은 보통주를 발행하여 자금을 조달하는 대가로 지급하는 비용이다.

The cost of equity is the return a firm pays to its equity investors to compensate for the risk they undertake by investing their capital.
The required return on the company's common stock in capital markets. It is also called the equity holders' required rate of return because it is what equity holders can expect to obtain in the capital market.

Corporations, big and small, need capital to do their business. The investors provide the capital to a corporation. A company may need a new factory to manufacture its products, or an airline a few more planes to expand into new territory. The firm acquires the money needed to build the factory or to buy the new planes from investors. The investors, of course, want a return on their investment.

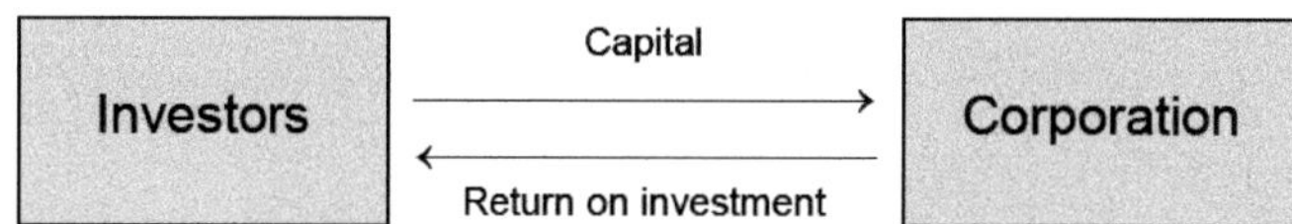

Capital comes in two forms: debt capital and equity capital. To raise debt capital the companies sell bonds to the public, and to raise equity capital the corporation sells the stock of the company. Both stock and bonds are financial instruments and they have a certain intrinsic value.

Intrinsic value

Intrinsic value refers to the true, underlying value of an asset, independent of its market price. It represents what an asset is really worth based on its fundamental characteristics, such as its earnings, cash flow, dividends, or other relevant factors.

For stocks, the intrinsic value is often estimated by analyzing the company's financial statements, growth prospects, competitive position, and other qualitative and quantitative factors.

Intrinsic value represents the underlying worth of an asset based on its fundamental characteristics, providing investors with a benchmark for evaluating whether an asset is overvalued, undervalued, or fairly priced in the market.

Capital

Capital typically refers to the funds a company uses to finance its operations and growth. There are two main types of capital: debt capital and equity capital.

Debt Capital: Debt capital is obtained by borrowing funds from lenders such as banks, bondholders, or other financial institutions. Companies borrow funds with the agreement to repay the principal amount plus interest over a specified period.

Equity Capital: Equity capital represents ownership in a company. It is raised by selling shares of ownership, known as stocks or equity, to investors. Unlike debt capital, equity capital does not require repayment of principal or payment of interest. Instead, investors expect to receive returns through dividends and capital appreciation.

The capital equation is a concept used to describe the relationship between the various sources of capital that a business utilizes to finance its operations and investments. I

Capital = Debt + Equity

In this equation:

Debt: Represents the funds borrowed by the company from external sources, such as loans from banks, bonds issued to investors, or other forms of debt financing. Debt typically incurs interest payments and must be repaid over time.

Equity: Refers to the ownership stake in the company held by its shareholders. Equity can be raised through the sale of common or preferred stock, as well as through retained earnings. Shareholders' equity represents the residual interest in the company's assets after deducting its liabilities.

Together, debt and equity constitute the total capital employed by the company to fund its operations, investments, and growth initiatives. The capital equation highlights the balance between debt financing, which involves taking on financial obligations with fixed repayment terms, and equity financing, which involves sharing ownership in the company with investors. Capital can also refer to physical assets used in production, such as machinery, equipment, buildings, and infrastructure.

Weighted Average

Weighted average is a calculation that takes into account the varying degrees of importance of the numbers in a data set. In calculating a weighted average, each number in the data set is multiplied by a predetermined weight before the final calculation is made.

A weighted average can be more accurate than a simple average in which all numbers in a data set are assigned an identical weight.

The weighted average takes into account the relative importance or frequency of some factors in a data set.

In calculating a simple average, or arithmetic mean, all numbers are treated equally and assigned equal weight. But a weighted average assigns weights that determine in advance the relative importance of each data point.

What is the weighted average weight of the fruits containing 10 apples with an average weight of 150 grams each and 5 oranges with an average weight of 200 grams each?

Solution

With 10 apples, each weighing an average of 150 grams, and 5 oranges, each averaging 200 grams, we can determine the weighted average weight of the fruits in the basket.

Apples: 10 apples, average weight = 150 grams

Oranges: 5 oranges, average weight = 200 grams

Given:

Number of apples: 10

Number of oranges: 5

Average weight of apples: 150 grams

Average weight of oranges: 200 grams

Since there are more apples, we'll assign them a higher weight in the calculation.

Let's give apples a weight of 2/3 and oranges a weight of 1/3.

Weighted average weight = (Average weight of apples * Weight of apples) + (Average weight of oranges * Weight of oranges)

= (150g * 2/3) + (200g * 1/3)

= (100g) + (66.67g)

= 166.67 grams

Therefore, the weighted average weight of the fruits is approximately 167 grams.

The weighted average weight of the fruits in the basket, considering 10 apples with an average weight of 150 grams and 5 oranges with an average weight of 200 grams, is approximately 167 grams.

Common Stock

Common stock is a form of corporate equity ownership, a type of security. It is called "common" to distinguish it from preferred stock. If both types of stock exist, common stock holders cannot be paid dividends until all preferred stockholders are paid.

Preferred stock

A type of stock whose holders are given certain priority over common stockholders in the payment of dividends. Preferred stockholders normally do not receive voting rights.

Net income can be distributed among holders of common stock as a dividend or held by the firm as an addition to retained earnings.

Dividend

Dividends are payments made by a corporation to its shareholders. It is the portion of corporate profits paid out to stockholders. When a corporation earns a profit, that money can be put to two uses: it can either be re-invested in the business, or it can be distributed to shareholders.

Retained Earnings

Retained earnings refers to the portion of net income which is retained by the corporation rather than distributed to its owners as dividends.

A dividend is a reward paid to the shareholders for their investment in a company's equity, and it usually originates from the company's net profits. Though profits can be kept within the company as retained earnings to be used for the company's ongoing and future business activities, a remainder can be allocated to the shareholders as a dividend.

DDM

The dividend discount model is a quantitative method used for predicting the price of a company's stock based on the theory that its present-day price is worth the sum of all of its future dividend payments when discounted back to their present value.
A procedure for valuing the price of a stock by using predicted dividends and discounting them back to present value.

$$S_0 = \frac{D_1}{1+r_S} + \frac{D_2}{(1+r_S)^2} + \frac{D_3}{(1+r_S)^3} + \cdots$$

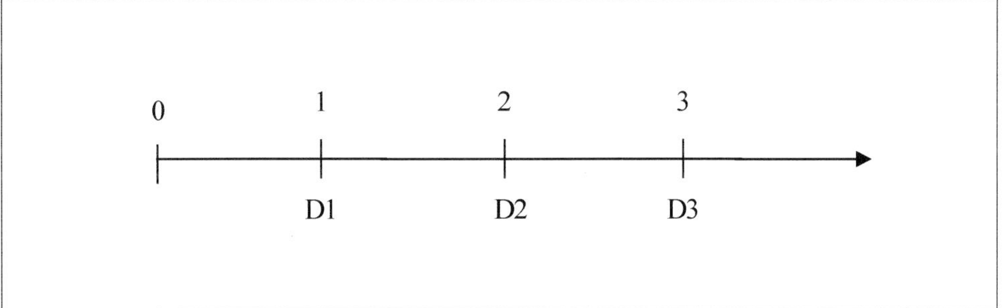

Example

Translate the sentence into an equation: The dividend discount model is a quantitative method used for predicting the price of a company's stock based on the theory that its present-day price is worth the sum of all of its future dividend payments when discounted back to their present value.

Solution

$$S_0 = \frac{D_1}{1+r_S} + \frac{D_2}{(1+r_S)^2} + \frac{D_3}{(1+r_S)^3} + \cdots$$

No-growth Dividend Discount Model

미래의 배당이 일정한 경우

This model assumes that all the dividends paid by the stock remain the same forever until infinite.

$$S_0 = \frac{D_1}{1+r_S} + \frac{D_1}{(1+r_S)^2} + \frac{D_1}{(1+r_S)^3} + \cdots = \frac{D_1}{r_S}$$

Example

Assume Company X will pay a dividend of 1,500 won per share after one year. The discount rate is 15%. Calculate a per-share value.

Solution

$$S_0 = \frac{D_1}{r_s} = \frac{1,500}{0.15} = 10,000$$

Example

서울기업은 매년 1,500원의 배당을 지급한다. 할인율이 15%라고 한다면, 이 기업의 주식가격은?

Solution

$$S_0 = \frac{D_1}{r_s} = \frac{1,500}{0.15} = 10,000$$

Example

The common stock of ABC pays an annual dividend of \$1.5 a share. The company has promised to maintain a constant dividend even though economic times are tough. How much are you willing to pay for one share of this stock if you want to earn a 15 percent annual return?

Solution

$$S_0 = \frac{D_1}{r_s} = \frac{1.5}{0.15} = 10$$

Example

The common stock of ABC pays an annual dividend of \$1.65 a share. The company has promised to maintain a constant dividend even though economic times are tough. How much are you willing to pay for one share of this stock if you want to earn a 12 percent annual return?

Solution

$$S_0 = \frac{D_1}{r_s} = \frac{1.65}{0.12} = 13.75$$

Constant Growth Model or Gordon Model

미래의 배당이 일정하게 성장하는 경우

This dividend discount model assumes dividends grow at a fixed percentage. They are not variable and are consistent throughout.

$$D_t = D_1(1+g)^{t-1}$$

$$S_0 = \frac{D_1}{1+r_S} + \frac{D_2}{(1+r_S)^2} + \frac{D_3}{(1+r_S)^3} + \cdots$$

$$S_0 = \frac{D_1}{1+r_S} + \frac{D_1(1+g)}{(1+r_S)^2} + \frac{D_1(1+g)^2}{(1+r_S)^3} + \cdots = \frac{D_1}{r_S - g}$$

Example

Assume Company Y will pay a dividend of 1,500 won per share after one year. The company expects dividends to grow in perpetuity at 10 percent per year, and the discount rate is 15%. Calculate a per-share value.

Solution

$D_1 = 1{,}500,\ \ D_2 = 1{,}650,\ \ \ D_3 = 1{,}815$

$$S_0 = \frac{D_1}{r_s - g}$$

$$S_0 = \frac{1{,}500}{0.15 - 0.1} = 30{,}000$$

Example

한라기업은 1년 후에 1,500원의 배당을 지급한다. 그리고 배당은 매년 10%의 비율로 성장한다고 한다. 이 때 할인율이 15%라고 한다면, 이 기업의 주식가격은?

Solution

$D_1 = 1{,}500,\ \ D_2 = 1{,}650,\ \ \ D_3 = 1{,}815$

$$S_0 = \frac{D_1}{r_s - g}$$

$$S_0 = \frac{1{,}500}{0.15 - 0.1} = 30{,}000$$

Example

Assume Company Y will pay a dividend of 1,000 won per share after one year. The company expects dividends to grow in perpetuity at 10 percent per year, and the discount rate is 15%. Calculate a per-share value.

Solution

$$S_0 = \frac{D_1}{r_S - g}$$

$$S_0 = 20,000$$

Example

한국기업은 1년 후에 1,000원의 배당을 지급한다. 그리고 배당은 매년 10%의 비율로 성장한다고 한다. 이 때 할인율이 15%라고 한다면, 이 기업의 주식가격은?

Solution

$$S_0 = \frac{D_1}{r_S - g}$$

$$S_0 = 20,000$$

Example

Assume Company K will pay a dividend of 560 won per share after one year. The company expects dividends to grow in perpetuity at 12 percent per year, and the discount rate is 17.6%. Calculate a per-share value.

Solution

$$S_0 = \frac{D_1}{r_s - g}$$

$$S_0 = \frac{560}{0.176 - 0.12} = 10,000$$

Example

How much are you willing to pay for one share of J stock if the company just paid a \$0.70 annual dividend, the dividends increase by 2.5 percent annually, and you require a 10 percent rate of return?

Solution

$$S_0 = \frac{0.7 \times (1+0.025)}{0.1-0.025} = 9.57$$

Example

K Enterprises paid a \$2.20 per share annual dividend last week. Dividends are expected to increase by 3.75 percent annually. What is one share of this stock worth to you today if your required rate of return is 15 percent?

Solution

$$S_0 = \frac{2.2 \times (1+0.0375)}{0.15-0.0375} = 20.29$$

Two-stage Dividend Discount Model

The two-stage growth model allows for two stages of growth – an initial phase where the growth rate is not a stable growth rate and a subsequent steady state where the growth rate is stable and is expected to remain so for the long term.

The two-stage model can be used to value companies where the first stage has an unstable initial growth rate. And, there is stable growth in the second stage, which lasts forever.

Example

A company has paid a dividend of $4 this year—assuming a higher growth for the next 3 years at 15% and stable growth of 4% thereafter.

Find the dividends for years 3 and 4.

Solution

Current Dividend = $ 4

Dividend after 1st year will be = $ 4.60 ($ 4 x 1.15 - growing at 15 %)

After 2nd year will be = $ 5.29 ($ 4.60 x 1.15 - growing at 15%)

After 3rd year will be = $ 6.0835 ($ 5.29 x 1.15 - growing at 15%)

Since the growth in the first three years was 15%, the value of the dividend declared after 3 years will be $6.0835, as calculated above.

The second stage has a growth rate of 4%, so the dividend value after the 4th year will be $6.0835 x 1.04 = $6.3268.

Retention ratio

addition to retained earnings divided by net income

The retention ratio refers to the percentage of net income that is retained to grow the business, rather than paid out as dividends.

The part of earnings not paid to investors is left for investment to provide for future earnings growth.

Dividend payout ratio

The dividend payout ratio is the fraction of net income a firm pays to its stockholders in dividends.

$$\text{Dividend payout ratio} = \frac{Dividends}{Net\,Income}$$

Retention ratio = 1 − Dividend Payout ratio

The dividend payout ratio is the complement of the retention ratio, also referred to as the plowback ratio.

The retention ratio is also called the plowback ratio.

The plowback ratio is a fundamental analysis ratio that measures how much earnings are retained after dividends are paid out. It is most often referred to as the retention ratio.

Example

K company had retained earnings of $2,122 at the beginning of the year. At the end of the year, the company had retained earnings of $2,696. Net income for the year was $1,374. What is the amount of dividends paid?

Solution

Dividends paid = 1,374 − (2,696 − 2,122) = 800

The payout ratio, also known as the dividend payout ratio, shows the percentage of a company's earnings paid out as dividends to shareholders.

For example, let's assume Company ABC has earnings per share of $1 and pays dividends per share of $0.60. In this scenario, the payout ratio would be 60%. Let's further assume that Company XYZ has earnings per share of $2 and dividends per share of $1.50. In this scenario, the payout ratio is 75%.

Note that br_A is the same as the rate of growth, g.

$$g = br_A$$

The growth rate is equal to the retention ratio multiplied by ROA.

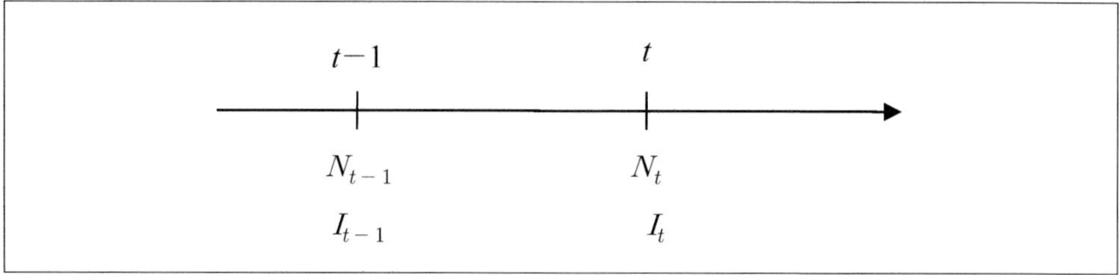

If we assume that a constant fraction, b, of earnings is retained for investment and the average rate of return, r_A, on all projects is the same, the fraction of earnings to be retained for investment is usually called the retention ratio.

$$b = \frac{I_t}{N_t}$$

The investment at time t is as follows:

$$I_t = bN_t$$

where I_t: the investment at time t

N_t: the earnings at time t

$$\begin{aligned} N_t &= N_{t-1} + r_A I_{t-1} \\ &= N_{t-1} + r_A b N_{t-1} \\ &= (1 + br_A) N_{t-1} \end{aligned}$$

The growth rate can be calculated as the percentage increase in earnings from time (t-1) to time t.

$$g = \frac{N_t - N_{t-1}}{N_{t-1}}$$

$$N_t = N_{t-1}(1+g)$$

$$N_t = N_{t-1}(1+g) = N_{t-1}(1+br_A)$$

Note that br_A is the same as the rate of growth, g.

$$g = br_A$$

Example

Translate the sentence into an equation: The new earings are determined by adding the old earnings to the product of ROA and the old investment.

Solution

$$N_t = N_{t-1} + r_A I_{t-1}$$

Example

Translate the sentence into an equation: The new earnings are equal to the sum of the old earnings and the product of the growth rate and the old earnings.

Solution

$$N_t = N_{t-1} + g N_{t-1}$$

Example

Translate the sentence into an equation: The new earnings are equal to the sum of the old earnings and the product of the retention ratio, ROA, and the old earnings.

Solution

$$N_t = N_{t-1} + b r_A N_{t-1}$$

Growth rate

The growth rate can be calculated as the percentage increase in earnings from time (t-1) to time t.

$$g = \frac{N_t - N_{t-1}}{N_{t-1}}$$

$$N_t = N_{t-1} + br_A N_{t-1}$$

Substituting the expression into the growth rate formula, we get:

$$g = br_A$$

Example

Translate the sentence into an equation: The growth rate is equal to the retention ratio multiplied by ROA.

Solution

$$g = br_A$$

Once your business begins to earn a profit, you'll need to reinvest some of those earnings. This will help your business grow and gain more profit.

Example

Gordon Model에서, 서울기업의 t년도 순이익이 10,000원이고, 유보율이 0.4, 투자수익률이 20%인 경우, $(t+1)$년도 순이익과 투자액, $(t+2)$년도 순이익과 투자액을 구하라.

Example

the earnings at time t: 10,000

retention ratio: 0.4,

The average rate of return on all projects is 20%.

Find the earnings at time (t+1).

Solution

$$I_t = 0.4 \times 10{,}000 = 4{,}000$$

$$N_{t+1} = N_t + r_A I_t = 10{,}000 + 0.2 \times 4{,}000 = 10{,}800$$

Example

the earnings at time t: 10,000

retention ratio: 0.4,

The average rate of return on all projects is 20%.

Find the retained earnings at time (t+1).

Solution

$$I_t = 0.4 \times 10{,}000 = 4{,}000$$

$$N_{t+1} = N_t + r_A I_t = 10{,}000 + 0.2 \times 4{,}000 = 10{,}800$$

$$I_{t+1} = 0.4 \times 10{,}800 = 4{,}320$$

Example

Given:

Earnings at time t: 10,000

Retention ratio: 0.4,

The average rate of return on all projects is 20%.

Find the earnings at time (t+2).

Solution

$I_t = 0.4 \times 10,000 = 4,000$

$N_{t+1} = N_t + r_A I_t = 10,000 + 0.2 \times 4,000 = 10,800$

$I_{t+1} = 0.4 \times 10,800 = 4,320$

$N_{t+2} = 10,800 + 0.2 \times 4,320 = 11,664$

Example

Given:

Earnings at time t: 10,000

Retention ratio: 0.4,

The average rate of return on all projects is 20%.

Find the asset values at time (t−1).

Solution

$r_A = 20\%$

$$r_A = \frac{N_t}{V_{t-1}}$$

$r_A V_{t-1} = N_t,\ V_{t-1} = 50,000$

Example

What is the asset value at time (t-1) if the earnings at time t are \$10,000, the retention ratio is 0.4, and the average rate of return on all projects is 20%?

Solution

$r_A = 20\%$

$$r_A = \frac{N_t}{V_{t-1}}$$

$r_A V_{t-1} = N_t, \ V_{t-1} = 50{,}000$

Example

What is the investment at time t if the earnings at time t are \$10,000, the retention ratio is 0.4, and the average rate of return on all projects is 20%?

Solution

When a company retains its earnings rather than distributing them to shareholders, it effectively allocates those funds towards various internal projects and initiatives aimed at growing the business.

Retained earnings represent an investment in the company's future growth and success.

$I_t = 0.4 \times 10{,}000 = 4{,}000$

Example

the earnings at time t: 10,000

retention ratio: 0.4,

The average rate of return on all projects is 20%.

Find the retained earnings at time t.

Solution

$I_t = 4,000$

Example

The earnings at time t are 10,000.

The retention ratio is 0.4.

The average rate of return on all projects is 20%.

Find the earnings at time (t+1).

Solution

$N_{t+1} = N_t + r_A I_t = 10,800$

Example

the earnings at time t: 10,000

retention ratio: 0.4,

The average rate of return on all projects is 20%.

Find the earnings at time (t+1).

Solution

$N_{t+1} = N_t + r_A I_t = 10,800$

Example

Gordon Model에서, 서울기업의 올해 순이익이 10,000원이고, 유보율이 0.4, 투자수익률이 20%인 경우, 작년의 자산가치와 올해 투자액, 내년의 순이익을 구하라.

Example

the earnings at time t: 1,000,000

retention ratio: 0.4,

The average rate of return on all projects is 20%.

Find the earnings at time (t+1).

Solution

$I_t = 0.4 \times 1,000,000 = 400,000$

$N_{t+1} = N_t + r_A I_t = 1,000,000 + 0.2 \times 400,000 = 1,080,000$

Example

the earnings at time t: 1,000,000

retention ratio: 0.4,

The average rate of return on all projects is 20%.

Find the rate of growth.

Solution

$I_t = 0.4 \times 1,000,000 = 400,000$

$N_{t+1} = N_t + r_A I_t = 1,000,000 + 0.2 \times 400,000 = 1,080,000$

$g = 8\%$

Example

What is the asset value at time (t-1) if the earnings at time t are \$200,000 and the average rate of return on all projects is 10%?

Solution

\$200,000

Example

Gordon Model에서, 관악기업의 올해 순이익이 20,000원이고, 유보율이 0.5, 투자수익률이 10%인 경우, 작년의 자산가치와 올해 투자액, 올해 자산가치, 내년의 순이익을 구하라.

Solution

$r_A = 10\%$

$$r_A = \frac{N_{t-1}}{V_{t-2}}$$

$r_A V_{t-2} = N_{t-1},\ V_{t-2} = 200,000$

$I_{t-1} = bN_{t-1} = 10,000$

$V_{t-1} = V_{t-2} + bN_{t-1} = 210,000$

$N_t = N_{t-1} + r_A I_{t-1} = 21,000$

Example

What is the investment at time t if the earnings at time t are \$50,000, the retention ratio is 0.8, and the average rate of return on all projects is 20%?

Solution

$I_t = 0.8 \times 50,000 = 40,000$

Example

Gordon Model에서, 강남기업의 t년도 순이익이 50,000원이고, 유보율이 0.8, 투자수익률이 20%인 경우, $(t+1)$년도 순이익과 투자액, 자산가치를 구하라.

Solution

$I_t = bN_t = 40,000$

$N_{t+1} = N_t + r_A I_t = 58,000$

$I_{t+1} = 46,400$

$r_A = 20\%$

$$r_A = \frac{N_{t+1}}{V_t}$$

$V_t = 290,000$

$V_{t+1} = V_t + bN_{t+1} = 336,400$

Dividend Policy

배당정책(dividend policy)이란 기업이 벌어들인 이익을 배당금과 유보이익으로 나누는 결정을 말한다.

유보이익(retained earnings)은 미래 기업의 투자를 위하여 필요한 기업내 자금의 원천으로서, 그리고 배당(dividend)은 주주가 제공한 자본을 사용한 대가로서 그 중요성을 갖는다. 기업이 너무 많은 배당을 하면, 성장기회를 잘 활용하지 못 할 수 있다. 기업의 성장을 위해서는 이익을 유보하여 재투자하는 것이 바람직하지만 주주의 입장에서는 배당도 중요하므로 이 상반되는 유보이익과 배당금의 영향을 잘 조화시켜 기업가치를 극대화하는 배당수준을 결정하는 것이 배당정책의 목표이다.

Geometric series

A geometric series is a series of numbers in which each term after the first is found by multiplying the previous term by a fixed, non-zero number called the common ratio. In mathematics, a geometric series is a series with a constant ratio between successive terms. For example, the series

$a + ar + ar^2 + \cdots$

is geometric, because each successive term can be obtained by multiplying the previous term by r.

The formula for the sum of an infinite geometric series is

$$a + ar + ar^2 + \cdots = \frac{a}{1-r}$$

$$\frac{a}{1+b} + \frac{a}{(1+b)^2} + \cdots = \frac{\frac{a}{1+b}}{1-\frac{1}{1+b}} = \frac{a}{b}$$

$$\frac{a}{1+b} + \frac{a(1+c)}{(1+b)^2} + \frac{a(1+c)^2}{(1+b)^3} + \cdots = \frac{\frac{a}{1+b}}{1-\frac{1+c}{1+b}} = \frac{a}{b-c}$$

Example

Simplify the expression $\dfrac{\frac{a}{1+b}}{1-\frac{1}{1+b}}$.

Solution

$$\frac{\frac{a}{1+b}}{1-\frac{1}{1+b}} = \frac{a}{b}$$

Finite Geometric Series

To find the sum of a finite geometric series, use the formula,

$$S=\frac{a(1-r^n)}{1-r}$$

where n is the number of terms, a is the first term and r is the common ratio.

Example

Prove $a+ar+ar^2+\cdots+ar^{n-1}=\frac{a(1-r^n)}{1-r}$.

Solution

$$S=a+ar+ar^2+\cdots+ar^{n-1}$$

$$rS=ar+ar^2+ar^3+\cdots+ar^n$$

$$(1-r)S=a(1-r^n)$$

$$S=\frac{a(1-r^n)}{1-r}$$

Example

Let's consider an example of a geometric series:

3+6+12+⋯

Find the sum of the first 5 terms of this series.

Solution

The sum of the first 5 terms of the given geometric series is 93.

Example

Find the sum of the first 8 terms of the geometric sequence 3,6,12,...

Solution

$2^7 = 128$

$3+6+12+\cdots+384 = 765$

$$S=3\frac{1-2^8}{-1}$$

$2^8 = 256$

$S=765$

Example

If the first term of an infinite geometric series is 4, and the common ratio is $\frac{1}{2}$, what is the sum?

Solution

$$S = \frac{4}{1-\frac{1}{2}} = 8$$

PMT

Dollar amount of each annuity payment

FVIFA

Future Value Interest Factor of Annuity

$1 per period at r% for n periods

$$\text{FVIFA} = \frac{\{(1+r)^n - 1\}}{r}$$

$$a+a(1+r)+a(1+r)^2+\cdots+a(1+r)^{n-1} = \frac{a\{(1+r)^n-1\}}{r} = aFVIFA$$

Example

An amount of $15,000 is to be invested annually at the end of each year for 3 years at 10% compounded interest per annum. Calculate the future value of the annuity.

Solution

$$15,000 + 15,000 \times 1.1 + 15,000 \times 1.1^2 = 49650$$

Example

Calculate FVIFA(10%,3).

Solution

$$\frac{1.1^3 - 1}{0.1} = 3.31$$

Financial instruments are monetary contracts between parties.

Financial instruments can be either cash instruments or derivative instruments:

Cash instruments - instruments whose value is determined directly by the markets. They can be securities, which are readily transferable, and instruments such as loans and deposits, where both borrower and lender have to agree on a transfer.

Derivative instruments - instruments which derive their value from the value and characteristics of one or more underlining entities such as an asset, index, or interest rate.

Bonds

채무자가 채권자에게 미래의 정해진 시점에서 일정한 이자와 원금을 지급하기로 약속한 증서

채권(bond)은 발행자가 자금을 조달하기 위하여 발행한 유가증권으로 일정한 이자를 지급함과 동시에 일정기간 후에는 액면금액을 상환할 것을 약속한 증서이다.
A bond is a long-term contract under which a borrower agrees to make payments of interest and principal, on specific dates, to the holders of the bond.
채권은 일반 대중 투자자들로부터 비교적 장기의 자금을 집단적, 대량적으로 조달하기 위하여 정부, 공공기관, 기업이 부담하는 채무를 표시하는 유가증권으로서 일종의 차용증서이다.

A bond is a fixed income investment in which an investor loans money to an entity that borrows the funds for a defined period of time at a fixed interest rate.

채권의 이자와 액면금액을 마지막으로 지급하기로 한 날을 만기일(maturity date)이라 한다.
Maturity date is a specific date on which the par value of a bond must be repaid.

Face Value

만기일에 지급하기로 증서에 기재된 금액을 액면금액 또는 액면가(face value 혹은 par value)라 한다.

Coupon rate

채권증서에는 액면금액 뿐만 아니라 만기일까지 매기간 지급하기로 약속한 이자율이 표시되어 있다. 이 이자율을 표면이자율(coupon rate)이라 하고, 실제로 지불하게 되는 금액을 표면이자(coupon) 또는 액면이자라 한다. 표면이자는 (액면금액×표면이자율)이다.
Coupon payment is the specific number of dollars of interest paid each period.
Coupon interest rate is the stated annual rate of interest on a bond.

Example

If you purchase a 5% bond from Company X with a face value of $1,000, how much will you receive in annual interest payments?

Solution

You purchase a 5% bond from Company X. The bond has a face value of $1,000. This means you will receive $50 in interest payments per year.

Example

An investor buys a $1,000 coupon bond from ABC Company with a 5% coupon rate. How much interest will the investor receive each year?

Solution

If an investor purchases a $1,000 ABC Company coupon bond and the coupon rate is 5%, the issuer provides the investor with a 5% interest every year. This means the investor gets $50, the face value of the bond derived from multiplying $1,000 by 0.05, every year.

채권은 다음의 세 종류로 구분된다. 첫째는 할인채권(discount bond 혹은 zero coupon bond)으로 만기까지 이자지급이 전혀 없고 만기일에 액면금액을 지급받는 채권이다. 둘째는 이표채(coupon bond)로 만기까지 매기간 일정액의 이자를 지급받고 만기일에 마지막 기의 이자와 액면금액을 받는 채권이다. 셋째는 영구채권(perpetual bond 혹은 consol)으로 만기가 없이 영원히 이자만을 받는 채권이다.

Coupon Bond

이자부채권

Zero coupon bond

A bond that has only one payment, which occurs at maturity

The present value of Zero Coupon Bond

$$B_0 = \frac{P}{(1+r)^T}$$

P: the par value of the bond

T: Maturity

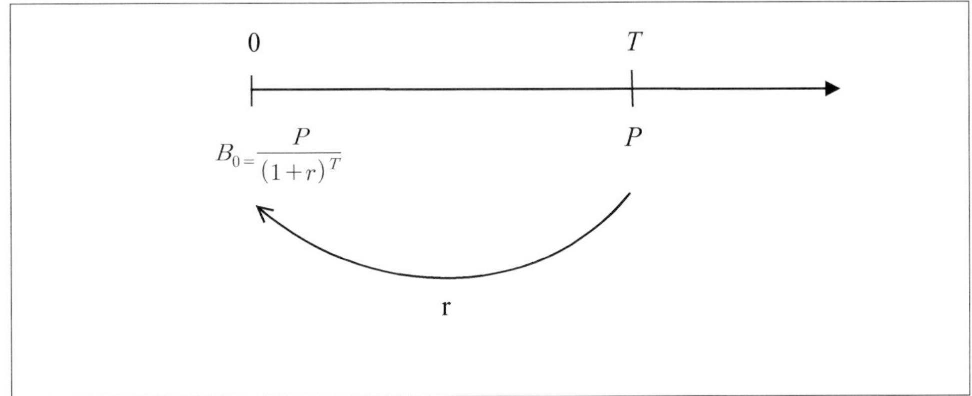

Example

Find the value of two-year maturity zero-coupon bonds with $100 face value if the current YTM is 10 percent.

Solution

$$B_0 = \frac{100}{1.1^2} = 82.6$$

Example

시장이자율이 10%일 때 액면가가 100만원이고 만기가 2년인 zero coupon bond의 현재가치는?

Solution

$$B_0 = \frac{100}{1.1^2} = 82.6$$

Example

A zero-coupon bond has a face value of $1,000, matures in 2 years, and offers a 10% annual yield. Approximately how much would an investor pay for this bond today?

Solution

A zero-coupon bond with a face amount of $1,000, that matures in 2 years, with a 10% yield, may be purchased for roughly $826. At the end of the 2 years, the investor will receive $1,000.

Example

Find the value of five-year maturity zero-coupon bonds with $100 face value if the current YTM is 10 percent.
1.1 to the power of 5 equals 1.611.

Solution

$$\frac{100}{1.1^5} = 62.1$$

Example

시장이자율이 10%일 때 액면가가 100만원이고 만기가 5년인 zero coupon bond의 현재가치는?

Solution

$$B_0 = \frac{100}{(1+0.1)^5} = 62.1$$

The present value of Coupon Bond

$$B_0 = \frac{C}{1+r} + \cdots + \frac{C}{(1+r)^T} + \frac{P}{(1+r)^T}$$

where C: the coupon payment

P: the par value of the bond

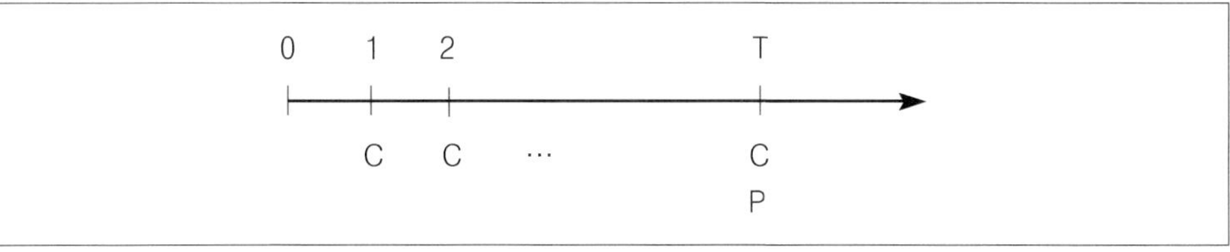

Example

A two-year bond with a face value of $100 pays an annual coupon of 10%. If the market interest rate is 5%, what is the value of the bond?

Solution

Given:

Face value = $100

Coupon rate = 10% → Coupon payment = $10 annually

Time to maturity = 2 years

Market interest rate = 5%

$$\text{Bond Value} = \frac{10}{1.05} + \frac{110}{1.05^2}$$

The value of the bond is $109.3.

Example

A two-year, $100 bond pays an annual coupon of 10 percent. What is the value of the coupon bond if the current YTM is 5 percent?

Solution

$$B_0 = \frac{10}{1.05} + \frac{110}{1.05^2} = 109.3$$

Example

Find the value of a corporate bond with an annual interest rate of 10%, making annual interest payments for 2 years. The face value is $100. Assume a YTM of 5%.

Solution

$$B_0 = \frac{10}{1.05} + \frac{110}{1.05^2} = 109.3$$

Example

액면가가 100만원이고 만기가 2년이며 표면이자율이 10%인 채권이 있다. 현재 시장이자율이 5%라면 이 채권의 가격은 얼마가 되어야 하는가?

Example

Find the sum of a finite geometric series.

$$\frac{15}{1+0.1} + \cdots + \frac{15}{(1+0.1)^{10}}$$

1.1 to the power of 10 is approximately equal to 2.59.

Solution

The sum of a finite geometric series: $\frac{C}{1+r} + \cdots + \frac{C}{(1+r)^T} = C\left\{\frac{1-\frac{1}{(1+r)^T}}{r}\right\}$

$$\frac{15}{1+0.1} + \cdots + \frac{15}{(1+0.1)^{10}} = 92.1$$

Example

액면가가 100만원이고 만기가 10년이며 표면이자율이 15%인 채권이 있다. 현재 시장이자율이 10%라면 이 채권의 가격은 얼마인가?

$1.1^{10} = 2.59$

Solution

The sum of a finite geometric series: $\frac{C}{1+r} + \cdots + \frac{C}{(1+r)^T} = C\left\{\frac{1-\frac{1}{(1+r)^T}}{r}\right\}$

$$\frac{15}{1+0.1} + \cdots + \frac{15}{(1+0.1)^{10}} = 92.1$$

$$B_0 = \frac{15}{1+0.1} + \cdots + \frac{15}{(1+0.1)^{10}} + \frac{100}{(1+0.1)^{10}} = 130.7 \text{ 만원}$$

채권의 가치

채권의 가치는, 채권을 보유하게 되면 얻게 될 미래 현금흐름을 적절한 할인율로 할인한 현재가치의 합이다.

A bond has coupon payments and a lump-sum payments.

Stock has dividend payments forever.

Coupon payments are fixed.

Stock dividends change over time.

Corporations sell bonds to borrow money from the investors. As a financial instrument, a bond represents a contractual agreement between the corporation and the bondholders. Eventually the corporation has to repay the principal to the investors and pay interest to them in the meantime.

Example

The par or face value of a corporate bond is typically stated as $1,000. If a corporate bond is issued at a discount, this means investors can purchase the bond below its par value. For example, if a corporate bond has a par value of $1,000 but is issued at a discount, investors may purchase the bond for, let's say, $950. In this case, investors pay less than the face value of the bond.

Example

ABC company has total sales of $1,349,800 and costs of $903,500. Depreciation is $42,700 and the tax rate is 34 percent. The firm does not have any interest expense. What is the operating cash flow?

Solution

OCF = EBIT(1−t) + Dep

Earnings before interest and taxes = $1,349,800 − $903,500 − $42,700 = $403,600

Tax = $403,600 × .34 = $137,224

Operating cash flow = $403,600 + $42,700 − $137,224 = $309,076

CF to Creditors

CF to Creditors = interest paid − net new borrowing

Interest Paid: This is the total value that you have paid as interest on the total liabilities during an accounting period.

Ending long term debt: End value of your long term debt in an accounting period. Beginning long term debt: The beginning value of a long term debt.

Net new borrowing is simply the difference between the firm's ending long-term debt and its beginning long-term debt.

Net new equity raised is computed as the increase in owner's equity from year-beginning to year end, other than retained earnings.

Percentage Change

If the value of the percent change is positive, then it referred to as percentage increase and when the value is negative, it is referred to as percentage decrease.

$$\text{Percentage change} = \frac{New\ Value - Old\ Value}{Old\ Value}$$

ΔV = New Value − Old Value

Percentage Increase calculation

First, find the increase by subtracting the original number from the new number.

Divide the result by the original number and multiply by 100 to get the percentage increase.

Increase = New Number − Original Number

If your answer is a negative number, then this is a percentage decrease.

Percentage Decrease calculation

Find the decrease by subtracting the new number from the original number.

Then find the percentage decrease by dividing the decrease by the original number and multiplying by 100.

Decrease = Original Number − New Number

If your answer is a negative number, then this is a percentage increase.

Example

The price of a bag of rice went up from $20 to $35. What is the percentage increase?

Solution

The price increased by 75%.

Example

Harry had $2000 in his bank account last week and now he has $2,200. What is the percentage increase?

Solution

Money in Harry's bank account increased by 10%.

Example

A factory went from producing 200 packs of its product to producing 180. What is the percentage decrease?

Solution

The percentage decrease is 10%.

Example

Increase $80 by 5%.

Solution

$80 increased by 5% is $84.

Accumulated depreciation

Accumulated depreciation is the total amount of depreciation expense allocated to a specific asset since the asset was put into use.

Assume that a company buys a machine at a cost of 1,500,000 won. The company decides on a salvage value of 300,000 won and a useful life of two years. The depreciable amount is (   ) and the annual depreciation using the straight-line method is (   ). At the end of year two, the accumulated depreciation would equal (   ).

Solution

Year	0	1	2
Book Value	1,500,000	900,000	300,000
Depreciation		600,000	600,000

The depreciable amount is 1,200,000 won and the annual depreciation using the straight-line method is 600,000 won.

At the end of year two, the accumulated depreciation would equal 1,200,000 won.

Example

Assume that a company buys a machine at a cost of 1,500,000 won. The company decides on a salvage value of 300,000 won and a useful life of three years. The depreciable amount is (   ) and the annual depreciation using the straight-line method is (   ). At the end of year two, the accumulated depreciation would equal (   ).

Solution

Year	0	1	2	3
Book Value	1,500,000	1,100,000	700,000	300,000
Depreciation		400,000	400,000	400,000

The depreciable amount is 1,200,000 won and the annual depreciation using the straight-line method is 400,000 won.

At the end of year two, the accumulated depreciation would equal 800,000 won.

NFA

Net Fixed Assets is the purchase price of all fixed assets less accumulated depreciation.

NFA = Gross Fixed Assets − Accumulated Depreciation

Example

If Gross Fixed Assets are $1,000,000 and Accumulated Depreciation is $200,000, Net Fixed Assets would be (   ).

Solution

$800,000

NCS

NCS = Ending net fixed assets − Beginning net fixed assets + Depreciation

Net Capital Spending is equal to the depreciation expense if the increase in the net fixed assets is equal to zero.

Net Capital Spending is equal to zero if the decrease in the net fixed assets is equal to the depreciation expense.

Example

ABC company had beginning net fixed assets of $1,644 and ending net fixed assets of $1,709. Depreciation for the year was $65. What is the amount of net capital spending?

Solution

NCS = ending net fixed assets − beginning net fixed assets + depreciation

= 1,709 − 1,644 + 65

= 130

Example

NFA increased from 1,644 in Y1 to 1,709 in Y2.

The company's income statement showed a depreciation expense of 65.

Compute NCS.

Solution

NCS = ending net fixed assets − beginning net fixed assets + depreciation

= 1,709 − 1,644 + 65

= 130

Example

Use the information from the balance sheet.

	2023	2024		2023	2024
			LTD	408	454
NFA	1,644	1,709	Common stock & APIC	600	640

Depreciation: 65

Compute NCS.

Solution

NCS = ending net fixed assets − beginning net fixed assets+depreciation

= 1,709 − 1,644 + 65 = 130

Example

A company's 2023 balance sheet showed net fixed assets of $2.2 million, and the 2024 balance sheet showed net fixed assets of $2.6 million. The company's income statement showed a depreciation expense of $900,000. What was the amount of the net capital spending for 2024?

Solution

Net capital spending = $2,600,000 − $2,200,000 + $900,000 = $1,300,000

Example

A company's 2023 balance sheet showed net fixed assets of $2.2 million, and the 2024 balance sheet showed net fixed assets of $2.2 million. The company's income statement showed a depreciation expense of $900,000. What was the amount of the net capital spending for 2024?

Solution

Net capital spending = $2,200,000 − $2,200,000 + $900,000 = $900,000

Example

A company's 2023 balance sheet showed net fixed assets of $2.2 million, and the 2024 balance sheet showed net fixed assets of $1.3 million. The company's income statement showed a depreciation expense of $900,000. What was the amount of the net capital spending for 2024?

Solution

Net capital spending = $1,300,000 − $2,200,000 + $900,000 = 0

Example

Use the information from the balance sheet.

	2011	2012		2011	2012
			CL	428	389
CA	1,112	1,403	LTD	408	454
NFA	1,644	1,709	Common stock & APIC	600	640

Compute Change in NWC.

Solution

beginning NWC = 1,112 − 428 = 684

ending NWC = 1,403 − 389 = 1,014

Change in NWC = ending NWC − beginning NWC

= 330

Company A has current assets of $1,403 and a current liability of $389 for the year 2024. The current asset and current liability for 2023 were $1,112 and $428, respectively. Compute Change in NWC.

Solution

Beginning NWC = 1,112 − 428 = 684

Ending NWC = 1,403 − 389 = 1,014

Change in NWC = Ending NWC − Beginning NWC

= 330

Example

Use the information from the balance sheet.

Current Assets (2017) = 1,112

Current Liabilities (2017) = 428

Current Assets (2018) = 1,403

Current Liabilities (2018) = 389

Compute Change in NWC.

Solution

beginning NWC = 1,112 − 428 = 684

ending NWC = 1,403 − 389 = 1,014

Change in NWC = ending NWC − beginning NWC

= 330

Example

Current assets increased from 1,112 in Y1 to 1,403 in Y2.

Current liabilities decreased from 428 in Y1 to 389 in Y2.

Compute Change in NWC.

Solution

beginning NWC = 1,112 − 428 = 684

ending NWC = 1,403 − 389 = 1,014

Change in NWC = ending NWC − beginning NWC

= 330

Example

	2011	2012
Long-term debt	408	454

Interest Expense: 70

Tax rate: 34%

Compute CF to creditors.

Solution

CF to Creditors = interest paid − net new borrowing

interest paid: $70(1-0.34)=46.2$

Net new borrowing = 454 − 408 = 46

CF to Creditors = 0.2

Example

Ending long term debt: 454

Beginning long term debt: 408

Interest Paid: 70

Compute CF to creditors.

Solution

CF to Creditors = interest paid − net new borrowing

interest paid: 70

Net new borrowing = 454 − 408 = 46

CF to Creditors = 24

CF to stockholders

Cash flow to stockholders = Dividend paid − Net new equity raised

Example

D company had net income of $121,600 of which 40 percent was distributed to the shareholders as dividends. During the year, the company sold $75,000 worth of common stock. What is the cash flow to stockholders?

Solution

Cash flow to stockholders = .40($121,600) − $75,000 = −$26,360

Example

Use the information from the balance sheet.

	2011	2012
Long-term debt	408	454
Common stock and paid-in surplus	600	640

Dividends paid: 102.84

Compute CF to Stockholders.

Solution

CF to Stockholders = dividends paid − net new equity raised

Net New Equity = 40

CF to Stockholders = 62.84

Example

Ending common stock and paid-in surplus: 640

Beginning common stock and paid-in surplus: 600

Dividends paid: 103

Compute CF to Stockholders.

Solution

CF to Stockholders = dividends paid − net new equity raised

Net New Equity = 40

CF to Stockholders = 63

Example

Use the information from the income statement.

Sales: 1,509

COGS: 750

Dep: 65

Taxes: 212

NCS: 130

Change in NWC = 330

Compute Cash Flow From Assets.

Solution

EBIT = 694

CFFA = EBIT + Dep − Taxes − NCS − ΔNWC = 87

Example

Use the information from the income statement.

Sales	1,600
COGS	700
Dep	60

Tax rate: 30%

NCS: 130

Change in NWC = 300

Compute Cash Flow From Assets.

Solution

EBIT = 840

CFFA = EBIT + Dep − Taxes − NCS − ΔNWC = 200

Example

EBIT = 1,000

Tax rate: 20%

Dep: 300

Compute OCF.

Solution

$$OCF = EBIT(1-t) + Dep$$

EBIT = 1,000

OCF = 1,100

Example

A company's 2010 balance sheet showed net fixed assets of $2,100, and the 2011 balance sheet showed net fixed assets of $2,200. The company's income statement showed a depreciation expense of $300. What was the amount of the net capital spending for 2011?

Solution

NCS = ending net fixed assets − beginning net fixed assets + depreciation

= 2,200 − 2,100 + 300

= 400

Example

Use the information from the balance sheet.

	2021	2022		2021	2022
CA	2,500	3,600	CL	1,700	2,200

Compute Change in NWC.

Solution

ending NWC = 3,600 − 2,200 = 1,400

beginning NWC = 2,500 − 1,700 = 800

Change in NWC = ending NWC − beginning NWC

= 600

Example

	2011	2012
Long-term debt	400	450

Interest Expense: 70

Tax rate: 20%

Compute CF to creditors.

Solution

CF to Creditors = interest paid − net new borrowing

interest paid: $70 \times (1-0.2) = 56$

Net new borrowing = 450 − 400 = 50

CF to Creditors = 6

Example

A firm has net working capital of $640. Long-term debt is $4,180, total assets are $6,230, and fixed assets are $3,910. What is the amount of the total liabilities?

Solution

Current assets = 6,230 − 3,910 = $2,320

Current liabilities = 2,320 − 640 = $1,680

Total liabilities = 1,680 + 4,180 = $5,860

Example

K Company has 5 million shares of common stock outstanding and Net Income of W30,000 million.

What's EPS of K Company?

Solution

EPS: W6,000

Example

K Company has 5 million shares of common stock outstanding and Dividend of 10,000 million won.

What's DPS of K Company?

Solution

DPS: 2,000 won

Example

The market price = $87.65 per share

Earnings per share = 3.61

Compute the PE ratio.

Solution

The PE ratio = Pice per share / Earnings per share

The PE ratio = 24.28

Example

K Company has 190.9 million shares of common stock outstanding.

The market price = $87.65 per share

The book value of the equity is $2,556 million.

Compute the market-to-book ratio.

Solution

Book value per share: $\frac{2,556}{190.9} = 13.39$

The market-to-book ratio: $\frac{87.65}{13.39} = 6.55$

Example

A company has a share price of $22.15 and 118 million shares outstanding. Its market-to-book ratio is 4.2, its book debt-equity ratio is 3.2, and it has cash of $800 million. How much would it cost to take over this business assuming you pay its enterprise value?

Solution

EV=Equity Value+Total Debt−Cash

Market cap $= 22.15 \times 118 = 2{,}614$ million

Book value of equity $= \frac{2{,}614}{4.2} = 622$ million

Debt $= 622 \times 3.2 = 1{,}990$ million

Market cap + Debt = 4,604

Enterprise value = 2,614 + 1,990 - 800 = $3,804 million

Profit margin is one of the commonly used profitability ratios to gauge the degree to which a company or a business activity makes money. It represents what percentage of sales has turned into profits. Simply put, the percentage figure indicates how many cents of profit the business has generated for each dollar of sale.

Example

If a company reports a 35% profit margin for the last quarter, how much net income did it earn for each dollar of sales?

Solution

$0.35

Example

A firm has annual sales of $320,000, a price-earnings ratio of 24, and a profit margin of 4.2 percent. There are 14,000 shares of stock outstanding. What is the price-sales ratio?

Solution

Profit Margin = 0.042

Sales = 320,000

Earnings = $320,000 \times 0.042 = 13,440$

Earnings per share $= \dfrac{13,440}{14,000}$ = $0.96

Price = $24 \times 0.96 = 23.04$

Per-Share Revenue $= \dfrac{320,000}{14,000} = 22.86$

Price-sales ratio $= \dfrac{23.04}{22.86} = 1.008$

Example

A company has annual sales of $220,000 with 10,000 shares of stock outstanding. The firm has a profit margin of 6 percent and a price-sales ratio of 1.2. What is the firm's price-earnings ratio?

Solution

Per-Share Revenue $= \dfrac{220,000}{10,000} = 22$

Price per share = 1.2 × 22 = $26.4

Earnings = $220,000 \times 0.06 = 13,200$

Earnings per share $= \dfrac{13,200}{10,000}$ = $1.32

Price-earnings ratio $= \dfrac{26.4}{1.32} = 20$

Tobin's Q

Tobin's Q relates the market value of a firm's assets to today's cost to duplicate those assets.

$$\frac{\textit{The market value of assets}}{\textit{The replacement value of assets}}$$

Tobin's Q equals the market value of a company divided by its assets' replacement cost. The ratio of the market value of assets to their replacement value at the end of the most recent fiscal year. The market value of assets is proxied by the book value of assets minus the book value of equity minus deferred taxes plus the market value of common stock. The replacement value of assets is proxied by the book value of assets.

Example

A firm has total assets with a current book value of $68,700, a current market value of $74,300, and a current replacement cost of $79,200. What is the value of Tobin's Q?

Solution

$$\text{Tobin's Q} = \frac{74,300}{79,200} = 0.94$$

Example

ABC company has a Tobin's Q of 0.96. The replacement cost of the firm's assets is $225,000 and the market value of the firm's debt is $101,000. The firm has 20,000 shares of stock outstanding and a book value per share of $2.09. What is the market to book ratio?

Solution

Market value of assets = 0.96 × 225,000 = $216,000

Market value of equity = 216,000 − 101,000 = $115,000

$$\text{Market value per share} = \frac{115,000}{20,000} = \$5.75$$

$$\text{Market-to-book ratio} = \frac{5.75}{2.09} = 2.75$$

Example

Given the following data, calculate the Tobin's Q:

Item	Company A
Stock price	20
Number of shares outstanding	12,500,000
Book value of debt	360,000,000
Book value of equity	225,000,000

Solution

$$\text{Tobin's Q} = \frac{12,500,000 \times 20 + 360,000,000}{225,000,000 + 360,000,000}$$
$$= 1.043$$

The price/earnings to growth ratio (PEG ratio) is a stock's price-to-earnings (P/E) ratio divided by the growth rate of its earnings for a specified time period.

$$\text{PEG Ratio} = \frac{P/E\ Ratio}{EPS\ Growth}$$

When calculating the PEG ratio, you should delete the percentage sign and use the growth rate as a whole number.

Example

A company's stock is trading at $46 per share. Its earnings per share (EPS) this year is $2.09, up from $1.74 last year.

What is the company's PEG Ratio?

Solution

$$\text{P/E ratio} = \frac{46}{2.09} = 22$$

$$\text{Earnings growth rate} = \frac{2.09}{1.74} - 1 = 20\%$$

$$\text{PEG ratio} = \frac{22}{20} = 1.1$$

Example

	2016	2017
Cash	84	146
A/R	165	188
Inventory	393	422
FA	2,731	2,880

Construct Common-size balance sheet.

Solution

	2016	2017	2016	2017
Cash	84	146	2.5%	4%
A/R	165	188	4.9	5.2
Inventory	393	422	11.7	11.6
FA	2,731	2,880	81	79.2
Assets	3,373	3,636	100%	100%

$$2.5\% = \frac{84}{3,373}$$

Example

A firm had cash of \$84, accounts receivable of \$165, inventory of \$393, and fixed assets of \$2,731.

Construct Common-size balance sheet.

Solution

Cash	84	2.5%
A/R	165	4.9
Inventory	393	11.7
FA	2,731	81
Assets	3,373	100%

$$2.5\% = \frac{84}{3,373}$$

$$4.9\% = \frac{165}{3,373}$$

Common-base year statement

Common-base year statement standardizes items on the income statement and balance sheet relative to their values as of a chosen point in time.

Example

	2016	2017
Cash	84	146
A/R	165	188
Inventory	393	422
FA	2,731	2,880

Construct Common-base year statement.

Solution

	2016	2017	2017
Cash	84	146	1.74
A/R	165	188	1.14
Inventory	393	422	1.07
FA	2,731	2,880	1.05

$$1.74 = \frac{146}{84}$$

Example

Last year, a firm had cash of $84, accounts receivable of $165, inventory of $393, and fixed assets of $2,731. This year, the firm had cash of $146, accounts receivable of $188, inventory of $393, and fixed assets of $2,880.

Construct Common-base year statement.

Solution

	2016	2017	2017
Cash	84	146	1.74
A/R	165	188	1.14
Inventory	393	422	1.07
FA	2,731	2,880	1.05

$$1.74 = \frac{146}{84}$$

Example

	2016	2017
Cash	84	146
A/R	165	188
Inventory	393	422
FA	2,731	2,880

Construct Combined common-size and base-year statement.

Solution

	2016	2017	2016	2017	2017
Cash	84	146	2.5%	4%	1.6
A/R	165	188	4.9	5.2	1.06
Inventory	393	422	11.7	11.6	0.99
FA	2,731	2,880	81	79.2	0.98

$$1.6 = \frac{4}{2.5}$$

Example

A firm has sales of $2,190, net income of $174, net fixed assets of $1,600, and current assets of $720. The firm has $310 in inventory. What is the common-size statement value of inventory?

Solution

Common-size inventory = $310/($1,600 + $720) = 13.36 percent

Example

Write T for True and F for False for the following statements. If the statement is false, correct the statement.

A decrease in net income will increase the return on equity, all else constant.

Solution

F; An increase in net income will increase the return on equity, all else constant.

chapter 3

Capital Budgeting

Capital Budgeting

자본예산(Capital Budgeting)은 투자대상에 대한 현금흐름을 측정하고 투자안의 경제성 분석을 통해 최적투자결정을 내리는 과정이다.

Investment decisions involving fixed assets.

Capital refers to long-term assets used in production, while a budget is a plan which details projected inflows and outflows during some future period. Thus, the capital budget is an outline of planned investments in fixed assets, and capital budgeting is the whole process of analyzing projects and deciding which ones to include in the capital budget.

Capital budgeting is the process of analyzing potential fixed asset investments. Capital budgeting decisions are probably the most important ones financial managers must make.

Capital budgeting is the process that companies use to evaluate and select long-term investments that are consistent with their goal of maximizing shareholder wealth.

Fixed asset

Long-lived property owned by a firm that is used by a firm in the production of its income. Tangible fixed assets include real estate, plant, and equipment. Intangible fixed assets include patents, trademarks, and customer recognition.

Property, plant, and equipment are also called fixed assets, meaning they are physical assets that a company cannot easily liquidate.

Purchases of PP&E are a signal that management has faith in the long-term outlook and profitability of its company.

Current asset

Asset that is in the form of cash or that is expected to be converted into cash in the next 12 months, such as inventory.

Financial capital

Financial capital is funds provided by investors to businesses to purchase real capital equipment for producing goods.

Real capital

Real capital comprises physical goods that assist in the production of goods.

Examples of "capital" include machinery, tools, highways, and factories.

투자안의 경제성 분석

투자안의 경제성 분석이란 투자안이 투자할 가치가 있는가를 분석하는 것이다.
자본예산기법(capital budgeting technique)이라고도 한다.
투자안의 경제성분석에는 다음과 같은 네 가지 기법이 자주 이용된다.

① 회수기간법(payback period method)
② 회계적이익률법(accounting rate of return method)
③ 순현가법(net present value method)
④ 내부수익률법(internal rate of return method)

Payback period method

Payback period

The length of time required to recover the original investment.
Length of time until initial investment is recovered
회수기간(payback period)이란 투자비용을 회수하는 데 걸리는 기간을 말한다.

$$Payback\ period = Year\ before\ full\ recovery + \frac{Unrecovered\ cost\ at\ start\ of\ year}{Cash\ flow\ during\ year}$$

The payback period is the number of years it takes to recover the original cost of the investment.
The Payback Period shows how long it takes for a business to recoup an investment.
The payback period provides a rough measure of a project's liquidity.

Decision criteria

Estimated Payback Period < Required Payback Period ⇒ Accept the project.

The shorter the payback period, the better.

투자안이 투자가치가 있느냐 없느냐의 판단은 기업 자체에서 정한 기준보다 짧으면 투자가치가 있다고 판단한다.

회수기간법은 투자로 인한 기업의 유동성을 나타내준다는 점은 회수기간법의 장점인 반면, 투자가치 판단의 기준이 되는 회수기간의 선정이 주관적이라는 점은 회수기간법의 단점이다.

Example

If a company invests $300,000 in a new production line and expects to generate an annual cash flow of $100,000, how many years will it take to recover the initial investment?

Solution

If a company invests $300,000 in a new production line, and the production line then produces positive cash flow of $100,000 per year, then the payback period is 3 years.

[Example]

If an initial investment of $400,000 is required to open new stores, and the expected annual cash flow from these stores is $200,000, what is the payback period for this investment?

Solution

If opening the new stores amounts to an initial investment of $400,000 and the expected cash flows from the stores would be $200,000 each year, then the period would be 2 years.

For example, suppose a business invests $100,000 in a project, and the expected annual cash inflow is $25,000. The payback period would be four years.

Example

Given the following cash flows,

Year	0	1	2	3	4	5
Project X	−500	200	300	100	150	170
Project Y	−500	50	150	100	200	300

Based on the payback period rule, which project should be chosen?

Solution

$200+300=500$

Project X: 2 years

$50+150+100+200=500$

Project Y: 4 years

Project X should be chosen.

Example

You are considering a project with an initial cost of $1,000. What is the payback period for this project if the cash inflows are $500, $400, $300, and $100 a year over the next four years, respectively?

Solution

To calculate the payback period for an investment with uneven cash flows:

Add up the cash inflows each year until their total equals the initial investment. If this occurs partway through a year, calculate how much of that year is needed to fully recover the investment by dividing the remaining amount by the cash inflow of that year.

By the end of Year 2, the cumulative cash flow is $900.

By the end of Year 3, the cumulative cash flow is $1,200.

During Year 3, the cumulative cash flow exceeds the initial investment. Calculate the fraction of Year 3 required to reach $1,000:

$$PP = 2 + \frac{100}{300} = 2.33 \text{ years}$$

Example

Given the following cash flows,

Year	0	1	2	3	4
Project X	−1,000	500	400	300	100
Project Y	−1,000	100	300	400	600

Based on the payback period rule, which project should be chosen?

Solution

Project X: $2+\dfrac{100}{300}=2.33$ years

Project Y: $3+\dfrac{200}{600}=3.33$ years

Project X should be chosen.

Example

Given the following cash flows,

(million won)

Year	0	1	2	3
Project X	−900	800	200	100
Project Y	−900	700	100	900

Find Payback Period of each project.

Solution

$$PP_X=1+\frac{100}{200}=1.5$$

$$PP_Y=2+\frac{100}{900}=2.11$$

Given the following cash flows,

(million won)

Year	0	1	2	3
Project X	−2,500	1,500	1,700	600
Project Y	−2,500	1,700	500	600

Find Payback Period of each project.

Solution

$$PP_X = 1 + \frac{1,000}{1,700} = 1.6$$

$$PP_Y = 2 + \frac{300}{600} = 2.5$$

Example

회수기간법은 회수기간 이후의 현금흐름을 고려하지 않는다. 회수기간법에 따르면, 투자안 X가 Y보다 좋은 투자안이다. 4년차와 5년차의 현금흐름을 보면, 투자안 Y가 훨씬 큰 값을 보이고 있다.

While Project X has a shorter payback period compared to Project Y, it fails to account for the higher cash flows of Project Y in the later years. This means Project Y may provide higher total returns over its lifespan.

Year	0	1	2	3	4	5
Project X	−500	200	300	50	30	20
Project Y	−500	100	150	250	530	720

Payback Method Disadvantages

The payback period method only considers cash flows until the initial investment is recovered. It ignores cash flows occurring after the payback period, which can lead to overlooking the long-term profitability of an investment.

The concept does not consider the presence of any additional cash flows that may arise from an investment in the periods after full payback has been achieved.

Example

It will cost $6,000 to acquire an ice cream cart. The cash flows are expected to be $3,600 a year for three years. What is the payback period?

Solution

1.67 years

Example

It will cost $6,000 to acquire an ice cream cart. Cart sales are expected to be $3,600 a year for three years. After the three years, the cart is expected to be worthless as the expected life of the refrigeration unit is only three years. What is the payback period?

Solution

1.67 years

Payback Period for Uneven Cash Flows

The process can be described in steps:

Calculate the cumulative cash flow for each period.

Determine the period in which the cumulative cash flow equals or exceeds the initial investment.

If the cumulative cash flow exceeds the initial investment in a particular period, determine the fraction of the period needed to recover the remaining investment.

Example

You are considering a project with an initial cost of $7,500. What is the payback period for this project if the cash inflows are $1,100, $1,640, $3,800, and $4,500 a year over the next four years, respectively?

Solution

To calculate the payback period for an investment with uneven cash flows:

Add up the cash inflows each year until their total equals the initial investment. If this occurs partway through a year, calculate how much of that year is needed to fully recover the investment by dividing the remaining amount by the cash inflow of that year.

By the end of Year 2, the cumulative cash flow is $2,740.

By the end of Year 3, the cumulative cash flow is $6,540.

By the end of Year 4, the cumulative cash flow is $11,040.

During Year 4, the cumulative cash flow exceeds the initial investment. Calculate the fraction of Year 4 required to reach $7,500:

$$PP = 3 + \frac{960}{4,500} = 3.21 \text{ years}$$

Example

A project has an initial cost of $7,500. The cash inflows are $1,100, $1,640, $3,800, and $4,500 over the next four years, respectively. What is the payback period?

Solution

$$PP = 3 + \frac{7,500 - 1,100 - 1,640 - 3,800}{4,500} = 3.21 \text{ years}$$

The decision process

Establish Decision Criteria: Determine the maximum acceptable payback period. This criterion serves as a threshold for evaluating projects.

Calculate Payback Period:

Compare to Decision Criteria: Compare the calculated payback period to the established decision criteria. If the payback period is shorter than or equal to the maximum acceptable payback period, the project may be considered for acceptance.

Make the Decision: Make an informed decision whether to accept or reject the project. If the project meets the established decision criteria, it may be accepted.

The Average Accounting Return

A project's average net income divided by its average book value is referred to as the project's average accounting return.

$$AAR = \frac{Average\ Net\ Income}{Average\ Investment}$$

$$\text{Average Net Income} = \frac{Total\ Net\ Incomes}{Project\ Life}$$

$$Average\ Investment = \frac{Total\ Book\ Values}{\Pr oject\ life + 1}$$

Decision criteria

If the firm had a targeted accounting rate of return less than the estimated AAR, the project would be accepted, and if its targeted return were greater than the estimated AAR, it would be rejected.

Given the following cash flows,

(million won)

Year	0	1	2	3	4
Project X	– 1,000	500	400	300	100
Project Y	– 1,000	100	300	400	600

Based on the AAR rule, which project should be chosen?

Solution

(million won)

Project X	0	1	2	3	4
Cash flow	– 1,000	500	400	300	100
Depreciation		250	250	250	250
Net Income		250	150	50	– 150
Book Value	1,000	750	500	250	0

$$Average\ Net\ Income = \frac{Total\ Net\ Incomes}{\Pr oject\ life} = 75$$

Average Investment= 500

$$AAR = \frac{Average\ Net\ Income}{Average\ Investment} = 15\%$$

(million won)

Project Y	0	1	2	3	4
Cash flow	–1,000	100	300	400	600
Depreciation		250	250	250	250
Net Income		–150	50	150	350
Book Value	1,000	750	500	250	0

$$Average\ Net\ Income = \frac{Total\ Net\ Incomes}{\Pr oject\ life} = 100$$

Average Investment= 500

$$AAR = \frac{Average\ Net\ Income}{Average\ Investment} = 20\%$$

Project Y should be chosen.

Accounting rate of return method

회계적 이익률법(accounting rate of return method)은 평균이익률법이라고도 한다.

$$Accounting\ Rate\ of\ \text{Re}turn = \frac{Yearly\ mean\ of\ Net\ Incomes}{Yearly\ mean\ of\ Amounts\ invested}$$

$$Yearly\ mean\ of\ Net\ Incomes = \frac{Total\ Net\ Incomes}{\text{Pr}oject\ life}$$

$$Yearly\ mean\ of\ Amonts\ Invested = \frac{Total\ Book\ Values}{\text{Pr}oject\ life + 1}$$

Example

어느 투자안의 현금흐름이 다음과 같다. 이 투자안의 잔존가치는 없으며 정액법으로 감가상각을 한다. 이 투자안의 회계적이익률은 얼마인가?

(million won)

Year	0	1	2	3	4
Cash flow	−1,100	300	400	400	300

Given the following cash flows,

Year	0	1	2	3	4
Cash flow	−1,100	300	400	400	300

What is the average accounting return of the investment?

Solution

Year	0	1	2	3	4
Cash flow	−1,100	300	400	400	300
Depreciation		275	275	275	275
Net Income		25	125	125	25

$$Yearly\ mean\ of\ Net\ Incomes = \frac{Total\ Net\ Incomes}{4} = 75\ million\ won$$

Year	0	1	2	3	4
Book Value	1,100	825	550	275	0

$$Yearly\ mean\ of\ Amonts\ Invested = \frac{1{,}100 + 825 + 550 + 275 + 0}{4+1}$$

$$Yearly\ mean\ of\ Amonts\ Invested = 550\, million\, won$$

$$Accounting\ Rate\ of\ \mathrm{Re}turn = 13.6\%$$

Example

Given the following cash flows,

(million won)

Year	0	1	2	3
Cash flow	−1,200	800	500	700

What is the average accounting return of the investment?

Solution

Year	0	1	2	3
Cash flow	−1,200	800	500	700
Dep		400	400	400
Net income		400	100	300

Average net income $= \frac{800}{3}$

Average investment: 600

AAR: 44.4%

Example

어느 투자안의 현금흐름이 다음과 같다. 이 투자안의 잔존가치는 없으며 정액법으로 감가상각을 한다. 이 투자안의 회계적이익률은 얼마인가?

(million won)

Year	0	1	2	3
Cash flow	−1,200	800	500	700

Solution

Year	0	1	2	3
Cash flow	−1,200	800	500	700
Dep		400	400	400
Net income		400	100	300

Average net income $= \frac{800}{3}$

Average investment: 600

AAR: 44.4%

Example

You are considering a project with an initial cost of $1,200. What is AAR for this project if the cash inflows are $800, $500, and $700 a year over the next three years, respectively?

Solution

Year	0	1	2	3
Cash flow	− 1,200	800	500	700
Dep		400	400	400
Net income		400	100	300

$$\text{Average net income} = \frac{800}{3}$$

Average investment: 600

AAR: 44.4%

Example

A project has an intial cost of $4,000 and a 4-year life. The projected net income from the project is $300, $350, $450, and $500 a year for the next 4 years, respectively. What is the average accounting return?

Solution

Year	1	2	3	4
Net Income	300	350	450	500

$$Average\ Net\ Income = \frac{Total\ Net\ Incomes}{\mathrm{Pr}oject\ life} = 400$$

Year	0	1	2	3	4
Book Value	4,000	3,000	2,000	1,000	0

Average Investment = 2,000

$$AAR = \frac{Average\ Net\ Income}{Average\ Investment} = 20\%$$

Example

대한기업은 4,000만원을 투자하여 새 기계를 구입하여 제품을 생산하려고 한다. 새 기계의 투자수명은 4년이고, 이후의 잔존가치는 없으며, 정액법으로 감가상각을 한다고 한다. 새 기계의 도입으로 인한 순이익은 첫해에 300만원, 둘째 해에 350만원, 셋째 해에 450만원, 넷째 해에 500만원이 될 것으로 예상하고 있다. 이 투자안의 회계적 이익률은 얼마인가?

Solution

20%

Example

대한기업은 새 기계를 구입하여 제품을 생산하려고 한다. 새 기계의 도입으로 인한 순이익은 첫해에 300만원, 둘째 해에 350만원, 셋째 해에 450만원, 넷째 해에 500만원이 될 것으로 예상하고 있다. 평균 장부가치는 2,000만원일 때, 이 투자안의 회계적 이익률은 얼마인가?

Solution

20%

Example

A project has an intial cost of $32,000 and a 3-year life. The projected net income from the project is $1,200, $2,300, and $1,800 a year for the next 3 years, respectively. What is the average accounting return?

Solution

Average NI = 1,766.7

Average Investment = 16,000

AAR = 11.04 percent

Example

You're trying to determine whether to expand your business by building a new manufacturing plant. The plant has an installation cost of $32,000. The plant has projected net income of $1,200, $2,300, and $1,800 over these 3 years. What is the average accounting return?

Solution

Average NI = 1,766.7

Average Investment = 16,000

AAR = 11.04 percent

Example

A project produces annual net income of $46,200, $51,800, and $62,900 over its 3-year life, respectively. The initial cost of the project is $675,000. What is the average accounting return?

Solution

AAR = 15.89 percent

Example

Given the following cash flows,

(million won)

Year	0	1	2	3
Project X	− 900	800	200	100
Project Y	− 900	700	100	900

Find AAR of each project.

Solution

Year	0	1	2	3
Project X	− 900	800	200	100
Dep		300	300	300
Net income		500	−100	−200
Book value	900	600	300	0

Project X: Average net income $= \frac{200}{3}$, Average investment $= 450$

$AAR_X = 15\%$

Year	0	1	2	3
Project Y	− 900	700	100	900
Dep		300	300	300
Net income		400	−200	600
Book value	900	600	300	0

Project Y: Average net income $= \frac{800}{3}$, Average investment $= 450$

$AAR_Y = 59\%$

Example

S Company has an opportunity to purchase a 2 million won new machine. It has an economic life of five years and will be worthless after that time. This new investment is expected to generate a cash flow of 500,000 won one year from today and the cash flow will grow at 5% per year subsequently. The company adopts a straight-line depreciation method. What is the average accounting return of the investment?

Solution

(thousand won)

Year	0	1	2	3	4	5
Cash flow	−2,000	500	525	551	579	608
Depreciation		400	400	400	400	400
Net Income		100	125	151	179	208

$$Average\ Net\ Income = \frac{Total\ Net\ Incomes}{\Pr oject\ life} = 152.6$$

$$AAR = \frac{Average\ Net\ Income}{Average\ Investment} = 15.26\%$$

Example

S Company has an opportunity to purchase a 3 million won new machine. It has an economic life of three years and will be worthless after that time. This new investment is expected to generate a cash flow of 1,500,000 won one year from today and the cash flow will grow at 10% per year subsequently. What is the average accounting return of the investment?

Solution

	0	1	2	3
Cash flow	−3000	1500	1650	1815
Dep		1000	1000	1000
Net income		500	650	815

Average Net Income: 655

Average Investment: 1,500

AAR: 43.7%

Example

Given the following cash flows,

(million won)

Year	0	1	2	3	4
Project X	−1,000	500	400	300	100
Project Y	−1,000	100	300	400	500

Based on the AAR rule, which project should be chosen?

Solution

(million won)

Project X	0	1	2	3	4
Cash flow	−1,000	500	400	300	100
Depreciation		250	250	250	250
Net Income		250	150	50	−150
Book Value	1,000	750	500	250	0

$$Average\ Net\ Income = \frac{Total\ Net\ Incomes}{Project\ life} = 75$$

Average Investment= 500

$$AAR = \frac{Average\ Net\ Income}{Average\ Investment} = 15\%$$

$$AAR_X = AAR_Y$$

Two projects have the same AAR.

Decision criteria

Establishing Acceptance Criteria: Organizations set specific thresholds or benchmarks for the AAR that investments must meet to be considered acceptable. This criterion is often based on internal targets, industry benchmarks, or comparative analysis.

Comparing AAR to Decision Criteria: Calculate the AAR for the investment by averaging the accounting returns over the investment's lifespan. Compare the calculated AAR to the established acceptance criteria.

Acceptance or Rejection Decision: If the calculated AAR meets or exceeds the acceptance criteria, the investment may be deemed acceptable and approved for implementation. If the AAR falls below the established threshold, the investment may be rejected.

Demerits of Using ARR

ARR treats cash flows received in different time periods equally, ignoring the time value of money. This means that a dollar received in the future is considered equal to a dollar received today, which may lead to incorrect investment decisions.

ARR method completely ignores the time value of money which states that a certain amount of money at present is worth more than the same amount of money in the future. The lack of adjustment of the time value of money makes ARR an inappropriate process to evaluate investments.

Example

Find the sum of the first n terms of the sequence 1,2,3,...

Solution

$$\frac{n(n+1)}{2}$$

Example

Write the following summation in expanded form:

$$\sum_{k=0}^{1}(A-kB)$$

Example

Write the following summation in expanded form:

$$\sum_{k=0}^{2}(A-kB)$$

Example

Write the following summation in expanded form:

$$\sum_{k=0}^{3}(A-kB)$$

Example

Write the following summation in expanded form:

$$\sum_{k=0}^{2}\left\{I-k\frac{I}{n}\right\}$$

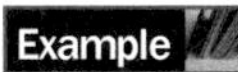

Given the following cash flow,

Year	0	1	2
Cash flow	−1,000	800	900

Find ARR.

Solution

Year	0	1	2
Cash flow	−1,000	800	900
Dep		500	500
NI		300	400

Yearly mean of Net Incomes: 350

Yearly mean of Amounts Invested: 500

$$ARR = \frac{350}{500} = 70\%$$

Example

Prove $\frac{B}{n+1}=\frac{I}{2}$.

In the Straight-line method with a zero salvage value.

B : Total Book Values

n : Project Life

I : Amounts invested

Solution

$$Depreciation\ Expense=\frac{Acquisition\ cost-Salvage\ value}{The\ Life\ of\ a\ machine}=\frac{I}{n}$$

Year	0	1	2	⋯	n−1	n
Book Value	I	$I-\frac{I}{n}$	$I-\frac{I}{n}-\frac{I}{n}$	⋯	$I-(n-1)\frac{I}{n}$	0

$$\frac{B}{n+1}=\frac{I+\left(I-\frac{I}{n}\right)+\left(I-2\frac{I}{n}\right)+\cdots+\left\{I-(n-1)\frac{I}{n}\right\}}{n+1}$$

$$=\frac{nI-\{1+2+\cdots+(n-1)\}\frac{I}{n}}{n+1}$$

$$=\frac{nI-\frac{(n-1)n}{2}\frac{I}{n}}{n+1}=\frac{\frac{n+1}{2}I}{n+1}=\frac{I}{2}$$

$\frac{B}{n+1}=\frac{I}{2}$ Q.E.D.

Q.E.D. is an initialism of the Latin phrase quod erat demonstrandum, meaning “which had to be proven”.

Example

In the Straight-line method with a zero salvage value.

I : Amounts invested

Project Life: n years

Determine the book value of the asset in year $(n-1)$.

Solution

Year	0	1	2	…	n−1	n
Book Value	I	$I-\frac{I}{n}$	$I-\frac{I}{n}-\frac{I}{n}$	…	$I-(n-1)\frac{I}{n}$	0

$$I-(n-1)\frac{I}{n}$$

Example

In the Straight-line method with a zero salvage value.

I : Amounts invested

Project Life: 2 years

Determine the total book values.

Solution

Depreciation Expense: $\frac{I}{2}$

Year	0	1	2
Book Value	I	$I-\frac{I}{2}$	0
Dep		$\frac{I}{2}$	$\frac{I}{2}$

BV : Total Book Values

$$\text{BV} = \frac{3}{2}I$$

Example

In the Straight-line method with a zero salvage value.

I : Amounts invested

Project Life: 2 years

Determine the average investment.

Solution

Depreciation Expense: $\frac{I}{2}$

Year	0	1	2
Book Value	I	$I-\frac{I}{2}$	0
Dep		$\frac{I}{2}$	$\frac{I}{2}$

BV : Total Book Values

$$\text{BV} = \frac{3}{2}I$$

$$\text{Average Investment} = \frac{BV}{3} = \frac{I}{2}$$

Example

Prove $\frac{B}{3}=\frac{I}{2}$.

In the Straight-line method with a zero salvage value.

B : Total Book Values

I : Amounts invested

Project Life: 2 years

Solution

Depreciation Expense: $\frac{I}{2}$

Year	0	1	2
Book Value	I	$I-\frac{I}{2}$	0
Dep		$\frac{I}{2}$	$\frac{I}{2}$

$$\frac{B}{3}=\frac{I+\left(I-\frac{I}{2}\right)}{3}$$

$$\frac{B}{3}=\frac{I}{2}$$

Example

In the Straight-line method with a zero salvage value.

I : Amounts invested

Project Life: 3 years

Determine the total book values.

Solution

Depreciation Expense: $\frac{I}{3}$

Year	0	1	2	3
Book Value	I	$I-\frac{I}{3}$	$I-\frac{2}{3}I$	0
Dep		$\frac{I}{3}$	$\frac{I}{3}$	$\frac{I}{3}$

BV : Total Book Values

BV = 2I

Example

In the Straight-line method with a zero salvage value.

I : Amounts invested

Project Life: 3 years

Determine the average investment.

Solution

Depreciation Expense: $\frac{I}{3}$

Year	0	1	2	3
Book Value	I	$I-\frac{I}{3}$	$I-\frac{2}{3}I$	0
Dep		$\frac{I}{3}$	$\frac{I}{3}$	$\frac{I}{3}$

BV : Total Book Values

BV = 2I

Average Investment $= \frac{BV}{4} = \frac{I}{2}$

Example

Prove $\frac{B}{4}=\frac{I}{2}$.

In the Straight-line method with a zero salvage value.

B : Total Book Values

I : Amounts invested

Project Life: 3 years

Solution

Depreciation Expense: $\frac{I}{3}$

Year	0	1	2	3
Book Value	I	$I-\frac{I}{3}$	$I-\frac{2}{3}I$	0
Dep		$\frac{I}{3}$	$\frac{I}{3}$	$\frac{I}{3}$

$$\frac{B}{4}=\frac{I+\left(I-\frac{I}{3}\right)+\left(I-\frac{2}{3}I\right)}{4}$$

$$\frac{B}{4}=\frac{I}{2}$$

NPV

Net Present Value method

The present value of future net cash flows, discounted at the cost of capital.

$$NPV = CF_0 + \sum_{t=1}^{n} \frac{CF_t}{(1+r)^t}$$

순현가법(net present value method)은 투자로 인하여 발생할 미래의 모든 현금흐름을 적절한 할인율로 할인하여 현가로 나타내서 투자결정에 이용하는 기법이다.

Decision criteria

$NPV > 0 \Rightarrow$ Accept the project.

An investment with a positive NPV will be profitable, and an investment with a negative NPV will result in a net loss.

The larger NPV, the better.

A project should only be undertaken if it has a positive NPV.

Example

Given the following cash flows,

Year	0	1
Project X	−100	110
Project Y	−100	120
Project Z	−100	130

Find NPV discounted at 20%.

Solution

$$NPV_X = -100 + \frac{110}{1.2} = -8$$

$$NPV_Y = -100 + \frac{120}{1.2} = 0$$

$$NPV_Z = -100 + \frac{130}{1.2} = 8$$

Example

Given the following cash flows,

(million won)

Year	0	1	2
Project X	−100	70	170
Project Y	−100	150	250

Based on the NPV rule, which project should be chosen? Suppose the discount rate is 20%.

Solution

$$NPV_X = -100 + \frac{70}{1.2} + \frac{170}{1.2^2} = 76$$

$$NPV_Y = -100 + \frac{150}{1.2} + \frac{250}{1.2^2} = 199$$

Project Y should be chosen.

Example

Given the following cash flows,

(million won)

Year	0	1	2
Project X	−110	100	120
Project Y	−110	150	250

Based on the NPV rule, which project should be chosen? Suppose the discount rate is 20%.

Solution

$$NPV_X = -110 + \frac{100}{1.2} + \frac{120}{1.2^2} = 57$$

$$NPV_Y = -110 + \frac{150}{1.2} + \frac{250}{1.2^2} = 189$$

$NPV_X = 57, \quad NPV_Y = 189$

Project Y should be chosen.

IRR

Internal Rate of Return method

내부수익률(internal rate of return : IRR)이란 미래현금흐름의 순현가를 0으로 만드는 할인율을 말한다.

The IRR is the discount rate that sets the NPV to 0.

The discount rate which equates the present value of cash inflows to the present value of cash outflows.

IRR is the interest rate that causes NPV for a series of cash flows to be zero.

$$CF_0 + \sum_{t=1}^{n} \frac{CF_t}{(1+r)^t} = 0$$

The IRR rule

Accept the project if IRR is greater than the discount rate.

Reject the project if IRR is less than the discount rate.

Hurdle Rate

The discount rate which the IRR must exceed if a project is to be accepted.

Once the internal rate of return is determined, it is typically compared to a company's hurdle rate or cost of capital. If the IRR is greater than or equal to the cost of capital, the company would accept the project as a good investment.

Example

Given the following cash flows,

Year	0	1
Project X	−50	51
Project Y	−50	52
Project Z	−50	53

Based on the IRR rule, which project should be chosen?

Solution

$$-50+\frac{51}{1+r_X}=0, \qquad r_X=2\%$$

$$-50+\frac{52}{1+r_Y}=0, \qquad r_Y=4\%$$

$$-50+\frac{53}{1+r_Z}=0, \qquad r_Z=6\%$$

Project Z should be chosen.

Factorization of quadratic equations

Factorization of quadratic equations is the part of finding the roots of a quadratic equation. Factoring quadratic equations means converting the given quadratic expression into the product of two linear factors.

Example

Factorize $3x^2+7x+4=0$

Solution

$(x+1)(3x+4)=0$

Example

Given the following cash flow,

(million won)

Year	0	1	2
Cash flow	−100	70	170

Find IRR.

Solution

$$-100+\frac{70}{1+r}+\frac{170}{(1+r)^2}=0$$

$$-10(1+r)^2+7(1+r)+17=0$$

$$-10r^2-13r+14=0$$

$$10r^2+13r-14=0$$

$$(r+2)(10r-7)=0$$

$$r=-2,\quad 0.7$$

Usually, we consider the positive IRR as the relevant one for investment decisions, so IRR = 70%.

Example

Given the following cash flow,

(million won)

Year	0	1	2
Cash flow	−100	150	250

Find IRR.

Solution

$$-100+\frac{150}{1+r}+\frac{250}{(1+r)^2}=0$$

$$-10(1+r)^2+15(1+r)+25=0$$

$$-10r^2-5r+30=0$$

$$2r^2+r-6=0$$

$$(r+2)(2r-3)=0$$

$$r=-2,\quad 1.5$$

Example

Solve $5x^2-6x+1=0$

Solution

Just put the values of a, b and c into the Quadratic Formula, and do the calculations.

$x=$ 0.2 or 1

Given the following cash flow,

(million won)

Year	0	1	2
Cash flow	−100	70	150

Find IRR.

Solution

$$-100+\frac{70}{1+r}+\frac{150}{(1+r)^2}=0$$

$$-10(1+r)^2+7(1+r)+15=0$$

$$10r^2+13r-12=0$$

$$r=\frac{-13\pm\sqrt{13^2+480}}{20}=\frac{-13\pm\sqrt{649}}{20}$$

$$r=0.624,\quad -1.924$$

62.4%

Cf.

The quadratic formula

For $ax^2+bx+c=0$, the values of x which are the solutions of the equation are given by:

$$x=\frac{-b\pm\sqrt{b^2-4ac}}{2a}$$

Example

Solve the quadratic equation below using the Quadratic Formula.

$x^2 + 5x - 14 = 0$

Solution

$x^2 + 5x - 14 = 0$

$$x = \frac{-b \pm \sqrt{b^2 - 4ac}}{2a}$$

What we need to do is simply identify the values of a, b, and c then substitute in the quadratic formula.

$$x = \frac{-5 \pm \sqrt{81}}{2}$$

$x = 2, \ -7$

Example

70,000원이 현재 소요되는 투자안으로부터 1년 후 78,400원의 현금유입이 예상된다. 다른 투자안을 수행할 때 연 10%의 이익을 올릴 수 있다면 이 투자안의 NPV, IRR은?

Solution

$$NPV = -70{,}000 + \frac{78{,}400}{1+0.1} = 1{,}273$$

$$-70{,}000 + \frac{78{,}400}{1+r} = 0$$

$r = 0.12$

IRR: 12%

Opportunity cost

The return on the best alternative use of an asset.
Opportunity cost is the value of what you forgo when you decide to give up one thing in favor of another.
Opportunity cost is the forgone benefit that would have been derived from an option not chosen.

Decision criteria in IRR

Establishing Acceptance Criteria: Organizations set specific thresholds or benchmarks for IRR that investment opportunities must meet to be considered acceptable. This criterion is often based on internal targets, minimum required rates of return, or comparative analysis.
Calculating IRR: Evaluate the IRR of each investment opportunity by finding the discount rate that makes the NPV of the investment equal to zero.
Comparing IRR to Decision Criteria: Compare the calculated IRR to the established acceptance criteria. If the IRR is equal to or greater than the acceptance threshold, the investment opportunity may be deemed acceptable and approved for implementation. If the IRR is less than the threshold, the investment opportunity may be rejected.

Example

Given the following cash flow,

Year	0	1
Cash flow	−10	A

Show that $\frac{dr}{dA} > 0$.

Solution

$$-10 + \frac{A}{1+r} = 0$$

$$r = \frac{1}{10}A - 1$$

$$\frac{dr}{dA} = \frac{1}{10} > 0$$

Example

다음과 같은 현금흐름을 가지는 투자안에서 현금흐름 A가 증가함에 따라 내부수익률이 증가함을 보여라.

Year	0	1
Cash flow	−10	A

Example

Suppose J Inc. plans to replace equipment worth $ 30,000 will result in additional revenues of $ 28,000 but also increased costs of $ 15,000 each year for the next three years. If the discount rate is 5% and the tax rate is 30%, what is NPV of this replacement project?

1.05 to the power of 2 equals 1.1025.

1.05 to the power of 3 equals 1.15763.

Solution

	0	1	2	3
Investment	−30,000			
Increase in Revenues		28,000	28,000	28,000
Increase in Costs		15,000	15,000	15,000
Increase in Depreciation		10,000	10,000	10,000
Increase in PBT		3,000	3,000	3,000
Tax		900	900	900
Increase in PAT		2,100	2,100	2,100
Add back Depreciation		10,000	10,000	10,000
Net cash flows	−30,000	12,100	12,100	12,100

$$NPV = -30,000 + \frac{12,100}{1.05} + \frac{12,100}{1.05^2} + \frac{12,100}{1.05^3} = 2,951$$

Comparison of the NPV and IRR methods

투자규모가 서로 다른 경우

Example

	0	1
Project A	−1,000,000	1,290,000
Project B	−100	130

Suppose the discount rate is 10%.

$$NPV_A = -1{,}000{,}000 + \frac{1{,}290{,}000}{1.1} = 172{,}727$$

$$NPV_B = -100 + \frac{130}{1.1} = 18$$

$$-1{,}000{,}000 + \frac{1{,}290{,}000}{1+r_A} = 0, \quad r_A = 29\%$$

$$-100 + \frac{130}{1+r_B} = 0, \quad r_B = 30\%$$

When there is a conflict between NPV and IRR, you should always use NPV. NPV is superior to the other methods of analysis.

Reinvestment Rate Assumption

The assumption that cash flows from a project can be reinvested at the cost of capital, if using the NPV method, or at the internal rate of return, if using the IRR method.

Example

Find if the quadratic equation $x^2 - 2x + 5 = 0$ has real solutions.

Solution

This quadratic equation has no real roots or solutions.

Example

Find if the quadratic equation $x^2 - 5x + 6 = 0$ has real solutions.

Solution

x = 2, 3

내부수익률이 존재하지 않는 경우

Example

Given the following cash flow,

Year	0	1	2
Cash flow	1,000	−2,000	3,000

Find IRR.

Solution

$$1,000 - \frac{2,000}{1+r} + \frac{3,000}{(1+r)^2} = 0$$

$$r^2 + 2 = 0$$

An IRR might not exist.

내부수익률이 존재하지 않는다.

내부수익률이 복수해가 존재하는 경우

Example

Given the following cash flow,

Year	0	1	2
Cash flow	− 1,000	2,300	− 1,320

Find IRR.

Solution

$$-1,000 + \frac{2,300}{1+r} - \frac{1,320}{(1+r)^2} = 0$$

$$100(1+r)^2 - 230(1+r) + 132 = 0$$

The investment has an IRR of both 10 and 20 percent.

There might be multiple internal rates of return.

Example

Given the following cash flow,

Year	0	1	2	3
Cash flow	−15,000	1,000	8,000	14,000

Find IRR.

Write your answer to three decimal places.

Solution

$$-15,000+\frac{1,000}{1+r}+\frac{8,000}{(1+r)^2}+\frac{14,000}{(1+r)^3}=0$$

$$NPV=-15,000+\frac{1,000}{1+r}+\frac{8,000}{(1+r)^2}+\frac{14,000}{(1+r)^3}$$

r	NPV
0.0%	8,000
5.0%	5,302
10.0%	3,039
15.0%	1,124
17.0%	440
18.0%	114
18.1%	82
18.2%	50
18.4%	−14
18.5%	−46
19.0%	−203
20.0%	−509

IRR must be calculated through trial-and-error.

$$NPV=-15,000+\frac{1,000}{1+r}+\frac{8,000}{(1+r)^2}+\frac{14,000}{(1+r)^3}$$

Try r=15%: NPV=1,124

We know that the IRR should be greater than 15%.

Try r=20%: $NPV=-509$

We could guess that the IRR should be lower than 20%.

Try r=18.2%: NPV=50

Try r=18.4%: NPV=-14

IRR is between 18.2% and 18.4%.

IRR=18.3%

Example

While using the trial and error approach to find a project's IRR, you first try 10% and find the present value of the inflows to be less than the cost of the project. From this you can conclude that

A. the IRR is below 10%

B. the IRR is above 10%

Solution

A

NPV Profile

The NPV Profile is a graphical illustration of a project's NPV graphed as a function of various discount rates.

A graph that plots the NPVs of a project to various discounts rates that could be applied to the project's cash flows.

The point where a project's net present value profile crosses the horizontal axis indicates a project's internal rate of return.

Example

Given the following cash flows,

Year	0	1
Cash flow	−10	15

Plot an NPV Profile.

Solution

$$-10+\frac{15}{1+r}=0$$

IRR: 50%

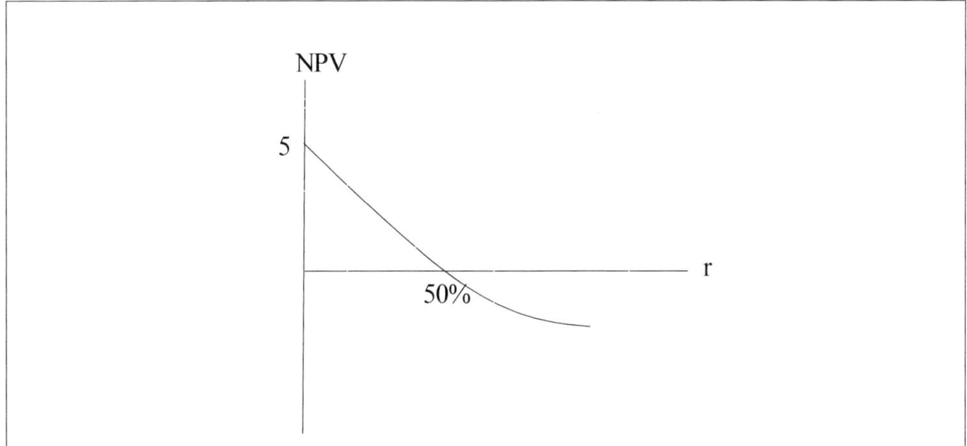

Discounted payback period

Length of time until intial investment is recovered on a discounted basis

A discounted payback period gives the number of years it takes to break even from undertaking the initial expenditure, by discounting future cash flows and recognizing the time value of money.

The discounted payback period formula shows how long it will take to recoup an investment based on observing the present value of the project's projected cash flows.

The shorter a discounted payback period is, means the sooner a project or investment will generate cash flows to cover the initial cost.

Example

Given the following cash flow,

Year	0	1	2
Cash flow	−1,000	800	900

Find Discounted PP discounted at 4%.

Solution

$PV_1 = 769$

$PV_2 = 832$

Year	0	1	2
Discounted Cash flow	−1,000	769	832

Discounted PP $= 1 + \dfrac{231}{832} = 1.28$

Value additivity principle

The net present value of various projects can be added.

The Value Additivity Principle in NPV states that the value of the total NPV of a bigger project is equal to the summation of all smaller NPVs of projects. In other words, the summation of all smaller NPVs provides the bigger NPV of an investment project. The NPV of a group of the independent projects will be equivalent to the NPV of all the independent projects. Value Additivity is an important principle because using it, we can find out the total NPV of an investment project by adding the smaller NPVs that are known to us. Alternately, if the total NPV and one project's NPVs are known, we can find the unknown project's NPV too.

Example

The cash flows for projects are given below:

Year	0	1	2	3
Project 1	−1,000	500	700	800
Project 2	−1,500	650	830	920
Project 3	−2,500	1,150	1,530	1,720

$NPV_1 = 559$

$NPV_2 = 380$

Compute NPV of Project 3.

Solution

Project 1, $NPV_1 = 559$

Project 2, $NPV_2 = 380$

Project 3 = Project 1 + Project 2,

$NPV_3 = NPV_1 + NPV_2$

$NPV_3 = 939$

Example

The cash flows for projects are given below:

Year	0	1	2	3
Project 1	−2,500	1,150	1,530	1,720
Project 2	−1,000	500	700	800
Project 3	−1,500	650	830	920

The NPV for Project 1 is 939.

The NPV for Project 2 is 559.

Compute NPV of Project 3.

Solution

$NPV_3 = NPV_1 - NPV_2$

$NPV_3 = 380$

Example

Given the following cash flow,

Year	0	1	2
Cash flow	−1,000	600	600

The cost of capital is 10%.

Find $NPV(2,\infty)$.

Solution

NPV = 41

Let $NPV(n,\infty)$ be the NPV of an n-year project with $NPV(n)$, replicated forever.

$$NPV(2,\infty) = 41 + \frac{41}{1.1^2} + \frac{41}{1.1^4} + \cdots = \frac{41}{1 - \frac{1}{1.1^2}} = 236$$

Example

Given the following cash flow,

Year	0	1	2	3
Cash flow	−1,000	400	400	474

The cost of capital is 10%.

Find $NPV(3,\infty)$.

Solution

NPV = 50

Let $NPV(n,\infty)$ be the NPV of an n-year project with $NPV(n)$, replicated forever.

$$NPV(3,\infty) = 50 + \frac{50}{1.1^3} + \frac{50}{1.1^6} + \cdots = \frac{50}{1 - \frac{1}{1.1^3}} = 201$$

Projects with different Lives

An NPV Technique for Evaluating Projects with different Lives

Example

The cash flows for projects with different lives are given below:

Year	0	1	2	3
Project M	−1,000	600	600	
project N	−1,000	400	400	474

The opportunity cost of capital is 10%.

Which project should be accepted?

Solution

$NPV_1 = 41$

$NPV_2 = 50$

To compare projects with different lives, we compute the NPV of an infinite stream of constant scale replications.

Let $NPV(n, \infty)$ be the NPV of an n-year project with $NPV(n)$, replicated forever.

$$NPV(2,\infty) = \frac{41}{1-\frac{1}{(1+0.1)^2}} = 236$$

$$NPV(3,\infty) = 50 + \frac{50}{1.1^3} + \frac{50}{1.1^6} + \cdots = \frac{50}{1-\frac{1}{1.1^3}} = 201$$

We would choose to accept Project M over Project N because when the cash flows are adjusted for different project lives, M provides the greater wealth.

Profitability Index

순현가는 투자규모가 다른 여러 투자안의 상대적인 성과를 비교하기가 어렵다. 이러한 단점을 보완하기 위하여 수익성지수(profitability index : PI)가 자주 사용된다.

$$PI = \frac{PV of\, future\, cash\, flows}{Inial\ investment}$$

Benefit-cost ratio

The present value of an investment's future cash flows divided by the initial cost of the investment.

The profitability index is calculated as the ratio between the present value of future expected cash flows and the initial amount invested in the project. A higher PI means that a project will be considered more attractive.

The PI is calculated by dividing the present value of future expected cash flows by the initial investment amount in the project.

A PI greater than 1 is deemed as a good investment, with higher values corresponding to more attractive projects.

The profitability index is helpful in ranking various projects because it lets investors quantify the value created per each investment unit. A profitability index of 1.0 is logically the lowest acceptable measure on the index, as any value lower than that number would indicate that the project's present value is less than the initial investment. As the value of the profitability index increases, so does the financial attractiveness of the proposed project.

The PI decision rule

Accept an independent project if PI > 1.

Reject if PI < 1.

Example

Given the following cash flow,

Year	0	1	2
Cash flow	−100	70	170

Find PI discounted at 20%.

Solution

$$NPV = -100 + \frac{70}{1.2} + \frac{170}{1.2^2} = 76$$

$$PV = \frac{70}{1.2} + \frac{170}{1.2^2} = 176$$

$$PI = \frac{176}{100} = 1.76$$

Example

어느 투자안의 현금흐름이 다음과 같다.

Year	0	1	2
Cash flow	100	70	170

할인율이 20%일 때, PI는 얼마인가?

Solution

$$NPV = -100 + \frac{70}{1.2} + \frac{170}{1.2^2} = 76$$

$$PV = \frac{70}{1.2} + \frac{170}{1.2^2} = 176$$

$$PI = 1.76$$

MIRR

Modified Internal Rate of Return

It is the interest rate that compares the future value of the cash flows with the cost of the project.

$$-PVCF+\frac{FVCF}{(1+r)^n}=0$$

Where:

FVCF: the future value of positive cash flows discounted at the reinvestment rate

PVCF: the present value of negative cash flows discounted at the financing rate

Example

Given the following cash flow,

Year	0	1	2
Cash flow	−100	70	170

Find MIRR discounted at 10%.

Solution

$70\times 1.1=77$

Year	0	1	2
Cash flow	−100	0	247

$$-100+\frac{247}{(1+r)^2}=0$$

$(1+r)^2=2.47$

$1+r=\sqrt{2.47}=1.5716$

MIRR = 57.16%

Example

어느 투자안의 현금흐름이 다음과 같다.

Year	0	1	2
Cash flow	−100	70	170

할인율이 10%일 때, MIRR은 얼마인가?

Crossover Rate

Crossover Rate is the rate of return at which the Net Present Values of two projects are equal. It represents the rate of return at which the net present value profile of one project intersects the net present value profile of another project.

Crossover rate is the cost of capital where two projects have the same net present values or where their NPV profiles intersect.

The crossover rate is the intersection between the rate of return of two different projects having equal net present value.

Example

Given the following cash flows,

Year	0	1
Project X	−10	15
Project Y	−20	26

Find Crossover Point.

Solution

$IRR_X = 50\%$

$IRR_Y = 30\%$

$$-10 + \frac{15}{1+r} = -20 + \frac{26}{1+r}$$

$$\frac{11}{1+r} = 10$$

Crossover Point = 10%

Mutually Exclusive Projects

If you choose one, you can't choose the other.

Mutually exclusive projects refer to a scenario in which a company must choose between two or more investment options, but it can only invest in one of them because the projects serve similar purposes or target the same resources. In other words, if one project is selected, it precludes the selection of the other projects.

Mutually exclusive projects are investment opportunities where undertaking one project precludes the possibility of pursuing the others. In other words, if you decide to invest in one project, you cannot simultaneously invest in another project that is mutually exclusive with it.

APV

adjusted present value method

조정현가법

조정현가법은 투자에 따른 현금흐름을 그 발생원천별로 분리한 후, 각 현금흐름의 순현가를 계산하고, 이를 모두 더하여 투자안의 가치를 평가하는 방법이다.

부채사용투자안의 경우는, 자기자본으로만 자본조달을 한 경우의 NPV를 구하고, 여기에 부채사용에 따른 이자비용의 법인세 감세효과를 더해 주게 된다.

APV = 자기자본으로만 조달한 경우의 NPV + 부채사용에 따른 효과의 NPV

APV = NPV + NPVF

The value of a project to the firm can be thought of as the value of the project to an unlevered firm plus the present value of the financing side effects.

The adjusted present value is the net present value of a project or company if financed solely by equity plus the present value of any financing benefits, which are the additional effects of debt. By taking into account financing benefits, APV includes tax shields such as those provided by deductible interest.

APV is a modified form of Net Present Value that takes into account the present value of leverage effects separately. APV splits financing and non-financing cash flows and discounts them separately.

The Adjusted Present Value is defined as the sum of the present value of a project assuming solely equity financing and the PV of all financing-related benefits.

Example

Consider a project of ABC Company, the timing and size of the cash flows for an all-equity firm are:

Year	0	1	2	3	4
Cash flow	−1,000	125	250	375	500

The unlevered cost of equity is 10%.

Now, imagine that the firm finances the project with $600 of debt at 8%.

The tax rate is 40%.

1.08 to the power of 2 equals 1.166.

1.08 to the power of 3 equals 1.26.

1.08 to the power of 4 equals 1.361.

Find APV.

Solution

NPV = −56.5

The tax rate is 40%, so they have an interest tax shield worth $tBr_B = 19.2$ each year.

NPV of Interest tax shield = 63.59

The net present value of the project under leverage is:

$$APV = -56.5 + \sum_{t=1}^{4} \frac{19.2}{1.08^t} = -56.5 + 63.59 = 7.09$$

chapter 4

Cost of Capital

Cost of Capital

자본비용(cost of capital)은 기업이 자본을 사용하는 대가로 자본제공자에게 지불하는 비용이다. 자본비용은 투자자들이 투자한 자본에 대하여 요구하는 수익률이므로 요구수익률(required rate of return)이라고도 한다.

요구수익률이란 투자자가 특정 투자대상에 투자할 때 기대하는 최소한의 만족할 수 있는 수익률을 말한다. 요구수익률이 얼마가 되어야 하는지에 대해서 다음과 같은 점을 생각해 볼 수 있다. 현재의 소비 일부를 희생한 대가로 얻어지는 투자수익은 현재와 미래 사이의 시간적 경과 속에서 미래의 일정시점까지 기다려야 얻어지는 것이므로, 최소한 일정한 시간을 기다려야 하는 것에 대한 시차보상이 있어야 한다. 또한 미래 얻어지는 투자수익은 불확실한 것이므로, 위험을 부담하는 데에 대한 위험보상이 있어야 한다.

Cost of Debt

The cost of debt is the firm's borrowing rate.

Cost of Equity

The required return on the company's common stock in capital markets. It is also called the equity holders' required rate of return because it is what equity holders can expect to obtain in the capital market.

Weight of debt

The weight of debt refers to the proportion of a company's capital structure that is financed by debt. It's calculated by dividing the market value of the company's debt by the total market value of the company's capital.

The weight of debt represents the percentage of the company's capital structure that comes from debt financing.

Example

Suppose a company, ABC Inc., has the following financial information:

Market value of debt (B): $2,000,000

Market value of equity (S): $6,000,000

Calculate the weight of debt.

Solution

The weight of debt for ABC Inc. is 0.25.

WACC

The Weighted Average Cost of Capital is calculated by multiplying the proportion of debt by the after-tax cost of debt and adding it to the proportion of equity multiplied by the cost of equity.

The "Proportion of equity" is the market value of the company's equity divided by the total market value of the company.

The "Proportion of debt" is the market value of the company's debt divided by the total market value of the company.

The "Cost of equity" is the rate of return required by equity investors.

The "Cost of debt" is the interest rate the company pays on its debt.

The definition of the weighted average cost of capital is to weight the after-tax cost of debt by the percentage of debt in the firm's capital structure and add the result to the cost of equity multiplied by the percentage of equity.

$$r_W = \frac{B}{V}(1-t)r_B + \frac{S}{V}r_S$$

V : the value of the firm

B : the market value of the Bonds

S : the market value of the Stocks

WACC = (Weight of debt)×(After-tax cost of debt)+(Weight of equity)×(Cost of equity)

WACC represents the average cost of capital for a company, considering both equity and debt financing. It's calculated by weighting the cost of equity and the after-tax cost of debt by their respective proportions in the company's capital structure, and then summing these values.

기업의 주요 자본조달원천에는 사채, 우선주, 보통주 등이 있다. 원천별 자본비용은 이 중 특정원천으로 자본을 조달하였을 때 부담하는 자본비용을 말한다. 그리고 가중평균자본비용(weighted average cost of capital : WACC)은 원천별 자본비용을 각 원천별 자본이 차지하는 구성비율로 가중평균한 값을 말한다.

Example

Asset 3,000	Debt	1,000
	Equity	2,000

The cost of equity is 10% and the cost of debt is 5%. The corporate tax rate is 30%. Find the WACC.

Solution

$$r_W = \frac{B}{V}(1-t)r_B + \frac{S}{V}r_S$$

$$r_W = \frac{1}{3}(1-0.3)5 + \frac{2}{3}\times 10 = 7.8(\%)$$

Example

K Company has 2,000 shares of common stock outstanding that are currently being sold for 10,000 won per share. The firm's debt is 10 million won.

The cost of equity is 10% and the cost of debt is 5%. The corporate tax rate is 30%.

Find the WACC.

Solution

$$r_W = \frac{B}{V}(1-t)r_B + \frac{S}{V}r_S$$

$$r_W = \frac{1}{3}(1-0.3)5 + \frac{2}{3} \times 10 = 7.8(\%)$$

Weighted Average

Weighted average is a calculation that takes into account the varying degrees of importance of the numbers in a data set. In calculating a weighted average, each number in the data set is multiplied by a predetermined weight before the final calculation is made.

A weighted average can be more accurate than a simple average in which all numbers in a data set are assigned an identical weight.

The weighted average takes into account the relative importance or frequency of some factors in a data set.

In calculating a simple average, or arithmetic mean, all numbers are treated equally and assigned equal weight. But a weighted average assigns weights that determine in advance the relative importance of each data point.

Cf.

	인원	kg
남자	500	70
여자	1,500	60

몸무게의 가중평균을 구하는 방법은 다음과 같다.

$$Weighted\ Average = \frac{500}{2,000}70kg + \frac{1,500}{2,000}60kg = 62.5kg$$

Example

Asset 10,000	Debt	2,000
	Equity	8,000

The cost of equity is 5% and the cost of debt is 10%. The corporate tax rate is 20%. Find the WACC.

Solution

$$r_W = \frac{B}{V}(1-t)r_B + \frac{S}{V}r_S$$

$$r_W = \frac{2}{10}(1-0.2)10 + \frac{8}{10} \times 5 = 5.6\%$$

Example

미정이는 그동안 저축한 돈 8,000만원과 은행에서 10%로 대출받은 2,000만원을 합쳐, 학교앞에 옷가게를 하나 차렸다. 미정이가 저축한 돈 8,000만원은 5% 예금이자를 받고 있었다. 세율 20%일 때, 옷가게의 자본비용을 계산하라.

Solution

$$r_W = \frac{B}{V}(1-t)r_B + \frac{S}{V}r_S$$

$$r_W = \frac{2}{10}(1-0.2)10 + \frac{8}{10} \times 5 = 5.6\ \%$$

Example

재영이는 그동안 저축한 돈 2,000만원과 은행에서 10%로 대출받은 8,000만원을 합쳐, 학교앞에 옷가게를 하나 차렸다. 재영이가 저축한 돈 2,000만원은 5% 예금이자를 받고 있었다. 세율 20%일 때, 옷가게의 자본비용을 계산하라.

Solution

$$r_W = \frac{B}{V}(1-t)r_B + \frac{S}{V}r_S$$

$$r_W = \frac{8}{10}(1-0.2)10 + \frac{2}{10} \times 5 = 7.4\ \%$$

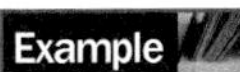

K Company

Assets	Debt	20,000
	Equity	30,000
50,000		50,000

The cost of equity is 5% and the cost of debt is 10%. The corporate tax rate is 30%. You are a financial analyst for K Company. The director of capital budgeting has asked you to analyze the following project. Should K Company take on the project?

Year	0	1	2
Cash flow	−1,000	700	500

Solution

$$\frac{B}{V} = \frac{2}{5}$$

$$\frac{S}{V} = \frac{3}{5}$$

$$r_W = \frac{B}{V}(1-t)r_B + \frac{S}{V}r_S$$

$$r_W = \frac{2}{5}(1-0.3)10 + \frac{3}{5} \times 5 = 5.8\ (\%)$$

$$NPV = -1000 + \frac{700}{1+0.058} + \frac{500}{(1+0.058)^2} = 108$$

Example

You are a financial analyst for K Company. The director of capital budgeting has asked you to analyze the following project. The firm has a debt-to-equity ratio of $\frac{2}{3}$. The cost of equity is 5% and the cost of debt is 10%. The corporate tax rate is 30%. Should K Company take on the project?

Year	0	1	2
Cash flow	−1,000	700	500

Solution

$$\frac{B}{S}=\frac{2}{3}$$

$$\frac{B}{V}=\frac{B}{B+\frac{3}{2}B}=\frac{2}{5}$$

$$\frac{S}{V}=\frac{3}{5}$$

$$r_W=\frac{B}{V}(1-t)r_B+\frac{S}{V}r_S$$

$$r_W=\frac{2}{5}(1-0.3)10+\frac{3}{5}\times 5=5.8\ (\%)$$

$$NPV=-1000+\frac{700}{1+0.058}+\frac{500}{(1+0.058)^2}=108$$

Example

Given that

$$\frac{B}{S} = 50\%,\ r_B = 12\%,\ r_S = 8\%,\ t = 30\% \ ,$$

Find the WACC.

Solution

$\frac{B}{S}$: the debt-to-equity ratio

$$2B = S$$

$$\frac{B}{V} = \frac{B}{B+2B} = \frac{1}{3}$$

$$\frac{S}{V} = \frac{2B}{B+2B} = \frac{2}{3}$$

$$r_W = \frac{B}{V}(1-t)r_B + \frac{S}{V}r_S$$

$$r_W = \frac{1}{3}(1-0.3)0.12 + \frac{2}{3} \times 0.08 = 8.13\%$$

Cf.

$\frac{B}{V}$: Debt ratio.

Debt ratios provide information about protection of creditors from insolvency and the ability of firms to obtain additional financing for potentially attractive investment opportunities.

Example

K Company has 2,000 shares of common stock outstanding that are currently being sold for 30,000 won per share. The firm's debt is 20 million won. The cost of debt is 10 percent and the cost of equity is 15 percent. The corporate tax rate is 40 percent. Calculate the weighted average cost of capital.

Solution

$S = 60{,}000{,}000 \quad B = 20{,}000{,}000$

$\frac{B}{V} = \frac{1}{4}$

$\frac{S}{V} = \frac{3}{4}$

$r_W = \frac{B}{V}(1-t)r_B + \frac{S}{V}r_S$

$r_W = \frac{1}{4}(1-0.4)0.1 + \frac{3}{4} \times 0.15 = 12.8\%$

Example

지영이와 수정이는 학교 앞에서 옷가게를 동업으로 운영하고 있다. 가게를 차리는데 들어간 돈은 1억원인데, 각각 반반씩 투자하였고 투자수익률은 20%이다. 그러던 중 지영이는 신촌에 독자적으로 가게 하나를 더 차릴 계획을 가지고 사업성분석을 하게 되었다. 신촌에 가게를 차리는데 필요한 돈은 1억6천만 원으로 1억2천만 원은 그동안 모은 돈으로 충당하고, 4천만 원은 은행에서 8% 이자율로 대출받을 예정이다. 신촌 옷가게에서 예상되는 현금흐름은 향후 3년간 매년 9천만 원이다. 세율 30%일 때, 지영이는 신촌에 옷가게를 차려도 될까?

Solution

$r_W = \frac{1}{4} \times 8 \times 0.7 + \frac{3}{4} \times 20 = 16.4\%$

$NPV = -16{,}000 + \frac{9{,}000}{1.16} + \frac{9{,}000}{1.16^2} + \frac{9{,}000}{1.16^3} = 4{,}213$

Example

You are a financial analyst for K Company. The director of capital budgeting has asked you to analyze the following project. The firm has a debt-to-equity ratio of 0.6. The cost of equity is 8% and the cost of debt is 5%. The corporate tax rate is 20%. Should K Company take on the project?

Year	0	1	2
Cash flow	−10,000	8,000	10,000

Solution

$$\frac{B}{S} = 0.6 = \frac{3}{5}$$

$$\frac{B}{V} = \frac{B}{B + \frac{5}{3}B} = \frac{3}{8}$$

$$\frac{S}{V} = \frac{5}{8}$$

$$r_W = \frac{B}{V}(1-t)r_B + \frac{S}{V}r_S$$

$$r_W = \frac{3}{8}(1-0.2)5 + \frac{5}{8}8 = 6.5\%$$

$$NPV = 6,328$$

Example

K Company has 30,000 shares of common stock outstanding that are currently being sold for 10,000 won per share. The firm's debt is 100 million won. The cost of debt is 14 percent and the cost of equity is 17.6 percent. The corporate tax rate is 40 percent. Calculate the weighted average cost of capital.

Solution

$S = 300,000,000, \qquad B = 100,000,000$

$\frac{B}{V} = \frac{1}{4}$

$\frac{S}{V} = \frac{3}{4}$

$$r_W = \frac{B}{V}(1-t)r_B + \frac{S}{V}r_S$$

$$r_W = \frac{1}{4}(1-0.4)14 + \frac{3}{4}17.6 = 15.3\%$$

Example

서울기업의 자본구조는 액면가 5,000원, 시장가격이 10,000원인 보통주 30,000주와 액면가 1억 원, 액면이자율 14%, 시장가격 1억 원인 회사채로 구성되어 있다. 서울기업의 전기말 당기순이익은 37,500,000원인데 이 중 40%가 배당되었고 재투자수익률은 20%이며 이러한 배당성향과 재투자수익률은 앞으로도 계속될 것이다. 법인세율이 40%일 경우 서울기업의 WACC는?

Solution

Gordon Model

$$S_0 = \frac{D_1}{r_S - g}$$

$$g = b \times r_A = 0.6 \times 0.2 = 0.12$$

b : 유보율

r_A : 재투자수익률

$$EPS_1 = EPS_0(1+g) = \frac{37,500,000}{30,000}(1+0.12) = 1,400$$

$$D_1 = EPS_1(1-b) = 560$$

$$10,000 = \frac{560}{r_s - 0.12}$$

$$r_S = 0.176$$

$$r_W = \frac{B}{V}(1-t)r_B + \frac{S}{V}r_S$$

$$r_W = \frac{1}{4}(1-0.4)0.14 + \frac{3}{4}0.176 = 0.153$$

FINANCIAL MANAGEMENT

chapter

5

Capital Structure

The value of an unlevered firm

Suppose the assets of a firm return the same distribution of net operating cash flows each time period for an infinite number of time periods. We can value this after-tax stream of cash flows by discounting its expected value at the appropriate risk-adjusted rate. The value of an unlevered firm, i.e., a firm with no debt, will be

$$V_U = \frac{FCF}{(1+r_0)} + \frac{FCF}{(1+r_0)^2} + \cdots + \frac{FCF}{(1+r_0)\infty}$$

$$V_U = \frac{FCF}{r_0}$$

where

FCF : the perpetual free cash flow after taxes,

r_0 : the discount rate for an all-equity firm of equivalent risk.

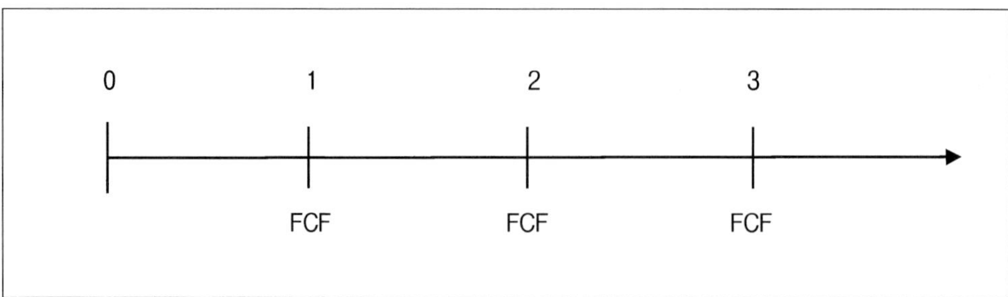

The Income Statement

무부채기업의 손익계산서는 다음과 같다.

Revenues
Cost of goods sold
SG & A
Depreciation
EBIT
Taxes
Net Income

SG & A

Selling, General, and Administrative expenses

판매비와 관리비는 상품과 용역의 판매활동 또는 기업의 관리와 유지에서 발생하는 비용으로 급여(임원급여, 급료, 임금 및 제수당을 포함한다), 퇴직급여, 복리후생비, 임차료, 접대비, 감가상각비, 무형자산상각비, 세금과공과, 광고선전비, 연구비, 경상개발비, 대손상각비 등 매출원가에 속하지 아니하는 모든 영업비용을 포함한다.

EBIT

Earnings Before Interest and Taxes

Free Cash Flow

$$FCF = NI + Dep - I$$

$$FCF = EBIT(1-t) + Dep - I$$

t : the corporate tax rate

I : investment

By assumption, depreciation each year must be replaced by investment in order to keep the same amount of capital in place.

Therefore $Dep - I$, and $FCF = EBIT(1-t)$.

$$V_U = \frac{FCF}{r_0} = \frac{EBIT(1-t)}{r_0}.$$

Steady state

Steady state is a theoretical construct that we use to consider a company with a growth rate of zero.

What are two main assumptions that we have to make in order to define steady state?

First, depreciation would need to be based on true replacement cost accounting and the annual depreciation expense would have to be reinvested in the business.

Second, all of the constant real profits achieved after charging this replacement cost depreciation must be paid out as dividends.

무부채기업의 기업가치는 미래에 벌어들일 자유현금흐름의 현재가치 합이다. 자유현금흐름은 순이익에 감가상각을 더하고 기업이 투자해야 하는 금액을 뺀 값이다. 기업규모가 일정하게 유지된다고 가정하면, 자유현금흐름과 순이익은 같아진다. 순이익은 세후영업이익과 같다. 무한등비급수공식을 이용하면, 무부채기업의 기업가치는 세후영업이익을 무부채기업의 할인율로 나누어 준 값과 같다.

Example

K Company, an all-equity firm, generates perpetual earnings before interest and taxes (EBIT) of 3 million won per year. K's after-tax, all-equity discount rate is 12%. The company's tax rate is 30%. What's the value of K Company?

Solution

$$V_U = \frac{EBIT(1-t)}{r_0}$$

$$V_U = \frac{3{,}000{,}000(1-0.3)}{0.12} = 17{,}500{,}000$$

The value of the levered firm

The Income Statement

Revenues
Cost of goods sold
SG & A
Depreciation
EBIT
Interest Expense
EBT
Taxes
Net Income

Depreciation: Noncash charges

Interest Expense: $r_B \cdot B$

The after-tax cash flows must be split up between debt holders and shareholders.

Shareholders receive $(NI + Dep - I)$.

Bondholders receive $r_B \cdot B$

Total cash flow available for payment: $(NI + Dep - I) + r_B \cdot B$

Given that $Dep = I$,

$$NI + r_B \cdot B = (EBIT - r_B \cdot B)(1-t) + r_B \cdot B$$

$$NI + r_B \cdot B = EBIT(1-t) - r_B \cdot B + r_B \cdot Bt + r_B \cdot B$$

$$NI + r_B \cdot B = EBIT(1-t) + r_B \cdot Bt$$

$EBIT(1-t)$ is assumed to be the same as the cash flows for the unlevered firm with the same risk.

Therefore we can discount $EBIT(1-t)$ at the rate appropriate for an unlevered firm, r_0.

$r_B Bt$ is assumed to be risk free.

Therefore we shall discount it at the before-tax cost of risk-free debt, r_B.

The value of the levered firm is the sum of the discounted value of the two types of cash flow.

$$V_L = \frac{EBIT(1-t)}{r_0} + \frac{r_B \cdot Bt}{r_B}.$$

$$V_L = V_U + t \cdot B.$$

부채기업의 총현금흐름은 채권자가 받아가는 몫과 주주가 받아가는 몫의 합이다. 채권자가 받아가는 금액은 이자비용이고, 주주가 받아가는 금액은 순이익에 감가상각을 더하고 기업이 투자를 해야 하는 금액을 뺀 금액이다. 기업규모가 일정하게 유지된다고 가정하면, 주주가 받아가는 금액은 순이익과 같다. 현재가치를 구하기 위해 총현금흐름을 정리하면, 세후영업이익과 이자비용에 세율을 곱한 값의 합이 된다. 세후영업이익의 현재가치를 구하기 위해 무부채기업의 할인율을 적용할 수 있다. 이자비용에 세율을 곱한 값의 현재가치를 구하기 위해 할인율로 타인자본비용을 적용할 수 있다. 그리고 무한등비급수 공식을 이용하여 정리하면 부채기업의 기업가치가 도출된다.

The interest tax shield

Tax rate times interest payment

$r_B Bt$

Present value of the interest tax shield

$$PV = \frac{r_B Bt}{1+r_B} + \frac{r_B Bt}{(1+r_B)^2} + \cdots$$

$$= \frac{\dfrac{r_B Bt}{1+r_B}}{1 - \dfrac{1}{1+r_B}} = tB$$

$$V_L = V_U + t \cdot B$$

Value of a levered firm = value of an unlevered firm + PV of interest tax shield

Derive the interest tax shield.

Solution

Tax = t × EBT

$$Tax = t(Rev - COGS - Dep - r_B B)$$
$$= t(Rev - COGS - Dep) - t r_B B$$

Modigliani-Miller Proposition 1

The value of the firm given corporate taxes only

$$V_L = V_U + t \cdot B$$

V_L : the value of the levered firm.

V_U : the value of an unlevered firm.

$t \cdot B$: the present value of the tax shield provided by debt.

The market value of the corporation can increase as it takes on more and more debt. The firm should take on 100% debt.
법인세를 고려하면, 타인자본을 사용한 기업의 가치는 자기자본만 사용한 기업의 가치보다 법인세 감세효과의 현가만큼 더 크며, 따라서 타인자본을 많이 사용할수록 기업의 가치는 증가한다.

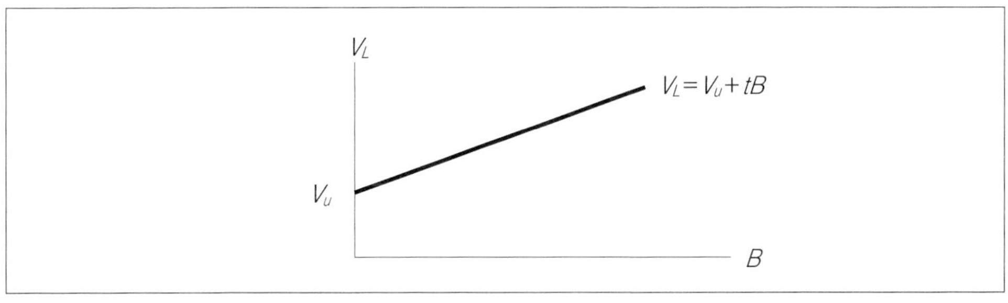

MM Proposition I with taxes is based on the concept that the value of a firm increases as the firm's debt increases because of the interest tax shield.

Example

An all-equity firm is subject to a 30% corporate tax rate. The firm's market value is 17,500,000 won. The firm issues 7 million won of bonds and uses the proceeds to repurchase common stock. According to MM, what's the new market value of the firm?

Solution

$V_L = V_U + t \cdot B$

$V_L = 17{,}500{,}000 + 0.3 \cdot 7{,}000{,}000$

$V_L = 19{,}600{,}000$

Example

H Company has common stock with a market value of 6,000,000 won and debt with a market value of 4,000,000 won.

The corporate tax rate is 30%.

The firm plans to sell the new shares of stock and to use the proceeds to repay debt. According to MM, what's the new market value of the firm?

Solution

$V_L = V_U + t \cdot B$

$10{,}000{,}000 = V_U + 0.3 \times 4{,}000{,}000$

$V_U = 8{,}800{,}000$

Example

한라기업의 자본구조는 자기자본 6,000,000원과 부채 4,000,000원으로 구성되어 있다. 신주를 발행하여 부채 4,000,000원을 상환한 경우, 신주발행 후 한라기업의 기업가치를 구하라. 법인세율은 30%이고, MM 명제가 성립한다고 가정한다.

Solution

$$V_L = V_U + t \cdot B$$

$$10{,}000{,}000 = V_U + 0.3 \times 4{,}000{,}000$$

$$V_U = 8{,}800{,}000$$

Example

K Company is currently an unlevered firm. The company expects to generate 3,000,000 won in EBIT, in perpetuity. The corporate tax rate is 30%. The firm is considering a capital restructuring to allow 7,000,000 won. Unlevered firms in the same industry have a cost of equity capital of 12%. What will the new value of K Company be? What will the value of levered equity be?

Solution

$$V_U = \frac{EBIT(1-t)}{r_0}$$

$$V_U = \frac{3{,}000{,}000(1-0.3)}{0.12} = 17{,}500{,}000$$

$$V_L = V_U + t \cdot B$$

$$V_L = 17{,}500{,}000 + 0.3 \cdot 7{,}000{,}000$$

$$V_L = 19{,}600{,}000$$

$$V_L = S + B$$

$$19{,}600{,}000 = S + 7{,}000{,}000$$

$$S = 12{,}600{,}000$$

Example

영업이익이 15,000원인 무부채기업이 20,000원의 차입금을 조달하여 자기주식을 매입소각하는 방법으로 자본구조를 변경하려고 계획하고 있다. 법인세율은 30%이고 무부채기업의 자본비용은 20%이다. 자본구조 변경 후의 기업가치와 자기자본가치를 구하라.

Solution

$$V_U = \frac{EBIT(1-t)}{r_0}$$

$$V_U = \frac{15{,}000(1-0.3)}{0.2} = 52{,}500$$

$$V_L = V_U + t \cdot B$$

$$V_L = 52{,}500 + 0.3 \cdot 20{,}000 = 58{,}500$$

$$V_L = S + B$$

$$58{,}500 = S + 20{,}000$$

$$S = 38{,}500$$

Example

K Company is currently an unlevered firm. The company expects to generate 30,000 won in EBIT, in perpetuity. The corporate tax rate is 30%. The firm is considering a capital restructuring to allow 40,000 won. Unlevered firms in the same industry have a cost of equity capital of 20%. What will the new value of K Company be? What will the value of levered equity be?

Solution

$$V_U = \frac{EBIT(1-t)}{r_0}$$

$$V_U = 105{,}000$$

$$V_L = V_U + t \cdot B$$

$$V_L = 117{,}000$$

$$V_L = S + B$$

$$S = 77{,}000$$

Without taxes

The value of the levered firm is the same as the value of the unlevered firm.

The value of the firm is completely independent of the type of financing used for its projects.

The market value of any firm is independent of its capital structure and is given by capitalizing its expected return at the rate r_0 appropriate to its risk class.

The method of financing is irrelevant.

$V_L = V_U$, $if \;\; t = 0$

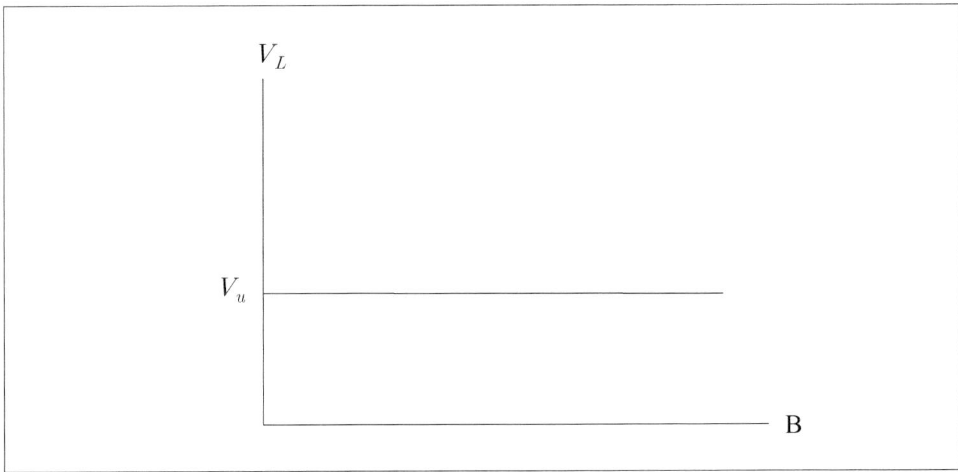

MM Proposition states that the value of a firm is unrelated to the firm's capital structure.

Example

The market value of an all-equity firm is 17,500,000 won. The firm issues 7 million won of bonds and uses the proceeds to repurchase common stock. According to MM, what's the new market value of the firm?

Solution

MM Proposition with No Corporate Taxes

$V_L = V_U$

$V_L = 17{,}500{,}000$

Example

The market value of an all-equity firm is 8,800,000 won. The firm issues 4 million won of bonds and uses the proceeds to repurchase common stock. According to MM, what's the new market value of the firm?

Solution

MM Proposition with No Corporate Taxes

$V_L = V_U$

$V_L = 8{,}800{,}000$

Example

고려기업의 자본구조는 자기자본 6,000,000원과 부채 4,000,000원으로 구성되어 있다. 신주를 발행하여 부채 4,000,000원을 상환한 경우, 신주발행 후 고려기업의 기업가치를 구하라. 법인세가 없는 MM 명제가 성립한다고 가정한다.

Solution

$V_L = V_U$

$10{,}000{,}000 = V_U$

$V_U = 10{,}000{,}000$

Example

K Company has common stock with a market value of 6,000,000 won and debt with a market value of 4,000,000 won.

The firm plans to sell the new shares of stock and to use the proceeds to repay debt. According to MM, what's the new market value of the firm?

Solution

$V_L = V_U$

$10{,}000{,}000 = V_U$

$V_U = 10{,}000{,}000$

Financial leverage

The higher the degree of financial leverage employed by a firm, the higher the probability that the firm will encounter financial distress.

Arbitrage strategy

$V_U < V_L$인 경우, 부채기업 주주는 자신의 주식을 매각하여 조달한 자금과 개인적인 차입으로 조달한 자금을 합쳐서 무부채기업의 주식을 매입함으로써 초과수익을 얻을 수 있다.

$V_U > V_L$인 경우, 무부채기업 주주는 자신의 주식을 매각하여 조달한 자금에서 개인적으로 대출해 준 자금을 차감한 금액으로 부채기업의 주식을 매입함으로써 초과수익을 얻을 수 있다.

If you own 1% of the shares in Y, you can earn a profit with no extra risk. Explain your arbitrage strategy and calculate the arbitrage profit.

($)

	Company X	Company Y
EBIT	10,000	10,000
S	100,000	80,000
B	0	40,000

Company Y has $40,000 of debt paying 10% interest.

Solution

	Company X	Company Y
EBIT	10,000	10,000
$r_B \times B$	0	4,000
NI	10,000	6,000

If we own 1% of the shares in Y, we can earn $60.

1. If we own 1% of the shares in Y, then we sell $800.
2. We borrow $400 at 10% interest.
3. We can invest $1,200 in shares of X.
   ① This brings our profit to $120.
   ② Pay interest on $400 of debt: $40.

This is exactly the same leverage and therefore the same risk as we started with when we had an equity investment in Y.

We can earn $80.

Arbitrage Profit: $20

Example

다음 정보와 관련한 차익거래전략을 설명하고, 차익거래이익을 계산하라.

(원)

	관악기업	강남기업
영업이익	10,000	10,000
자본	100,000	80,000
부채	0	40,000

강남기업 주식 1%를 소유하고 있으며, 차입이자율은 10%이다.

Solution

	Company X	Company Y
EBIT	10,000	10,000
$r_B \times B$	0	4,000
NI	10,000	6,000

If we own 1% of the shares in Y, we can earn $60.

1. If we own 1% of the shares in Y, then we sell $800.
2. We borrow $400 at 10% interest.
3. We can invest $1,200 in shares of X.
   ① This brings our profit to $120.
   ② Pay interest on $400 of debt: $40.

This is exactly the same leverage and therefore the same risk as we started with when we had an equity investment in Y.

We can earn $80.

Arbitrage Profit: $20

Example

Company X is an unlevered firm. The market value of an all-equity firm is $100,000. Company Y has common stock with a market value of $60,000 and debt with a market value of $60,000. Both firms have EBIT=$10,000.

Company Y has $60,000 of debt paying 10% interest.

If you own 1% of the shares in Y, you can earn a profit with no extra risk.

Explain your arbitrage strategy and calculate the arbitrage profit.

Solution

($)

	Company X	Company Y
EBIT	10,000	10,000
S	100,000	60,000
B	0	60,000

	Company X	Company Y
EBIT	10,000	10,000
$r_B \times B$	0	6,000
NI	10,000	4,000

If we own 1% of the shares in Y, we can earn $40.

1. If we own 1% of the shares in Y, then we sell $600.
2. We borrow $600 at 10% interest.
3. We can invest $1,200 in shares of X.
   ① This brings our profit to $120.
   ② Pay interest on $600 of debt: $60.

This is exactly the same leverage and therefore the same risk as we started with when we had an equity investment in Y.

We can earn $60.

Arbitrage Profit: $20

If you own 1% of the shares in X, you can earn a profit with no extra risk.
Explain your arbitrage strategy and calculate the arbitrage profit.

	Company X	Company Y
EBIT	10,000	10,000
S	100,000	50,000
B	0	30,000

Company Y has $30,000 of debt paying 5% interest.

Solution

	Company X	Company Y
EBIT	10,000	10,000
Interest Expense	0	1,500
NI	10,000	8,500

If we own 1% of the shares in X, we can earn $100.

1. If we own 1% of the shares in X, then we sell $1,000.
2. We lend $375 at 5% interest.

$$375 = 1{,}000 \times \frac{30{,}000}{80{,}000}$$

3. We can invest $625 in shares of Y.

This brings our profit to $106.25.

Receive interest on $375 of debt: $18.75.

This is exactly the same leverage and therefore the same risk as we started with when we had an equity investment in X.

We can earn $125.

Arbitrage Profit: $25.

Homemade leverage

Homemade leverage is the borrowing or lending of money by individual shareholders as a means of adjusting their level of financial leverage.

Homemade leverage is used by an individual investor to artificially adjust the leverage of a company. Individuals can use homemade leverage to recreate the effects of corporate leverage.

Homemade leverage refers to the use of borrowing on the personal level as opposed to the corporate level.

Modigliani-Miller Proposition 2

The levered firm with corporate taxes

$V_L = S + B$

S : Stockholders' claim

B : Bondholders' claim

Shareholders receive $(NI + Dep - I)$.

Given that $Dep = I$,

$NI = (EBIT - r_B \cdot B)(1-t)$

자기자본비용은 연간 순이익을 자기자본 시장가치로 나눈 값이다.

$$S = \frac{NI}{r_S}$$

$$S = \frac{NI}{r_S} = \frac{(EBIT - r_B \cdot B)(1-t)}{r_S}$$

$$V_L = V_U + t \cdot B = S + B$$

$$V_U = S + (1-t)B$$

$$V_U = \frac{EBIT(1-t)}{r_0}$$

$$EBIT(1-t) = r_0 \cdot V_U$$

$$EBIT(1-t) = r_0\{S + (1-t)B\}$$

$$S = \frac{(EBIT - r_B B)(1-t)}{r_s} = \frac{r_0\{S + (1-t)B\} - r_B B(1-t)}{r_s}$$

$$r_S = \frac{r_0\{S + (1-t)B\} - r_B \cdot B(1-t)}{S}$$

$$r_S = r_0 + (1-t)(r_0 - r_B)\frac{B}{S}$$

The cost of equity is a linear function of the firm's debt-equity ratio.

부채의 사용이 증가함에 따라 자기자본비용의 상승률이 법인세가 없을 때보다 법인세가 있을 때 더 작게 나타난다.

MM proposition Ⅱ states that a firm's cost of equity is directly and proportionally related to the firm's capital structure.

Example

K Company is currently an unlevered firm. The firm's equity is worth 17,500,000 won. The cost of equity is 12%. The corporate tax rate is 30%. The firm plans to issue 7,000,000 won in debt and to use the proceeds to repurchase stock. The cost of debt is 10%. After the repurchase, what will the cost of equity be?

Solution

$V_U = 17{,}500{,}000$

$V_L = V_U + t \cdot B$

$V_L = 17{,}500{,}000 + 0.3 \cdot 7{,}000{,}000$

$V_L = 19{,}600{,}000$

$V_L = S + B$

$19{,}600{,}000 = S + 7{,}000{,}000$

$S = 12{,}600{,}000$

$$r_S = r_0 + (1-t)(r_0 - r_B)\frac{B}{S}$$

$$r_S = 0.12 + (1-0.3)(0.12-0.1)\frac{7{,}000{,}000}{12{,}600{,}000} = 12.8\%$$

Weighted Average Cost of Capital

$$r_W = \frac{B}{V}(1-t)r_B + \frac{S}{V}r_S$$

$$r_S = r_0 + (1-t)(r_0 - r_B)\frac{B}{S}$$

$$r_W = \frac{B}{V}(1-t)r_B + \frac{S}{V}\{r_0 + (1-t)(r_0 - r_B)\frac{B}{S}\}$$

$$r_W = \frac{B}{V}(1-t)r_B + \frac{S}{V}r_0 + (1-t)(r_0 - r_B)\frac{B}{V}$$

$$r_W = \frac{B}{V}(1-t)r_B + \frac{S}{V}r_0 + (1-t)r_0\frac{B}{V} - (1-t)r_B\frac{B}{V}$$

$$r_W = r_0(\frac{S}{V} + \frac{B}{V} - t\frac{B}{V})$$

$$r_W = r_0(1 - t\frac{B}{V})$$

Example

K Company is currently an unlevered firm. The firm's equity is worth 17,500,000 won. The cost of equity is 12%. The corporate tax rate is 30%. The firm plans to issue 7,000,000 won in debt and to use the proceeds to repurchase stock.

After the repurchase, what will the cost of capital be?

Solution

$$V_U = 17{,}500{,}000$$

$$V_L = V_U + t \cdot B$$

$$V_L = 17{,}500{,}000 + 0.3 \cdot 7{,}000{,}000$$

$$V_L = 19{,}600{,}000$$

$$V_L = S + B$$

$$19{,}600{,}000 = S + 7{,}000{,}000$$

$$S = 12{,}600{,}000$$

$$r_W = r_0(1 - t\frac{B}{V})$$

$$r_W = 0.12(1 - 0.3 \times \frac{7{,}000{,}000}{19{,}600{,}000}) = 10.7\%$$

Example

J Company has common stock with a market value of 1,000,000 won and debt with a market value of 250,000 won.

The cost of capital is 12%. The corporate tax rate is 30%.

The firm plans to sell the new shares of stock and to use the proceeds to repay debt. What will the all-equity discount rate be?

Solution

$$r_W = r_0(1 - t\frac{B}{V})$$

$$r_W = r_0(1 - 0.3\frac{250}{1,250}) = 12\%$$

$$r_0 = 12.8\%$$

Example

L Company has common stock with a market value of 6,000,000 won and debt with a market value of 3,000,000 won.

The cost of capital is 10%. The corporate tax rate is 30%.

The firm plans to sell the new shares of stock and to use the proceeds to repay debt. What will the all-equity discount rate be?

Solution

$$r_W = r_0(1 - t\frac{B}{V})$$

$$r_W = r_0\left(1 - 0.3\frac{3,000,000}{9,000,000}\right) = 10\%$$

$$r_0 = 11.1\%$$

Example

Calculate the cost of capital from the following data.

$\frac{B}{S}: 1.5$

Corporate tax rate : 40%

r_0 : 10%

Solution

$$\frac{B}{B+S} = \frac{3}{5}$$

$$r_W = r_0(1 - t\frac{B}{V}) = 7.6\%$$

Example

다음 자료를 이용하여 가중평균자본비용을 구하라.

$\frac{B}{S}: 1.5$

법인세율 : 40%

무부채기업의 자기자본비용 : 10%

Solution

$$\frac{B}{B+S} = \frac{3}{5}$$

$$r_W = r_0(1 - t\frac{B}{V}) = 7.6\%$$

Example

관악기업은 새로운 시설투자를 하기 위하여 5:7의 비율로 사채와 보통주를 발행할 예정이다. Proxy company로 사용할 수 있는 신림기업이 부채를 사용하지 않았을 경우의 자기자본비용이 18%라면 법인세율이 40%일 때 관악기업이 새로운 투자에 대해 적용할 할인율은?

Solution

$$\frac{B}{B+S}=\frac{5}{12}$$

$$r_W = r_0(1-t\frac{B}{V}) = 15\%$$

Example

관악기업은 새로운 시설투자를 하기 위하여 5:5의 비율로 사채와 보통주를 발행할 예정이다. Proxy company로 사용할 수 있는 신림기업이 부채를 사용하지 않았을 경우의 자기자본비용이 10%라면 법인세율이 40%일 때 관악기업이 새로운 투자에 대해 적용할 할인율은?

Solution

$$\frac{B}{V}=\frac{1}{2}$$

$$r_W = r_0\left(1-t\frac{B}{V}\right)= 8\%$$

순이익접근법

Net income approach

The equity value of the company is equal to the net income divided by the cost of equity.

$$S = \frac{NI}{1+r_S} + \frac{NI}{(1+r_S)^2} + \cdots$$

$$S = \frac{NI}{r_S} = \frac{EBIT - r_B B}{r_S}$$

$$V = B + \frac{EBIT - r_B B}{r_S} = B\left(1 - \frac{r_B}{r_S}\right) + \frac{EBIT}{r_S}$$

순영업이익접근법

EBIT approach

$$V = \frac{EBIT}{1+r_W} + \frac{EBIT}{(1+r_W)^2} + \cdots$$

$$V = \frac{EBIT}{r_W}$$

The firm value is equal to the Earnings Before Interest and Taxes divided by the cost of capital.

Bankruptcy

State of being unable to pay debts. Thus, the ownership of the firm's assets is transferred from the stockholders to the bondholders.

Bankruptcy cost

기업의 자산가치가 부채가치보다 작고 기업이 실제로 이러한 상태를 벗어나기 어렵다고 판단되는 경우에 채권자는 법원에 파산신청을 하게 되고 법원의 선고에 의해 기업은 해산되는데, 이와 같은 상태를 가리켜 파산(bankruptcy)이라 한다. 파산이 된 기업은 일정한 절차를 거쳐 정리되는데, 이러한 과정에서 여러 가지 비용이 발생한다. 이러한 비용을 파산비용(bankruptcy cost)이라 한다.

Example

The explicit costs, such as legal and administrative expenses, associated with corporate default are classified as _____ costs.

Solution

direct bankruptcy

Example

The costs incurred by a business in an effort to avoid bankruptcy are classified as _____ costs.

Solution

indirect bankruptcy

파산에 따르는 직접비용

기업이 파산에 이르게 되면 법적 처리나 관리에 많은 비용이 발생한다. 대표적인 것이 변호사와 공인회계사 등에게 돌아가는 비용이다.

파산에 따르는 간접비용

파산선고를 받은 기업이 정해진 파산절차를 밟는 과정에서 또는 파산 후 재정비를 한다고 하여도 기업이미지의 실추 때문에 고객을 잃고 거래처를 상실하게 된다. 그 결과 판매량이 감소하고 영업활동이 위축되어 손해를 보게 된다. 또한 새로운 자본조달도 어렵게 되며, 자본조달이 가능하더라도 높은 조달비용을 지불하게 된다. 이러한 비용을 파산의 간접비용이라 한다.

Bankruptcy cost theory

파산비용이론 또는 재무적 곤경비용이론
부채사용의 증가는 이자비용에 대한 절세효과가 존재하는 반면 파산위험을 증가시키는 상충관계가 성립하게 되어 기업가치를 극대화할 수 있는 자기자본과 타인자본의 최적결합이 존재할 수 있다는 이론이다.

$V_L = V_U + Bt - PVFD$

Bt : 세금효과의 현재가치

$PVFD$: 재무적 곤경비용의 현가

Example

부채를 사용하는 기업의 가치가 5,000백만원이고, 부채가 없는 기업의 가치가 4,780백만원이며 파산비용과 대리인비용의 현재가치가 160백만원일 때 파산비용이론에서 법인세 절감액의 현재가치는?

Solution

$V_L = V_U + Bt - PVFD$

$5{,}000 = 4{,}780 + Bt - 160$

$Bt = 380$

Example

Which form of financing do firms prefer to use first according to the pecking-order theory?

a. regular debt

b. common stock

c. preferred stock

d. internal funds

Solution

d

Business Risk

The risk associated with projections of a firm's future returns on assets.

Business risk depends on a number of factors, including the following:

(1) Demand variability: Utility companies, because of their stable demand, have historically been able to use more financial leverage than industrial firms.

(2) Sales price variability

(3) Input price variability

(4) Ability to adjust output prices for changes in input prices

(5) The extent to which costs are fixed

Financial Risk

The additional risk placed on the common stockholders as a result of financial leverage.

Firms generally consider the following factors when making capital structure decisions.

(1) Business Risk

(2) The firm's tax position

(3) Financial flexibility

(4) Management attitudes: Some managements tend to be more conservative than others, and thus use less debt than the average firm in their industry.

(5) Asset structure

Firms whose assets are suitable as security for loans tend to use debt rather heavily.

(6) Growth rate

Other things the same, faster-growing firms must rely more heavily on external capital.

(7) Profitability

One often observes that firms with very high rates of return on investment use relatively little debt.

(8) Taxes

The higher a firm's tax rate, the greater the advantage of debt.

Business risk is the equity risk arising from the nature of the firm's operating activity and is directly related to the systematic risk of the firm's assets. Financial risk is the equity risk that is due entirely to the firm's chosen capital structure.

The utility sector is a category of company stocks that provide basic services including electricity, natural gas, and water.

Target debt-equity ratios

Since Modigliani and Miller's irrelevance proposition in 1958, researchers have investigated firms' decisions about how to finance their operations.
Firms would select target debt-equity ratios, trading off their costs and benefits of leverage.
Survey evidence by Graham and Harvey(2001) shows that 81% of firms consider a target debt ratio or range when making debt decisions.

Modigliani and Miller

Modigliani, F., and M.H.Miller, The cost of capital, corporation finance, and the theory of investment, American Economic Review, June 1958
Modigliani, F., and M.H.Miller, Corporate income taxes and the cost of capital, American Economic Review, June 1963

Nobel Prize Laureates

Modigliani won the Nobel Prize in economics in 1985 for his pioneering analyses of savings and financial markets.
1985 Franco Modigliani
1990 Harry M. Markowitz, Merton H. Miller, William F. Sharpe

Target Capital Structure

The mix of debt and equity with which then firm plans to raise capital.

chapter 6

Risk & Return

위험(risk)은 미래 수익(return)의 불확실성(uncertainty) 또는 불확실성에의 노출(exposure to uncertainty)로 정의된다.

An investment is an asset or item acquired with the goal of generating income or appreciation. Appreciation refers to an increase in the value of an asset over time. When an individual purchases a good as an investment, the intent is not to consume the good but rather to use it in the future to create wealth.

Dividends are payments made by a corporation to its shareholders, usually derived from the company's profits. These payments represent a portion of the company's earnings that is distributed to its investors as a reward for their ownership.

What Is the Dividend Yield?

Dividend yield is a ratio that demonstrates a company's annual dividends relative to its shares' market price.

A stock's dividend yield is a ratio showing how much a company pays out in dividends each year relative to its stock price.

The dividend yield is the amount of money a company pays shareholders for owning a share of its stock divided by its current stock price.

Examples of Dividend Yield

Suppose Company A's stock is trading at $20 and pays annual dividends of $1 per share to its shareholders. Suppose that Company B's stock is trading at $40 and also pays an annual dividend of $1 per share.

This means Company A's dividend yield is 5%, while Company B's dividend yield is only 2.5%.

The dividend payout ratio represents how much of a company's net earnings are paid out as dividends.

What Is Capital Appreciation?

Capital appreciation is a rise in an investment's market price. Capital appreciation is the difference between the purchase price and the selling price of an investment. If an investor buys a stock for $10 per share, for example, and the stock price rises to $12, the investor has earned $2 in capital appreciation. When the investor sells the stock, the $2 earned becomes a capital gain.

Capital appreciation is a rise in an investment's market price.
Capital appreciation is the difference between the purchase price and the selling price of an investment.

Example of Capital Appreciation
An investor purchases a stock for $10, and the stock pays an annual dividend of $1, equating to a dividend yield of 10%. A year later, the stock is trading at $15 per share, and the investor has received a dividend of $1. The investor has a return of $5 from capital appreciation as the price of the stock went from the purchase price or cost basis of $10 to a current market value of $15 per share. In percentage terms, the rise in the stock price led to a 50% return from capital appreciation. The dividend income return is $1, equating to a return of 10% in line with the original dividend yield. The return from capital appreciation combined with the return from the dividend leads to a total return on the stock of $6 or 60%.

What Is Capital Gains Yield (CGY)?

A capital gains yield is the rise in the price of a security, such as common stock. For common stock holdings, the CGY is the rise in the stock price divided by the original price of the security.

Capital gains yield is a simple formula to calculate as the only components needed are as follows:
The original price of the security
The current price of the security

A capital gains yield is the rise in the price of an investment such as a stock or bond, calculated as the rise in the security's price divided by the original price of the security. The total return on a share of common stock includes CGY and dividend yield.

The total return on a share of common stock includes CGY and dividend yield.

CGY equals the total return if the investment generates no cash flow.

$$CGY = \frac{P_1 - P_0}{P_0}$$

where:

P_0 = original purchase price of the security

P_1 = current market price of the security

For example, Peter buys a share of company ABC for $200 and then sells the share for $220. The CGY for the share in company ABC equals 10%.

Example

The common stock of K company is expected to earn 20 percent in a normal economy and lose 20 percent in a recession. The probability of a normal economy is 60 percent while the probability of a recession is 40 percent.
What is the expected rate of return?

Solution

Probability	Return
0.4	−20%
0.6	20%

$$E(r) = 0.4 \times (-20) + 0.6 \times 20 = 4$$

$$E(r) = 4\%$$

Example

If the economy is normal, K stock is expected to return 20 percent. If the economy falls into a recession, the stock's return is projected at a negative 20 percent. The probability of a normal economy is 60 percent while the probability of a recession is 40 percent. What is the expected rate of return?

Solution

Probability	Return
0.4	−20%
0.6	20%

$$E(r) = 0.4 \times (-20) + 0.6 \times 20 = 4$$

$$E(r) = 4\%$$

Example

A stock is currently priced at ₩30,000 per share. At the end of the period, there is a 40% chance it will be worth ₩24,000 and a 60% chance it will be worth ₩36,000. What is the expected rate of return? The variance of end-of-period returns?

Solution

Probability	Stock Price	Return
0.4	24,000	−20%
0.6	36,000	20%

$$E(r) = 0.4 \times (-20) + 0.6 \times 20 = 4$$

$$E(r) = 4.0\%$$

$$Var(r) = 0.4 \times (-20-4)^2 + 0.6 \times (20-4)^2 = 384$$

Example

A stock is currently priced at W30,000 per share.

Given the following end-of-period return:

Probability	Return
0.4	−10%
0.6	10%

What is the expected price? The variance of price?

Solution

Probability	Return	Stock Price
0.4	−10%	27,000
0.6	10%	33,000

$$E(P) = 0.4 \times 27{,}000 + 0.6 \times 33{,}000 = 30{,}600$$

$$E(P) = 30{,}600$$

$$Var(P) = 0.4 \times (27{,}000 - 30{,}600)^2 + 0.6 \times (33{,}000 - 30{,}600)^2$$

$$Var(P) = 8{,}640{,}000$$

Example

If you toss the coin 3 times, what is the probability of getting 3 Heads?

Solution

When you toss a coin, there are two equally likely outcomes: Heads (H) or Tails (T).

Sample Space is the set of all possible outcomes.

S = {HHH, HHT, HTH, HTT, THH, THT, TTH, TTT}

$P(H)=\frac{1}{2}$, $P(HHH)=\frac{1}{8}$

The probability of getting 3 Heads in 3 coin tosses is 0.125.

A coin is tossed repeatedly until the first head appears.

What is the probability that the first head occurs on the 4th toss?

Example

You recently purchased a stock that is expected to earn 20 percent in a booming economy, 0 percent in a normal economy, and lose 20 percent in a recessionary economy. There is a 50 percent probability of a boom and a 30 percent chance of a normal economy. What is your expected rate of return on this stock?

Solution

Probability	Return
0.2	−20%
0.3	0%
0.5	20%

$E(r) = 0.2 \times (-20) + 0.3 \times 0 + 0.5 \times 20 = 6$

$E(r) = 6\%$

Example

The rate of return on the common stock of J company is expected to be 20 percent in a boom economy, 0 percent in a normal economy, and a negative 20 percent in a recessionary economy. The probabilities of these economic states are 50 percent for a boom, 30 percent for a normal economy, and 20 percent for a recession.

What is your expected rate of return on this stock?

Solution

Probability	Return
0.2	−20%
0.3	0%
0.5	20%

$$E(r) = 0.2 \times (-20) + 0.3 \times 0 + 0.5 \times 20 = 6$$

$$E(r) = 6\%$$

Example

A stock is currently priced at 20,000 won per share.

Given the following end-of-period prices,

Stock Price	18,000	24,000
Probability	$\frac{1}{2}$	$\frac{1}{2}$

What is the expected return? The variance of return?

Solution

Return	−10%	20%
Probability	$\frac{1}{2}$	$\frac{1}{2}$

$$E(r) = \frac{1}{2}(-10) + \frac{1}{2}20 = 5\%$$

$$Var(r) = \frac{1}{2}(-15)^2 + \frac{1}{2}15^2 = 225$$

Standard deviation & Expected rate of return

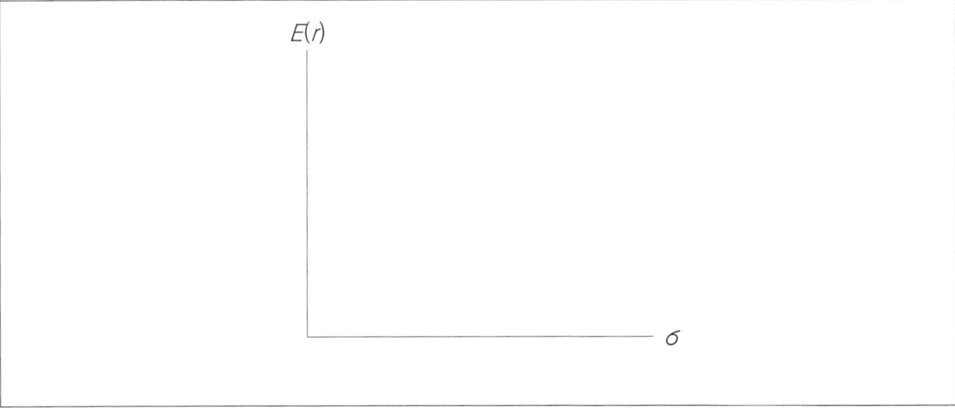

The standard deviation of a random variable is a measure of the spread or dispersion of the values of the random variable. In many applications it is preferable to the variance as such a measure since it will have the same measurement units as the random variable itself. Standard deviation is the positive square root of the variance. Standard deviation is one of the basic methods of statistical analysis. Standard deviation is commonly abbreviated as SD and denoted by 'σ' and it tells about the value that how much it has deviated from the mean value. If we get a low standard deviation then it means that the values tend to be close to the mean whereas a high standard deviation tells us that the values are far from the mean value.

The lowercase Greek letter sigma represents standard deviation.

The variance is typically designated as Var(X), or sometimes as V(X), or symbolically as σ_X^2.

The expected return is the profit or loss that an investor anticipates on an investment that has known historical rates of return. It is calculated by multiplying potential outcomes by the chances of them occurring and then totaling these results.

An expected return is calculated by multiplying potential outcomes by the odds of them occurring and then totaling these results.

Rate of Return

Capital Gain

If an investment is sold at a price that exceeds the original price paid on the date of initial investment, then there is a capital gain.

Capital Gain = Current Market Price – Original Purchase Price

Realized Capital Gain

If the security is sold, i.e. the investor exited the position, the gain is considered to be a "realized" capital gain.

Unrealized Capital Gain

If the security has not yet been sold, the paper gain is an "unrealized" capital gain.

Holding Period Return

Calculating the HPR starts by subtracting the beginning value of an investment from the ending value to arrive at the capital appreciation value, i.e. the capital gain.

The capital appreciation formula – i.e. ending value minus beginning value – measures how much an investment how grown in price since the initial purchase.

Capital Appreciation = Ending Value – Beginning Value

A capital gain occurs if the sale price exceeds the purchase price, whereas if the security was sold for less than the initial price paid on the original date of purchase, the investment would be sold for a capital loss.
The amount of income received is then added to the capital appreciation in the next step.

The Holding Period Return measures the total return earned on an investment, inclusive of the capital gain and income.

Conceptually, HPR refers to the return received on an investment throughout the period during which the investment was held.

The holding period return metric is comprised of two-income sources: capital appreciation and dividend income.

Generally expressed as a percentage, there are two components to the total HPR:

Capital Appreciation: Sale Price > Purchase Price

Income: Dividends or Interest Income

More specifically, an investor can earn returns in the form of capital appreciation and receive income, such as dividends or interest income.

If the investment is in a company's shares, dividends represent the income source of the equity shareholders.

If the investment is in debt securities, interest would be the income received by the bondholders.

HPR = Capital Gains Yield + Dividend Yield

Example

One year ago, you purchased a stock at a price of $33. The stock pays quarterly dividends of $0.2 per share. Today, the stock is selling for $38 per share. What is your capital gain on this investment?

Solution

Capital gain = 38 − 33 = $5

Example

What is the HPR for an investor, who bought a stock a year ago at $50 and received $5 in dividends over the year, if the stock is now trading at $60?

Solution

$$HPR = \frac{(60-50)+5}{50} = 30\%$$

A dividend is a portion of a company's earnings that is distributed to its shareholders, usually in the form of cash or additional shares of stock. Dividends are typically paid on a regular basis, such as quarterly or annually, and they represent a way for companies to share their profits with their investors.

Dividends are a way for companies to distribute a portion of their profits to their shareholders, providing them with regular income in addition to any gains from increases in the stock price.

If a company pays dividends multiple times a year, the annual dividend is the sum of these payments. For example, if a company pays \$0.5 per share each quarter, the annual dividend would be $\$0.5 \times 4 = \$2$ per share.

Quarterly dividend

A quarterly dividend is a dividend payment made by a company to its shareholders every quarter, typically as a portion of its profits.

Example

Let's say a company called XYZ Corp has declared a quarterly dividend of \$0.25 per share. If you own 100 shares of XYZ Corp, you would receive a dividend payment of \$25 every quarter.

Example

Six months ago, you purchased 100 shares of stock at a price of \$38.7 a share. The stock pays a quarterly dividend of \$0.15 a share. Today, you sold all of your shares for \$40.2 per share. What is the total amount of your dividend income on this investment?

Solution

Dividend income $= 0.15 \times 2 \times 100 = \$30$

Example

If the company pays \$2.45 in dividends per share and the current price per share is \$35, the dividend yield is 7%.

Example

You own 400 shares of GH stock valued at \$51.2 per share. What is the dividend yield if your annual dividend income is \$352?

Solution

$$\frac{352}{400} = 0.88$$

The company pays \$0.88 in dividends per share.

$$\text{Dividend yield} = \frac{0.88}{51.2} = 1.72 \text{ percent}$$

Example

WXY stock is currently selling for \$48 a share. The stock has a dividend yield of 3.2 percent. How much dividend income will you receive per year if you purchase 200 shares of this stock?

Solution

Dividend income = 48 × 0.032 × 200 = \$307.2

Example

One year ago, you purchased a stock at a price of \$47.5 a share. Today, you sold the stock and realized a total loss of 22.1 percent. Your capital gain was −\$12.7 a share. What was your dividend yield?

Solution

Total loss = 0.221

$$\text{Capital gain yield} = -\frac{12.7}{47.5} = -0.267$$

$-0.221 = -0.267 + \text{Dividend yield}$

Dividend yield = −0.221 − (−0.267) = 4.6 percent

Example

You just sold 600 shares of W stock at a price of \$32.04 a share. Last year, you paid \$30.92 a share to buy this stock. Over the course of the year, you received dividends totaling \$1.20 per share. What is your total capital gain on this investment?

Solution

Total capital gain = (32.04 − 30.92) × 600 = \$672

Example

Last year, you purchased 500 shares of ABC stock for \$11.16 a share. You have received a total of \$120 in dividends and \$7,190 from selling the shares. What is your capital gains yield on this stock?

Solution

$$\text{Sale Price} = \frac{7,190}{500} = 14.38$$

$$\text{Capital gains yield} = \frac{14.38 - 11.16}{11.16} = 28.85 \text{ percent}$$

Example

Today, you sold 200 shares of P stock. Your total return on these shares is 6.2 percent. You purchased the shares one year ago at a price of $31.1 a share. You have received a total of $100 in dividends over the course of the year. What is your capital gains yield on this investment?

Solution

$$\text{Dividend Yield} = \frac{0.5}{31.1} = 0.016$$

Total return = Capital gains yield + 0.016

Capital gains yield = 0.062 − 0.016 = 4.6 percent

Example

One year ago, you purchased 500 shares of ABC stock at a price of $9.75 a share. The company pays an annual dividend of $0.1 per share. Today, you sold all of your shares for $15.6 a share. What is your total percentage return on this investment?

Solution

$$\text{Total percentage return} = \frac{15.6 - 9.75 + 0.1}{9.75} = 61.03 \text{ percent}$$

Example

1 년 전 주가가 11,000원이었고, 올 해 주가가 13,200원, 배당금이 600원인 경우, 수익률은?

Solution

$$\frac{(13{,}200 - 11{,}000) + 600}{11{,}000} = 25.45\%$$

Example

Three years ago, Tom invested $10,000 in the shares of ABC Corp. Each year, the company distributed dividends to its shareholders. Each year, Tom received $100 in dividends. Note that since Tom received $100 in dividends each year, his total income is $300. Today, Tom sold his shares for $12,000, and he wants to determine the HPR of his investment.

Solution

$$\frac{(12,000-10,000)+300}{10,000} = 23\%$$

Holding period return is the total return received from holding an asset or portfolio of assets over a period of time, known as the holding period.
Holding period return is the total return earned on an investment during the time that it has been held.

Example

What is the HPR for an investor who bought a stock a year ago at $50 and received $5 in dividends over the year if the stock is now trading at $60?

Solution

HPR = 30%

Geometric average return

The geometric average return, also known as the geometric mean return, is a measure of the average rate of return on an investment over multiple periods, considering the effects of compounding.

Example

A stock has annual returns of 6 percent and 14 percent for the past two years. Calculate the geometric average return for the period.

Solution

$(1+r)^2 = 1.06 \times 1.14$

$1+r = \sqrt{1.06 \times 1.14}$

$r = \sqrt{1.06 \times 1.14} - 1 = 9.93\%$

Geometric average return = 9.93%

Calculating HPR for Multiple Periods

To calculate the Holding Period Return for multiple periods, you need to calculate the HPR for each individual period first, and then combine them to find the overall HPR. This can be done by either compounding the individual HPRs or by using the beginning and ending values of the entire period.

Holding period return for the multiple periods

보유기간수익률

The Holding Period Return for multiple periods measures the total return on an investment over a series of time periods.

일별수익률이 r_{t-1}과 r_t인 경우, 이들간의 보유기간수익률은 다음과 같다.

$(1+r_{t-1})(1+r_t) - 1$

Example

What is the total return on an investment over two years if the yearly returns were 20% and −10%?

Solution

$$HPR = (1+0.2)(1-0.1)-1$$
$$= 1.2 \times 0.9 - 1 = 0.08$$

8%

Example

$(t-2)$일, $(t-1)$일, t일의 종가가 각각 100원, 125원, 100원인 경우, 일별수익률은 다음과 같다.

$r_{t-1} = 25\%,\ r_t = -20\%$

이틀간의 보유기간수익률은 0%이다.

Example

Our investment had a price appreciation of 20% and -10% over the two day period. Calculate the holding period return for the multiple periods.

Solution

$$HPR = (1+0.2)(1-0.1)-1$$
$$= 1.2 \times 0.9 - 1 = 0.08$$

8%

Example

일별 수익률이 20%, -10% 일 때, 이틀간의 보유기간수익률은?

Solution

$1.2 \times 0.9 - 1 = 0.08$

8%

Example

Our investment had a price appreciation of 10% and -5% over the two day period. Calculate the holding period return for the multiple periods.

Solution

4.5%

Example

일별 수익률이 10%, -5% 일 때, 이틀간의 보유기간수익률은?

Solution

4.5%

Example

Returns varied with 21% growth for the first year, followed by 30% returns for the second year and -15% returns for the third year.

Calculate HPR for the stock over a period of 3 years.

Solution

$HPR = (1+0.21)(1+0.3)(1-0.15)-1 = 33.7\%$

The result would be HPR of 33.7% for all 3 years.

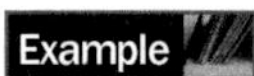 Probability distribution

A listing of all possible outcomes with a probability assigned to each outcome.

Example

Given the following end-of-period prices,

Stock Price	13,700	14,500
Probability	$\frac{1}{2}$	$\frac{1}{2}$

What is the expected price? The variance of prices? The standard deviation of prices?

Solution

$$E(P)=\frac{1}{2}\times 13{,}700+\frac{1}{2}\times 14{,}500=14{,}100$$

$$Var(P)=(-400)^2\times\frac{1}{2}+400^2\times\frac{1}{2}=160{,}000$$

$$\sigma=400$$

Example

삼성전자 주가가 현재 50만원이다. 한 달 후 45만원이 될 확률이 0.4이고, 55만원이 될 확률이 0.6이다. 기대가격, 가격의 분산, 기대수익률, 수익률의 분산을 구하라.

Solution

Probability	Price
0.4	45
0.6	55

$E(P)=51$, $Var(P)=24$

현재주가 50만원이 45만원이 될 때의 수익률은 $\frac{45-50}{50}$ 이다.

현재주가 50만원이 55만원이 될 때의 수익률은 $\frac{55-50}{50}$ 이다.

(%)

Probability	Return
0.4	−10
0.6	10

$E(r)=2\%$, $Var(r)=96$

Expectation

기댓값은 어떤 사건이 일어날 확률에 그 사건에서 얻게 되는 이득을 곱해서 계산한다.

In probability theory, the sample space of an experiment or random trial is the set of all possible outcomes or results of that experiment.
For example, if the experiment is tossing a coin, the sample space is typically the set {heads, tails}, commonly written {H,T}. For tossing two coins, the corresponding sample space would be {(heads,heads), (heads,tails), (tails,heads), (tails,tails)}, commonly written {HH,HT,TH, TT}.

Consider a probability distribution in which the outcomes of a random event are not equally likely to happen. If random variable, Y, is the number of heads we get from tossing two coins, then Y could be 0, 1, or 2. This means that we could have no heads, one head, or both heads on a two-coin toss.
The two coins land in four different ways: TT, HT, TH, and HH. Therefore, the P(Y=0) $= \frac{1}{4}$ since we have one chance of getting no heads. Similarly, the probability of getting two heads (HH) is also 1/4. Notice that getting one head has a likelihood of occurring twice: in HT and TH. In this case, P(Y=1) $= \frac{1}{2}$.

A random experiment is a mechanism that produces a definite outcome that cannot be predicted with certainty. The sample space associated with a random experiment is the set of all possible outcomes.

Example

Construct a sample space for the experiment that consists of tossing a single coin.

Solution

$\{H, T\}$

A coin is tossed three times.

What is the probability of getting the sequence TTH?

$$P(TTH)=\frac{1}{8}$$

A box contains 5 red balls and 3 blue balls.

One ball is drawn at random from the box.

What is the probability that the ball drawn is blue?

$$P(Blue)=\frac{3}{8}$$

Example

Construct a sample space for the experiment that consists of rolling a single die.

Solution

$\{1, 2, 3, 4, 5, 6\}$

Example

Consider the experiment of tossing two coins.

Let X denote the number of heads.

Find the Probability distribution of X.

Solution

X	0	1	2
Probability	$\frac{1}{4}$	$\frac{1}{2}$	$\frac{1}{4}$

Example

Consider the experiment of tossing two coins.

Let X denote the number of heads.

Find $E(X)$, $Var(X)$, and σ_X .

Solution

X	0	1	2
Probability	$\frac{1}{4}$	$\frac{1}{2}$	$\frac{1}{4}$

$$E(X)=\frac{1}{4}\times 0+\frac{1}{2}\times 1+\frac{1}{4}\times 2=1$$

$$E(X)=1$$

$$Var(X)=(0-1)^2\frac{1}{4}+(1-1)^2\frac{1}{2}+(2-1)^2\frac{1}{4}=\frac{1}{2}$$

$$\sigma_X=\frac{1}{\sqrt{2}}$$

Example

Consider the experiment of tossing two coins.

Let X denote the number of heads.

Find the expectation of X, the variance of X, and the standard deviation of X.

Solution

X	0	1	2
Probability	$\frac{1}{4}$	$\frac{1}{2}$	$\frac{1}{4}$

$$E(X) = \frac{1}{4}\times 0 + \frac{1}{2}\times 1 + \frac{1}{4}\times 2 = 1$$

$$E(X) = 1$$

$$Var(X) = (0-1)^2\frac{1}{4} + (1-1)^2\frac{1}{2} + (2-1)^2\frac{1}{4} = \frac{1}{2}$$

$$\sigma_X = \frac{1}{\sqrt{2}}$$

Consider the flip of two fair coins; let A and B be discrete random variables associated with the outcomes of the first and second coin flips respectively. Each coin flip is a Bernoulli trial and has a Bernoulli distribution. If a coin displays "heads" then the associated random variable takes the value 1, and it takes the value 0 otherwise.

Example

Consider the experiment of tossing two coins.

Let X denote the number of heads.

Find the expectation of (3X+2) and the variance of (3X+2).

Solution

X	0	1	2
Probability	$\frac{1}{4}$	$\frac{1}{2}$	$\frac{1}{4}$

$$E(X)=1$$

$$Var(X)=(0-1)^2\frac{1}{4}+(1-1)^2\frac{1}{2}+(2-1)^2\frac{1}{4}=\frac{1}{2}$$

$$E(3X+2)=5$$

3X+2	2	5	8
Probability	$\frac{1}{4}$	$\frac{1}{2}$	$\frac{1}{4}$

$$E(3X+2)=\frac{1}{4}\times 2+\frac{1}{2}\times 5+\frac{1}{4}\times 8=5$$

$$Var(3X+2)=9Var(X)=\frac{9}{2}$$

Example

Consider the experiment of tossing two coins.

Let X denote the number of heads.

Find the probability distribution of (3X+2).

Solution

X	0	1	2
Probability	$\frac{1}{4}$	$\frac{1}{2}$	$\frac{1}{4}$

3X+2	2	5	8
Probability	$\frac{1}{4}$	$\frac{1}{2}$	$\frac{1}{4}$

Variance

분산

$Var(X) = E(X - \mu_X)^2$

$Var(X) = E[(X - E[X])^2]$

분산은 어떤 사건이 일어날 확률에 그 사건에서 얻게 되는 이득과 기댓값의 차의 제곱을 곱해서 계산한다.

Variance is the expectation of the squared deviation of a random variable from its mean. The variance of a random variable X is the expected value of the squared deviation from the mean of X, $\mu = E(X)$.

The variance of a random variable X will be a measure of the spread or dispersion of the density of X.

If values of a random variable X tend to be far from their mean, the variance of X will be larger than the variance of a comparable random variable Y whose values tend to be near their mean.

Example

Translate the sentence into an equation: Variance is the expectation of the squared deviation of a random variable from its mean.

Solution

$Var(X) = E[(X - E[X])^2]$

For any random variable X, $Var(X) = E(X^2) - [E(X)]^2$

The variance of X is equal to the mean of the square of X minus the square of the mean of X.

For any constants a and b, $Var(aX + b) = a^2 Var(X)$

Example

Prove $Var(X) = E(X^2) - [E(X)]^2$.

Solution

$$\begin{aligned} Var(X) &= E\left[(X-\mu_X)^2\right] \\ &= E\left[X^2 - 2\mu_X X + \mu_X^2\right] \\ &= E(X^2) - 2\mu_X E(X) + \mu_X^2 \\ &= E(X^2) - [E(X)]^2 \end{aligned}$$

Example

Expand E[(X−3)(X−3)].

Solution

$$E\left[(X-3)^2\right] = E\left[X^2 - 6X + 9\right] = E(X^2) - 6E(X) + 9$$

Example

Prove $Var(3X+2) = 9\,Var(X)$.

Solution

$$\begin{aligned} Var(3X+2) &= E[3X+2-E(3X+2)]^2 \\ &= 9\,Var(X) \end{aligned}$$

Example

Express the variance of 2X+3 using expectation.

Solution

$$Var(2X+3) = E[2X+3-E(2X+3)]^2$$

Example

The probability for $X=-4$ and Y=5 is $\frac{1}{3}$.

The probability for X=14 and Y=5 is $\frac{1}{3}$.

The probability for X=26 and Y=5 is $\frac{1}{3}$.

Find Var(X) and Var(Y).

Solution

Probability	X	Y
$\frac{1}{3}$	−4	5
$\frac{1}{3}$	14	5
$\frac{1}{3}$	26	5

$E(X)=12$

$Var(X)=\frac{1}{3}(16^2+2^2+14^2)=152$

$Var(Y)=0$

Example

Consider one roll of a die. Let X be the number that turns up.

Find the expected value of X.

Find Var(X).

Solution

$E(X)=\frac{1}{6}(1+2+3+4+5+6)=\frac{7}{2}$

$Var(X)=\frac{1}{6}\left(\frac{25}{4}+\frac{9}{4}+\frac{1}{4}+\frac{1}{4}+\frac{9}{4}+\frac{25}{4}\right)$

$Var(X)=\frac{35}{12}$

Example

A die is rolled. If an odd number turns up, we win an amount equal to this number; if an even number turns up, we lose an amount equal to this number.
Find the expected value of X.

Solution

For example, if a two turns up we lose 2, and if a three comes up we win 3.

$$E(X)=\frac{1}{6}(1-2+3-4+5-6)=-\frac{1}{2}$$

Covariance

공분산

For random variables X and Y, the covariance of X and Y is defined to be

$Cov(X,Y) = E[(X-\mu_X)(Y-\mu_Y)]$

The covariance is defined as the expected value of the product of their deviations from their individual expected values.

It measures linear association between X and Y.

$Cov(X,Y) = Cov(Y,X)$

$Cov(aX,bY) = abCov(X,Y)$

[Theorem]

$Cov(X,Y) = E(XY) - E(X)E(Y)$

[Proof]

$$
\begin{aligned}
Cov(X,Y) &= E[(X-\mu_X)(Y-\mu_Y)] \\
&= E[XY - X\mu_Y - \mu_X Y + \mu_X\mu_Y] \\
&= E(XY) - \mu_X\mu_Y - \mu_X\mu_Y + \mu_X\mu_Y \\
&= E(XY) - \mu_X\mu_Y
\end{aligned}
$$

Example

Expand $E[(X-2)(Y-3)]$.

Solution

$E[(X-2)(Y-3)] = E[XY-3X-2Y+6] = E(XY)-3E(X)-2E(Y)+6$

If X and Y are independent, then $Cov(X,Y)=0$.

Example

Prove $Cov(aX+bY,Z)=aCov(X,Z)+bCov(Y,Z)$.

Solution

$$Cov(aX+bY,Z)=E[(aX+bY-a\mu_X-b\mu_Y)(Z-\mu_Z)]$$
$$=E[a(X-\mu_X)(Z-\mu_Z)+b(Y-\mu_Y)(Z-\mu_Z)]$$
$$=a\cdot Cov(X,Z)+b\cdot Cov(Y,Z)$$

Example

Expand $Cov(2X+3Y,Z)$.

Solution

$$Cov(2X+3Y,Z)=2Cov(X,Z)+3Cov(Y,Z)$$

Correlation

상관계수

$$\rho_{XY} = \frac{\sigma_{XY}}{\sigma_X \sigma_Y}$$

The correlation coefficient is covariance divided by the product of the two variables' standard deviations.

The covariance of the standardized deviations.

The correlation coefficient removes the individual variability of each X and Y by dividing the covariance by the product of the standard deviations, and thus the correlation coefficient is a better measure of the linear relationship of X and Y than is the covariance.

$$-1 \leq \rho_{XY} \leq 1$$

The correlation coefficient's values range between -1 and 1.

Example

Translate the sentence into an equation: The correlation coefficient is covariance divided by the product of the two variables' standard deviations.

Solution

$$\rho_{XY} = \frac{\sigma_{XY}}{\sigma_X \sigma_Y}$$

Example

Translate the sentence into an inequality: The correlation coefficient's values range between -1 and 1.

Solution

$$-1 \leq \rho_{XY} \leq 1$$

Variance

$$Var(X) = E[(X - \mu_X)(X - \mu_X)]$$

Covariance

$$Cov(X, Y) = E[(X - \mu_X)(Y - \mu_Y)]$$

Correlation

$$Corr(X, Y) = \frac{Cov(X, Y)}{\sqrt{Var(X)}\ \sqrt{Var(Y)}}$$

Joint Probability Distribution

A joint probability distribution gives the probability that two or more random variables take on a specific set of values simultaneously.

Example

Given the following end-of-period returns,

(%)

Probability	Security X	Security Y
0.5	5	9
0.5	3	3

Find σ_{XY}.

Solution

$E(X) = 4, \quad E(Y) = 6$

Probability	$X - E(X)$	$Y - E(Y)$
0.5	1	3
0.5	−1	−3

$$\sigma_{XY} = 0.5 \times 1 \times 3 + 0.5 \times (-1) \times (-3) = 3$$

Example

P(X=5,Y=9) = 0.5.

P(X=3,Y=3) = 0.5.

Find the covariance of X and Y.

Example

The probability for X=5 and Y=9 is 0.5.

The probability for X=3 and Y=3 is 0.5.

Find the covariance of X and Y.

Solution

Probability	X	Y
0.5	5	9
0.5	3	3

$E(X)=4,\quad E(Y)=6$

Probability	$X-E(X)$	$Y-E(Y)$
0.5	1	3
0.5	−1	−3

$\sigma_{XY}=0.5\times1\times3+0.5\times(-1)\times(-3)=3$

Example

두 주식의 확률분포가 다음과 같을 때, 공분산을 계산하면?

(%)

X \ Y	3	9
3	0.5	0
5	0	0.5

Solution

$E(X)=4,\quad E(Y)=6$

Probability	$X-E(X)$	$Y-E(Y)$
0.5	1	3
0.5	−1	−3

$\sigma_{XY}=0.5\times1\times3+0.5\times(-1)\times(-3)=3$

Example

The probability for X=2 and Y=8 is 0.5.

The probability for X=4 and Y=2 is 0.5.

Find the covariance of X and Y.

Solution

Probability	X	Y
0.5	2	8
0.5	4	2

$E(X)=3,\quad E(Y)=5,\quad \sigma_X=1,\quad \sigma_Y=3$

Probability	$X-E(X)$	$Y-E(Y)$
0.5	−1	3
0.5	1	-3

$\sigma_{XY}=0.5\times(-1)\times3+0.5\times1\times(-3)=-3$

Example

The probability for X=2 and Y=8 is 0.5.

The probability for X=4 and Y=2 is 0.5.

Find the correlation of X and Y.

Solution

Probability	X	Y
0.5	2	8
0.5	4	2

$E(X)=3,\quad E(Y)=5,\quad \sigma_X=1,\quad \sigma_Y=3$

Probability	$X-E(X)$	$Y-E(Y)$
0.5	−1	3
0.5	1	-3

$\sigma_{XY}=0.5\times(-1)\times3+0.5\times1\times(-3)=-3$

$\rho_{XY}=-1$

Joint probability distribution

Joint probability is the probability of two events happening together.

Example

하나의 동전을 세 번 던질 때, X와 Y를

X = 처음 두 번에서 나오는 앞면의 개수

Y = 세 번째에 나오는 앞면의 개수로 정의할 경우

X와 Y의 공분산을 구하라.

Solution

X \ Y	0	1	행의 합
0	$\frac{1}{8}$	$\frac{1}{8}$	$\frac{1}{4}$
1	$\frac{1}{4}$	$\frac{1}{4}$	$\frac{1}{2}$
2	$\frac{1}{8}$	$\frac{1}{8}$	$\frac{1}{4}$
열의 합	$\frac{1}{2}$	$\frac{1}{2}$	1

X	0	1	2
Probability	$\frac{1}{4}$	$\frac{1}{2}$	$\frac{1}{4}$

$E(X)=1$

Y	0	1
Probability	$\frac{1}{2}$	$\frac{1}{2}$

$E(Y)=\frac{1}{2}$

XY	0	1	2
Probability	$\frac{5}{8}$	$\frac{1}{4}$	$\frac{1}{8}$

$E(XY)=\frac{1}{2}$

$$Cov(X,Y)=E(XY)-E(X)E(Y)=\frac{1}{2}-1\times\frac{1}{2}=0$$

Example

A container holds three balls numbered 1, 2, and 3. A ball is drawn at random and the number X noted. A second ball is drawn at random and the number Y noted. The drawing is without replacement. Construct a sample space for the experiment.

Solution

$\{(1,2),(1,3),(2,1),(2,3),(3,1),(3,2)\}$

Example

A container holds three balls numbered 1, 2, and 3. A ball is drawn at random and the number X noted. A second ball is drawn at random and the number Y noted. The drawing is without replacement. Compute the correlation coefficient.

Solution

X \ Y	1	2	3
1	0	$\frac{1}{6}$	$\frac{1}{6}$
2	$\frac{1}{6}$	0	$\frac{1}{6}$
3	$\frac{1}{6}$	$\frac{1}{6}$	0

X	1	2	3
Probability	$\frac{1}{3}$	$\frac{1}{3}$	$\frac{1}{3}$

$E(X)=2,\ \sigma_X=\sqrt{\frac{2}{3}}$

$E(Y)=2,\ \sigma_Y=\sqrt{\frac{2}{3}}$

XY	2	3	6
Probability	$\frac{1}{3}$	$\frac{1}{3}$	$\frac{1}{3}$

$E(XY)=\frac{11}{3}$

$Cov(X,Y)=-\frac{1}{3}$

$\rho_{XY}=-\frac{1}{2}$

Example

항아리에 공이 세 개가 있고, ①, ②, ③의 번호가 매겨져 있다. 항아리에서 임의로 공을 꺼내서 나온 공의 번호를 X라 한다. 두 번째로 항아리에서 공을 꺼낼 때는 항아리에 공이 두 개가 남아 있는데, 항아리에서 두 번째로 공을 꺼내서 나온 공의 번호를 Y라 할 때, X와 Y의 공분산을 구하라.

Example

A container holds three balls numbered 1, 2, and 3. A ball is drawn at random and the number X noted. A second ball is drawn at random and the number Y noted. The drawing is with replacement. Construct a sample space for the experiment.

Solution

$\{(1,1),(1,2),(1,3),(2,1),(2,2),(2,3),(3,1),(3,2),(3,3)\}$

Example

A container holds three balls numbered 1, 2, and 3. A ball is drawn at random and the number X noted. A second ball is drawn at random and the number Y noted. The drawing is with replacement. Compute the correlation coefficient.

Solution

X \ Y	1	2	3
1	$\frac{1}{9}$	$\frac{1}{9}$	$\frac{1}{9}$
2	$\frac{1}{9}$	$\frac{1}{9}$	$\frac{1}{9}$
3	$\frac{1}{9}$	$\frac{1}{9}$	$\frac{1}{9}$

X	1	2	3
Probability	$\frac{1}{3}$	$\frac{1}{3}$	$\frac{1}{3}$

$E(X) = 2,\ \sigma_X = \sqrt{\frac{2}{3}}$

$E(Y) = 2,\ \sigma_Y = \sqrt{\frac{2}{3}}$

XY	1	2	3	4	6	9
Probability	$\frac{1}{9}$	$\frac{2}{9}$	$\frac{2}{9}$	$\frac{1}{9}$	$\frac{2}{9}$	$\frac{1}{9}$

$E(XY) = 4$

$Cov(X,Y) = E(XY) - E(X)E(Y) = 0$

If X and Y are independent, then $Cov(X, Y) = 0$.

$$\rho_{XY} = \frac{\sigma_{XY}}{\sigma_X \sigma_Y} = 0$$

Perfect Correlation

Perfect correlation will result in a correlation coefficient equal to 1.
Y is a linear function of X.

If we are given the value of X, we know for sure what the corresponding value of Y will be.

Example

Let $Y = 3 + 2X$.
Expand Cov(X,Y).

Solution

$\sigma_{XY} = E[(X - E(X))(Y - E(Y))] = E[(X - E(X))(3 + 2X - E(3 + 2X))]$
$= E[(X - E(X))(3 + 2X - 3 - 2E(X))] = 2\sigma_X^2$

Example

$Y = 3 + 2X$ 일 때, $\rho_{XY} = 1$임을 증명하시오.

Example

$Y = 3 - 2X$일 때, $\rho_{XY} = -1$임을 증명하시오.

Solution

$$Var(Y) = E[(Y - E(Y))^2] = E[(3 - 2X - E(3 - 2X))^2]$$
$$= E[(3 - 2X - 3 + 2E(X))^2] = E[(-2(X - E(X)))^2] = 4\,Var(X)$$

$$\sigma_Y = 2\sigma_X$$

$$\sigma_{XY} = E[(X - E(X))(Y - E(Y))] = E[(X - E(X))(3 - 2X - E(3 - 2X))]$$
$$= E[(X - E(X))(3 - 2X - 3 + 2E(X))] = -2\sigma_X^2$$

$$\rho_{XY} = \frac{-2\sigma_X^2}{\sigma_X \times 2\sigma_X} = -1$$

The possible range of values for the correlation coefficient is -1.0 to 1.0. In other words, the values cannot exceed 1.0 or be less than -1.0. A correlation of -1.0 indicates a perfect negative correlation, and a correlation of 1.0 indicates a perfect positive correlation. If the correlation coefficient is greater than zero, it is a positive relationship. Conversely, if the value is less than zero, it is a negative relationship. A value of zero indicates that there is no relationship between the two variables.

Prove that coefficient of correlation lies between -1 and 1.

Example

Prove $\frac{2\sqrt{xy}}{x+y} \leq 1$

Solution

$\sqrt{xy} \leq \frac{x+y}{2}$

$0 \leq (a\sqrt{x} - b\sqrt{y})^2 = a^2x + b^2y - 2ab\sqrt{xy}$

$2ab\sqrt{xy} \leq (a^2x + b^2y)$

If we let $a = 1$, $b = 1$, then

$2\sqrt{xy} \leq (x+y)$

$\sqrt{xy} \leq \frac{x+y}{2}$

Example

What is the geometric mean of 4 and 9?

Solution

The geometric mean of 4 and 9 is 6.

Example

What is the geometric mean of 4 and 25?

Solution

The geometric mean of 4 and 25 is 10.

The AM-GM inequality

the inequality of arithmetic and geometric means

$$\frac{x+y}{2} \geq \sqrt{xy}$$

In mathematics, the AM - GM inequality states that the arithmetic mean of a list of non-negative real numbers is greater than or equal to the geometric mean of the same list.

Example

Prove the AM-GM inequality.

Solution

The square of a real number is always non-negative.

$$0 \leq (x-y)^2$$
$$= (x+y)^2 - 4xy$$

Hence $(x+y)^2 \geq 4xy$.

The AM - GM inequality then follows from taking the positive square root of both sides and then dividing both sides by 2.

$$\frac{x+y}{2} \geq \sqrt{xy}$$

Example

Prove the AM-GM inequality in 2 variables using the Cauchy-Schwarz inequality.

Solution

Let's consider the case of 2 terms. Then by Cauchy-Schwarz inequality we have

$(a^2+b^2)(c^2+d^2) \geq (ac+bd)^2$

If we let $a=1$, $b=1$, $c=\sqrt{x}$, $d=\sqrt{y}$, then

$2(x+y) \geq (\sqrt{x}+\sqrt{y})^2$

$2\sqrt{xy} \leq (x+y)$

$\sqrt{xy} \leq \frac{x+y}{2}$

the AM-GM inequality

Cauchy-Schwarz inequality

Let's consider the case of 2 terms. Then by Cauchy-Schwarz inequality we have

$(a^2+b^2)(c^2+d^2) \geq (ac+bd)^2$

The equality holds when $\frac{c}{a}=\frac{d}{b}$.

Example

Find the maximum value of x+2y, given that $x^2+y^2=1$.

Solution

$(a^2+b^2)(c^2+d^2) \geq (ac+bd)^2$

$x^2+y^2=1$

$x+2y \leq \sqrt{5}$

The equality holds when $x=\frac{y}{2}$.

$x=\frac{1}{\sqrt{5}}, y=\frac{2}{\sqrt{5}}$

Dominance principle

The dominance principle is a concept used in decision theory, finance, and economics to compare different options or investments. It states that one option is considered better or dominant over another if it provides a higher return or outcome with the same or lower level of risk, or if it provides the same return with lower risk.

Investors use the dominance principle to select portfolios or investments. A portfolio that offers higher returns with the same or lower risk is preferred.

Same variance. → The bigger the mean is, the better.

If two options or investments have the same variance, then the dominance principle suggests that the option with the higher mean return is preferable.

Same mean. → The smaller the variance is, the better.

If two options or investments have the same mean return, then the dominance principle suggests that the option with the smaller variance is preferable.

X dominates Y if

$E(r_X) \geq E(r_Y)$ and $\sigma_X \leq \sigma_Y$ and at least one inequality is strict.

Strict inequality is a concept in mathematics that describes a relationship between two quantities where one is always less than or greater than the other, but never equal.

Example

Given the following end-of-period returns,

(%)

Probability	Security X	Security Y	Security Z
0.5	7	5	9
0.5	5	3	3

which asset is preferred?

Solution

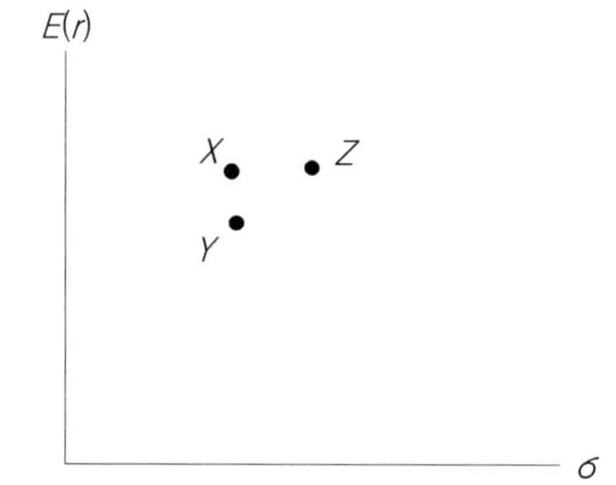

$E(r_X) = 6, \quad \sigma_X = 1$

$E(r_Y) = 4, \quad \sigma_Y = 1$

$E(r_Z) = 6, \quad \sigma_Z = 3$

X dominates Y.

X dominates Z.

Example

The probability for X=7, Y=5, and Z=9 is 0.5.

The probability for X=5, Y=3, and Z=3 is 0.5.

Which asset is preferred?

Solution

Probability	Security X	Security Y	Security Z
0.5	7	5	9
0.5	5	3	3

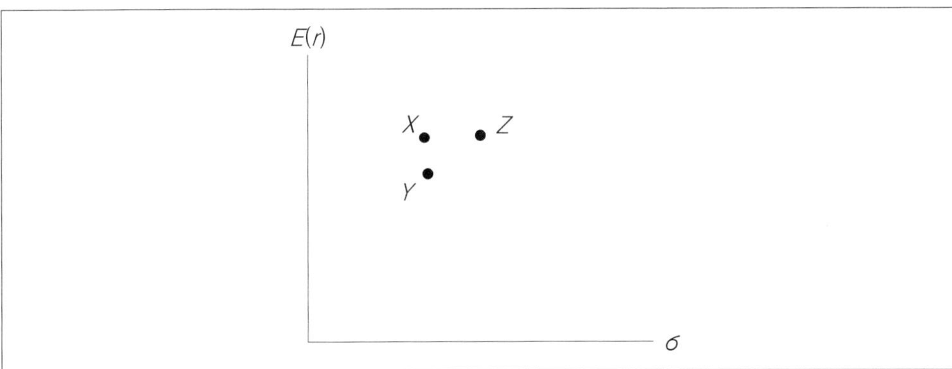

$E(r_X) = 6, \quad \sigma_X = 1$

$E(r_Y) = 4, \quad \sigma_Y = 1$

$E(r_Z) = 6, \quad \sigma_Z = 3$

X dominates Y.

X dominates Z.

Example

Given the following probability distribution for Stocks related to Ice cream and Umbrella:

(%)

Weather	Probability	Ice cream	Umbrella
Shiny	$\frac{3}{4}$	10	7
Rainy	$\frac{1}{4}$	8	15

If the only available choice is 100% of your wealth in Stock related to Ice cream or 100% in Stock related to Umbrella and you choose on the basis of mean and variance, which asset is preferred?

Solution

Ice cream: $E(r) = 9.5\%$,

$$Var(r) = \frac{3}{4}0.25 + \frac{1}{4}2.25 = \frac{3}{4}$$

$\sigma = 0.87$

Umbrella: $E(r) = 9\%$,

$$Var(r) = \frac{3}{4}4 + \frac{1}{4}36 = \frac{48}{4} = 12$$

$\sigma = 3.46$

Stock related to Ice cream is preferred.

Example

The probability for X=6 and Y=5 is 0.5.

The probability for X=2 and Y=3 is 0.5.

Which asset is preferred?

Solution

(%)

Probability	Security X	Security Y
0.5	6	5
0.5	2	3

$E(r_X) = 4\%$, $\sigma_X = 2$

$E(r_Y) = 4\%$, $\sigma_Y = 1$

Same mean. → The smaller the variance is, the better.

Y is preferred.

투자자산

투자자의 부를 증식하게 하는 투자대상은 실물자산과 금융자산으로 구분할 수 있다. 실물자산(real assets)은 토지, 건물, 재고자산 등과 같이 그 자체가 미래이익발생능력이 있는 자산을 말한다. 반면에 금융자산(financial assets)은 주식, 국공채, 회사채 등과 같이 그 자체는 이익발생능력이 없고, 실물자산이 벌어들이는 이익이나 자산에 대하여 청구권(claims)을 행사할 수 있는 자산을 말한다. 주식에 투자한 사람은 투자지분에 따라 배당지급을 받을 권리가 있고, 채권에 투자한 사람은 당해 기업의 실물자산이 벌어들이는 이익에 대하여 이자지급을 받을 권리가 있다.

Two-Asset Portfolio

Expectation & Variance

$E(X+Y)=E(X)+E(Y)$

$E(aX+bY)=aE(X)+bE(Y)$

[Theorem]

$Var(X+Y)=Var(X)+Var(Y)+2Cov(X,Y)$

[Proof]

$Var(X+Y)=E[X+Y-E(X+Y)]^2$

$Var(X+Y)=E[(X+Y-\mu_X-\mu_Y)^2]$

$=E[(X-\mu_X)^2+(Y-\mu_Y)^2+2(X-\mu_X)(Y-\mu_Y)]$

$Var(X+Y)=Var(X)+Var(Y)+2Cov(X,Y)$

[Theorem]

$Var(aX+bY)=a^2Var(X)+b^2Var(Y)+2abCov(X,Y)$

[Proof]

$$Var(aX+bY)=E[(aX+bY-a\mu_X-b\mu_Y)^2]$$

$$=E[a^2(X-\mu_X)^2+b^2(Y-\mu_Y)^2+2ab(X-\mu_X)(Y-\mu_Y)]$$

$$=a^2Var(X)+b^2Var(Y)+2abCov(X,Y)$$

[Theorem]

$Var(X-Y)=Var(X)+Var(Y)-2Cov(X,Y)$

[Theorem]

$Var(aX-bY)=a^2Var(X)+b^2Var(Y)-2abCov(X,Y)$

[Proof]

$$Var(aX-bY)=E[(aX-bY-a\mu_X+b\mu_Y)^2]$$

$$=E[a^2(X-\mu_X)^2+b^2(Y-\mu_Y)^2-2ab(X-\mu_X)(Y-\mu_Y)]$$

$$=a^2Var(X)+b^2Var(Y)-2abCov(X,Y)$$

Example

Prove

$Var(2X+3Y)=4Var(X)+9Var(Y)+12Cov(X,Y)$

Solution

$$
\begin{aligned}
Var(2X+3Y) &= E[2X+3Y-E(2X+3Y)]^2 \\
&= E[2X-2E(X)+3Y-3E(Y)]^2
\end{aligned}
$$

$= 4E[X-E(X)]^2+9E[Y-E(Y)]^2+12E[(X-E(X))(Y-E(Y))]$

$= 4Var(X)+9Var(Y)+12Cov(X,Y)$

Cf.

$(a+b-c-d)^2=(a-c)^2+(b-d)^2+2(a-c)(b-d)$

$(a-b-c+d)^2=(a-c)^2+(b-d)^2-2(a-c)(b-d)$

Example

Let the fraction of X be w_1 and the fraction of Y be w_2.

$w_1+w_2=1$

$E(w_1X+w_2Y)=w_1E(X)+w_2E(Y)$

$Var(w_1X+w_2Y)=w_1^2Var(X)+w_2^2Var(Y)+2w_1w_2Cov(X,Y)$

Example

$E[wX+(1-w)Y]=wE(X)+(1-w)E(Y)$

$Var[wX+(1-w)Y]=w^2Var(X)+(1-w)^2Var(Y)+2w(1-w)Cov(X,Y)$

Example

Suppose you hold two assets in your portfolio, X and Y.

Let the fraction of X be w and the fraction of Y be $(1-w)$.

If $w=1$, you hold only X,

If $w=0$, you hold only Y,

If $w=0.5$, you have an equally weighted or naively diversified portfolio.

Example

Given the following end-of-period returns,

(%)

Probability	Security X	Security Y
0.5	5	9
0.5	3	3

Find the expected return and standard deviation of Equally Weighted Portfolio.

Solution

$E(X)=4, \quad \sigma_X=1$

$E(Y)=6, \quad \sigma_Y=3$

$$E(r_p)=E\left(\frac{1}{2}X+\frac{1}{2}Y\right)=\frac{1}{2}E(X)+\frac{1}{2}E(Y)=5\%$$

$$\sigma_p^2=Var(\frac{1}{2}X+\frac{1}{2}Y)$$

$$Var(\frac{1}{2}X+\frac{1}{2}Y)=(\frac{1}{2})^2Var(X)+(\frac{1}{2})^2Var(Y)+2(\frac{1}{2})(\frac{1}{2})Cov(X,Y)$$

$$\rho_{XY}=\frac{\sigma_{XY}}{\sigma_X\sigma_Y}=1$$

$$Var(\frac{1}{2}X+\frac{1}{2}Y)=(\frac{1}{2})^2Var(X)+(\frac{1}{2})^2Var(Y)+2(\frac{1}{2})(\frac{1}{2})\sigma_X\sigma_Y=4$$

$$\sigma_p=2$$

Example

Suppose security X has expected return of 4% and standard deviation of 1%, Security Y has expected return of 6% and standard deviation of 3%. Consider the expected return and standard deviation of a portfolio of securities X and Y when the correlation between them is 1. Plot the set of feasible mean-variance combinations of return.

Solution

$E(X)=4,\ E(Y)=6,\ \sigma_X=1,\ \sigma_Y=3$

$\rho_{XY}=1$

$E(r_p)=E[wX+(1-w)Y]=wE(X)+(1-w)E(Y)=w\cdot 4+(1-w)6$

$E(r_p)=-2w+6$

$\sigma_p^2=Var[wX+(1-w)Y]$

$\sigma_p^2=w^2\sigma_X^2+(1-w)^2\sigma_Y^2+2w(1-w)\sigma_{XY}$

$\rho_{XY}=\dfrac{\sigma_{XY}}{\sigma_X\sigma_Y}=1$

$\sigma_p^2=w^2\sigma_X^2+(1-w)^2\sigma_Y^2+2w(1-w)\sigma_X\sigma_Y$

$\sigma_p^2=\{w\ \sigma_X+(1-w)\ \sigma_Y\}^2$

$\sigma_p=w\ \sigma_X+(1-w)\ \sigma_Y$

$\sigma_p=w\ \cdot 1+(1-w)\ 3=-2w+3$

$E(r_p)=\sigma_p+3$

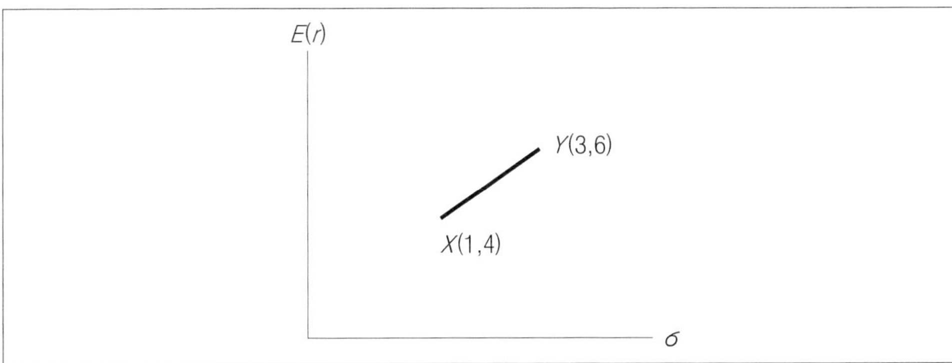

Example

Suppose security X has expected return of 4% and standard deviation of 1%,

Security Y has expected return of 6% and standard deviation of 3%.

Consider the expected return and standard deviation of a portfolio of securities X and Y when the correlation between them is -1.

Plot the set of feasible mean-variance combinations of return.

If you want to minimize risk, how much of your portfolio will you invest in security X?

Solution

$E(X)=4,\ E(Y)=6,\ \sigma_X=1,\ \sigma_Y=3$

$\rho_{XY}=-1$

$E(r_p)=E[wX+(1-w)Y]=wE(X)+(1-w)E(Y)=w\cdot 4+(1-w)6$

$E(r_p)=-2w+6$

$\sigma_p^2=Var[wX+(1-w)Y]$

$\sigma_p^2=w^2\sigma_X^2+(1-w)^2\sigma_Y^2+2w(1-w)\sigma_{XY}$

$\rho_{XY}=\dfrac{\sigma_{XY}}{\sigma_X\sigma_Y}=-1$

$\sigma_p^2=w^2\sigma_X^2+(1-w)^2\sigma_Y^2-2w(1-w)\sigma_X\sigma_Y$

$\sigma_p^2=\{w\sigma_X-(1-w)\sigma_Y\}^2$

$\sigma_p^2=\{w-(1-w)3\}^2=(4w-3)^2$

$\sigma_p=4w-3,\quad \dfrac{3}{4}\le w\le 1$

$\sigma_p=-(4w-3),\quad 0\le w\langle\dfrac{3}{4}$

$$0 \le w \langle \frac{3}{4}, \qquad w = \frac{-\sigma_p + 3}{4}$$

$$\frac{3}{4} \le w \le 1, \qquad w = \frac{\sigma_p + 3}{4}$$

$$0 \le w \langle \frac{3}{4}, \qquad E(r_p) = \frac{1}{2}\sigma_p + \frac{9}{2}$$

$$\frac{3}{4} \le w \le 1, \qquad E(r_p) = -\frac{1}{2}\sigma_p + \frac{9}{2}$$

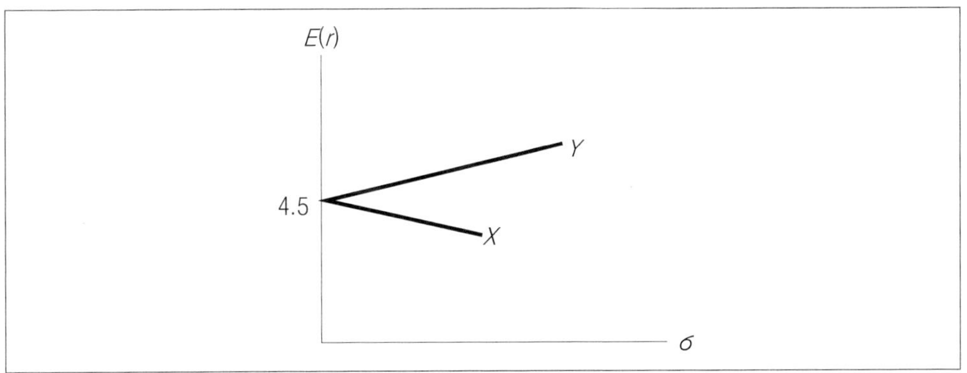

Zero Variance Portfolio

$$w = \frac{3}{4} = 75\%$$

$$\sigma_p = 0, \quad E(r_p) = \frac{9}{2} = 4.5$$

I put 75% of my wealth into security X and 25% of my wealth into security Y.

Example

Find the value of y that minimizes x:

$$x^2 = (4y-3)^2$$

where both x and y are nonnegative.

Solution

$$y = \frac{3}{4}$$

Example

Consider the quadratic function $y = x^2 - 4x + 7$.

Find the value of x that minimizes the function.

Example

Suppose security X has expected return of 4% and standard deviation of 1%,

Security Y has expected return of 6% and standard deviation of 3%.

Consider the expected return and standard deviation of a portfolio of securities X and Y when the correlation between them is 0.

Plot the set of feasible mean-variance combinations of return.

If you want to minimize risk, how much of your portfolio will you invest in security X?

Solution

$$E(r_p) = E[wX + (1-w)Y] = wE(X) + (1-w)E(Y) = w \cdot 4 + (1-w)6$$

$$E(r_p) = -2w + 6$$

$$\sigma_p^2 = Var[wX + (1-w)Y]$$

$$\sigma_p^2 = w^2\sigma_X^2 + (1-w)^2\sigma_Y^2 + 2w(1-w)\sigma_{XY}$$

$$\rho_{XY} = \frac{\sigma_{XY}}{\sigma_X \sigma_Y} = 0$$

$$\sigma_p^2 = w^2 1^2 + (1-w)^2 3^2$$

$$w = \frac{-E(r_p) + 6}{2}$$

$$\sigma_p^2 = \{\frac{-E(r_p) + 6}{2}\}^2 + (1 - \frac{-E(r_p) + 6}{2})^2 3^2$$

Minimum Variance Portfolio

$$\frac{\partial \sigma_p^2}{\partial w} = 2w - 2(1-w)9 = 0$$

$$w = \frac{18}{20}$$

$$\sigma_p = 0.95, \quad E(r_p) = 4.2$$

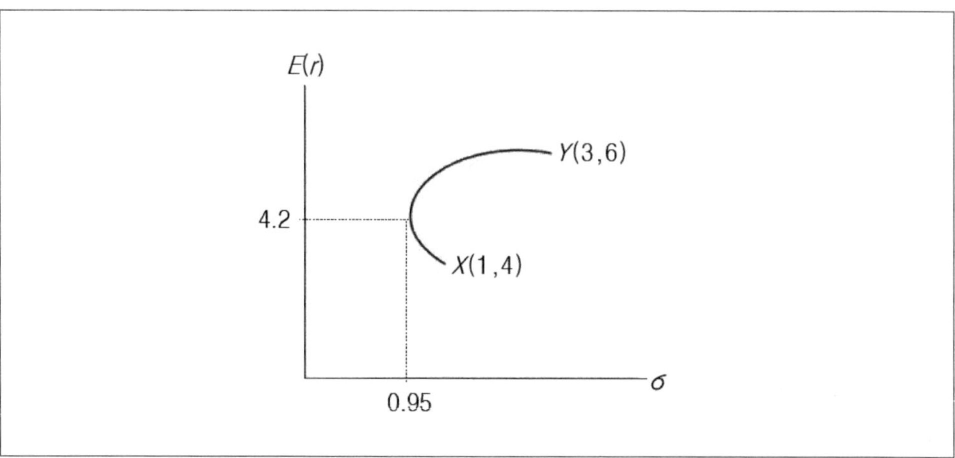

We put 90% of our wealth into security X and 10% of our wealth into security Y.

Example

Find the value of y that minimizes x:

$x = y^2 + 9(1-y)^2$

Solution

$$\frac{dx}{dy} = 2y - 18(1-y) = 0$$

y=0.9

Example

두 주식의 수익률 상관계수가 −1일 때 다음 자료를 이용하여 두 주식으로 구성되는 포트폴리오의 기대수익률과 표준편차의 관계를 그림으로 나타내라.

	기대수익률	표준편차
주식 1	28%	30%
주식 2	16	10

Solution

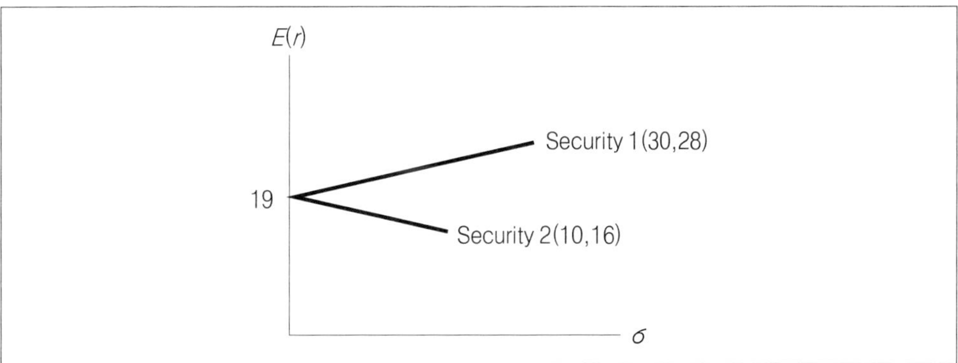

$$E(r_p) = E[wr_1 + (1-w)r_2] = wE(r_1) + (1-w)E(r_2)$$

$$\sigma_p^2 = Var[wr_1 + (1-w)r_2]$$

$$Var[wr_1 + (1-w)r_2] = w^2\sigma_1^2 + (1-w)^2\sigma_2^2 + 2\cdot w\cdot(1-w)\sigma_{12}$$

$$\rho_{12} = \frac{\sigma_{12}}{\sigma_1\sigma_2} = -1$$

$$Var[wr_1 + (1-w)r_2] = w^2\sigma_1^2 + (1-w)^2\sigma_2^2 - 2\cdot w\cdot(1-w)\sigma_1\sigma_2$$

$$Var[wr_1 + (1-w)r_2] = \{w\ \sigma_1 - (1-w)\ \sigma_2\}^2$$

$$Var[wr_1 + (1-w)r_2] = \{w\ 30 - (1-w)\ 10\}^2$$

$$E(r_p) = 16 + 12w$$

$$\sigma_p^2 = (40w - 10)^2$$

If $w \geq 0.25,\quad \sigma_p = 40w - 10$

If $w < 0.25$, $\sigma_p = -40w + 10$

If $w \geq 0.25$, $E(r_p) = 19 + 0.3\sigma_p$

If $w < 0.25$, $E(r_p) = 19 - 0.3\sigma_p$

Zero Variance Portfolio

$\sigma_p^2 = (40w - 10)^2 = 0$

$w = 0.25$

$E(r_p) = 0.25 \times 28 + 0.75 \times 16 = 19$ (%)

We put 25% of our wealth into security 1 and 75% of our wealth into security 2.

Example

Given the parametric equations

$u = 2w + 3$

$v = 4(w+1)^2 + 2, \ 0 \leq w \leq 1$

Express v in terms of u.

Solution

$$w = \frac{u-3}{2}$$

$$v = 4\left(\frac{u}{2} - \frac{1}{2}\right)^2 + 2$$

$$v = (u-1)^2 + 2, \ 3 \leq u \leq 5$$

Example

Suppose you hold 10 shares of Samsung stock and 30 shares of Hyundai stock. Samsung stock is currently sold at 80,000 won per share, while Hyundai stock is sold at 40,000 won. The expected return of Samsung stock is 15%, while that of Hyundai stock is 20%. The standard deviation of Samsung is 8%, while that of Hyundai is 20%. The correlation coefficient between the stocks is 0.3.

① Calculate the expected return and standard deviation of your portfolio.

② Today you sold 20 shares of Hyundai stock. Calculate the expected return and standard deviation of your new portfolio.

Solution

① The expected return and standard deviation

삼성주식에 투자한 돈은 800,000원이고, 현대주식에 투자한 돈은 1,200,000원이다.

$$w_S = \frac{8}{20},\quad w_H = \frac{12}{20}$$

$$E(r_p) = \frac{2}{5} \times 15 + \frac{3}{5} \times 20 = 18\%$$

$$\sigma_p^2 = (\frac{2}{5})^2 \cdot (8)^2 + (\frac{3}{5})^2 \cdot (20)^2 + 2(\frac{2}{5})(\frac{3}{5})(0.3)(8 \cdot 20) = 177.28$$

$$\sigma_p = 13.31$$

② The expected return and standard deviation

삼성주식에 투자한 돈은 800,000원이고, 현대주식에 투자한 돈은 400,000원이다.

$$w_S = \frac{8}{12},\quad w_H = \frac{4}{12}$$

$$E(r_p) = \frac{2}{3} \times 15 + \frac{1}{3} \times 20 = 16.7\%$$

$$\sigma_p^2 = (\frac{2}{3})^2 \cdot (8)^2 + (\frac{1}{3})^2 \cdot (20)^2 + 2(\frac{2}{3})(\frac{1}{3})(0.3)(8 \cdot 20) = 94.22$$

$$\sigma_p = 9.71$$

Example

Let us take the example of a portfolio that consists of two stocks. The value of stock A is W800,000, and its standard deviation is 8%, while the value of stock B is W1,200,000, and its standard deviation is 20%. There is a correlation of 0.3 between the two stocks. Determine the variance.

Solution

$$\sigma_p^2 = (\frac{2}{5})^2 \cdot (8)^2 + (\frac{3}{5})^2 \cdot (20)^2 + 2(\frac{2}{5})(\frac{3}{5})(0.3)(8 \cdot 20) = 177.28$$

Example

Suppose you hold 20 shares of Samsung stock and 10 shares of Hyundai stock. Samsung stock is currently sold at 30,000 won per share, while Hyundai stock is sold at 20,000 won. The expected return of Samsung stock is 12%, while that of Hyundai stock is 15%. The standard deviation of Samsung is 8%, while that of Hyundai is 10%. The correlation coefficient between the stocks is 0.2.
Calculate the expected return and standard deviation of your portfolio.

Solution

삼성주식에 투자한 돈은 600,000원이고, 현대주식에 투자한 돈은 200,000원이다.

$$w_S = \frac{6}{8}, \quad w_H = \frac{2}{8}$$

$$E(r_p) = \frac{6}{8} \times 12 + \frac{2}{8} \times 15 = 12.75\%$$

$$\sigma_p^2 = (\frac{6}{8})^2 \cdot (8)^2 + (\frac{2}{8})^2 \cdot (10)^2 + 2(\frac{6}{8})(\frac{2}{8})(0.2)(8 \cdot 10) = 48.25$$

$$\sigma_p = 6.95$$

Example

송승헌은 삼성주식 20주와 현대주식 10주를 갖고 있다. 삼성의 현재주가는 30,000원이고, 현대의 현재주가는 20,000원이다. 삼성주식의 기대수익률은 12%이고, 현대주식의 기대수익률은 15%이다. 삼성의 표준편차는 8%이고, 현대의 표준편차는 10%이다. 두 주식의 상관계수는 0.2이다. 송승헌의 포트폴리오 기대수익률과 표준편차를 구하시오.

Solution

삼성주식에 투자한 돈은 600,000원이고, 현대주식에 투자한 돈은 200,000원이다.

$$w_S = \frac{6}{8}, \quad w_H = \frac{2}{8}$$

$$E(r_p) = \frac{6}{8} \times 12 + \frac{2}{8} \times 15 = 12.75\%$$

$$\sigma_p^2 = (\frac{6}{8})^2 \cdot (8)^2 + (\frac{2}{8})^2 \cdot (10)^2 + 2(\frac{6}{8})(\frac{2}{8})(0.2)(8 \cdot 10) = 48.25$$

$$\sigma_p = 6.95$$

Example

장동건은 삼성주식 20주와 롯데주식 40주를 갖고 있다. 삼성의 현재주가는 30,000원이고, 롯데의 현재주가는 10,000원이다. 삼성주식의 기대수익률은 12%이고, 롯데주식의 기대수익률은 15%이다. 삼성의 표준편차는 8%이고, 롯데의 표준편차는 10%이다. 두 주식의 상관계수는 0.2이다. 장동건의 포트폴리오 기대수익률과 표준편차를 구하라.

Solution

$$w_S = \frac{3}{5}, \; w_H = \frac{2}{5}$$

$$E(r_p) = 13.2\%$$

$$\sigma_p^2 = 46.72$$

$$\sigma_p = 6.84$$

Example

$0 \le x \le 1$, $y \ge 0$ 일 때, 다음 함수를 그림 그리시오.

$y^2 = (3x+1)^2$

Example

Graph this function.

$y^2 = (3x+1)^2$, $0 \le x \le 1$, $y \ge 0$

Solution

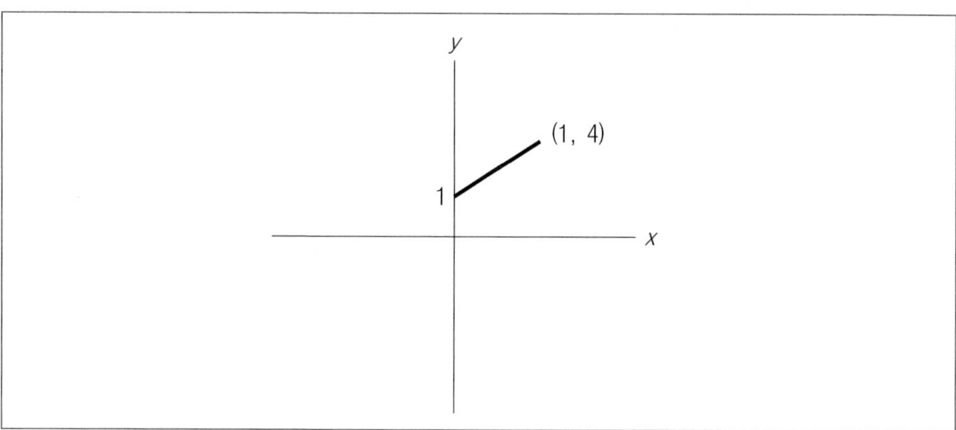

$y = 3x + 1, \qquad 0 \le x \le 1$

Example

$0 \le x \le 1$, $y \ge 0$일 때, 다음 함수를 그림 그리시오.

$y^2 = (3x-1)^2$

Example

$0 \le x \le 1$, $y \ge 0$,

$y^2 = (3x-1)^2$

Plot the set of x−y combinations.

Solution

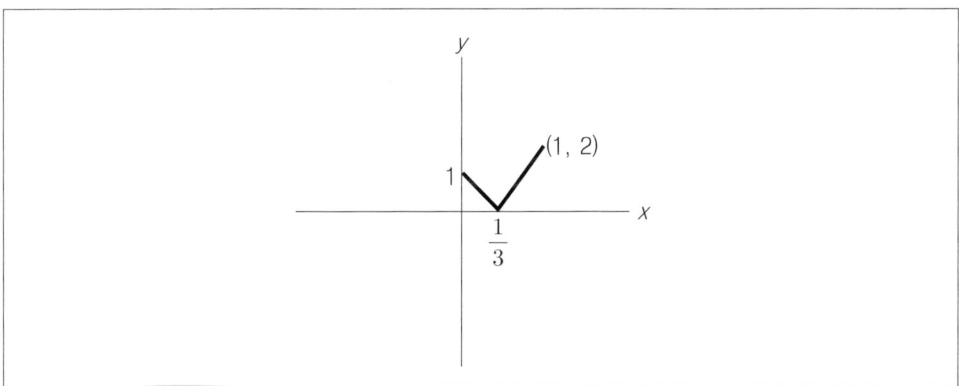

$y = -3x + 1, \quad 0 \le x < \frac{1}{3}$

$y = 3x - 1, \quad \frac{1}{3} \le x \le 1$

Example

$0 \le w \le 1$일 때, 다음 함수를 x, y 평면에 그림 그리시오.

$x = 2w + 1$

$y = 3w + 5$

Example

$0 \le w \le 1$,

$x = 2w + 1$

$y = 3w + 5$

Plot the set of x−y combinations.

Solution

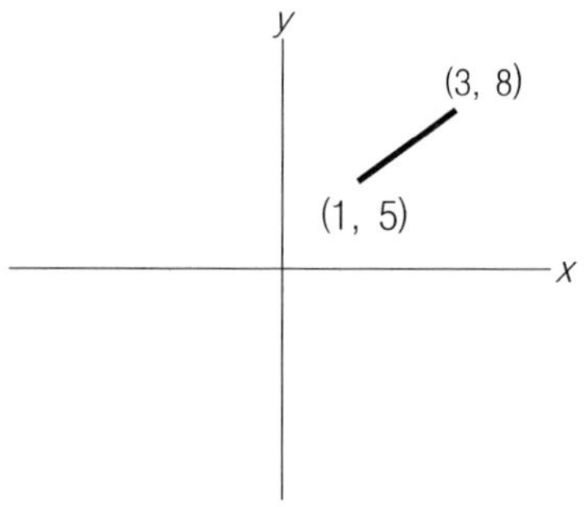

y
(3, 8)
(1, 5)
x

$$y = \frac{3}{2}x + \frac{7}{2}, \quad 1 \le x \le 3$$

Example

$0 \leq w \leq 1,$

$x = -2w + 3$

$y = -2w + 6$

Plot the set of x−y combinations.

Solution

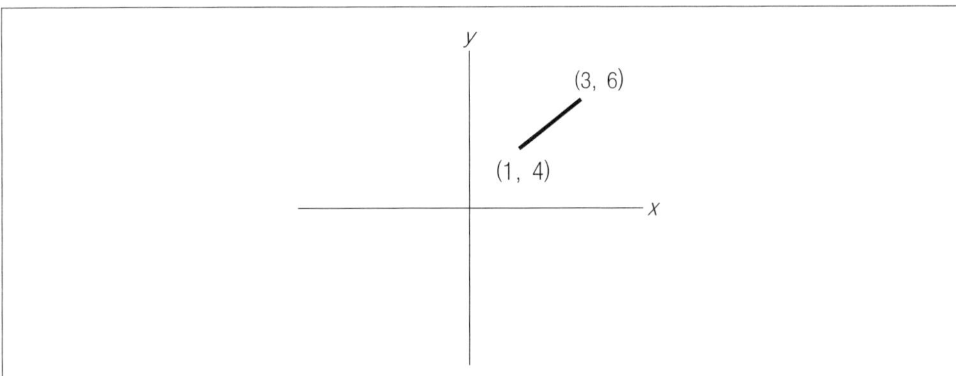

Three-Asset Portfolio

Expectation & Variance

$$E(aX + bY + cZ) = aE(X) + bE(Y) + cE(Z)$$

$$Var(aX + bY + cZ) = a^2\sigma_X^2 + b^2\sigma_Y^2 + c^2\sigma_Z^2 + 2(ab\sigma_{XY} + bc\sigma_{YZ} + ca\sigma_{ZX})$$

[Proof]

$$Var(aX + bY + cZ) = E[\{aX + bY + cZ - E(aX + bY + cZ)\}^2]$$

$$= a^2E[\{X - E(X)\}^2] + b^2E[\{Y - E(Y)\}^2] + c^2E[\{Z - E(Z)\}^2]$$

$$+ 2ab \cdot E[\{X - E(X)\}\{Y - E(Y)\}] + 2bc \cdot E[\{Y - E(Y)\}\{Z - E(Z)\}]$$

$$+ 2ca \cdot E[\{Z - E(Z)\}\{X - E(X)\}]$$

$$Var(aX + bY + cZ) = a^2\sigma_X^2 + b^2\sigma_Y^2 + c^2\sigma_Z^2 + 2(ab\sigma_{XY} + bc\sigma_{YZ} + ca\sigma_{ZX})$$

Example

Prove

$$Var(2X+3Y+4Z)=4\sigma_X^2+9\sigma_Y^2+16\sigma_Z^2+2(6\sigma_{XY}+12\sigma_{YZ}+8\sigma_{ZX})$$

Solution

$$Var(2X+3Y+4Z)=E[\{2X+3Y+4Z-E(2X+3Y+4Z)\}^2]$$

$$Var(2X+3Y+4Z)=4\sigma_X^2+9\sigma_Y^2+16\sigma_Z^2+2(6\sigma_{XY}+12\sigma_{YZ}+8\sigma_{ZX})$$

Example

다음 표와 같은 수익률과 확률을 갖는 주식 X, Y, Z에 각각 0.2, 0.5, 0.3의 비율로 투자한 portfolio의 기대수익률과 분산을 구하라.

(%)

Probability	X	Y	Z
0.1	11	−3	18
0.4	9	15	5
0.2	25	2	12
0.3	7	20	4

Solution

$E(X)=11.8,\quad E(Y)=12.1,\quad E(Z)=7.4$

$E(0.2X+0.5Y+0.3Z)=0.2E(X)+0.5E(Y)+0.3E(Z)=10.6$

$Var(0.2X+0.5Y+0.3Z)$

$=0.2^2\sigma_X^2+0.5^2\sigma_Y^2+0.3^2\sigma_Z^2+2(0.2\cdot 0.5\cdot\sigma_{XY}+0.5\cdot 0.3\cdot\sigma_{YZ}+0.3\cdot 0.2\cdot\sigma_{ZX})$

$\sigma_X^2=45.0,\quad \sigma_Y^2=65.3,\quad \sigma_Z^2=21.2$

$\sigma_{XY}=-40.1,\quad \sigma_{YZ}=-36.1,\quad \sigma_{ZX}=18.9$

$Var(0.2X+0.5Y+0.3Z)=3.4$

Example

Write 1+2+3+···+10 using sigma notation.

Solution

$$\sum_{n=1}^{10} n$$

$$\sum_{i=1}^{n} x_i$$

This expression means that the sum of all the terms x_i takes the values from 1 to n.

Portfolio effect

분산효과(diversification effect).
포트폴리오를 구성함으로써 위험이 감소되는 효과.

As the number of assets in the portfolio increases, the portfolio variance decreases and approaches the average covariance.

The symbol for summation, which represents the addition of a series of terms, is denoted by the uppercase Greek letter sigma.
The uppercase Greek letter sigma represents summation.

Example

Write the following summation in expanded form:

$$\sum_{i=1}^{2}\sigma_i^2$$

Solution

$$\sum_{i=1}^{2}\sigma_i^2=\sigma_1^2+\sigma_2^2$$

Example

Write the following summation in expanded form:

$$\underbrace{\sum_{i=1}^{2}\sum_{j=1}^{2}}_{i\neq j}\sigma_{ij}$$

Solution

$$\underbrace{\sum_{i=1}^{2}\sum_{j=1}^{2}}_{i\neq j}\sigma_{ij}=\sigma_{12}+\sigma_{21}$$

Two-Asset Portfolio

$$Var\left(\frac{1}{2}R_1+\frac{1}{2}R_2\right)=\left(\frac{1}{2}\right)^2\sigma_1^2+\left(\frac{1}{2}\right)^2\sigma_2^2+2\left(\frac{1}{2}\right)\left(\frac{1}{2}\right)\sigma_{12}$$

$$=\left(\frac{1}{2}\right)^2\sigma_1^2+\left(\frac{1}{2}\right)^2\sigma_2^2+\left(\frac{1}{2}\right)\left(\frac{1}{2}\right)\sigma_{12}+\left(\frac{1}{2}\right)\left(\frac{1}{2}\right)\sigma_{21}$$

$$=\sum_{i=1}^{2}\left(\frac{1}{2}\right)^2\sigma_i^2+\sum_{i=1}^{2}\sum_{\substack{j=1\\(i\neq j)}}^{2}\left(\frac{1}{2}\right)\left(\frac{1}{2}\right)\sigma_{ij}$$

$$=\left(\frac{1}{2}\right)\sum_{i=1}^{2}\frac{\sigma_i^2}{2}+\left(\frac{1}{2}\right)\sum_{i=1}^{2}\sum_{\substack{j=1\\(i\neq j)}}^{2}\left(\frac{1}{2}\right)\sigma_{ij}$$

$$=\left(\frac{1}{2}\right)\left(\frac{\sigma_1^2+\sigma_2^2}{2}\right)+\left(\frac{1}{2}\right)\left(\frac{\sigma_{12}+\sigma_{21}}{2}\right)$$

$$Var\left(\frac{1}{2}r_1+\frac{1}{2}r_2\right)=\frac{1}{2}\overline{\sigma_i^2}+\frac{1}{2}\overline{\sigma_{ij}}$$

Example

Write T for True and F for False for the following equation. If the equation is false, correct the equation.

$$Var\left(\frac{1}{2}R_1+\frac{1}{2}R_2\right)=\left(\frac{1}{2}\right)^2\sigma_1^2+\left(\frac{1}{2}\right)^2\sigma_2^2+\left(\frac{1}{2}\right)\left(\frac{1}{2}\right)\sigma_{12}$$

Solution

F,

$$Var\left(\frac{1}{2}R_1+\frac{1}{2}R_2\right)=\left(\frac{1}{2}\right)^2\sigma_1^2+\left(\frac{1}{2}\right)^2\sigma_2^2+2\left(\frac{1}{2}\right)\left(\frac{1}{2}\right)\sigma_{12}$$

A series can be represented in a compact form, called summation or sigma notation. The Greek capital letter, Σ , is used to represent the sum.

Example

Write $Var\left(\frac{1}{2}r_1+\frac{1}{2}r_2\right)$ using sigma notation.

Solution

$$Var\left(\frac{1}{2}r_1+\frac{1}{2}r_2\right)=\sum_{i=1}^{2}\left(\frac{1}{2}\right)^2\sigma_i^2+\underbrace{\sum_{i=1}^{2}\sum_{j=1}^{2}}_{i\neq j}\left(\frac{1}{2}\right)\left(\frac{1}{2}\right)\sigma_{ij}$$

Example

You have a portfolio consisting of two assets, and each asset is equally weighted. Express the variance using sigma notation.

Solution

$$\sigma_p^2=\sum_{i=1}^{2}\left(\frac{1}{2}\right)^2\sigma_i^2+\underbrace{\sum_{i=1}^{2}\sum_{j=1}^{2}}_{i\neq j}\left(\frac{1}{2}\right)\left(\frac{1}{2}\right)\sigma_{ij}$$

Example

Write T for True and F for False for the following equation. If the equation is false, correct the equation.

$$Var\left(\frac{1}{2}r_1+\frac{1}{2}r_2\right)=\sum_{i=1}^{2}\left(\frac{1}{2}\right)^2\sigma_i^2+\underbrace{\sum_{i=1}^{2}\sum_{j=1}^{2}}_{i\neq j}\left(\frac{1}{2}\right)\sigma_{ij}$$

Solution

F,

$$Var\left(\frac{1}{2}r_1+\frac{1}{2}r_2\right)=\sum_{i=1}^{2}\left(\frac{1}{2}\right)^2\sigma_i^2+\underbrace{\sum_{i=1}^{2}\sum_{j=1}^{2}}_{i\neq j}\left(\frac{1}{2}\right)\left(\frac{1}{2}\right)\sigma_{ij}$$

Example

Write T for True and F for False for the following equation. If the equation is false, correct the equation.

$$Var\left(\frac{1}{2}R_1 + \frac{1}{2}R_2\right) = \left(\frac{1}{2}\right)\left(\frac{\sigma_1^2 + \sigma_2^2}{2}\right) + \left(\frac{\sigma_{12} + \sigma_{21}}{2}\right)$$

Solution

F,

$$Var\left(\frac{1}{2}R_1 + \frac{1}{2}R_2\right) = \left(\frac{1}{2}\right)\left(\frac{\sigma_1^2 + \sigma_2^2}{2}\right) + \left(\frac{1}{2}\right)\left(\frac{\sigma_{12} + \sigma_{21}}{2}\right)$$

Example

$$Var\left(\frac{1}{2}r_1 + \frac{1}{2}r_2\right) = \sum_{i=1}^{2}\left(\frac{1}{2}\right)^2 \sigma_i^2 + (\quad)\underbrace{\sum_{i=1}^{2}\sum_{j=1}^{2}}_{i \neq j}\left(\frac{1}{2}\right)\sigma_{ij}$$

Solution

$$Var\left(\frac{1}{2}r_1 + \frac{1}{2}r_2\right) = \sum_{i=1}^{2}\left(\frac{1}{2}\right)^2 \sigma_i^2 + \left(\frac{1}{2}\right)\underbrace{\sum_{i=1}^{2}\sum_{j=1}^{2}}_{i \neq j}\left(\frac{1}{2}\right)\sigma_{ij}$$

Example

Write $Var\left(\frac{1}{3}r_1 + \frac{1}{3}r_2 + \frac{1}{3}r_3\right)$ using sigma notation.

Solution

$$Var\left(\frac{1}{3}r_1 + \frac{1}{3}r_2 + \frac{1}{3}r_3\right) = \sum_{i=1}^{3}\left(\frac{1}{3}\right)^2\sigma_i^2 + \underbrace{\sum_{i=1}^{3}\sum_{j=1}^{3}}_{i \neq j}\left(\frac{1}{3}\right)\left(\frac{1}{3}\right)\sigma_{ij}$$

$\overline{y}$

The y bar symbol is used in statistics to represent the sample mean of a distribution.

Average variance

$\overline{\sigma_i^2}$

Example

Translate the sentence into an equation: The average variance of an equally weighted portfolio with two assets is calculated as half the sum of the variances of the individual assets.

Solution

$$\overline{\sigma_i^2} = \sum_{i=1}^{2}\left(\frac{1}{2}\right)\sigma_i^2$$

Example

Translate the sentence into an equation: The average variance of an equally weighted portfolio with three assets is calculated as one-third of the sum of the variances of the individual assets.

Solution

$$\overline{\sigma_i^2} = \sum_{i=1}^{3}\left(\frac{1}{3}\right)\sigma_i^2$$

Average covariance

$\overline{\sigma_{ij}}$

Example

Translate the sentence into an equation: The average covariance of an equally weighted portfolio with two assets is calculated as half of the sum of the covariances between each pair of assets in the portfolio.

Solution

$$\overline{\sigma_{ij}} = \underbrace{\sum_{i=1}^{2}\sum_{j=1}^{2}}_{i \neq j}\left(\frac{1}{2}\right)\sigma_{ij}$$

Example

Translate the sentence into an equation: The average covariance of an equally weighted portfolio with three assets is calculated as one-sixth of the sum of the covariances between each pair of assets in the portfolio.

Solution

$$\overline{\sigma_{ij}} = \underbrace{\sum_{i=1}^{3}\sum_{j=1}^{3}}_{i \neq j}\left(\frac{1}{3}\right)\left(\frac{1}{2}\right)\sigma_{ij}$$

Example

Write $Var\left(\frac{1}{2}r_1 + \frac{1}{2}r_2\right)$ using bar notation.

Solution

$$Var\left(\frac{1}{2}r_1 + \frac{1}{2}r_2\right) = \frac{1}{2}\overline{\sigma_i^2} + \frac{1}{2}\overline{\sigma_{ij}}$$

Example

You have a portfolio consisting of two assets, and each asset is equally weighted. Express the variance using bar notation.

Solution

$$\sigma_p^2 = \frac{1}{2}\overline{\sigma_i^2} + \frac{1}{2}\overline{\sigma_{ij}}$$

$$\text{Portfolio Variance} = \frac{1}{2}\text{Average Variance} + \frac{1}{2}\text{Average Covariance}$$

Example

You have a portfolio consisting of two assets, and each asset is equally weighted. Portfolio variance equals one-half times (   ) plus one-half times the average covariance.

Solution

the average variance

Example

The variance of asset 1 is 1.

The variance of asset 2 is 1.

The covariance between asset 1 and 2 is 0.2.

Find the variance of a Naively Diversified Portfolio.

Solution

The variance of the naively diversified portfolio is 0.6.

Three–Asset Portfolio

$$Var\left(\frac{1}{3}R_1+\frac{1}{3}R_2+\frac{1}{3}R_3\right)=\left(\frac{1}{3}\right)^2\sigma_1^2+\left(\frac{1}{3}\right)^2\sigma_2^2+\left(\frac{1}{3}\right)^2\sigma_3^2+2\left(\frac{1}{3}\right)\left(\frac{1}{3}\right)(\sigma_{12}+\sigma_{23}+\sigma_{31})$$

$$Var\left(\frac{1}{3}r_1+\frac{1}{3}r_2+\frac{1}{3}r_3\right)=\sum_{i=1}^{3}\left(\frac{1}{3}\right)^2\sigma_i^2+\underbrace{\sum_{i=1}^{3}\sum_{j=1}^{3}}_{i\neq j}\left(\frac{1}{3}\right)\left(\frac{1}{3}\right)\sigma_{ij}$$

$$Var\left(\frac{1}{3}r_1+\frac{1}{3}r_2+\frac{1}{3}r_3\right)=\left(\frac{1}{3}\right)\sum_{i=1}^{3}\left(\frac{1}{3}\right)\sigma_i^2+\left(\frac{2}{3}\right)\underbrace{\sum_{i=1}^{3}\sum_{j=1}^{3}}_{i\neq j}\left(\frac{1}{3}\right)\left(\frac{1}{2}\right)\sigma_{ij}$$

$$=\left(\frac{1}{3}\right)\sum_{i=1}^{3}\frac{\sigma_i^2}{3}+\left(\frac{2}{3}\right)\sum_{i=1}^{3}\sum_{\substack{j=1\\(i\neq j)}}^{3}\left(\frac{1}{3}\right)\left(\frac{1}{2}\right)\sigma_{ij}$$

$$Var\left(\frac{1}{3}R_1+\frac{1}{3}R_2+\frac{1}{3}R_3\right)=\frac{1}{3}\overline{\sigma_i^2}+\frac{2}{3}\overline{\sigma_{ij}}$$

Portfolio variance equals one-third times the average variance plus two-thirds times the average covariance.

Example

Write T for True and F for False for the following equation. If the equation is false, correct the equation.

$$Var\left(\frac{1}{3}R_1+\frac{1}{3}R_2+\frac{1}{3}R_3\right)=\left(\frac{1}{3}\right)^2\sigma_1^2+\left(\frac{1}{3}\right)^2\sigma_2^2+\left(\frac{1}{3}\right)^2\sigma_3^2+\left(\frac{1}{3}\right)\left(\frac{1}{3}\right)(\sigma_{12}+\sigma_{23}+\sigma_{31})$$

Solution

F,

$$Var\left(\frac{1}{3}R_1+\frac{1}{3}R_2+\frac{1}{3}R_3\right)=\left(\frac{1}{3}\right)^2\sigma_1^2+\left(\frac{1}{3}\right)^2\sigma_2^2+\left(\frac{1}{3}\right)^2\sigma_3^2+2\left(\frac{1}{3}\right)\left(\frac{1}{3}\right)(\sigma_{12}+\sigma_{23}+\sigma_{31})$$

Example

Write T for True and F for False for the following equation. If the equation is false, correct the equation.

$$Var\left(\frac{1}{3}X+\frac{1}{3}Y+\frac{1}{3}Z\right)=\left(\frac{1}{3}\right)\left(\frac{\sigma_X^2+\sigma_Y^2+\sigma_Z^2}{3}\right)+\left(\frac{1}{3}\right)\left(\frac{\sigma_{XY}+\sigma_{YZ}+\sigma_{ZX}}{3}\right)$$

Solution

F,

$$Var\left(\frac{1}{3}X+\frac{1}{3}Y+\frac{1}{3}Z\right)=\left(\frac{1}{3}\right)\left(\frac{\sigma_X^2+\sigma_Y^2+\sigma_Z^2}{3}\right)+\left(\frac{2}{3}\right)\left(\frac{\sigma_{XY}+\sigma_{YZ}+\sigma_{ZX}}{3}\right)$$

Example

$$Var\left(\frac{1}{3}r_1+\frac{1}{3}r_2+\frac{1}{3}r_3\right)=\left(\frac{1}{3}\right)\sum_{i=1}^{3}\left(\frac{1}{3}\right)\sigma_i^2+(\quad)\underbrace{\sum_{i=1}^{3}\sum_{j=1}^{3}}_{i\neq j}\left(\frac{1}{3}\right)\left(\frac{1}{2}\right)\sigma_{ij}$$

Solution

$$Var\left(\frac{1}{3}r_1+\frac{1}{3}r_2+\frac{1}{3}r_3\right)=\left(\frac{1}{3}\right)\sum_{i=1}^{3}\left(\frac{1}{3}\right)\sigma_i^2+\left(\frac{2}{3}\right)\underbrace{\sum_{i=1}^{3}\sum_{j=1}^{3}}_{i\neq j}\left(\frac{1}{3}\right)\left(\frac{1}{2}\right)\sigma_{ij}$$

Example

$$Var\left(\frac{1}{4}r_1+\frac{1}{4}r_2+\frac{1}{4}r_3+\frac{1}{4}r_4\right)$$

$$\sigma_p^2=\sum_{i=1}^{4}\left(\frac{1}{4}\right)^2\sigma_i^2+\sum_{i=1}^{4}\sum_{\substack{j=1\\(i\neq j)}}^{4}\left(\frac{1}{4}\right)\left(\frac{1}{4}\right)\sigma_{ij}$$

$$\sigma_p^2=\left(\frac{1}{4}\right)\sum_{i=1}^{4}\left(\frac{1}{4}\right)\sigma_i^2+\left(\frac{3}{4}\right)\sum_{i=1}^{4}\sum_{\substack{j=1\\(i\neq j)}}^{4}\left(\frac{1}{4}\right)\left(\frac{1}{3}\right)\sigma_{ij}$$

$$\sigma_p^2=\frac{1}{4}\overline{\sigma_i^2}+\frac{3}{4}\overline{\sigma_{ij}}$$

Portfolio variance equals one-fourth times the average variance plus three-fourths times the average covariancc.

Example

$\sigma_i^2 = 1, \quad i = 1,2,3,4$

$\sigma_{ij} = 0.2, \quad i = 1,2,3,4, \quad j = 1,2,3,4 \quad (i \neq j)$

Find the variance of a Naively Diversified Portfolio.

Solution

$$Var(\frac{1}{4}R_1 + \frac{1}{4}R_2 + \frac{1}{4}R_3 + \frac{1}{4}R_4)$$

$$\sigma_p^2 = \frac{1}{4}\overline{\sigma_i^2} + \frac{3}{4}\overline{\sigma_{ij}} = \frac{1}{4} + \frac{3}{4} \times 0.2 = 0.4$$

Example

The variance of the ith asset = 1, i=1,2,3,4

The covariance between assets i and j = 0.2,

i = 1,2,3,4, j = 1,2,3,4 (i<j)

Find the variance of a Naively Diversified Portfolio.

Solution

$$Var(\frac{1}{4}R_1 + \frac{1}{4}R_2 + \frac{1}{4}R_3 + \frac{1}{4}R_4)$$

$$\sigma_p^2 = \frac{1}{4}\overline{\sigma_i^2} + \frac{3}{4}\overline{\sigma_{ij}} = \frac{1}{4} + \frac{3}{4} \times 0.2 = 0.4$$

Example

What is the variance of a naively diversified portfolio consisting of four assets, where the variance of each asset is 1, the covariance between any two assets is 0.2, and all assets are equally weighted?

Solution

$$Var\left(\frac{1}{4}r_1 + \frac{1}{4}r_2 + \frac{1}{4}r_3 + \frac{1}{4}r_4\right)$$

$$\sigma_p^2 = \frac{1}{4}\overline{\sigma_i^2} + \frac{3}{4}\overline{\sigma_{ij}} = \frac{1}{4} + \frac{3}{4} \times 0.2 = 0.4$$

Example

The average variance is 1.

The average covariance is 0.2.

The number of assets in the portfolio is 4.

Find the variance of a Naively Diversified Portfolio.

Solution

$$Var(\frac{1}{4}R_1 + \frac{1}{4}R_2 + \frac{1}{4}R_3 + \frac{1}{4}R_4)$$

$$\sigma_p^2 = \frac{1}{4}\overline{\sigma_i^2} + \frac{3}{4}\overline{\sigma_{ij}} = \frac{1}{4} + \frac{3}{4} \times 0.2 = 0.4$$

Example

$\sigma_i^2 = 1,\ i = 1,2,3,4,5$

$\sigma_{ij} = 0.2,\ \ i = 1,2,3,4,5,\ \ j = 1,2,3,4,5\ \ (i \neq j)$

Find the variance of a Naively Diversified Portfolio.

Solution

Portfolio variance equals one-fifth times the average variance plus four-fifths times the average covariance.

$$\sigma_p^2 = \frac{1}{5}\overline{\sigma_i^2} + \frac{4}{5}\overline{\sigma_{ij}} = 0.36$$

Example

$\sigma_i^2 = 1,\ \ i = 1,2,3,\cdots,10$

$\sigma_{ij} = 0.2,\ \ i = 1,2,3,\cdots,10,\ \ j = 1,2,3,\cdots,10\ (i \neq j)$

Find the variance of a Naively Diversified Portfolio.

Solution

$$\sigma_p^2 = \frac{1}{10}\overline{\sigma_i^2} + \frac{9}{10}\overline{\sigma_{ij}} = 0.28$$

N–Asset Portfolio

$$\sigma_p^2 = \sum_{i=1}^{n}(\frac{1}{n})^2\sigma_i^2 + \sum_{i=1}^{n}\sum_{\substack{j=1 \\ (i \neq j)}}^{n}(\frac{1}{n})(\frac{1}{n})\sigma_{ij}$$

$$\sigma_p^2 = (\frac{1}{n})\sum_{i=1}^{n}(\frac{1}{n})\sigma_i^2 + (\frac{n-1}{n})\sum_{i=1}^{n}\sum_{\substack{j=1 \\ (i \neq j)}}^{n}(\frac{1}{n})(\frac{1}{n-1})\sigma_{ij}$$

$$\sigma_p^2 = \frac{1}{n}\overline{\sigma_i^2} + \frac{n-1}{n}\overline{\sigma_{ij}}$$

$$\sigma_p^2 = \frac{1}{n}(\overline{\sigma_i^2} - \overline{\sigma_{ij}}) + \overline{\sigma_{ij}}$$

Example

Write the variance of n-asset equally weighted portfolio using sigma notation.

Solution

$$\sigma_p^2 = \sum_{i=1}^{n}(\frac{1}{n})^2\sigma_i^2 + \sum_{i=1}^{n}\sum_{\substack{j=1 \\ (i \neq j)}}^{n}(\frac{1}{n})(\frac{1}{n})\sigma_{ij}$$

Example

Write the variance of n-asset equally weighted portfolio using bar notation.

Solution

$$\sigma_p^2 = \frac{1}{n}\overline{\sigma_i^2} + \frac{n-1}{n}\overline{\sigma_{ij}}$$

Portfolio variance equals one over n times the average variance plus n minus one over n times the average covariance.

Infinite-Asset Portfolio

$$\lim_{n \to \infty} \sigma_p^2 = \overline{\sigma_{ij}}$$

Example

Translate the sentence into an equation: As the number of assets in the portfolio increases, the portfolio variance decreases and approaches the average covariance.

Solution

$$\lim_{n \to \infty} \sigma_p^2 = \overline{\sigma_{ij}}$$

Variance of a Naively Diversified Portfolio

$\overline{\sigma_{ij}}$

Total Risk

Total Risk = Unsystematic Risk + Systematic Risk

$$\sigma_p^2 = \frac{1}{n}(\overline{\sigma_i^2} - \overline{\sigma_{ij}}) + \overline{\sigma_{ij}}$$

Total risk is unsystematic risk plus systematic risk.

Total risk equals systematic risk plus unsystematic risk.

Unsystematic Risk

$$\frac{1}{n}(\overline{\sigma_i^2} - \overline{\sigma_{ij}})$$

포트폴리오의 위험 중에서 분산투자로써 제거할 수 있는 위험을 분산가능한 위험(diversifiable risk)이라고 한다. diversifiable risk는 개별주식을 발행한 기업의 특수한 상황과 관련이 있는 것으로서, 비체계적 위험(unsystematic risk) 또는 기업 고유의 위험(company specific risk)이라고 한다.

It can be eliminated by diversification.

This is the risk that can be diversified away by holding a diversified portfolio of assets.

Systematic Risk

$$\overline{\sigma_{ij}}$$

분산투자로써 감소시킬 수 없는 위험을 분산불가능한 위험(non-diversifiable risk)이라고 한다. non-diversifiable risk는 시장의 전반적인 상황과 관련되어 나타나는 위험으로 체계적 위험(systematic risk)이라고 한다.

It cannot be eliminated by diversification.

This is the portion of total risk that cannot be eliminated through diversification.

The portfolio's total risk consists of unsystematic and systematic risk.

Example

Translate the sentence into an equation: The portfolio's total risk consists of unsystematic and systematic risk.

Solution

$$\sigma_p^2 = \frac{1}{n}\left(\overline{\sigma_i^2} - \overline{\sigma_{ij}}\right) + \overline{\sigma_{ij}}$$

Example

The variance of asset 1 is 3.

The variance of asset 2 is 5.

The covariance between asset 1 and 2 is 0.2.

Find the variance of a Naively Diversified Portfolio.

Solution

$\sigma_1^2 = 3,\ \ \sigma_2^2 = 5,\ \ \sigma_{12} = 0.2$

$\sigma_p^2 = 2.1$

Example

$\sigma_1^2 = 3,\ \ \sigma_2^2 = 5,\ \ \sigma_3^2 = 2,\ \ \sigma_4 = 1$

$\sigma_{12} = 0.2,\ \ \sigma_{13} = 0.1,\ \ \sigma_{14} = 0.3,\ \ \sigma_{23} = 0.5,\ \ \sigma_{24} = 0.2,\ \ \sigma_{34} = 0.6$

Find the variance of a Naively Diversified Portfolio.

Solution

$$Var(\frac{1}{4}R_1 + \frac{1}{4}R_2 + \frac{1}{4}R_3 + \frac{1}{4}R_4)$$

$$\overline{\sigma_i^2} = 2.75,\ \ \overline{\sigma_{ij}} = 0.32$$

$$\sigma_p^2 = \frac{1}{4}\overline{\sigma_i^2} + \frac{3}{4}\overline{\sigma_{ij}} = 0.93$$

Sum of series

$$\sum_{k=1}^{n} k = 1 + 2 + \cdots + n = \frac{n(n+1)}{2}$$

Example

Find the sum of the series:

1 + 2 + 3 + 4 + 5

Solution

1 + 2 + 3 + 4 + 5 = 15

Example

the average variance: 46.619

the average covariance: 7.058

the number of assets in the portfolio: 25

Find the variance of a Naively Diversified Portfolio.

Solution

$\sigma_p^2 = 8.64$

Example

What is the variance of a naively diversified portfolio with 25 assets if the average variance is 46.619, the average covariance is 7.058, and all assets are equally weighted?

Example

$\overline{\sigma_i^2} = 46.619$, $\overline{\sigma_{ij}} = 7.058$ 일 때, 25개의 주식에 균등투자한 포트폴리오의 분산을 구하라.

Solution

$\sigma_p^2 = 8.64$

Example

the average variance: 20

the average covariance: 14.4

the number of assets in the portfolio: 2

Find the variance of a Naively Diversified Portfolio.

Solution

$\frac{1}{2}\overline{\sigma_i^2} + \frac{1}{2}\overline{\sigma_{ij}} = 17.2$

Example

the average variance: 20

the average covariance: 14.4

the number of assets in the portfolio: 4

Find the variance of a Naively Diversified Portfolio.

Solution

$\frac{1}{4}\overline{\sigma_i^2} + \frac{3}{4}\overline{\sigma_{ij}} = 15.8$

Example

다음의 포트폴리오 분산효과표에서 (　)에 적절한 값은?

포트폴리오의 구성주식수	포트폴리오의 분산
2	17.2
4	15.8
∞	(　)

Solution

$$\sigma_p^2 = \frac{1}{n}\overline{\sigma_i^2} + \frac{n-1}{n}\overline{\sigma_{ij}}$$

$$17.2 = \frac{1}{2}\overline{\sigma_i^2} + \frac{1}{2}\overline{\sigma_{ij}}$$

$$15.8 = \frac{1}{4}\overline{\sigma_i^2} + \frac{3}{4}\overline{\sigma_{ij}}$$

$$\overline{\sigma_{ij}} = 14.4$$

Example

Find the solution of the following system.

$$17.2 = \frac{1}{2}x + \frac{1}{2}y$$

$$15.8 = \frac{1}{4}x + \frac{3}{4}y$$

Solution

$$34.4 = x + y$$

$$63.2 = x + 3y$$

x=20, y=14.4

Example

Graph this function.

$$y = 2 + \frac{1}{x}$$

x is greater than zero.

Solution

x = 1, y = 3

x = 2, y = 2.5

x = 3, y = $\frac{7}{3}$

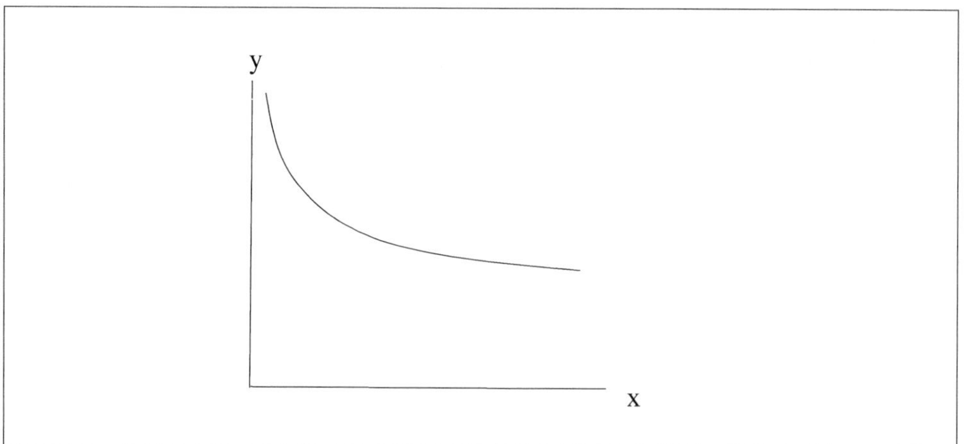

Example

As x increases in the equation $y = 2 + \frac{1}{x}$, y decreases and approaches 2.

Example

As x increases in the equation $y = a + \frac{b}{x}$ where $b > 0$, y decreases and approaches a.

Example

As x increases in the equation $y = a + \frac{1}{x}(b-a)$ where $b > a$, y decreases and approaches a.

Example

Statistics for four stocks are shown in the following table.

Covariance	Stock 1	Stock 2	Stock 3	Stock 4
Stock 1	3	0.2	0.1	0.3
Stock 2		5	0.5	0.2
Stock 3			2	0.6
Stock 4				1

Find the variance of a Naively Diversified Portfolio.

Solution

$\sigma_1^2 = 3,\ \ \sigma_2^2 = 5,\ \ \sigma_3^2 = 2,\ \ \sigma_4 = 1$

$\sigma_{12} = 0.2,\ \ \sigma_{13} = 0.1,\ \ \sigma_{14} = 0.3,\ \ \sigma_{23} = 0.5,\ \ \sigma_{24} = 0.2,\ \ \sigma_{34} = 0.6$

$Var(\frac{1}{4}R_1 + \frac{1}{4}R_2 + \frac{1}{4}R_3 + \frac{1}{4}R_4)$

$\overline{\sigma_i^2} = 2.75,\ \ \overline{\sigma_{ij}} = 0.32$

$\sigma_p^2 = \frac{1}{4}\overline{\sigma_i^2} + \frac{3}{4}\overline{\sigma_{ij}} = 0.93$

Market value

Market value—also known as market cap—is calculated by multiplying a company's outstanding shares by its current market price.
If XYZ Company trades at $25 per share and has 1 million shares outstanding, its market value is $25 million.

Market Capitalization

The market cap of a company is calculated by taking the current stock price and multiplying it by the company's outstanding shares.
For example, a company with 20 million shares selling at $100 a share would have a market cap of $2 billion. A second company with a share price of $1,000 but only 10,000 shares outstanding, on the other hand, would only have a market cap of $10 million.

A company's market cap is first established via an initial public offering. Before an IPO, the company that wishes to go public enlists an investment bank to employ valuation techniques to derive a company's value and to determine how many shares will be offered to the public and at what price.

For example, a company whose IPO value is set at $100 million by its investment bank may decide to issue 10 million shares at $10 per share or they may equivalently want to issue 20 million at $5 a share. In either instance, the initial market cap would be $100 million.

Capitalization-Weighted Index

A capitalization-weighted index is an index construction methodology where individual components are weighted according to their relative total market capitalization.

Calculation of a Capitalization-Weighted Index

To find the value of a capitalization-weighted index, first multiply each component's market price by its total outstanding shares to arrive at the total market value. The proportion of the stock's value to the overall total market value of the index components provides the weighting of the company in the index.

Example

Consider the following five companies:

Company A: 1 million shares outstanding, the current price per share equals $45

Company B: 300,000 shares outstanding, the current price per share equals $125

Company C: 500,000 shares outstanding, the current price per share equals $60

Company D: 1.5 million shares outstanding, the current price per share equals $75

Company E: 1.5 million shares outstanding, the current price per share equals $5

Find the weightings for each company in the index.

Solution

The total market value of each company would be calculated as:

Company A market value = 1,000,000 × 45 = $45,000,000

Company B market value = 300,000 × 125 = $37,500,000

Company C market value = 500,000 × 60 = $30,000,000

Company D market value = 1,500,000 × 75 = $112,500,000

Company E market value = 1,500,000 × 5 = $7,500,000

The entire market value of the index components equals $232,500,000 with the following weightings for each company:

Company A has a weight of 19.4% (45,000,000 / 232,500,000)

Company B has a weight of 16.1% (37,500,000 / 232,500,000)

Company C has a weight of 12.9% (30,000,000 / 232,500,000)

Company D has a weight of 48.4% (112,500,000 / 232,500,000)

Company E has a weight of 3.2% (7,500,000 / 232,500,000)

Market portfolio

A portfolio consisting of all stocks.

$$w_i = \frac{V_i}{\sum_{i=1}^{N} V_i}$$

w_i : the weight of the ith asset in the market portfolio.

V_i : the market value of the ith asset.

$\sum_{i=1}^{N} V_i$: the total market value of all assets.

Example

Translate the sentence into an equation: In the calculation of the weight of the ith asset, it is determined by dividing the total market value of the portfolio by the market value of the ith asset.

Solution

$$w_i = \frac{V_i}{\sum_{i=1}^{N} V_i}$$

Example

Write the following summation in expanded form.

$$\sum_{i=1}^{2} V_i$$

Solution

$$\sum_{i=1}^{2} V_i = V_1 + V_2$$

Example

Assume two companies exist in the stock market.

w_i : the weight of the ith asset in the market portfolio.

V_i : the market value of the ith asset.

The weight of Stock 1 in the market portfolio is $w_1 = \frac{V_1}{V_1 + V_2}$.

The weight of Stock 2 in the market portfolio is $w_2 = \frac{V_2}{V_1 + V_2}$.

Example

In Congo's stock market, suppose there are two companies, Company 1 and Company 2, each with market values of $40 million and $60 million, respectively. How would an investor calculate the weights of these companies in a portfolio?

Solution

$w_1 = 0.4$

$w_2 = 0.6$

Example

In an African country with two companies, let's call them Company P and Company Q, having market values of $40 million and $60 million, how does an investor calculate the weight of each company in a market portfolio?

Solution

$w_P = 0.4$

$w_Q = 0.6$

Example

In a scenario where there are only two companies in the stock market, let's call them Company P and Company Q, with market values of $40 million and $60 million, respectively, how would an investor determine the weight of each company in a portfolio?

Solution

$w_P = 0.4$

$w_Q = 0.6$

Example

How are the weights of two companies, Company P and Company Q, calculated in a market portfolio with market values of $40 million and $60 million, respectively?

Solution

$w_P = 0.4$

$w_Q = 0.6$

Example

Assume three companies exist in the stock market.
The market values of these assets are $50 million, $30 million, and $20 million, respectively.
Calculate the weight of each company in the portfolio.

[Solution]
0.5, 0.3, 0.2

N-Asset Equally Weighted Portfolio

$$E(\frac{1}{n}r_1+\frac{1}{n}r_2+\cdots+\frac{1}{n}r_n)=\frac{1}{n}E(r_1)+\frac{1}{n}E(r_2)+\cdots+\frac{1}{n}E(r_n)$$

$$Var(\frac{1}{n}r_1+\frac{1}{n}r_2+\cdots+\frac{1}{n}r_n)=\sum_{i=1}^{n}(\frac{1}{n})^2\sigma_i^2+\sum_{\substack{i=1\\(i\neq j)}}^{n}\sum_{j=1}^{n}(\frac{1}{n})(\frac{1}{n})\sigma_{ij}$$

N-Asset Portfolio

$$E(w_1r_1+w_2r_2+\cdots+w_nr_n)=w_1E(r_1)+w_2E(r_2)+\cdots+w_nE(r_n)$$

$$Var(w_1r_1+w_2r_2+\cdots+w_nr_n)=\sum_{i=1}^{n}(w_i)^2\sigma_i^2+\sum_{\substack{i=1\\(i\neq j)}}^{n}\sum_{j=1}^{n}(w_i)(w_j)\sigma_{ij}$$

The weights of the assets are $w_1, w_2, \cdots, w_n$.

Example

Write the variance of a three-asset portfolio using sigma notation.

Solution

$$Var(w_1r_1+w_2r_2+w_3r_3)=\sum_{i=1}^{3}(w_i)^2\sigma_i^2+\underbrace{\sum_{i=1}^{3}\sum_{j=1}^{3}}_{i\neq j}(w_i)(w_j)\sigma_{ij}$$

Example

Write the variance of a four-asset portfolio using sigma notation.

Solution

$$Var(w_1r_1+w_2r_2+w_3r_3+w_4r_4)=\sum_{i=1}^{4}(w_i)^2\sigma_i^2+\underbrace{\sum_{i=1}^{4}\sum_{j=1}^{4}}_{i\neq j}(w_i)(w_j)\sigma_{ij}$$

Example

Assume two companies exist in the stock market: Company A and Company B. The market capitalization of Company A is $8 billion and the market capitalization of Company B is $2 billion.

What is the weight of each company in the market portfolio?

Solution

The total market capitalization : $10 billion.

The market portfolio consists of each of these companies, which are weighed in the portfolio as follows:

Company A portfolio weight = $8 billion / $10 billion = 80%

Company B portfolio weight = $2 billion / $10 billion = 20%

Example

The data below describe a two-stock financial market.

	Price	Shares Outstanding
J	20,000	400
K	10,000	200

Construct a market portfolio with 150,000 won.

Solution

Market capitalization of J company: 8,000,000 won

Market capitalization of K company: 2,000,000 won

Total market capitalization: 10,000,000 won

Weight of J company: 80%

Weight of K company: 20%

Therefore, to construct the market portfolio with a budget of 150,000 won, you would allocate 80% to company J and 20% to company K.

Amounts invested in J company: 120,000 won

Amounts invested in K company: 30,000 won

I will buy 6 shares of J company and 3 shares of K company.

Example

In the stock market, shares of companies J and K are being traded, with the stock price of company J at 20,000 won and company K at 10,000 won. Construct a market portfolio with a total investment of 150,000 won available. Note that the outstanding shares for company J are 400, and for company K, they are 200.

Solution

Market capitalization of J company: 8,000,000 won
Market capitalization of K company: 2,000,000 won

Total market capitalization: 10,000,000 won
Weight of J company: 80%
Weight of K company: 20%
Therefore, to construct the market portfolio with a budget of 150,000 won, you would allocate 80% to company J and 20% to company K.
Amounts invested in J company: 120,000 won
Amounts invested in K company: 30,000 won

I will buy 6 shares of J company and 3 shares of K company.

Example

주식시장에는 J기업 주식과 K기업 주식이 거래되고 있고, J기업의 주가는 20,000원이고 K기업의 주가는 10,000원이다. 150,000원으로 시장포트폴리오를 구성하라.
단, J기업의 발행주식 수는 400주, K기업의 발행주식 수는 200주이다.

Solution

J기업 시장가치: $20,000 \times 400 = 8,000,000$ 원
K기업 시장가치: $10,000 \times 200 = 2,000,000$ 원
주식시장 총가치: 10,000,000원
J기업 주식의 비율: 80%
K기업 주식의 비율: 20%
J기업 주식 투자금액: $0.8 \times 150,000 = 120,000$ 원
K기업 주식 투자금액: $0.2 \times 150,000 = 30,000$ 원
J기업 주식 6주, K기업 주식 3주를 구입하면 시장포트폴리오를 구성한 것이 된다.

Example

In the stock market, shares of companies J, K, and L are being traded, with the stock prices of company J at 20,000 won, company K at 10,000 won, and company L at 30,000 won. Construct a market portfolio with a total investment of 1,500,000 won available. Note that the outstanding shares for company J are 400, for company K they are 200, and for company L, they are 500.

Solution

The market value of each company is determined by multiplying its respective stock price by the number of outstanding shares. For Company J, with a stock price of 20,000 won per share and 400 shares outstanding, the market value is 8,000,000 won. Company K, with a stock price of 10,000 won per share and 200 shares outstanding, has a market value of 2,000,000 won. Finally, Company L, with a stock price of 30,000 won per share and 500 shares outstanding, has a market value of 15,000,000 won.

The total market value of the portfolio is 25,000,000 won.

The weight of each company in the portfolio is determined by dividing its market value by the total market value of all companies. For Company J, with a market value of 8,000,000 won, its weight is 32% of the total portfolio. Company K, with a market value of 2,000,000 won, contributes 8% to the portfolio. Company L, with a market value of 15,000,000 won, represents 60% of the total portfolio.

To construct the market portfolio with a budget of 1,500,000 won, you would allocate 32% (480,000 won) to company J, 8% (120,000 won) to company K, and 60% (900,000 won) to company L.

The stock prices for the companies are 20,000 won per share for Company J, 10,000 won per share for Company K, and 30,000 won per share for Company L.

Therefore, you would buy 24 shares of Company J, 12 shares of Company K, and 30 shares of Company L to construct the market portfolio.

Example

주식시장에는 J기업 주식, K기업 주식, L기업 주식이 거래되고 있고, J기업의 주가는 20,000원이고 K기업의 주가는 10,000원, L기업의 주가는 30,000원이다. 1,500,000원으로 시장포트폴리오를 구성하라.
단, J기업의 발행주식 수는 400주, K기업의 발행주식 수는 200주, L기업의 발행주식 수는 500주이다.

Solution

J기업 시장가치: $20,000 \times 400 = 8,000,000$ 원

K기업 시장가치: $10,000 \times 200 = 2,000,000$ 원

L기업 시장가치: $30,000 \times 500 = 15,000,000$ 원

주식시장 총가치: 25,000,000원

J기업 주식의 비율: 32%

K기업 주식의 비율: 8%

L기업 주식의 비율: 60%

J기업 주식 투자금액: $0.32 \times 1,500,000 = 480,000$ 원

K기업 주식 투자금액: $0.08 \times 1,500,000 = 120,000$ 원

L기업 주식 투자금액: $0.60 \times 1,500,000 = 900,000$ 원

J기업 주식 24주, K기업 주식 12주, L기업 주식 30주를 구입하면 시장포트폴리오를 구성한 것이 된다.

Market capitalization is the total value of a company's outstanding shares of stock. It is calculated by multiplying the current share price by the total number of outstanding shares. The KOSPI market, which is a benchmark stock market of Korea, has listed global corporations such as Samsung Electronics, Hyundai Motor, POSCO and LG Electronics since its opening back in 1956.

The Korea Composite Stock Price Index is the main stock market index of South Korea, representing the performance of common stocks traded on the Korea Exchange. Established in 1983, the KOSPI serves as a barometer for the South Korean economy, similar to how the S&P 500 functions in the United States.

It refers to the stock composite price index for the KRX main board, and the main board market is called the KOSPI market as well. KOSPI is calculated based on the market capitalization with its base index at 100 on January 4, 1980.

KOSPI = Current Market Capitalization / Base Market Capitalization

The S&P 500 is a stock market index that tracks the performance of 500 of the largest publicly traded companies in the United States. It is widely regarded as one of the best representations of the U.S. stock market and overall economy.

Companies are weighted by their market capitalization, meaning larger companies have a greater impact on the index's movement.

The S&P 500 is commonly used by investors and financial professionals to gauge the overall health of the U.S. stock market and as a benchmark for investment performance.

KOSPI

Korea Composite Stock Price Index

The KOSPI is a representative indicator in the Korean securities market. The KOSPI is a market value weighted index for all of listed common stocks.

종합주가지수(KOSPI)는 증권거래소에 상장된 전종목을 대상으로 산출 발표하는 지수로 1980년 1월 4일의 시가총액을 100으로 하고 비교시점의 시가총액과 비교하여 산출하는 지수이다. 따라서 KOSPI가 현재 1,000포인트라 하면 1980년 1월 4일에 비해 주가가 10배 올랐다는 뜻이다. 또 KOSPI 200 지수는 상장 전 종목 중에서 시장을 대표할 수 있는 우량주 200종목만을 선정하여 1990년 1월 3일을 기준 100으로 하여 산출하는 지수이다.

Base date

January 4, 1980

Base index

100.00

Calculation formula

KOSPI = Current aggregated Market Value / Base aggregated Market Value × 100

DJIA

DOW JONES INDUSTRIAL AVERAGE

The DJIA, introduced in 1896 by Charles H. Dow, is the oldest stock price measure in continuous use. Today, it's the most widely followed measurement of the stock market. The average is comprised of 30 stocks that represent leading companies in major industries. These stocks, widely held by both individual and institutional investors, are all blue-chip companies.

S&P 500 Index

A capitalization weighted index of 500 stocks. The index is a standard by which investors measure the performance of the large cap U.S stock market. The 500 stocks of this index are selected for being a representative sample of leading companies in leading industries. Many money managers index their portfolios to match the S&P 500, so the return on their investments keep pace with the performance of the index.

Riskfree assets

무위험 자산

정기예금, 국공채와 같이 미래 현금흐름이 확정적인 자산을 무위험 자산이라 한다.

The riskless asset has a standard deviation of zero.

Example

Given the following probability distribution,

(%)

Probability	X	Y
0.2	−4	5
0.5	10	5
0.3	26	5

Find σ_{XY}.

Solution

$E(X) = 12$, $E(Y) = 5$

$\sigma_{XY} = 0$

Example

The probability for X=-4 and Y=5 is 0.2.

The probability for X=10 and Y=5 is 0.5.

The probability for X=26 and Y=5 is 0.3.

Find the covariance of X and Y.

Solution

Probability	X	Y
0.2	−4	5
0.5	10	5
0.3	26	5

$E(X)=12,\ E(Y)=5$

$\sigma_{XY}=0$

Example

Express the equation for the line passing through the points (0, 3) and (2, 7).

Solution

y=2x+3

Example

Express the equation for the line passing through the points (0, a) and (b, c).

Solution

$$y=\frac{c-a}{b}x+a$$

CAL

Capital Allocation Line

자본배분선

위험자산과 무위험자산을 결합하여 구성한 포트폴리오의 자취를 그린 직선.

Derivation of CAL

$$E(r_p) = E(wr_f + (1-w)r_i) = wr_f + (1-w)E(r_i)$$

$$\sigma_p = (1-w)\sigma_i$$

$$w = 1 - \frac{\sigma_p}{\sigma_i}$$

$$E(r_p) = r_f + \frac{E(r_i) - r_f}{\sigma_i}\sigma_p$$

The capital allocation line is a line created on a graph of all possible combinations of risk-free and risky assets. The graph displays the return investors might possibly earn by assuming a certain level of risk with their investment. The slope of the CAL is known as the reward-to-variability ratio.

The slope of the CAL measures the trade-off between risk and return. A higher slope means that investors receive a higher expected return in exchange for taking on more risk. The value of this calculation is known as the Sharpe ratio.

Derivation of CAL

To derive the equation for the CAL, we consider a portfolio that combines a risk-free asset and a risky asset with weights w and (1—w), respectively.

The expected return of this portfolio is given by the weighted average of the expected returns of the risk-free asset and the risky asset:

$$E(r_p) = E(wr_f + (1-w)r_i) = wr_f + (1-w)E(r_i)$$

The standard deviation of the portfolio is determined by multiplying the standard deviation of the risky asset by the weight (1—w).

$$\sigma_p = (1-w)\sigma_i$$

The equation can be transformed into an equation for w.

$$w = 1 - \frac{\sigma_p}{\sigma_i}$$

Substitute this expression for w into the equation for $E(r_p)$.

$$E(r_p) = r_f + \frac{E(r_i) - r_f}{\sigma_i}\sigma_p$$

Example

Translate the sentence into an equation: To derive the equation for the CAL, we consider a portfolio that combines a risk-free asset and a risky asset with weights w and (1−w), respectively.

The expected return of this portfolio is given by the weighted average of the expected returns of the risk-free asset and the risky asset.

Solution

$$E(r_p) = E(wr_f + (1-w)r_i) = wr_f + (1-w)E(r_i)$$

Example

Translate the sentence into an equation: To derive the equation for the CAL, we consider a portfolio that combines a risk-free asset and a risky asset with weights w and (1−w), respectively.

The standard deviation of the portfolio is determined by multiplying the standard deviation of the risky asset by the weight (1−w).

Solution

$$\sigma_p = (1-w)\sigma_i$$

Example

Translate the sentence into an equation: To derive the equation for the CAL, we consider a portfolio that combines a risk-free asset and a risky asset with weights w and (1−w), respectively.

The standard deviation of the portfolio is determined by multiplying the standard deviation of the risky asset by the weight (1—w).

The equation can be transformed into an equation for w.

Solution

$$\sigma_p = (1-w)\sigma_i$$

$$w = 1 - \frac{\sigma_p}{\sigma_i}$$

Example

Assume that the return of the Treasury bill is 3%.

The expected return of the stock is 7% and its standard deviation is 2%.

Find the CAL.

Solution

$$E(r_p) = 3 + 2\sigma_p$$

Example

The risk-free asset has a return of 0.03. A risky portfolio, X, has an expected return of 0.07 and a standard deviation of 0.02.

Find the CAL.

Solution

$$E(r_p) - r_f + \frac{E(r_i) - r_f}{\sigma_i}\sigma_p$$

$$E(r_p) = 3 + 2\sigma_p$$

Example

Assume that the return of the Treasury bill is 3%.

The expected return of the stock is 10% and its standard deviation is 20%.

Find the CAL.

Solution

$$E(r_p) = r_f + \frac{E(r_i) - r_f}{\sigma_i}\sigma_p$$

$$E(r_p) = 3 + 0.35\sigma_p$$

Example

Assume that the return of the Treasury bill is 3%.

The expected return of the stock is 10% and its standard deviation is 20%.

Calculate the portfolio expected return and risk if the investor allocated 25% to the risk-free asset and 75% to the risky asset.

Solution

$$E(r_p) = E(wr_f + (1-w)r_i) = wr_f + (1-w)E(r_i)$$

ER of portfolio = $0.25 \times 3 + 0.75 \times 10$ = 0.75 + 7.5 = 8.25%

$$\sigma_p = (1-w)\sigma_i$$

Risk of portfolio = $75\% \times 20 = 15$

Example

The risk-free asset has a return of 0.05. A risky portfolio, X, has an expected return of 0.12 and a standard deviation of 0.20.

Find the CAL.

Solution

$$E(r_p) = r_f + \frac{E(r_i) - r_f}{\sigma_i}\sigma_p$$

$$E(r_p) = 5 + 0.35\sigma_p$$

Example

The risk-free asset has a return of 0.05. A risky portfolio, X, has an expected return of 0.12 and a standard deviation of 0.20. Find the expected return for a portfolio that is 60% X and 40% risk-free asset.

Solution

$E(r_p) = E(wr_f + (1-w)r_i) = wr_f + (1-w)E(r_i)$

$= 0.4 \times 5 + 0.6 \times 12$

$E(r_P) = 9.2\%$

In constructing portfolios, investors often combine risky assets with risk-free assets to reduce risks. A complete portfolio is defined as a combination of a risky asset portfolio, with return Rp, and the risk-free asset, with return Rf.

Example

You invest $20,000 in a portfolio. The portfolio is composed of a risky asset with an expected rate of return of 15% and a standard deviation of 21% and a Treasury bill with a rate of return of 5%. How much money should be invested in the risky asset to form a portfolio with an expected return of 12%?

Solution

$5w + 15(1-w) = 12$

$w = 0.3$

$14,000

Risky assets

주식과 같이 미래 현금흐름이 변동가능한 자산을 위험자산이라 한다.

Example

Suppose you hold a risk free asset worth $1,000 which returns 4% each year. This means that you get a return of $40 each year, year after year.

The risky asset, on the other hand, will give you a return that varies from year to year.

Tobin's Two-fund Separation

When the risk-free asset is introduced, all investors prefer to move from their originally optimal portfolios to a combination of the risk-free asset and the market portfolio. Alternatively stated, combinations of the risk-free asset and the market portfolio dominate all other assets and portfolios.

Utility Theory

In the context of investments, "utility" typically refers to the satisfaction or happiness that an investor derives from their investment choices. Utility theory is a concept from finance that aims to quantify and understand the preferences and decision-making of individuals based on their satisfaction.

The utility of an investment can be calculated as:

Utility = $E(r) - 0.5A\sigma^2$

where:

A = measure of risk aversion

Utility Score = Expected Return $-0.5A\sigma^2$

where A is the risk aversion coefficient (a number proportionate to the amount of risk aversion of the investor). It is positive for a risk-averse investor, zero for a risk-neutral investor, and negative for a risk seeker.

A: aversion index, larger A is, the more compensation is needed for an increase in risk

Example

A person is given the choice between two scenarios, one with a guaranteed payoff and one without. In the guaranteed scenario, the person receives $50. In the uncertain scenario, a coin is flipped to decide whether the person receives $100 or nothing.

A person is said to be:

risk averse - if they would accept a certain payment of less than $50, rather than taking the gamble and possibly receiving nothing.

risk neutral - if they are indifferent between the bet and a certain $50 payment.

risk loving - if they would accept the bet even when the guaranteed payment is more than $50.

Example

Utility Score = Expected Return $- 0.5A\sigma^2$

An investor's risk aversion coefficient is 2.

What should the investor choose, the 4% risk-free investment, or XYZ stock with an expected return of 12% and a standard deviation of 25%?

Solution

His utility score of XYZ stock is equal to 5.75%

U=$12\% - 0.25^2 = 5.75\%$

The investor will invest in XYZ stock.

For the risk-free investment, the risk-free return is 4%, and the variance is zero. i.e. U = 4%.

He would choose the risky investment.

U=$12\% - 0.25^2 = 5.75\%$

vs. 4% for the risk-free return.

Derivation of Capital Market Line

A portfolio consisting of w% invested in risk-free asset and $(1-w)$% in the market portfolio will have the following mean and standard deviation:

$$E(R_p) = wE(R_f) + (1-w)E(R_m) = wR_f + (1-w)E(R_m)$$

$$\sigma_p^2 = w^2\sigma_f^2 + (1-w)^2\sigma_m^2 + 2w(1-w)\sigma_{mf}$$

$$\sigma_f^2 = 0, \qquad \sigma_{mf} = 0$$

$$\sigma_p^2 = (1-w)^2\sigma_m^2$$

$$w = 1 - \frac{\sigma_p}{\sigma_m}$$

$$E(R_p) = (1 - \frac{\sigma_p}{\sigma_m})R_f + \frac{\sigma_p}{\sigma_m}E(R_m)$$

$$E(r_p) = r_f + \frac{E(r_m) - r_f}{\sigma_m}\sigma_p$$

Derivation of Capital Market Line

투자자금의 일부 w를 무위험자산에 투자하고 나머지 $(1-w)$를 시장포트폴리오에 투자하여 구성한 포트폴리오의 기대수익률과 분산은 다음과 같다.

$$E(R_p) = wE(R_f) + (1-w)E(R_m) = wR_f + (1-w)E(R_m)$$

$$\sigma_p^2 = w^2\sigma_f^2 + (1-w)^2\sigma_m^2 + 2w(1-w)\sigma_{mf}$$

R_f 는 상수이므로, $\sigma_f^2 = 0, \quad \sigma_{mf} = 0$

$$\sigma_p^2 = (1-w)^2\sigma_m^2$$

$$w = 1 - \frac{\sigma_p}{\sigma_m}$$

$$E(R_p) = (1 - \frac{\sigma_p}{\sigma_m})R_f + \frac{\sigma_p}{\sigma_m}E(R_m)$$

$$E(r_p) = r_f + \frac{E(r_m) - r_f}{\sigma_m}\sigma_p$$

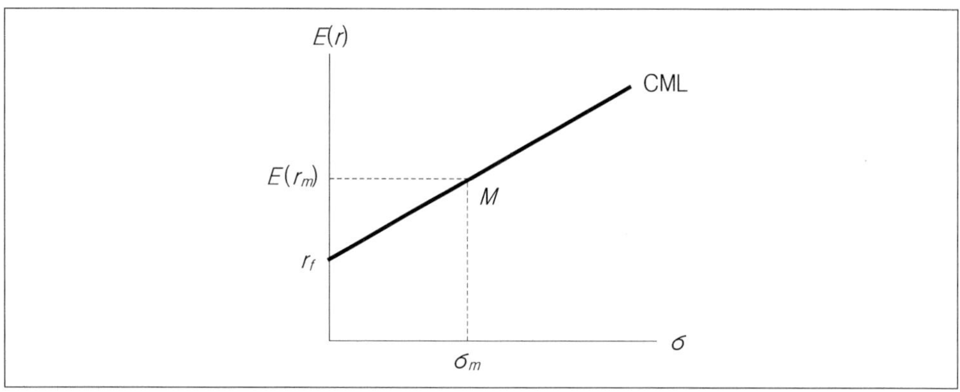

CML을 도출하기 위하여는 투자자금의 일부를 무위험자산에 투자하고 나머지를 시장포트폴리오에 투자하여 구성한 포트폴리오의 기대수익률과 분산을 설정한 후, 매개변수 w를 소거한다.

Example

Risk-free rate is 5% and the expected return on the market is 12%.

The market index has a standard deviation of 10.6%.

Find the CML.

Solution

$E(r_m) = 12\%, \qquad \sigma_m = 10.6$

$$E(R_p) = R_f + \frac{E(R_m) - R_f}{\sigma_m}\sigma_p$$

$$E(R_p) = 5 + \frac{12 - 5}{10.6}\sigma_p$$

$$E(R_p) = 5 + 0.66\sigma_p$$

Lending portfolio

대출 포트폴리오.
보유자금의 일부를 무위험자산에 대출하고 나머지는 시장 포트폴리오에 투자함으로써 구성된 포트폴리오를 대출 포트폴리오라 한다.

An investor holds a positive proportion of the two funds if the tangency between an indifference curve and the capital market line lies between the two funds.

Example

Risk-free rate is 5% and the expected return on the market is 12%.
The market index has a standard deviation of 10.6%.
Suppose you decide to invest 1,000 thousand won in a portfolio of Risk-free asset (200 thousand won) and Market Portfolio (800 thousand won).
Find the expected return and the standard deviation of your portfolio.

Solution

$E(r_m) = 12\%, \quad \sigma_m = 10.6$

$$E(R_p) = \frac{1}{5} \times 5 + \frac{4}{5} \times 12 = 10.6$$

$$E(R_p) = 5 + 0.66\sigma_p$$

$$10.6 = 5 + 0.66\sigma_p$$

$$\sigma_p = 8.48$$

Example

Risk-free rate is 10% and the expected return on the market is 18%.

The market index has a standard deviation of 20%.

Suppose you decide to invest 1,000 thousand won in a portfolio of Risk-free asset (400 thousand won) and Market Portfolio (600 thousand won).

Find the expected return and the standard deviation of your portfolio.

Solution

$E(R_p) = 0.4 \times 10 + 0.6 \times 18 = 14.8\%$

$$E(R_p) = R_f + \frac{E(R_m) - R_f}{\sigma_m}\sigma_p$$

$E(r_p) = 10 + 0.4\sigma_p$

$14.8 = 10 + 0.4\sigma_p$

$\sigma_p = 12\ (\%)$

Borrowing portfolio

차입 포트폴리오.

무위험자산을 차입하여 보유자금과 합쳐서 시장 포트폴리오에 투자함으로써 구성된 포트폴리오를 차입 포트폴리오라 한다.

An investor borrows at the risk-free rate and invests in the market portfolio if the tangency between an indifference curve and the capital market line lies to the right of the two funds.

Example

Risk-free rate is 5% and the expected return on the market is 12%.

The market index has a standard deviation of 10.6%.

Suppose you borrow 200 thousand won at the risk-free rate and invest 1,200 thousand won in Market Portfolio.

Find the expected return and the standard deviation of your portfolio.

Solution

$E(r_m) = 12\%, \quad \sigma_m = 10.6$

$$E(r_p) = \left(-\frac{1}{5}\right) \times r_f + \frac{6}{5} \times E(r_m)$$

$E(r_p) = 13.4\%$

$$E(r_p) = r_f + \frac{E(r_m) - r_f}{\sigma_m} \sigma_p$$

$E(r_p) = 5 + 0.66\sigma_p$

$13.4 = 5 + 0.66\sigma_p$

$\sigma_p = 12.7$

Example

시장 포트폴리오의 기대수익률이 18%, 표준편차가 20%이며, 무위험이자율이 10%인 경우, 1,000천원을 가지고 있는 투자자가 무위험 이자율로 400천원을 차입하여 1,400천원을 시장 포트폴리오에 투자하여 구성한 포트폴리오의 기대수익률과 표준편차를 구하라.

Solution

$E(R_p) = (-0.4) \times 10 + 1.4 \times 18 = 21.2\%$

$$E(R_p) = R_f + \frac{E(R_m) - R_f}{\sigma_m}\sigma_p$$

$$21.2 = 10 + \frac{18 - 10}{20}\sigma_p$$

$\sigma_p = 28\,(\%)$

Example

시장 포트폴리오의 기대수익률이 18%, 표준편차가 20%이며, 무위험이자율이 8%인 경우, 100만원을 가지고 있는 투자자가 무위험 이자율로 80만원을 차입하여 180만원을 시장 포트폴리오에 투자하여 구성한 포트폴리오의 기대수익률과 표준편차를 구하라.

Solution

$E(R_p) = (-0.8) \times 8 + 1.8 \times 18 = 26\%$

$$E(R_p) = R_f + \frac{E(R_m) - R_f}{\sigma_m}\sigma_p$$

$$26 = 8 + \frac{18 - 8}{20}\sigma_p$$

$\sigma_p = 36\,(\%)$

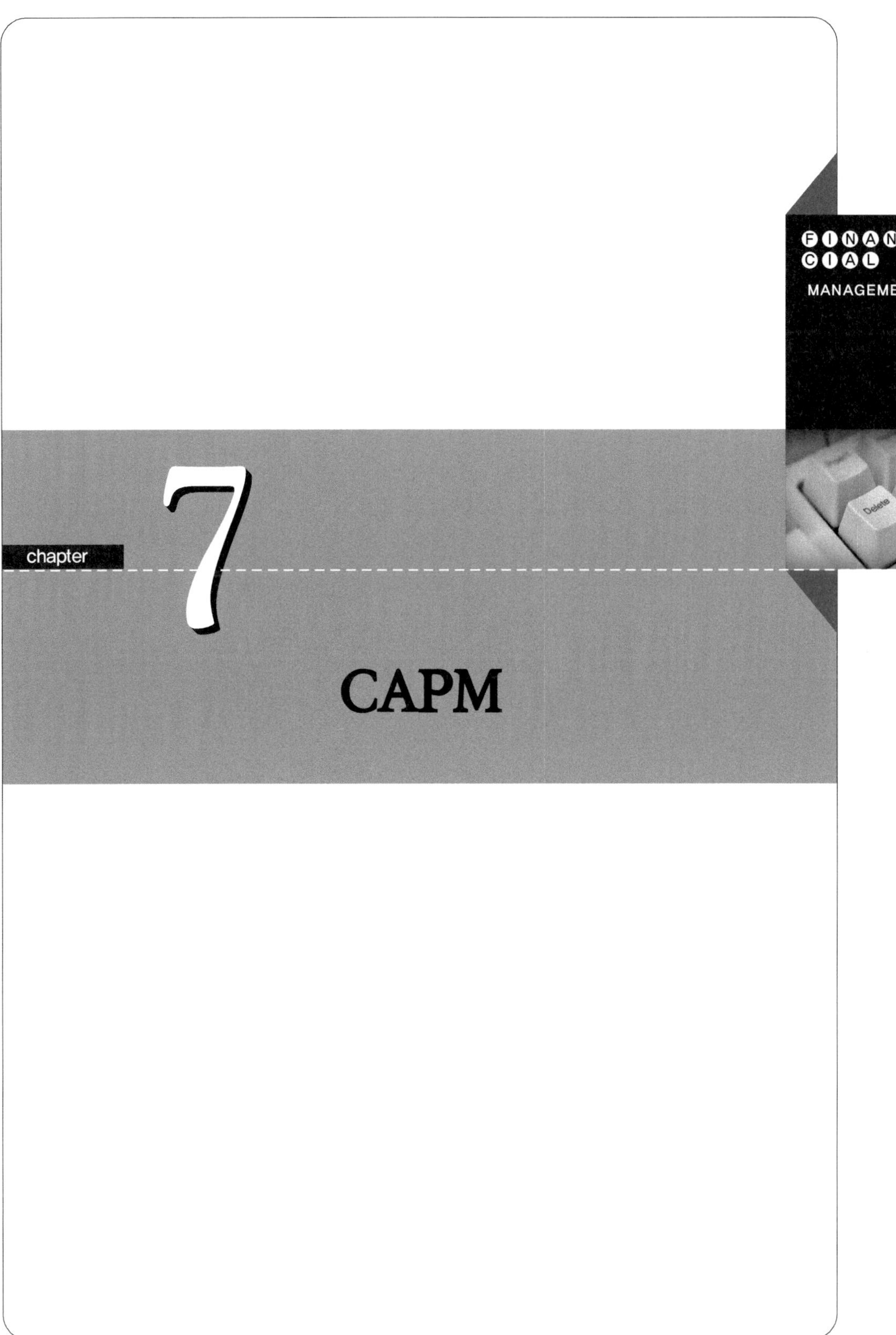

chapter

7

CAPM

CAPM

자본자산가격결정모형(capital asset pricing model : CAPM).

An equilibrium asset pricing theory that shows that equilibrium rates of expected return on all risky assets are a function of their covariance with the market portfolio.

자본자산가격 결정모형이란 시장이 균형상태를 이룰 때 자본자산의 가격이 어떻게 결정되는가를 설명하는 모형이다. 자본자산(capital asset)이란 미래의 수익을 얻을 수 있는 권리를 갖는 자산을 말하며, 주식 사채 등의 유가증권을 가리킨다.

The CAPM predicts that security rates of return will be linearly related to a single common factor, the rate of return on the market portfolio.

SML

Graphical representation of the expected return-beta relationship of the CAPM.

증권시장선(security market line : SML)

The line on a graph that shows the relationship between risk as measured by beta and the required rate of return for individual securities.

$$E(r_i) = r_f + \{E(r_m) - r_f\}\beta_i$$

$$\begin{matrix} Required\ return \\ on\ Stock\ i \end{matrix} = Riskfree\ rate + [Market\ risk\ premium](Stock\ i's\ \beta)$$

$$\beta_i = \frac{Cov(r_i, r_m)}{\sigma_m^2}$$

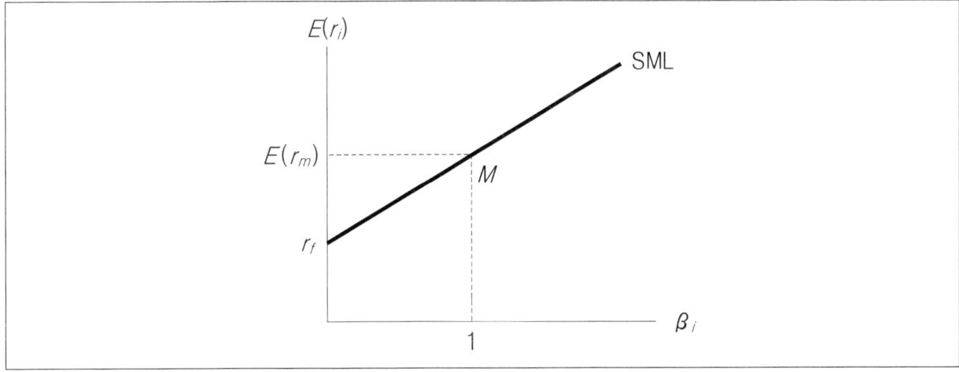

Beta

A measure of the extent to which the returns on a given stock move with the stock market.

β is the sensitivity of the share price on market movements.

Market premium & Risk premium

$E(r_m) - r_f$: Market premium.

The market risk premium is the difference between the expected return on a market portfolio and the risk-free rate.

$\{E(r_m) - r_f\}\beta_i$: Risk premium.

Example

Risk-free rate is 5% and the expected return on the market is 12%.

Find the SML.

Solution

$E(r_m) = 12\%$

$E(r_i) = r_f + \{E(r_m) - r_f\}\beta_i$

$E(r_i) = 5 + 7\beta_i$

Example

The market has a 30% probability of giving a 26% return, a 50% probability of generating a 10% return, and a 20% probability of resulting in a 4% loss.

Risk-free rate is 5%.

Find the SML.

Solution

$E(r_m) = 12\%$

$E(r_i) = r_f + \{E(r_m) - r_f\}\beta_i$

$E(r_i) = 5 + 7\beta_i$

Example

Risk-free rate is 5% and the expected return on the market is 12%. What's the expected return of a stock with beta of 0.9?

Solution

$E(r_i) = 5 + 7\beta_i$

$E(r_i) = 11.3\%$

Example

Risk-free rate is 5% and the expected return on the market is 12%. What's the expected return of a stock with beta of 1.5?

Solution

$E(r_i) = 5 + 7\beta_i$

$E(r_i) = 15.5\%$

Example

Risk-free rate is 5% and the expected return on the market is 12%.

The current price of a stock is 30,000 won.

What's the expected price of a stock with beta of 1.5?

Solution

$$E(r_i) = 5 + 7\beta_i$$

$$E(r_i) = 15.5\%$$

$$\frac{E(P) - 30{,}000}{30{,}000} = 0.155$$

$$E(P) = 34{,}650$$

Example

Risk-free rate is 6% and the expected return on the market is 17%.

The current price of a stock is 30,000 won.

What's the expected price of a stock with beta of 0.4?

Solution

$$E(r_i) = 6 + 11\beta_i$$

$$E(r_i) = 10.4\ (\%)$$

$$\frac{E(P) - 30{,}000}{30{,}000} = 0.104$$

$$E(P) = 33{,}120$$

Example

Given the following market return,

(%)

Probability	Market Return
0.5	5
0.5	15

$r_f = 4\%$.

Find the SML.

Solution

$E(r_i) = 4 + 6\beta_i$

Example

The market has a 50% probability of giving a 5% return and a 50% probability of generating a 15% return.

Risk-free rate is 4%.

Find the SML.

Solution

$E(r_i) = 4 + 6\beta_i$

Example

The market has a 50% probability of giving a 5% return and a 50% probability of generating a 15% return.

Risk-free rate is 4%.

What's the expected return of a stock with beta of 1.5?

Solution

$E(r_i) = 4 + 6\beta_i$

13%

Example

다음 표를 보고 증권시장선의 방정식을 구하라. 무위험 수익률은 6%이다.

상태	확률	시장수익률
1	0.1	−0.15
2	0.3	0.05
3	0.4	0.15
4	0.2	0.2

Solution

$E(r_m) = 10\%$

$E(r_i) = 6 + 4\beta_i$

Example

Risk-free rate is 5% and expected return on the market is 12%.

What's the expected return of a stock with beta of 0.8?

Solution

$E(r_i) = r_f + \{E(r_m) - r_f\}\beta_i$

$E(r_i) = 5 + 7 \times 0.8$

$E(r_i) = 10.6\%$

Example

시장포트폴리오의 기대수익률이 12%이며 무위험자산의 수익률이 5%인 경우에 K기업 주식의 베타계수가 0.8로 측정되었다면, K기업 주식의 기대수익률은?

Solution

$E(r_i) = r_f + \{E(r_m) - r_f\}\beta_i$

$E(r_i) = 5 + 7 \times 0.8$

$E(r_i) = 10.6\%$

Example

시장포트폴리오의 기대수익률이 18%이며 무위험자산의 수익률이 10%인 경우에 관악기업 주식의 베타계수가 1.2로 측정되었다면, 관악기업 주식의 기대수익률은?

Solution

$E(r_i) = r_f + \{E(r_m) - r_f\}\beta_i$

$E(r_i) = 19.6\%$

Example

시장포트폴리오의 기대수익률이 10%이며 무위험자산의 수익률이 4%인 경우에 서울기업 주식의 베타계수가 1.5로 측정되었다면, 서울기업 주식의 기대수익률은?

Solution

$E(r_i) = 4 + 6\beta_i$

$E(r_i) = 13\%$

Example

시장포트폴리오의 기대수익률이 10%이며 무위험자산의 수익률이 4%인 경우에 서울기업 주식의 베타계수가 1.5로 측정되었다면, 현재주가가 50,000원인 서울기업 주식의 기대가격은?

Solution

$E(r_i) = 4 + 6\beta_i$

$E(r_i) = 13\%$

$E(P) = 56,500$

β의 크기와 자산의 성격

If $\beta_i = 0$, we have the risk-free asset.
If $\beta_i = 1$, we have the market portfolio.

The market portfolio has a beta of one because the covariance of the market portfolio with itself is identical to the variance of the market portfolio:

$$\beta_i = \frac{Cov(R_i, R_m)}{\sigma_m^2}$$

$$\beta_m = \frac{Cov(R_m, R_m)}{\sigma_m^2} = \frac{\sigma_m^2}{\sigma_m^2} = 1$$

If $\beta_i = 2$, we have an asset two times as risky as the market portfolio.
If $\beta_i = 0.5$, we have an asset half as risky as the market portfolio.

Example

Prove $Cov(X, X) = Var(X)$.

Solution

$$Cov(X, X) = E(X - E(X))(X - E(X))$$
$$Cov(X, X) = Var(X)$$

Example

Prove $Cov(X, 2X) = 2Var(X)$.

Solution

$$Cov(X, 2X) = E(X - E(X))(2X - 2E(X))$$
$$= 2E(X - E(X))(X - E(X))$$
$$Cov(X, 2X) = 2Var(X)$$

Example

Prove $Cov\left(X, \frac{1}{2}X\right) = \frac{1}{2}Var(X)$

Solution

$$Cov(X, 2X) = E(X - E(X))\left(\frac{1}{2}X - \frac{1}{2}E(X)\right)$$
$$= \frac{1}{2}E(X - E(X))(X - E(X))$$
$$Cov\left(X, \frac{1}{2}X\right) = \frac{1}{2}Var(X)$$

Single index model: purely statistical regression model.

In the single index model, we explain a stock's return using one common factor: the market index.

$$R_i = \alpha_i + \beta_i R_M + \epsilon_i$$

R_i : excess return of stock i $(r_i - r_f)$

R_M : excess return of the market index

β_i : sensitivity to the market

ϵ_i : firm-specific shock

Example

You observe the following statistics for Stock A and the market index:

Covariance between Stock A's returns and the market returns: 18

Variance of the market returns: 12

Calculate the beta of Stock A.

$\beta_A = 1.5$

Stock A has a beta of 1.5, meaning it is 50% more volatile than the market.

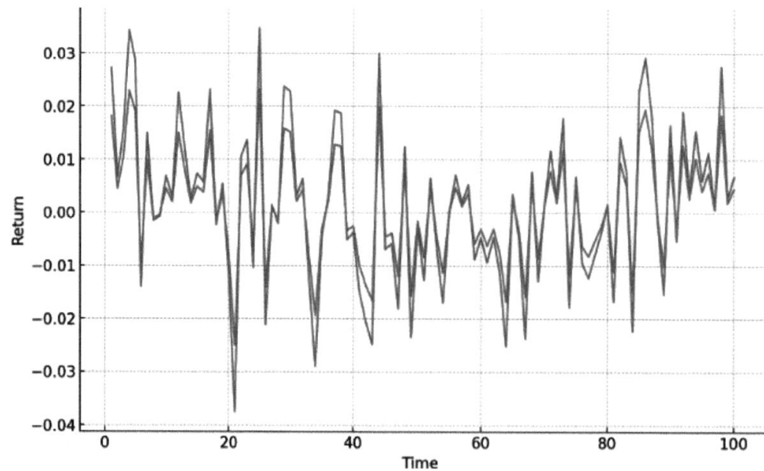

Beta = 2 return simulation graph

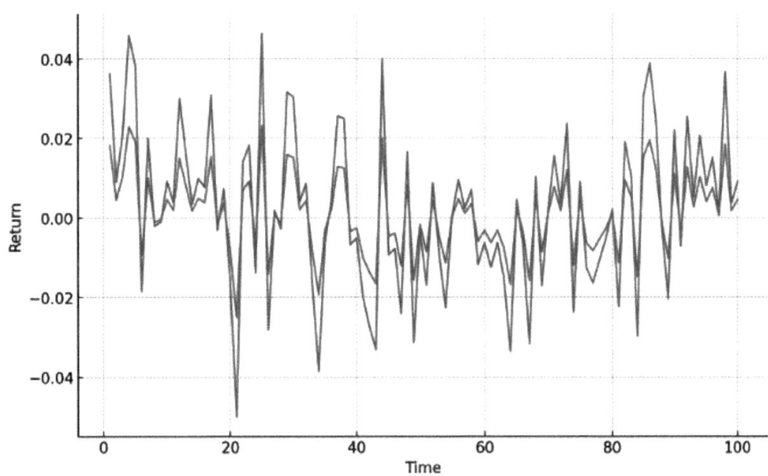

Beta = 3 return simulation graph

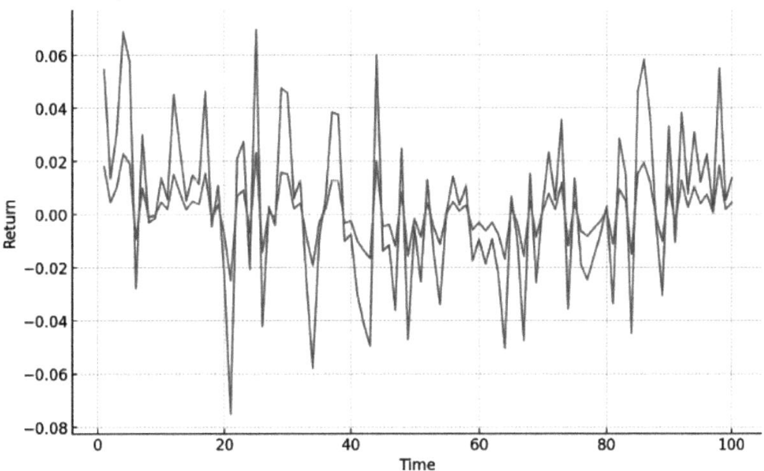

Example

Given the following data,

(%)

Probability	Market Return	Security X
0.2	−4	−8
0.5	10	20
0.3	26	52

Find β_X.

Solution

$E(r_m) = 12\%,\quad E(r_X) = 24\%$

$\sigma_m = \sqrt{112},\quad \sigma_X = \sqrt{448}$

$\beta_i = \dfrac{Cov(r_i, r_m)}{\sigma_m^2}$

$Cov(r_X, r_m) = 224$

$\beta_X = 2.$

Example

Given the following data,

(%)

Probability	Market Return	Security Y
0.2	−4	−2
0.5	10	5
0.3	26	13

Find β_Y.

Solution

$E(r_m) = 12\%,\quad E(r_Y) = 6\%$

$\sigma_m = \sqrt{112},\quad \sigma_Y = \sqrt{28}$

$\beta_i = \dfrac{Cov(r_i, r_m)}{\sigma_m^2}$

$Cov(r_Y, r_m) = 56$

$\beta_Y = 0.5.$

Example

Given the following data,

(%)

Probability	Market Return	Security X
0.5	5	7
0.5	10	14

Find β_X.

Solution

$\beta_X = 1.4$

Aggressive asset

$\beta > 1$

자산의 수익률 변동이 시장수익률 변동보다 크게 나타난다.

Defensive asset

$\beta < 1$

자산의 수익률 변동이 시장수익률 변동보다 작게 나타난다.

Under-priced or Over-priced Stock

시장이 균형상태일 때 각 개별증권의 β_i가 결정되면 각 개별증권의 기대수익률이 SML 상에 놓이게 되도록 가격이 결정된다.

그런데, 만약 SML 상에 놓이지 못한 증권 U가 존재할 경우, 증권 U는 증권 U의 위험수준에 비하여 기대수익률이 너무 높은 상태로 가격이 과소평가(under-priced)되어 있으므로 증권 U에 대한 수요가 증가하여 증권 U의 가격이 상승하게 된다. 그 결과 증권 U의 가격은 기대수익률이 U'에 이를 때까지 상승하게 되어 균형을 이루게 된다.

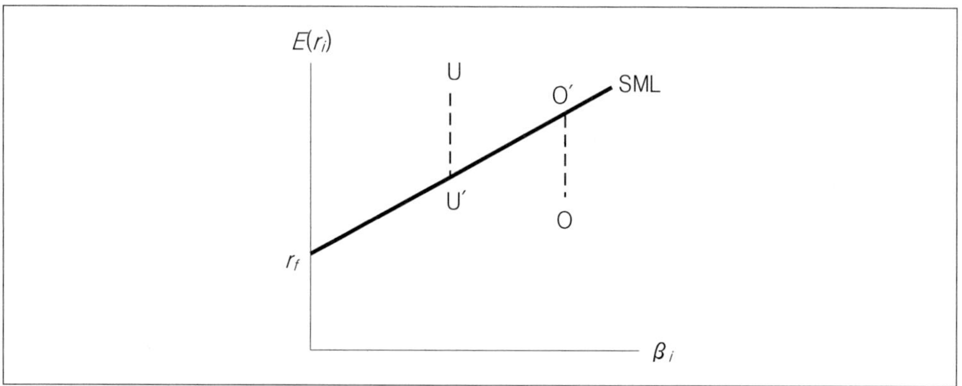

만약 SML 상에 놓이지 못한 증권 O가 존재할 경우, 증권 O는 증권 O의 위험수준에 비하여 기대수익률이 너무 낮은 상태로 가격이 과대평가(overpriced)되어 있으므로 증권 O에 대한 수요가 감소하여 증권 O의 가격이 하락하게 된다. 그 결과 증권 O의 가격은 기대수익률이 O'에 이를 때까지 하락하게 되어 균형을 이루게 된다.

Example

Given the following data on the market and security X:

(%)

Probability	Market Return	Security X
0.2	−4	−8
0.5	10	20
0.3	26	52

$r_f = 5\%$. $E(P) = 30{,}000$.

Provide an evaluation of the investment performance of security X.

Solution

$\sigma_m = 10.6,\ \ \sigma_X = 21.2$

$$\beta_i = \frac{Cov(r_i, r_m)}{\sigma_m^2}$$

$E(r_m) = 12\%,\ \ E(r_X) = 24\%$

$\beta_X = 2$

SML

$E(r_i) = r_f + \{E(r_m) - r_f\}\beta_i$

$E(r_i) = 5 + 7\beta_i$

$E(r_X) = 19\%$

$\frac{30{,}000 - P_0}{P_0} = 0.24$, $P_0 = 24{,}194$, Under-priced.

$\frac{30{,}000 - P_0}{P_0} = 0.19$, $P_0 = 25{,}210$

Example

Given the following data on the market and security Y:

(%)

Probability	Market Return	Security Y
0.2	−4	−2
0.5	10	5
0.3	26	13

$r_f = 5\%$. $E(P) = 30{,}000$.

Provide an evaluation of the investment performance of security Y.

Solution

$\sigma_m = 10.6, \quad \sigma_Y = 5.3$

$$\beta_i = \frac{Cov(r_i, r_m)}{\sigma_m^2}$$

$E(r_m) = 12\%, \quad E(r_Y) = 6\%$

$\beta_Y = 0.5$

SML

$E(r_i) = r_f + \{E(r_m) - r_f\}\beta_i$

$E(r_i) = 5 + 7\beta_i$

$E(r_Y) = 8.5\%$

$\frac{30{,}000 - P_0}{P_0} = 0.06$, $P_0 = 28{,}302$, Over-priced.

$\frac{30{,}000 - P_0}{P_0} = 0.085$, $P_0 = 27{,}650$

Example

10개의 투자대상에 천만원씩 1억원을 투자한 포트폴리오가 있다. 현재 포트폴리오의 β는 1.64이다. β가 2.0인 주식을 매각하고 β가 0.6인 주식을 매입한 경우, 새로운 포트폴리오의 β는 얼마인가?

Solution

$$\frac{1}{10}2+\sum_{i=1}^{9}\left(\frac{1}{10}\beta_i\right)=1.64$$

$$\frac{1}{10}0.6+\sum_{i=1}^{9}\left(\frac{1}{10}\beta_i\right)=x$$

$$x=1.5$$

Example

10개의 투자대상에 천만원씩 1억원을 투자한 포트폴리오가 있다. 현재 포트폴리오의 β는 1.64이다. β가 2.0인 주식을 매각하고 새로운 주식을 매입하니 새로운 포트폴리오의 β는 1.5가 되었다. 새로운 주식의 β는 얼마인가?

Solution

$$\frac{1}{10}2+\sum_{i=1}^{9}\left(\frac{1}{10}\beta_i\right)=1.64$$

$$\frac{1}{10}x+\sum_{i=1}^{9}\left(\frac{1}{10}\beta_i\right)=1.5$$

$$x=0.6$$

Single-factor model

Suppose that we summarize all relevant economic factors by one macroeconomic indicator. We further assume that, beyond this common effect, all remaining uncertainty in stock returns is firm specific.

We can summarize the distinction between macroeconomic and firm-specific factors.

$r_i = E(r_i) + m_i + \varepsilon_i$

where r_i: the holding period return on security i

$E(r_i)$: the expected return on the security as of the beginning of the holding period

m_i: the impact of unanticipated macro events on the security's return

ε_i: the impact of unanticipated firm-specific events

$E(m_i) = 0$

$E(\varepsilon_i) = 0$

If we denote the unanticipated components of the macro factor by F, and denote the responsiveness of security i to macro events by b_i, then

$m_i = b_i F$.

$r_i = E(r_i) + b_i F + \varepsilon_i$

This is known as a single-factor model.

A single-factor model classifies sources of uncertainty as systematic factors or firm-specific factors.

Single-index model

It uses the market index to proxy for the systematic factor.

$$Z_i = \alpha_i + \beta_i Z_M + \varepsilon_i$$

where $Z_i = r_i - r_f$

α_i: the stock's expected return if $(r_M - r_f) = 0$.

$Z_M = r_M - r_f$

$$r_i - r_f = \alpha_i + \beta_i (r_M - r_f) + \varepsilon_i$$

ϵ_i is defined as firm specific, that is, independent of movements in the market.

$$Cov(r_M, \epsilon_i) = 0$$

Since α_i is a constant,

$$\sigma_i^2 = \beta_i^2 \sigma_M^2 + Var(\varepsilon_i).$$

$\beta_i^2 \sigma_M^2$: The variance attributable to the uncertainty of the common macroeconomic factor

$Var(\varepsilon_i)$: The variance attributable to firm-specific uncertainty

The index model assumes that the macro factor can be represented by a broad index of stock returns.

$$Cov(Z_i, Z_j) = Cov(\alpha_i + \beta_i Z_M + \varepsilon_i, \alpha_j + \beta_j Z_M + \varepsilon_j)$$

$$= Cov(\beta_i Z_M, \beta_j Z_M) = \beta_i \beta_j \sigma_M^2$$

R–square

The R-square gives the fraction of the variance of the dependent variable that is explained by movements in the independent variable.

The R-square is systematic variance over total variance, which tells us what fraction of a firm's volatility is attributable to market movements:

$$R^2 = \frac{\beta^2 \sigma_M^2}{\sigma^2}$$

Example

Consider the results of an index model regression where the R-squared is 0.576 and the residual standard deviation is 10.3%. What is the standard deviation of the asset's returns?

Solution

$$R^2 = \frac{\beta^2 \sigma_M^2}{\sigma^2} = 1 - \frac{Var(\epsilon_i)}{\sigma_i^2}$$

$$0.576 = 1 - \frac{10.3^2}{\sigma_i^2}$$

$$\sigma_i = 15.82$$

Sharpe's measure

샤프척도

$$\frac{\overline{r_p} - \overline{r_f}}{\sigma_p}$$

RVAR : reward to variability ratio

The Sharpe ratio was developed by Nobel laureate William F. Sharpe and is used to help investors understand the return of an investment compared to its risk. The ratio is the average return earned in excess of the risk-free rate per unit of volatility or total risk. Volatility is a measure of the price fluctuations of an asset or portfolio.

Treynor's measure

$$\frac{\overline{r_p} - r_f}{\beta_p}$$

RVOL: reward to volatility ratio

Jensen's measure

$$\overline{r_p} - \left[\overline{r_f} - \left(\overline{r_m} - \overline{r_f}\right)\beta_p\right]$$

Adjusted closing price

Adjusted closing price is a financial term referring to a stock's closing price on a particular day, which has been modified to account for corporate actions that could affect the stock's value. Its purpose is to provide a clear picture of the stock's true value and help make informed investment decisions.

A dividend payment represents a distribution of the company's earnings to shareholders, effectively reducing the company's total value.
To reflect this reduction in value, the stock's price is adjusted downward by the exact amount of the dividend payment.

Adjusted closing price after a dividend payout

Company ABC's closing price at the end of the day is $500. Following, the company distributes a $10 dividend per share. The corporate action will affect the closing price, and therefore, an adjusted closing price will be calculated. In such a case, the calculation would be $500 – $10 to equal an adjusted closing price of $490.

Adjusted closing price after a stock split

For example, a company's board of directors may decide to split the company's stock 3-for-1. Therefore, the company's shares outstanding increase by a multiple of three, while its share price is divided by three. Suppose a stock closed at $300 the day before its stock split. In this case, the closing price is adjusted to $100 per share to maintain a consistent standard of comparison.

Example

Suppose a company's shares sell for $40 and they undergo a 2-for-1 stock split. You'd use the split ratio, which is 2-to-1 in this case, to determine the adjusted closing value. The stock's closing price would be $40, while its adjusted closing price would be $20.

Degrees of freedom (DOF)

The number of items in a sample that are free to vary.

In statistics, the number of degrees of freedom is the number of values in the final calculation of a statistic that are free to vary.

The degree of freedom is defined as the number of variables that are free to vary in a statistical setting. In statistical testing, degrees of freedom refer to the number of values in a sample that are free to vary without changing the number of samples or observations.

df = $n-1$

n = sample size

Example

Suppose there are two items in a sample, and we know the mean. We are free to specify only one of the two values because the other value is automatically determined. If the mean is 6, we are free to choose only one value. Choosing 4 makes the other value 8. So there is 1 degree of freedom in this illustration.

Example

Consider a data sample consisting of five positive integers. The values of the five integers must have an average of six. If four items within the data set are {3, 8, 5, and 4}, the fifth number must be 10. Because the first four numbers can be chosen at random, the degree of freedom is four.

Example

Pick a set of numbers that have a mean of 10.

Some sets of numbers you might pick: 9, 10, 11 or 8, 10, 12 or 5, 10, 15.

Once you have chosen the first two numbers in the set, the third is fixed. In other words, you can't choose the third item in the set. The only numbers that are free to vary are the first two. You can pick 9 + 10 or 5 + 15, but once you've made that decision you must choose a particular number that will give you the mean you are looking for. So degrees of freedom for a set of three numbers is TWO.

Example

Consider the following set of data:

Weights of 5 items in a box weighing 12KG = {4, 2.5, 3.5, 1, 1}

There are 5 items in the box with four degrees of freedom. This means that only four items are free to vary in terms of weights because the weight of fifth item must be equal to difference between 12 KG and sum of weights of four items.

Example

Suppose there are two items in a sample, and we know the mean. We are free to specify only one of the two values because the other value is automatically determined.

If the mean is 6, we are free to choose only one value. Choosing 3 makes the other value 9. So there is 1 degree of freedom in this illustration.

Example

If the mean of two numbers is 6, and one of the numbers is 3, what is the other number?

Solution

9

Population Mean

$$\mu = \frac{\sum_{i=1}^{N} x_i}{N}$$

N is the number of terms in the population.

Sample Mean

$$\bar{x} = \frac{\sum_{i=1}^{n} x_i}{n}$$

n is the number of terms in the sample.

A population is a collection of persons, objects or items of interest.

A sample is a portion of the whole and, if properly taken, is representative of the whole.

Sample variance

The sample variance, s^2, is used to calculate how varied a sample is. A sample is a select number of items taken from a population.

Example

You are given the following three data points from a sample:

3, 5, 7

Calculate the sample variance.

Solution

Sample size (n):

n=3

Sample mean :

$\overline{X}$ =5

Sum of squared deviations:

4+0+4=8

Sample variance formula:

$$s^2 = \frac{\sum(x_i - \overline{X})^2}{n-1}$$

$$s^2 = 4$$

Historical Variance

A stock's historical variance measures the difference between the stock's returns for different periods and its average return.

$$\sigma_H^2 = \sum_{t=1}^{n} \frac{(r_t - \overline{r_t})^2}{n-1}$$

Example

Let's say returns for stock in Company ABC are 10% in Year 1, 20% in Year 2, and −15% in Year 3.

Calculate the Sum of Squared Deviations.

Solution

$\overline{r_t} = 5\%$

The differences between each return and the average are 5%, 15%, and −20% for each consecutive year.

Squaring these deviations yields 25, 225, and 400, respectively. If we add these squared deviations, we get a total of 650.

$\sum(r_t - \overline{r_t})^2 = 650$

Example

Let's say returns for stock in Company ABC are 10% in Year 1, 20% in Year 2, and −15% in Year 3. Find the historical variance.

Solution

$\overline{r_t} = 5\%$

The average of these three returns is 5%. The differences between each return and the average are 5%, 15%, and −20% for each consecutive year.

Squaring these deviations yields 25, 225, and 400, respectively. If we add these squared deviations, we get a total of 650.

$\sum(r_t - \overline{r_t})^2 = 650$

When you divide the sum of 650 by one less the number of returns in the data set, as this is a sample, it gives us a variance of 325.

Example

You've observed the following returns on K stock over the past five years: 2 percent, −12 percent, 16 percent, 22 percent, and 18 percent. What is the historical variance of these returns?

Solution

Average = (2 − 12 + 16 + 22 + 18)/5 = 9.2%

$$\text{Variance} = \frac{1}{4}\{(2-9.2)^2+(-12-9.2)^2+(16-9.2)^2+(22-9.2)^2+(18-9.2)^2\}$$

$$= 197.2$$

Example

Suppose a data set is given as 3, 21, 98, 17, and 9. The mean of the data set is 29.6. The mean is subtracted from each data point and the summation of the square of the resulting values is taken. This gives 6043.2. To get the sample variance, this number is divided by one less than the total number of observations. Thus, the sample variance is 1510.8.

$$\sum_{i=1}^{5}\left(x_i-\overline{x}\right)^2 = 6043.2$$

Example

You've observed the following returns: 25 percent, 10 percent, 3 percent, 15 percent and 17 percent. What is the historical variance of these returns?

Solution

Add together the historical annual returns. Divide your result by the number of years of returns to calculate the historical average annual return. In this example, add 25, 10, 3, 15 and 17 to get 70. Divide 70 by 5 years of returns to get an average annual return of 14 percent.

Subtract the average annual return from each actual annual return to calculate the difference between each actual return and the average return. In this example, subtract 14 from 25 to get 11. Subtract the average return from each remaining annual return to get −4, −11, 1 and 3.

Calculate the square of each difference. In this example, square 11 to get 121. Square each of the remaining results to get 16, 121, 1 and 9.

Add together each result. In this example, add 121, 16, 121, 1 and 9 to get 268.

Subtract 1 from the number of years of returns. In this example, subtract 1 from 5 to get 4.

Continuing with the example, divide 268 by 4 to get 67.

Example

You've observed the following returns: 11.54%, 5.46%, and -2%.

Calculate the historical variance of these annual returns.

Solution

Add 11.54 plus 5.46 minus 2 to get 15 percent. Then, divide 15 percent by 3 to get an average return of 5 percent.

Calculate the difference between the average return and each annual return. In this example, the difference between 11.54 and 5 is 6.54; the difference between 5.46 and 5 is 0.46, and the difference between minus 2 and 5 is 7.

Square each of the differences. In this example, square 6.54 to get 42.7716, square 0.46 to get 0.2116 and square 7 to get 49.

Add each of the results. In this example, add 42.7716 plus 0.2116 plus 49 to get 91.9832.

Divide the sum by the number of years minus 1. In this example, divide 91.9832 by 2 to find the variance is 45.9916.

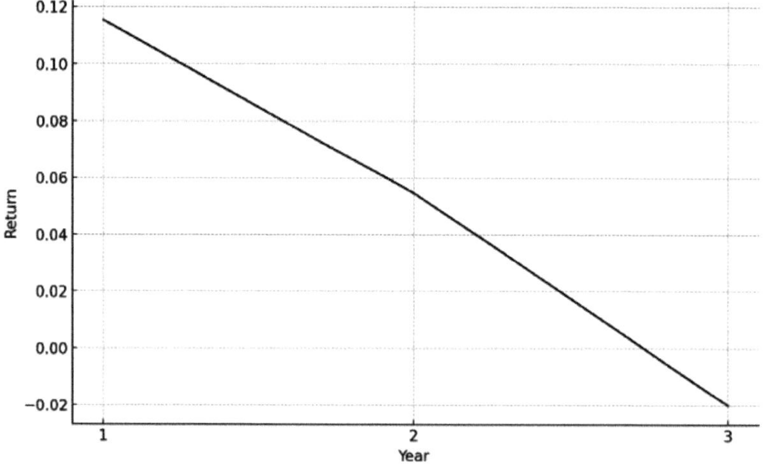

Sample Variance

$$s^2 = \frac{1}{n-1}\sum_{i=1}^{n}\left(X_i - \overline{X}\right)^2$$

The capital sigma symbol signifies the summation of all of the calculations.

Sample Covariance

$$s_{XY} = \frac{1}{n-1}\sum_{i=1}^{n}\left(X_i - \overline{X}\right)\left(Y_i - \overline{Y}\right)$$

Where:

n is the number of data points.

Sample covariance measures how two random variables vary together in a sample dataset. It quantifies the strength and direction of the linear relationship between the two variables. If the covariance is positive, the variables tend to increase together, while a negative covariance indicates that one variable tends to increase when the other decreases. A covariance of zero suggests no linear relationship between the variables.

Steps to Calculate Sample Covariance

Calculate the means of X and Y.

Subtract the mean from each data point to get the deviations.

Multiply the deviations for each pair of corresponding data points.

Sum up these products.

Divide by n−1 to get the sample covariance.

Example

Suppose you have the following data:

X=[2,4,6,8]

Y=[1,3,5,7]

Calculate the sample covariance.

Solution

Calculate the means:

$\overline{X}=5,\ \overline{Y}=4$

Subtract the means:

$(X_i-\overline{X})$=[−3,−1,1,3],

$(Y_i-\overline{Y})$=[−3,−1,1,3]

Multiply the deviations:

[−3×−3,−1×−1,1×1,3×3]=[9,1,1,9]

Sum the products:

9+1+1+9=20

Divide by 3.

The sample covariance is 6.67.

Historical Covariance

$$\sum_{t=1}^{n} \frac{(X_t - \overline{X})(Y_t - \overline{Y})}{n-1}$$

Example

Calculate the covariance between two stocks, assume you have the stock prices for a period of four days.

Day	X	Y
1	1.2%	3.1%
2	1.8%	4.2%
3	2.2%	5%
4	1.5%	4.2%

Solution

We need to calculate the average return for each stock.

For X, it would be 1.675.

For Y, it would be 4.125.

Day 1 : (1.2 − 1.675)(3.1 − 4.125) = 0.487

Day 2 : (1.8 − 1.675)(4.2 − 4.125) = 0.009

Day 3 : (2.2 − 1.675)(5 − 4.125) = 0.459

Day 4 : (1.5 − 1.675)(4.2 − 4.125) = −0.013

Add each day's result to the previous result:

0.487 + 0.009 + 0.459 − 0.013 = 0.942

Your sample size is four, so subtract one from four and divide the previous result by it.

This sample has a covariance of 0.314.

Example

Calculate the covariance between two stocks.

Day	ABC Returns	XYZ Returns
1	1.1%	3%
2	1.7%	4.2%
3	2.1%	4.9%
4	1.4%	4.1%
5	0.2%	2.5%

Solution

We need to calculate the average return for each stock:

For ABC, it would be $\frac{1.1+1.7+2.1+1.4+0.2}{5}=1.3.$

For XYZ, it would be $\frac{3+4.2+4.9+4.1+2.5}{5}=3.74.$

Using our example of ABC and XYZ above, the covariance is calculated as:

= 0.148 + 0.184 + 0.928 + 0.036 + 1.364

= 2.66

In this situation, we are using a sample, so we divide by the sample size minus one.

The covariance between the two stock returns is 0.665.

Example

Calculate the historical covariance for the returns of X and Y over these three days: Over three days, Stock X had returns of 2%, 1%, and 3%, while Stock Y had returns of 1%, 2%, and 9%, respectively.

Solution

Day	1	2	3
Stock X	2%	1%	3%
Stock Y	1%	2%	9%

Day	Stock X	Stock Y
1	2%	1%
2	1%	2%
3	3%	9%

Calculate the Mean Return for Each Stock:

$$\text{Mean of X} = \frac{2+1+3}{3} = 2\%$$

$$\text{Mean of Y} = \frac{1+2+9}{3} = 4\%$$

Calculate the Deviations from the Mean for Each Day:

Day 1:

X deviation: 2 - 2 = 0

Y deviation: 1 - 4 = -3

Day 2:

X deviation: 1 - 2 = -1

Y deviation: 2 - 4 = -2

Day 3:

X deviation: 3 - 2 = 1

Y deviation: 9 - 4 = 5

Sum the Products of Deviations:

Sum = 0 + 2 + 5 = 7

Cov(X,Y) = 3.5

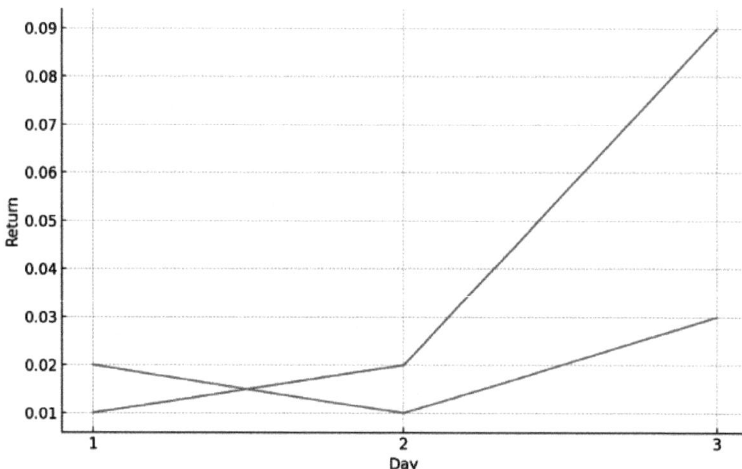

Volatility is a statistical measure of the dispersion of returns for a given security or market index. It represents the degree of variation in the price of a financial instrument over time. Higher volatility indicates a higher degree of risk and uncertainty, as prices can change significantly in a short period, while lower volatility suggests a more stable price movement. The most common measure of volatility is the standard deviation of returns. It quantifies the amount of variation or dispersion from the average return.

Volatility is a fundamental concept in finance, reflecting the degree of price variation over time.

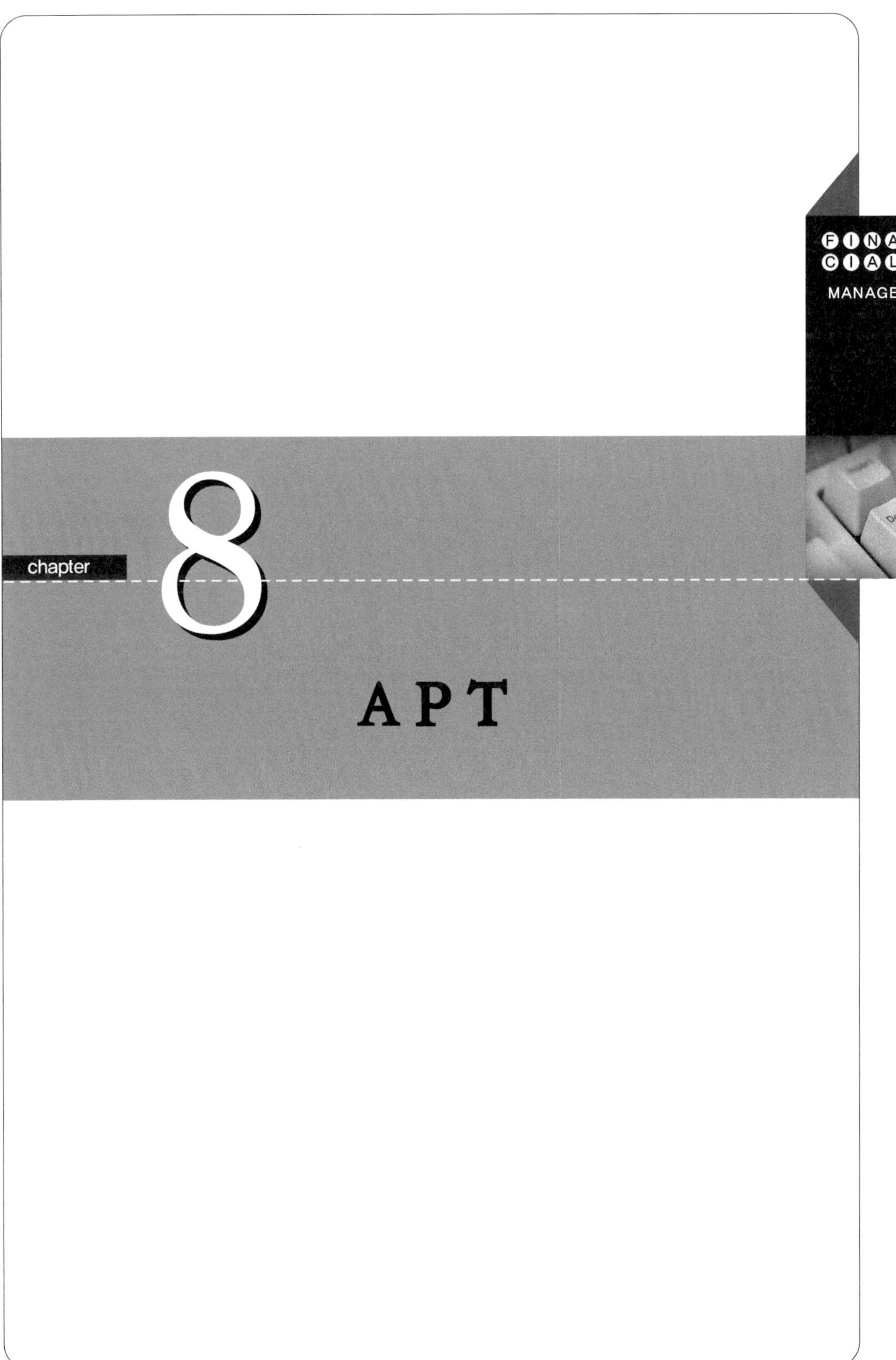

8 APT

APT

the arbitrage pricing theory

$E(r_i) - r_f = \lambda_1 b_{i1} + \cdots + \lambda_k b_{ik}$

where $\lambda_k = E(r_{Fk}) - r_f$.

$E(r_{Fk})$ is the expected return on a portfolio with unit sensitivity to the *k*th factor and zero sensitivity to all other factors.

b_{ik} is the sensitivity of the *i*th asset's returns to the *k*th factor.

An equilibrium asset pricing theory that is derived from a factor model by using diversification and arbitrage. It shows that the expected return on any risky asset is a linear combination of various factors.

λ: lambda

One-factor APT

One-factor APT assumes that the rate of return on any asset is a linear function of one factor as shown below:

$r_i = E(r_i) + b_i F + \varepsilon_i$

where $E(r_i)$: the expected return on stock i

F : the mean zero factor

ε_i: a random zero mean noise term

A special case of the arbitrage pricing theory that is derived from the one-factor model by using diversification and arbitrage. It shows the expected return on any risky asset is a linear function of a single factor. The CAPM can be expressed as one-factor APT in which a single factor is the market portfolio.

$$r_i = E(r_i) + b_i F + \varepsilon_i$$

where $E(r_i)$: the expected return on stock i

F: the deviation of the common factor from its expected value

b_i: the sensitivity of firm i to that factor

The factor model states that the actual return on firm *i* will equal its initially expected return plus a random amount attributable to unanticipated economywide events, plus another random amount attributable to firm-specific events.

Example

Suppose that F is taken to be the unexpected percentage change in GDP, and that the consensus is that GDP will increase by 4% this year. Suppose also that a stock's β value is 1.2. If GDP increases by only 3%, then the value of F would be — 1%, representing a 1% disappointment in actual growth versus expected growth. This disappointment would translate into a return on the stock that is 1.2% lower than previously expected. This macro surprise together with the firm-specific disturbance determines the total departure of the stock's return from its originally expected value.

Well-diversified portfolio

A portfolio spread out over many securities in such a way that the weight in any security is close to zero.

Portfolios are called "well-diversified" if they include a large number of securities and the investment proportion in each is sufficiently small.

If a portfolio is well diversified, its non-factor risk can be diversified away.

Only factor risk remains.

The rate of return on the portfolio is as follows:

$$r_p = E(r_p) + \beta_p F + \varepsilon_p$$

where $\beta_p = \sum_{i=1}^{n} w_i \beta_i$, $\varepsilon_p = \sum_{i=1}^{n} w_i \varepsilon_i$.

The portfolio variance is

$$\sigma_p^2 = \beta_p^2 \sigma_F^2 + Var(\varepsilon_p).$$

$$Var(\varepsilon_p) = Var\left(\sum_{i=1}^{n} w_i \varepsilon_i\right) = \sum_{i=1}^{n} w_i^2 \times Var(\varepsilon_i)$$

A well-diversified portfolio is diversified over a large enough number of securities that $Var(\varepsilon_p)$ is negligible.

For a well-diversified portfolio.

$$\sigma_p^2 = \beta_p^2 \sigma_F^2.$$

Example

$Var(2+3X+Y)$ 를 전개하시오

Solution

$Var(2+3X+Y) = 9\,Var(X) + Var(Y) + 6\,Cov(X, Y)$

Zero-investment portfolio

A portfolio of zero net value, established by buying and shorting component securities.

Systems of Linear Equations

The system of equations

$$a_{11}x_1 + a_{12}x_2 + \cdots + a_{1n}x_n = b_1$$

$$a_{21}x_1 + a_{22}x_2 + \cdots + a_{2n}x_n = b_2$$

$$\vdots$$

$$a_{m1}x_1 + a_{m2}x_2 + \cdots + a_{mn}x_n = b_m$$

$$A = \begin{pmatrix} a_{11} & \cdots & a_{1n} \\ \vdots & \vdots & \vdots \\ a_{m1} & \cdots & a_{mn} \end{pmatrix}$$

$$x = \begin{pmatrix} x_1 \\ \vdots \\ x_n \end{pmatrix} \text{ and } b = \begin{pmatrix} b_1 \\ \vdots \\ b_m \end{pmatrix}$$

The system may be rewritten as a single matrix equation

$Ax = b$.

Example

$$2x_1 + 3x_2 + 4x_3 = 5$$

$$3x_1 + 3x_2 + 5x_3 = 7$$

$$7x_1 + 5x_2 + 8x_3 = 3$$

$$\begin{pmatrix} 2 & 3 & 4 \\ 3 & 3 & 5 \\ 7 & 5 & 8 \end{pmatrix} \begin{pmatrix} x_1 \\ x_2 \\ x_3 \end{pmatrix} = \begin{pmatrix} 5 \\ 7 \\ 3 \end{pmatrix}$$

Homogeneous System

A system $Ax = b$ of m linear equations in n unknowns is said to be homogeneous if $b = 0$.

Trivial solution

Any homogeneous system has at least one solution, namely, the zero vector. This solution is called the trivial solution.

[Theorem]

If $m < n$, the system $Ax = 0$ has a nonzero solution.

Example

Find the solution of the following system.

$x_1 + 2x_2 + x_3 = 0$

$x_1 - x_2 - x_3 = 0$

Solution

$$A = \begin{pmatrix} 1 & 2 & 1 \\ 1 & -1 & -1 \end{pmatrix}$$

The solution set of this system

$$k\begin{pmatrix} 1 \\ -2 \\ 3 \end{pmatrix}$$

Example

Find the solution set of the following system.

$$\begin{pmatrix} 2 & 3 & 4 \\ 3 & 3 & 5 \\ 7 & 5 & 8 \end{pmatrix}\begin{pmatrix} x \\ y \\ z \end{pmatrix} = \begin{pmatrix} 0 \\ 0 \\ 0 \end{pmatrix}$$

Solution

$$\begin{pmatrix} 0 \\ 0 \\ 0 \end{pmatrix}$$

Example

Find the solution set of the following system.

$$\begin{pmatrix} 2 & 3 & 4 \\ 3 & 3 & 5 \\ 5 & 6 & 9 \end{pmatrix}\begin{pmatrix} x \\ y \\ z \end{pmatrix} = \begin{pmatrix} 0 \\ 0 \\ 0 \end{pmatrix}$$

Solution

$$k\begin{pmatrix} 3 \\ 2 \\ -3 \end{pmatrix}$$

Example

Given that $\{(a+b)x+a+4b\}(x+3)=2x^2+5x-3$ is an algebraic identity in x, what are the values of a and b?

Solution

$a+b-2=0$

$4a+7b-5=0$

$3a+12b+3=0$

$a=3,\ b=-1$

Example

항등식 $\{(a+b)x+a+4b\}(x+3)=2x^2+5x-3$ 에서 a,b를 구하여라.

Solution

$a+b-2=0$

$4a+7b-5=0$

$3a+12b+3=0$

$a=3,\ b=-1$

Vectors

Vectors are represented by arrows in which the length of the arrow denotes the magnitude of the vector and the direction of the arrow represents the direction of the vector.

A set of vectors is said to be linearly dependent if there is a nontrivial linear combination of the vectors that equals the zero vector. If no such linear combination exists, then the vectors are said to be linearly independent.

Example

Determine whether or not the first vector can be expressed as a linear combination of the other two.

$(-2,0,3), (1,3,0), (2,4,-1)$

Solution

$(-2,0,3) = \lambda_0(1,3,0) + \lambda_1(2,4,-1)$

$\lambda_0 = 4, \lambda_1 = -3$

The first vector can be expressed as a linear combination of the other two.

Example

Let $V_1 = (-2,0,3)$, $V_2 = (1,3,0)$, and $V_3 = (2,4,-1)$. Determine whether vectors V_1, V_2, V_3 are linearly independent.

Solution

$(-2,0,3) = \lambda_0 (1,3,0) + \lambda_1 (2,4,-1)$

$\lambda_0 = 4, \lambda_1 = -3$

Vectors V_1, V_2, V_3 are linearly dependent.

Example

Determine whether or not the first vector can be expressed as a linear combination of the other two.

$(-2,0,3), (1,3,0), (2,4,1)$

Solution

$(-2,0,3) = \lambda_0 (1,3,0) + \lambda_1 (2,4,1)$

The first vector cannot be expressed as a linear combination of the other two.

Example

Assume that the returns of individual securities are generated by the following one-factor model:

$r_1 = 12\% + 2F + \varepsilon_1$

$r_2 = 15\% + 3F + \varepsilon_2$

$r_3 = 21\% + 5F + \varepsilon_3$

In addition, assume that there is a capital market for three securities.

Derive One-factor APT.

Solution

Arbitrage portfolio

$w_1 + w_2 + w_3 = 0$

$2w_1 + 3w_2 + 5w_3 = 0$

$\lambda_0(w_1 + w_2 + w_3) + \lambda_1(2w_1 + 3w_2 + 5w_3) = 0$

$w_1(\lambda_0 + 2\lambda_1) + w_2(\lambda_0 + 3\lambda_1) + w_3(\lambda_0 + 5\lambda_1) = 0$

Arbitrage portfolio return

In equilibrium all portfolios that satisfy the condition of using no wealth and having no risk must earn no return on average.

$w_1r_1 + w_2r_2 + w_3r_3 = 0$

$w_1 \cdot 12 + w_2 \cdot 15 + w_3 \cdot 21 = 0$

$\lambda_0 + 2\lambda_1 = 12$

$\lambda_0 + 3\lambda_1 = 15$

$\lambda_0 + 5\lambda_1 = 21$

$\lambda_0 = 6,\ \lambda_1 = 3$

$E(r_i) = 6 + 3b_i$

chapter 9

Bonds

Comparing IOUs and Bonds: Acknowledging Debts in Different Forms

An IOU is an informal note that promises to pay a debt. It is so-called as it is a phonetic match for "I Owe You" and it also abbreviates the first letters of each word.
An IOU, a phonetic acronym of the words "I owe you," is a document that acknowledges the existence of a debt.
An IOU is often viewed as an informal written agreement rather than a legally binding commitment.
IOUs are the most basic of notes payable but in order to have any validity, they must contain a number of important details. This includes the following information about a debt:
The names of the debtor and the lender
The amount of money that has been loaned
Interest that will be paid
When the money must be repaid
The signature of the debtor

Bonds are technically a form of IOU, whereby an individual loans an amount of money to a company or government and is given a contract promising to repay the money with interest by a certain date.

IOU: This is a simple written acknowledgment of a debt. It is an informal document that one person uses to acknowledge a debt to another. For example, if you borrow money from a friend, you might give them an IOU as a promise to repay the borrowed amount.

Bond: In finance, a bond is a debt security that represents the borrowing of money. When you buy a bond, you are essentially lending money to the issuer in exchange for periodic interest payments and the return of the principal amount when the bond matures.

A bond is a long-term contract under which a borrower agrees to make payments of interest and principal, on specific dates, to the holders of the bond.

A bond is a fixed income investment in which an investor loans money to an entity that borrows the funds for a defined period of time at a fixed interest rate.

Maturity date is a specific date on which the par value of a bond must be repaid.

Coupon payment is the specific number of dollars of interest paid each period.
Coupon interest rate is the stated annual rate of interest on a bond.

Example

A bond has a face value of $1,000 and an annual coupon rate of 5%. How much does the bond pay in total coupon payments each year?

Solution

If a bond has a face value of $1,000 and a coupon rate of 5%, then it pays total coupons of $50 per year.

YTM

만기수익률

The yield to maturity is the internal rate of return earned by an investor who buys the bond today at the market price, assuming that the bond is held until maturity, and that all coupon and principal payments are made on schedule.

Yield to maturity is the overall interest rate earned by an investor who buys a bond at the market price and holds it until maturity. Mathematically, it is the discount rate at which the sum of all future cash flows equals the price of the bond.

The term yield to maturity refers to the total return anticipated on a bond if the bond is held until it matures.

A bond's yield to maturity is the percentage rate of return for a bond, assuming that the investor holds the asset until its maturity date and receives all its remaining coupon payments and return of the principal at maturity.

현재 거래가격으로 채권을 구입하여 만기까지 보유할 경우에 미래의 현금흐름을 가져다주는 내부수익률이다.

Example

액면가액이 10,000원이고 액면이자율이 10%, 만기가 2년인 채권의 현재 거래가격이 9,000원이다. 이 채권의 만기수익률을 구하라.

Example

Write T for True and F for False the following equation. If the equation is false, correct the equation.

Let's say you have a bond with a face value of $10,000, a coupon rate of 10%, and 2 years until maturity. The bond is currently selling for $9,000.

The equation to calculate the YTM is

$$9,000 = \frac{1,000}{1+r} + \frac{10,000}{(1+r)^2}$$

Solution

F,

$$9,000 = \frac{1,000}{1+r} + \frac{11,000}{(1+r)^2}$$

Example

Company ABC's 2-year bond with par value of W10,000 and coupon of 10% is currently trading at W9,000.

Find the yield to maturity on the bond.

Solution

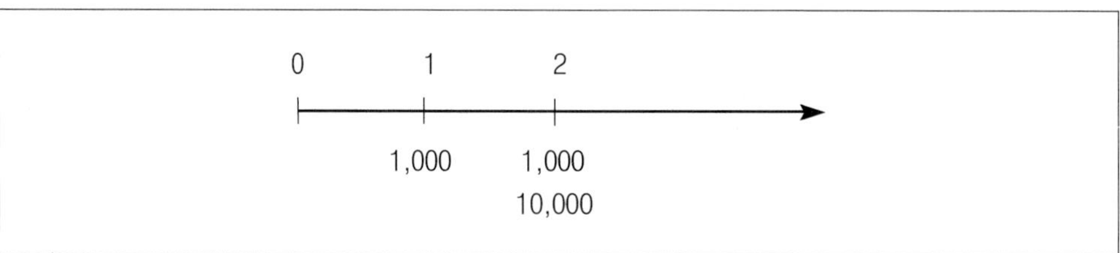

$$9{,}000 = \frac{1{,}000}{1+r} + \frac{11{,}000}{(1+r)^2}$$

$$9(1+r)^2 - (1+r) - 11 = 0$$

$$9r^2 + 17r - 3 = 0$$

$$r = \frac{-17 \pm \sqrt{17^2 + 4 \times 27}}{18}$$

$$r = \frac{-17 + \sqrt{397}}{18} = 16.25\%$$

Example

Suppose the price of two-year maturity coupon bonds with a face value of 10,000 won and a coupon rate of 10% is 9,000 won.

Calculate YTM.

Solution

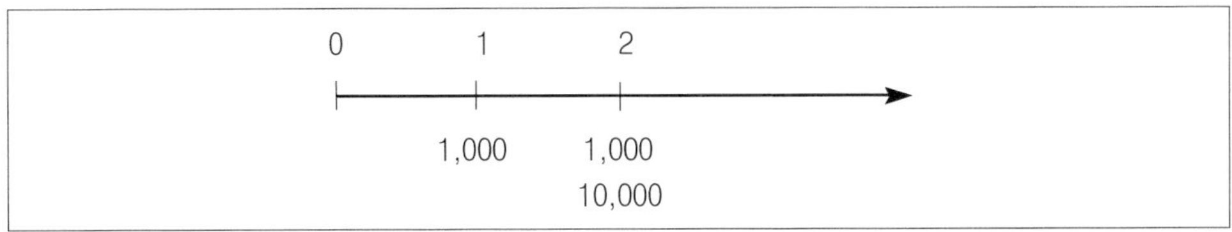

$$9{,}000 = \frac{1{,}000}{1+r} + \frac{11{,}000}{(1+r)^2}$$

$$9(1+r)^2 - (1+r) - 11 = 0$$

$$9r^2 + 17r - 3 = 0$$

$$r = \frac{-17 \pm \sqrt{17^2 + 4 \times 27}}{18}$$

$$r = \frac{-17 + \sqrt{397}}{18} = 16.25\%$$

Example

Suppose the price of two-year maturity coupon bonds with a face value of 10,000 won and a coupon rate of 5% is 9,000 won.

Calculate YTM.

Solution

$$9{,}000 = \frac{500}{1+r} + \frac{10{,}500}{(1+r)^2}$$

10.8%

Example

Suppose the price of one-year maturity coupon bonds with a face value of 10,000 won and a coupon rate of 5% is 9,000 won.
Calculate YTM.

Solution

$$9,000 = \frac{10,500}{1+r}$$

16.7%

Example

Suppose the price of one-year maturity coupon bonds with a face value of 10,000 won and a coupon rate of 5% is 8,750 won.
Calculate YTM.

Solution

20%

Example

Suppose the price of two-year maturity coupon bonds with a face value of 10,000 won and a coupon rate of 15% is 9,800 won.
Calculate YTM.

Solution

$$9,800 = \frac{1,500}{1+r} + \frac{11,500}{(1+r)^2}$$

$$98r^2 + 181r - 32 = 0$$

$$r = \frac{-181 \pm \sqrt{181^2 + 4 \times 98 \times 32}}{196}$$

$$r = \frac{-181 + \sqrt{45305}}{196}$$

$$r = \frac{-181 + 213}{196}$$

r = 16.3%

Example

액면가액이 10,000원이고 액면이자율이 15%, 만기가 2년인 채권의 현재 거래가격이 9,800원이다. 이 채권의 만기수익률을 구하라.

Solution

$$9,800 = \frac{1,500}{1+r} + \frac{1,500}{(1+r)^2} + \frac{10,000}{(1+r)^2}$$

$$98r^2 + 181r - 32 = 0$$

$$r = \frac{-181 \pm \sqrt{181^2 + 4 \times 98 \times 32}}{196}$$

$r = 16.3\%$

Example

A three-year, \$10,000 bond pays an annual coupon of 10%. What is the value of the coupon bond if the current YTM is 11%.

Solution

$$B_0 = \frac{1,000}{1+r} + \frac{1,000}{(1+r)^2} + \frac{11,000}{(1+r)^3}$$

The present value of our bond is equal to W9,756 when the YTM is at 11%.

Example

Suppose the price of three-year maturity coupon bonds with a face value of 10,000 won and a coupon rate of 10% is 9,500 won.
Calculate YTM.

Solution

$$9,500 = \frac{1,000}{1+r} + \frac{1,000}{(1+r)^2} + \frac{11,000}{(1+r)^3}$$

$$B_0 = \frac{1,000}{1+r} + \frac{1,000}{(1+r)^2} + \frac{11,000}{(1+r)^3}$$

YTM must be calculated through trial-and-error.
The present value of our bond is equal to W9,756 when the YTM is at 11%.
The present value of our bond is equal to W9,520 when the YTM is at 12%.
The present value of our bond is equal to W9,473 when the YTM is at 12.2%.
The present value of our bond is equal to W9,292 when the YTM is at 13%.
$r = 12.1\%$

Example

액면가액이 10,000원이고 액면이자율이 10%, 만기가 3년인 채권의 현재 거래가격이 9,500원이다. 이 채권의 만기수익률을 구하라.

The term structure of interest rates

The term structure of interest rates is the relationship between bonds yields and maturities.

동일한 발행주체에 의해 발행된 채권의 잔존기간과 수익률의 관계를 나타내는 개념을 수익률의 기간구조라고 한다. 그리고 이를 그래프로 나타낸 것을 수익률곡선(yield curve)이라고 한다.

Forward Rate

선도이자율
현재 시점에서 기대되는 미래의 특정시점부터 일정기간 동안의 이자율
미래의 일정시점부터 그 이후 일정시점까지의 기간 동안에 대한 금리
A forward rate is an interest rate applicable to a financial transaction that will take place in the future.
The forward rate is the future yield on a bond.

A spot rate is the borrowing or lending interest rate today for a specified period of time.
A forward rate is the interest rate for the future.

R_2: The spot rate from year 0 to year 2 represents the interest rate for the entire two-year period.
${}_1r_2$: The forward rate from year 1 to year 2 represents the interest rate agreed upon today for a loan or investment that will start in year 1 and extend to year 2.
The forward interest rate from Year 1 to Year 2 is the interest rate applicable for the period from Year 1 to Year 2.

Example

You decide to deposit \$100 in a savings account with a 1-year term. The bank offers a 1-year deposit rate of 6%.

The 1-year deposit interest rate refers to the annualized percentage yield or interest rate offered by financial institutions on a deposit with a maturity of one year. It represents the rate at which an individual or entity can earn interest on their deposit over a one-year period.

$R_1 = {}_0r_1 = 6\%$

Example

You deposit \$100 in a bank for 1 year. If the future value of your deposit after 1 year is \$106, what is the 1-year deposit rate offered by the bank?

Solution

The 1-year deposit rate offered by the bank is exactly 6%, as the future value of the \$100 deposit after 1 year is \$106.

Example

Find the 1-year deposit rate offered by the bank if you deposit \$100, and the future value of your investment after 1 year is \$106.

Solution

The 1-year deposit rate offered by the bank is exactly 6%, as the future value of the \$100 deposit after 1 year is \$106.

Example

You deposit \$100 in a bank for 2 years at 10%.

The 2-year deposit rate refers to the annualized interest rate at which funds are deposited in a financial institution for a period of two years.

The future value of a \$100 deposit in a bank after 2 years at a 10% annual interest rate is \$121.

The 2-year deposit rate is 10%.

$R_2 = 10\%$

Example

Find the 2-year deposit rate offered by the bank if you deposit \$100, and the future value of your investment after 2 years is \$121.

Solution

The 2-year deposit rate is 10%.

$R_2 = 10\%$

Example

You decide to invest $200 in a 2-year fixed-term deposit. If the future value of your deposit after 2 years is $242, what is the 2-year deposit rate offered by the bank?

Solution

The 2-year deposit rate offered by the bank is 10%, as the future value of the $200 deposit after 2 years is $242.

R_2: 2년 만기 현물이자율

${}_1r_2$: 시점 1에서 1기간 동안의 선도이자율

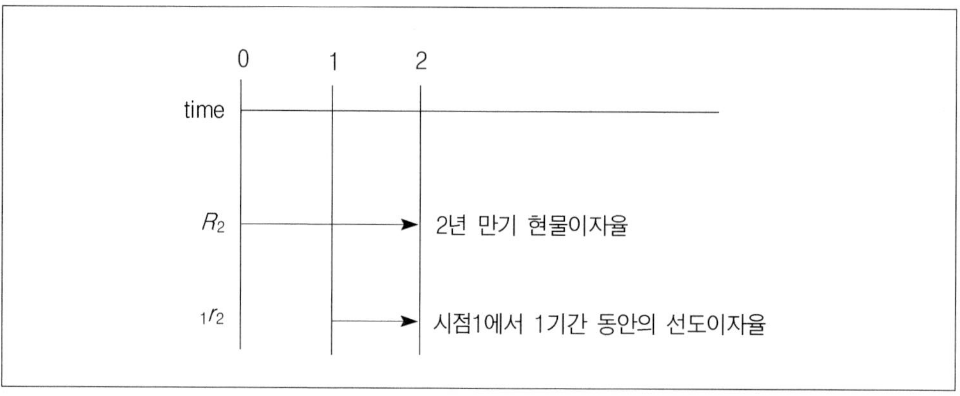

Unbiased Expectation Hypothesis

불편기대가설
장기채권의 수익률은 미래의 단기채권에 대한 선도이자율의 기하평균이라는 가설.

$$(1+R_n)^n = (1+{}_0r_1)(1+{}_1r_2)\cdots(1+{}_{n-1}r_n)$$

The Unbiased Expectations Hypothesis for a 2-period scenario is as follows.

$$(1+R_2)^2 = (1+{}_0r_1)(1+{}_1r_2)$$

If n is equal to 2 in the equation for the Unbiased Expectation Hypothesis, the equation becomes:

$$(1+R_2)^2 = (1+{}_0r_1)(1+{}_1r_2)$$

The Unbiased Expectations Hypothesis for a 3-period scenario is as follows.

$$(1+R_3)^3 = (1+{}_0r_1)(1+{}_1r_2)(1+{}_2r_3)$$

If n is equal to 3 in the equation for the Unbiased Expectation Hypothesis, the equation becomes:

$$(1+R_3)^3 = (1+{}_0r_1)(1+{}_1r_2)(1+{}_2r_3)$$

Example

The current one-year interest rate is 4%, and the forward rate from year 1 to year 2 is 8%.

What should be the spot rate from year 0 to year 2?

Answer as a decimal with four decimal places.

Solution

$$(1+R_2)^2 = 1.04 \times 1.08$$

5.98%

Example

Suppose the price of one-year maturity zero-coupon bonds with face value $1,000 is $950 and the price of two-year zeros with $1,000 face value is $880. What is the forward rate for the two year?

Solution

$$950 = \frac{1,000}{1+R_1}, \quad R_1 = 5.3\%$$

$$880 = \frac{1,000}{(1+R_2)^2}, \quad R_2 = 6.6\%$$

$$(1+0.066)^2 = (1+0.053)(1+{}_1r_2)$$

$${}_1r_2 = 7.92\%$$

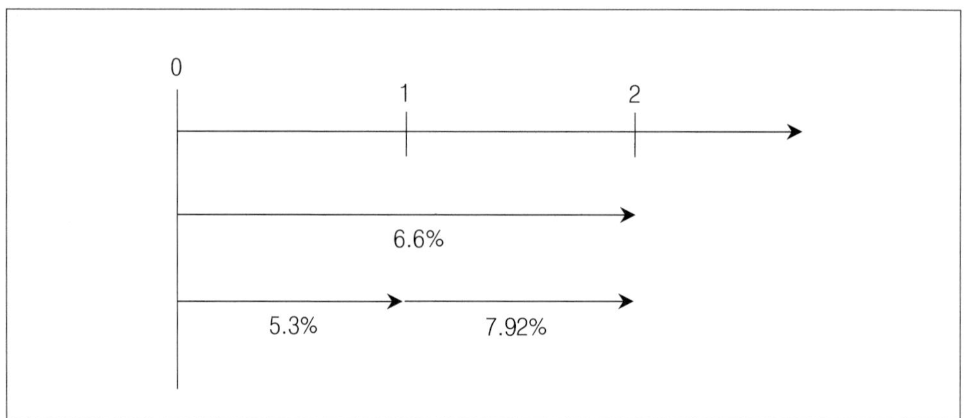

Example

Suppose the price of one-year maturity zero-coupon bonds with face value \$1,000 is \$925.93 and the price of two-year zeros with \$1,000 face value is \$841.68. What is the forward rate for the two year?

Solution

$$925.93 = \frac{1{,}000}{1+R_1}, \quad R_1 = 8\%$$

$$841.68 = \frac{1{,}000}{(1+R_2)^2}, \quad R_2 = 9\%$$

$$1.09^2 = 1.08 \times (1 + {}_1r_2)$$

$${}_1r_2 = 10.01\%$$

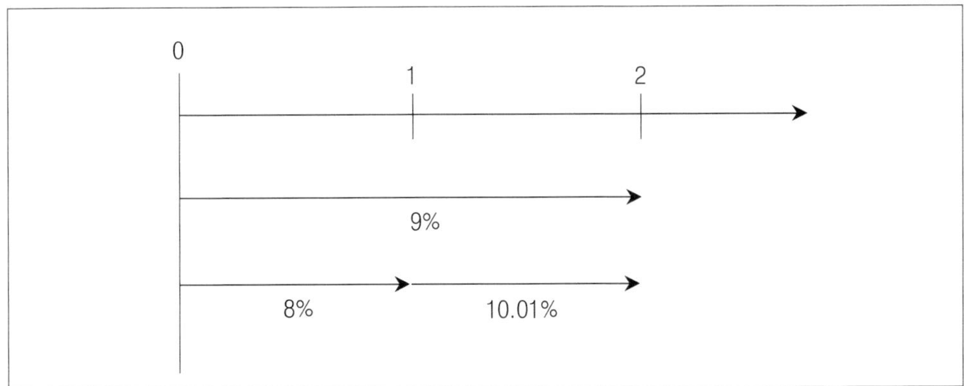

Example

현재 채권시장에서 액면금액이 10,000원인 할인채권이 1년 만기짜리는 9,091원에 거래되고 2년 만기짜리는 7,831원에 거래되고 있다. 1년 후 시점에서의 선도이자율을 구하라.

Solution

$$9{,}091 = \frac{10{,}000}{1+R_1},\quad R_1 = 10\%$$

$$7{,}831 = \frac{10{,}000}{(1+R_2)^2},\quad R_2 = 13\%$$

$$(1+0.13)^2 = (1+0.1)(1+{}_1r_2)$$

$${}_1r_2 = 16.08\%$$

Example

Suppose the price of one-year maturity zero-coupon bonds with face value W100,000 is W95,238 and the price of two-year zeros with W100,000 face value is W88,183. What is the forward rate for the two year?

Solution

$$\frac{100{,}000}{1+{}_0r_1} = 95{,}238$$

$${}_0r_1 = 0.05$$

$$\frac{100{,}000}{(1+0.05)(1+{}_1r_2)} = 88{,}183$$

$${}_1r_2 = 0.08$$

Example

Suppose the price of one-year maturity zero-coupon bonds with face value W100,000 is W95,238 and the price of two-year zeros with W100,000 face value is W88,183. The price of three-year zeros with W100,000 face value is W80,167. What is the forward rate for the three year?

Solution

$$\frac{100,000}{1+{}_0r_1} = 95,238$$

$${}_0r_1 = 0.05$$

$$\frac{100,000}{(1+0.05)(1+{}_1r_2)} = 88,183$$

$${}_1r_2 = 0.08$$

$$\frac{100,000}{(1+0.05)(1+0.08)(1+{}_2r_3)} = 80,167$$

$${}_2r_3 = 0.1$$

Example

액면 100,000원에 대한 채권의 가격이 다음과 같다. 불편기대가설이 성립한다고 가정하고 다음의 물음에 답하라.

종류	만기	현재시장가치	표면이자율
a	1년	95,238	0%
b	2년	88,183	0%
c	3년	80,167	0%

1) 1년 후 시점에서 액면 100,000원, 1년 만기 할인사채의 가격을 구하면?

2) 1년 후 시점에서 액면 100,000원, 2년 만기 할인사채의 가격을 구하면?

Solution

1) $\dfrac{100,000}{1+{}_0r_1}=95,238$

$${}_0r_1=0.05$$

$$\frac{100,000}{(1+0.05)(1+{}_1r_2)}=88,183$$

$${}_1r_2=0.08$$

1년 후, 1년 만기 할인채의 가격: $\dfrac{100,000}{1+{}_1r_2}=92,593$원

2) $\dfrac{100,000}{(1+0.05)(1+0.08)(1+{}_2r_3)}=80,167$

$${}_2r_3=0.1$$

1년 후, 2년 만기 할인채의 가격: $\dfrac{100,000}{(1+0.08)(1+0.1)}=84,175$원

Liquidity preference theory

유동성 선호이론에서의 선도이자율은 기대현물이자율에 유동성 프리미엄까지 포함된다.

Example

The current 1-year deposit interest rate is 4%, and the 2-year deposit interest rate is 6%. What is the forward rate from year 1 to year 2?

Solution

$(1+0.06)^2 = (1+0.04)(1+{}_1r_2)$

${}_1r_2 = 8.04\%$

Example

The current 1-year deposit interest rate is 4%, and the current 2-year deposit interest rate is 6%. If you plan to invest in a 1-year deposit after one year, what is the expected interest rate?

Solution

$(1+0.06)^2 = (1+0.04)(1+{}_1r_2)$

${}_1r_2 = 8.04\%$

Example

Given the current 1-year deposit interest rate is 4%, and the current 2-year deposit interest rate is 6%, if you plan to invest in a 1-year deposit after one year, what is the expected interest rate for the 1-year deposit according to the Unbiased Expectations Hypothesis?

Solution

$(1+0.06)^2 = (1+0.04)(1+{}_1r_2)$

${}_1r_2 = 8.04\%$

Example

수진이가 은행에 갔더니, 1년 만기 정기예금 금리가 연 4%이고, 2년 만기 정기예금 금리가 연 6%였다. 수진이가 1년 후 1년 만기 정기예금에 가입한다면, 예상되는 금리는 얼마인가?

Solution

$$(1+0.06)^2 = (1+0.04)(1+{}_1r_2)$$

$${}_1r_2 = 8.04\%$$

Example

In the current bond market, zero-coupon bonds with a face value of 10,000 won are trading at 9,091 won for a 1-year maturity and 7,831 won for a 2-year maturity. Draw the yield curve.

Solution

$$9,091 = \frac{10,000}{1+R_1},\ R_1 = 10\%$$

$$7,831 = \frac{10,000}{(1+R_2)^2},\ R_2 = 13\%$$

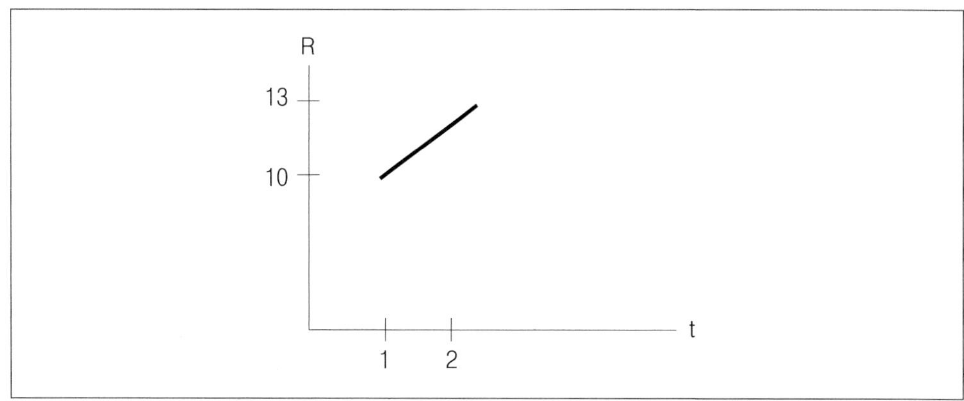

Example

현재 채권시장에서 액면금액이 10,000원인 할인채권이 1년 만기짜리는 9,091원에 거래되고 2년 만기짜리는 7,831원에 거래되고 있다. 수익률곡선을 그리시오.

The yield curve is a graph showing the relationship between bond yields (interest rates) and their maturities.

A yield curve plots the yield (Y-axis) against the term to maturity (X-axis).

A yield curve is a line that plots the yields (interest rates) of bonds with equal credit quality but different maturity dates. It is a graphical representation of the relationship between bond yields and the time remaining until their maturity. The yield is plotted on the vertical axis, and the time to maturity is plotted on the horizontal axis.

Example

The yield on a 1-year Zero-Coupon Bond is 10%, while the yield on a 2-year Zero-Coupon Bond is 13%.

Draw the yield curve based on the data above.

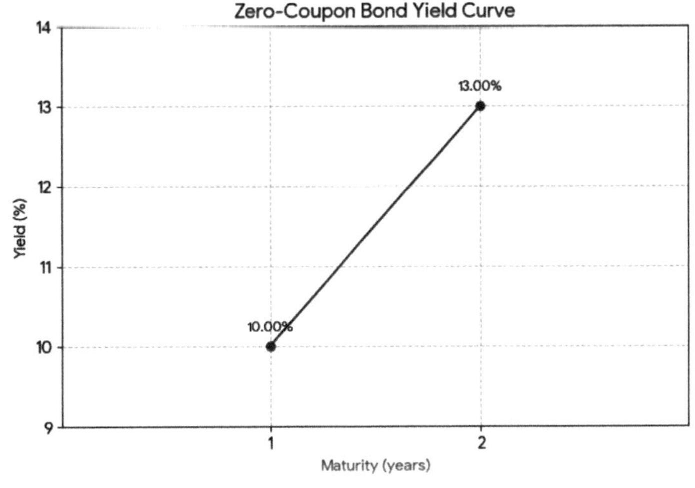

T–note

T-note은 만기 1~10년의 미국 재무부채권이며, T-bond는 만기 10~30년의 미국 재무부채권이다. 호가와 관련하여, 1%의 $\frac{1}{32}$ 단위로 표시하여, 99-05는 액면가의 $\left(99+\frac{5}{32}\right)$% 를 의미한다.

채권매매일과 이자지급일이 일치하지 않는 경우, 채권매입자는 전 이자지급일로부터 매매일까지 발생한 이자, 즉 경과이자(accrued interest)를 호가(quoted price)에 더하여 매도자에게 지불하여야 한다.

A Treasury Bill is a short-term debt obligation backed by the U.S. Treasury Department with a maturity of one year or less.

Treasury Bonds vs. Treasury Notes vs. Treasury Bills

Treasury bills are one of several types of debt issued by the U.S. Department of the Treasury. In addition to T-bills, there are also Treasury bonds and Treasury notes, each referring to different debt products. All three represent fixed-term debt over a period of time.

The main difference between these types of debt is the time to maturity. Treasury bills represent short-term obligations that mature anywhere between a few days to 52 weeks. Treasury notes are medium-term securities that take between two and 10 years to mature. Treasury bonds have the longest lifetime and mature in 30 years.

Note and bond prices are quoted in dollars and fractions of a dollar. By market convention, the normal fraction used for Treasury security prices is 1/32.

Example

A Treasury bond has a bid quote of 93-12. What is the total dollar value of the bid for a $100,000 face value bond?

Solution

The bid quote of 93-12 means $93,375 per $100,000 face value of T-bond.

$$100,000\times\left(93+\frac{12}{32}\right)\times\frac{1}{100}=93,375$$

Example

액면 100,000달러의 T-bond를 93-12에 매입하였다. 이를 금액으로 환산하면 얼마인가?

Solution

$$100,000 \times \left(93 + \frac{12}{32}\right) \times \frac{1}{100} = 93,375\text{달러}$$

Example

A Treasury bond has a bid quote of 92-07. What is the total dollar value of the bid for a $100,000 face value bond?

Solution

The bid quote of 92-07 means $92,219 per $100,000 face value of T-bond.

$$100,000 \times \left(92 + \frac{7}{32}\right) \times \frac{1}{100} = 92,219$$

Example

액면 100,000달러의 T-bond를 92-07에 매입하였다. 이를 금액으로 환산하면 얼마인가?

Solution

$$100,000 \times \left(92 + \frac{7}{32}\right) \times \frac{1}{100} = 92,219\text{달러}$$

Duration

Duration is the weighted-average time to maturity on the loan using the relative present values of the cash flows as weights.
듀레이션이란 현재가치 개념으로 투자원금이 회수되는 평균기간이다.

$$D=\frac{PV_1\times 1+PV_2\times 2+\cdots+PV_n\times n}{PV_1+PV_2+\cdots+PV_n}$$

PV_t: t년도에 실현되는 현금흐름의 현재가치

CF_t: t 년도에 실현되는 현금흐름

y: 만기수익률

$$PV_t=\frac{CF_t}{(1+y)^t}$$

The duration for a bond with 2 periods can be calculated using the following formula:

$$D=\frac{PV_1\times 1+PV_2\times 2}{PV_1+PV_2}$$

$$PV_2=\frac{CF_2}{(1+y)^2}$$

CF_t is the cash flow in period t.

y is the yield to maturity.

The duration for a bond with 3 periods can be calculated using the following formula:

$$D=\frac{PV_1\times 1+PV_2\times 2+PV_3\times 3}{PV_1+PV_2+PV_3}$$

A two-year, $1,000 bond pays an annual coupon of 10 percent. What is the duration of the coupon bond if the current YTM is 8 percent?

Solution

$$D=\frac{\frac{100}{1.08}+\frac{1,100}{1.08^2}\times 2}{\frac{100}{1.08}+\frac{1,100}{1.08^2}}=1.911$$

Example

Consider a two-year bond with a face value of $1,000 and an annual coupon rate of 10%. What is the duration of the coupon bond if the current YTM is 8 percent?

Solution

$$D=\frac{\frac{100}{1.08}+\frac{1,100}{1.08^2}\times 2}{\frac{100}{1.08}+\frac{1,100}{1.08^2}}=1.911$$

Example

Two bonds are available for purchase in the financial markets. The first bond is a two-year, $1,000 bond that pays an annual coupon of 10 percent. The second bond is a two-year, $1,000 zero-coupon bond.

1) What is the duration of the coupon bond if the current YTM is 8 percent?

2) Calculate the duration of zero-coupon bond with a YTM of 8 percent.

Solution

1) $$D = \frac{\frac{100}{1.08} \times 1 + \frac{1{,}100}{(1.08)^2} \times 2}{\frac{100}{1.08} + \frac{1{,}100}{(1.08)^2}} = 1.911$$

2) $$D = \frac{\frac{1{,}000}{(1.08)^2} \times 2}{\frac{1{,}000}{(1.08)^2}} = 2$$

Example

A two-year, $1,000 bond pays an annual coupon of 10 percent. What is the duration of the coupon bond if the current YTM is 10 percent?

Solution

$$D = \frac{\frac{100}{1.1} \times 1 + \frac{1{,}100}{1.1^2} \times 2}{\frac{100}{1.1} + \frac{1{,}100}{1.1^2}} = 1.909 \text{ years}$$

Example

A two-year, $1,000 bond pays an annual coupon of 10 percent. What is the duration of the coupon bond if the current YTM is 12 percent?

Solution

$$D = \frac{\frac{100}{1.12}\times 1 + \frac{1{,}100}{(1.12)^2}\times 2}{\frac{100}{1.12} + \frac{1{,}100}{(1.12)^2}} = 1.908$$

Example

A three-year, W10,000 bond pays an annual coupon of 5 percent. The bond's current YTM is 8 percent. What is the duration of the coupon bond if the current YTM is 8 percent?

Solution

$$D = \frac{\frac{500}{1.08} + \frac{500}{1.08^2}\times 2 + \frac{10,500}{1.08^3}\times 3}{\frac{500}{1.08} + \frac{500}{1.08^2} + \frac{10,500}{1.08^3}} = 2.853$$

Example

액면가액이 10,000원이고 액면이자율이 5%, 만기가 3년인 채권의 만기수익률이 8%일 때, 듀레이션을 계산하라.

Solution

$$D = \frac{\frac{500}{1.08} + \frac{500}{1.08^2}\times 2 + \frac{10,500}{1.08^3}\times 3}{\frac{500}{1.08} + \frac{500}{1.08^2} + \frac{10,500}{1.08^3}} = 2.853$$

Example

Write T for True and F for False equation. If the equation is false, correct the equation. A five-year, $1,000 bond pays an annual coupon of 12 percent. The bond's current YTM is 15 percent.

$$D=\frac{\frac{120}{1.15}+\frac{120}{1.15^2}\times 2+\cdots+\frac{1,120}{1.15^5}\times 3}{\frac{120}{1.15}+\frac{120}{1.15^2}+\cdots+\frac{1,120}{1.15^5}}$$

Solution

F,

$$D=\frac{\frac{120}{1.15}+\frac{120}{1.15^2}\times 2+\cdots+\frac{1,120}{1.15^5}\times 5}{\frac{120}{1.15}+\frac{120}{1.15^2}+\cdots+\frac{1,120}{1.15^5}}$$

Example

만기수익률이 15%일 때, 액면이자율 12%, 액면금액 1,000원, 만기 5년인 채권의 듀레이션을 계산하시오.

Solution

$$D=\frac{\frac{120}{1.15}+\frac{120}{1.15^2}\times 2+\cdots+\frac{1,120}{1.15^5}\times 5}{\frac{120}{1.15}+\frac{120}{1.15^2}+\cdots+\frac{1,120}{1.15^5}}=3.98$$

듀레이션은 3.98년이다.

The percentage change in bond price

Let cash flows be CF_1, CF_2.

The bond price at yield R is

$$P=\frac{C}{1+R}+\frac{C+F}{(1+R)^2}.$$

Differentiate P(R) w.r.t. R

$$\frac{dP}{dR}=\frac{-C}{(1+R)^2}+\frac{-2(C+F)}{(1+R)^3}$$

$$\frac{dP}{dR}=-\frac{1}{1+R}\left\{\frac{C}{1+R}+\frac{2(C+F)}{(1+R)^2}\right\}$$

Define Duration

$$D=\frac{\frac{C}{1+R}+2\frac{C+F}{(1+R)^2}}{P}$$

Express $\frac{dP}{dR}$ in terms of P and D

$$\frac{dP}{dR}=-\frac{1}{1+R}PD$$

Convert to a proportional change

$$\frac{dP}{P}=-D\left(\frac{dR}{1+R}\right)$$

where C: the coupon payment

F: the face value of the bond

For small changes in interest rates, bond prices move in an inversely proportional fashion according to the size of D.

Example

A bond has a duration of 6 years and a yield of 5%.

If the market interest rate increases by 0.2 percentage points,

estimate the percentage change in the bond's price.

Solution

$$\frac{dP}{P}=-D\frac{dR}{1+R}=-6\frac{0.002}{1.05}=-0.0114=-1.14\%$$

So, the bond's price is expected to decrease by approximately 1.14%.

The Duration Gap for a Financial Institution

For a bank or financial institution,

an asset refers to anything the institution owns that will generate future cash inflows.

The Duration Gap is a key concept in asset - liability management (ALM) for financial institutions such as banks, insurance companies, and pension funds. It measures the mismatch between the durations (interest rate sensitivities) of assets and liabilities.

Let:

A = market value of assets,

L = market value of liabilities,

E=A−L = equity (market value of equity).

$$A = L + E$$

$$\Delta A = \Delta L + \Delta E$$

$$\frac{\Delta A}{A}=-D_A\frac{\Delta R}{1+R}$$

$$\frac{\Delta L}{L}=-D_L\left(\frac{\Delta R}{1+R}\right)$$

$$\Delta E = -(D_A - D_L k)A\frac{\Delta R}{1+R}$$

where $k = \frac{L}{A}$

The effect of interest rate changes on the market value of an FI's equity or net worth breaks down into three effects.

$[D_A - D_L k]$: the leverage adjusted duration gap

A : the size of the FI's assets

$\frac{\Delta R}{1+R}$: the size of the interest rate shock

Example

A bank has total assets of ₩100 billion and total liabilities of ₩90 billion.

The average duration of its assets is 4.5 years, and the average duration of its liabilities is 2.5 years.

The current market interest rate is 5%.

If interest rates increase by 1 percentage point, estimate the approximate change in the market value of the bank's equity using the duration gap model.

Solution

$$\Delta E = -(D_A - D_L k)A\frac{\Delta R}{1+R}$$

$$= -\left(4.5 - 2.5\frac{90}{100}\right)100\frac{0.01}{1.05} = -2.14$$

So the market value of equity falls by approximately ₩2.14 billion when interest rates rise by 1%.

Taylor's Theorem

Taylor's Theorem is a fundamental result in calculus that provides a way to approximate a function near a specific point using a polynomial.

The second-order Taylor expansion of f(x) around a

$$f(x) \approx f(a) + f'(a)(x-a) + \frac{1}{2}f''(a)(x-a)^2$$

Example

Find the second-order Taylor expansion of the function

f(x)= $\sqrt{x}$ around the point a=4.

$$f(x) \approx 2 + \frac{1}{4}(x-4) - \frac{1}{64}(x-4)^2$$

Modified Duration

$$D_M = \frac{D}{1+r}$$

Convexity

$$Convexity = \frac{\frac{d^2P}{dr^2}}{P}$$

Convexity and Taylor's theorem

$$\frac{dP}{P} = -D\left(\frac{dr}{1+r}\right)$$

$$\frac{dP}{dr} \times \frac{1}{P} = -\frac{D}{1+r}$$

$$\frac{dP}{dr} \times \frac{1}{P} = -D_m$$

$$\Delta P \fallingdotseq \frac{dP}{dr}\Delta r + \frac{1}{2}\frac{d^2P}{dr^2}(\Delta r)^2$$

$$\frac{\Delta P}{P} = (-D_m)\Delta r + \frac{1}{2}C(\Delta r)^2$$

Example

A bond has a modified duration of 7 and a convexity of 50.

If the interest rate increases by 0.1%, what is the approximate percentage change in the bond's price?

Answer as a decimal with the six decimal places.

Solution

$$\frac{\Delta P}{P} = (-D_m)\Delta r + \frac{1}{2}C(\Delta r)^2$$

$$= (-7) \times 0.001 + \frac{1}{2} \times 50 \times (0.001)^2 = -0.6975\%$$

If the interest rate rises by 0.1%, the bond's price will decrease by approximately 0.6975%.

Rate Sensitive Assets (RSA) are those assets whose values or returns change when market interest rates change. They are typically part of a bank or financial institution's balance sheet and are crucial for measuring interest rate risk — that is, how changes in interest rates affect the bank's profitability and equity.

Rate Sensitive Assets are financial assets that reprice (mature or have their interest rates reset) within a specific time frame, usually within one year.

These are compared with Rate Sensitive Liabilities (RSL) to determine the institution's Interest Rate Gap or Duration Gap.

Interest Rate Gap=RSA−RSL

Example

A bank has the following items on its balance sheet (in ₩ million):

Item	Amount
Variable−rate loans	1,200
Treasury bills (6 months)	400
Adjustable−rate mortgages (ARM, 6m reset)	600
Fixed−rate 3−year bonds	800
Fixed−rate mortgages (20−year FRM)	900
Demand deposits	1,000
Fixed 2−year deposits	600

Calculate the bank's Rate Sensitive Assets (RSA), Rate Sensitive Liabilities (RSL), and the Interest Rate Gap.

Solution

Item	Amount	Repricing ≤ 1 year?	Category
Variable−rate loans	1,200	Yes	RSA
Treasury bills (6 months)	400	Yes	RSA
Adjustable−rate mortgages	600	Yes	RSA
Fixed−rate 3−year bonds	800	No	Non−RSA
Fixed−rate mortgages	900	No	Non−RSA
Demand deposits	1,000	Yes	RSL
Fixed 2−year deposits	600	No	Non−RSL

RSA = 1,200 + 400 + 600 = ₩2,200 million

RSL = 1,000 = ₩1,000 million

Interest Rate Gap = RSA − RSL = 2,200− 1,000 = ₩1,200 million

Convertible Bonds

전환사채소유자의 의사에 따라 사채를 발행한 기업의 주식으로 전환할 수 있는 권리가 부여된 사채이다. 사채에 주식으로 전환할 수 있는 권리인 전환권이 부가되어 있다.

A convertible bond is a fixed-income corporate debt security that yields interest payments, but can be converted into a predetermined number of common stock or equity shares. The conversion from the bond to stock can be done at certain times during the bond's life and is usually at the discretion of the bondholder.
A convertible bond pays fixed-income interest payments, but can be converted into a predetermined number of common stock shares.
A convertible bond offers investors a type of hybrid security that has features of a bond, such as interest payments, while also having the option to own the underlying stock.
From the issuer's perspective, the key benefit of raising money by selling convertible bonds is a reduced cash interest payment. The advantage for companies of issuing convertible bonds is that, if the bonds are converted to stocks, companies' debt vanishes. However, in exchange for the benefit of reduced interest payments, the value of shareholder's equity is reduced due to the stock dilution expected when bondholders convert their bonds into new shares.

Parity

$$Parity = \frac{\text{주가}}{\text{전환가격}}$$

CR
Conversion ratio
전환비율
전환사채 1개를 전환할 때 받게 되는 주식의 수
The number of shares that you'll receive at conversion is calculated by dividing the face value of the security by the conversion price.
The conversion ratio is the number of common shares that the holder of a convertible security could receive by submitting the security to the issuer for conversion.
Conversion ratio = Par value of convertible bond / Conversion price of equity

Example

An investor has a convertible bond that has a par value of $2,000. The conversion price for each stock share is $10. By dividing $2,000 by $10, the investor determines they will receive 200 shares of the issuer's common stock.

Example

For example, when the holder of a convertible bond with a face value of $1,000 can trade it in for a conversion price of $20 per share, the holder will receive 50 shares of the issuer's common stock.

Conversion price
전환가격

$$Conversion\ price = \frac{\text{액면금액}}{\text{전환비율}}$$

A conversion price is the predetermined price, set at the time of issue, at which you can exchange a convertible bond for common stock.

The conversion price is determined when the convertible security is issued and can be found in the bond indenture. The conversion price is essential in determining the number of shares to be received, by computing the quotient of the principal value of the convertible security divided by the conversion price.

Example

액면가 10,000원인 전환사채의 전환가격은 20,000원일 때, 전환비율은 얼마인가?

Solution

$$\text{전환비율} = \frac{10,000}{20,000} = 0.5$$

Example

액면가 10,000원인 전환사채의 전환가격은 20,000원이고, 주가는 18,000원일 때, 패리티는 얼마인가?

Solution

$$\frac{18,000}{20,000} = 90\%$$

The difference between the bond price and the conversion parity price is the conversion premium.

Conversion Premium = Bond Price − (Stock Price × Conversion Ratio)

Example

If a bond, with a conversion ratio of 20, is currently selling in the secondary market for $1,200 and the common stock is selling for $50, what is the conversion premium?

Solution

Conversion Premium = $1,200 − ($50 × 20) = $1,200 − $1,000 = $200.

Example

If a bond, with a conversion ratio of 2, is currently selling in the secondary market for 15,000 won and the common stock is selling for 7,000 won, what is the conversion premium?

Solution

Conversion Premium = 1,000

Example

Assume, for example, that a $1,000 IBM convertible bond has a market price of $1,200, and the bond is convertible into 20 shares of IBM common stock. The parity price is:
$1,200 / 20 shares = $60 per share
If the market price of IBM common stock is above $60 per share, the investor can profit by converting it into common stock.

CPP

The conversion parity price is calculated by dividing the current value of the convertible security by the conversion ratio, which is the number of shares a convertible security can be converted into.

Conversion Parity Price = Value of Convertible Security / Conversion Ratio

Example

Suppose an investor had a convertible bond with a current market price of $1,000 that could be converted into 20 shares of common stock in the issuing company. The conversion parity price would be $50. If the current value of the company's stock is considerably higher than $50, then the investor can profit from exercising the conversion option.

Example

For example, Mary holds convertible bonds of Co. ABC bearing a face value of $5,000. Co. ABC issues an option for the conversion of bonds to common stock at a conversion price of $25. Thus, Mary would be entitled to 200 equity shares of Co ABC.

Example

The convertible bonds of Apple Corp trade at $2500 in the open market. The management has pre-set the conversion ratio at 10. Also, the common shares of Apple Corp are currently trading at $265.

Therefore, the conversion parity price = 2500/10 = $250.

This means that a bondholder holding a single bond worth $2500 prior to the exercise of an option would now hold 10 shares at a value of $250 each.

In order for the investor to make a profit, the conversion parity price must always be less than the current market price of the equity shares. As in this case, upon conversion, the investor receives 10 shares worth $250 each, whereas the market price stands at $265 each. Therefore, the investor can make a profit of $150 with this trade. Had the market price been any lower than $250, the investor would either have to square off this trade in a loss or hold a position till the price picks up.

Example

The convertible bonds of Apple Corp trade at 15,000 won in the open market. The management has pre-set the conversion ratio at 2. Also, the common shares of Apple Corp are currently trading at 7,000.

Therefore, the conversion parity price = 7,500.

As in this case, upon conversion, the investor receives 2 shares worth 7,500 won each, whereas the market price stands at 7,000 won each. Therefore, the investor can make a loss of 1,000 won with this trade.

패리티가격

패리티에 액면 10,000원을 곱한 가격

Disparate Ratio

$$괴리율 = \frac{전환사채\ 시장가격 - 패리티가격}{패리티가격}$$

패리티가격보다 낮은 가격에 전환사채를 매입한 후 주식으로 전환하여 매각하면 매매차익이 발생하고, 패리티가격보다 높은 가격에 매입한 후 주식으로 전환하여 매각하면 매매손실이 발생하게 된다. 괴리율이 음(−)이면 주식에 직접 투자하는 것보다 전환사채를 매입하여 주식으로 전환하는 것이 유리하다.

Example

액면가 10,000원인 한라기업 전환사채의 시장가격은 15,000원이다. 한라기업의 현재 주가가 7,000원이고 전환사채의 전환가격은 5,000원이라면,

1) 전환사채의 괴리율은 얼마인가?

2) 전환사채 1개를 매입하여 주식으로 전환한 후, 주식을 매각할 때의 이익 또는 손실을 계산하라.

Solution

1) $패리티가격 = \frac{7,000}{5,000} \times 10,000 = 14,000$

$괴리율 = \frac{15,000 - 14,000}{14,000} = 0.071$

2) 전환사채 1개를 15,000원에 매입하여 주식 2개로 전환한 후, 주식을 매각하면 14,000원이 되므로 1,000원 손실이 발생한다.

Example

액면가 10,000원인 전환사채의 전환가격은 5,000원일 때, 전환비율은 얼마인가?

Solution

$$전환비율 = \frac{10,000}{5,000} = 2$$

Altman Z Score

$Z_i = \beta_1 X_1 + \cdots + \beta_5 X_5$

Z_i: 기업 i의 판별점수

X_1 : 순운전자본/총자산 (Working Capital / TA)

X_2 : 유보이익/총자산 (Retained earnings / TA)

X_3 : 영업이익/총자산 (EBIT / TA)

X_4 : 자기자본시장가치/총부채장부가치 (Market value of equity / Book value of debt)

X_5 : 매출액/총자산 (Sales / TA)

The Altman z-score quantifies the financial stability of a company to predict how likely a company will become insolvent.

The Altman Z-score is the output of a credit-strength test that gauges a publicly traded manufacturing company's likelihood of bankruptcy.

Altman's Z-score Model is a numerical measurement that is used to predict the chances of bankruptcy.

Altman's Z-score model combines five financial ratios to predict the probability of a company becoming insolvent in the next two years.

The following are the key financial ratios that make up the Z-score model:

X1 = Working Capital ÷ Total Assets

Working capital is the difference between the current assets of a company and its current liabilities. The value of a company's working capital determines its short-term financial health. A positive working capital means that a company can meet its short-term financial obligations and still make funds available to invest and grow.

In contrast, negative working capital means that a company will struggle to meet its short-term financial obligations because there are inadequate current assets.

The working capital to total assets ratio measures the company's short-term liquidity.

X2 = Retained Earnings ÷ Total Assets

The retained earnings/total assets ratio shows the amount of retained earnings or losses in a company. If a company reports a low retained earnings to total assets ratio, it means that it is financing its expenditure using borrowed funds rather than funds from its retained earnings.

On the other hand, a high retained earnings to total assets ratio shows that a company uses its retained earnings to fund capital expenditure. It shows that the company achieved profitability over the years, and it does not need to rely on borrowings.

The retained earnings to total assets ratio measure a company's reliance on debt financing to fund operations, so a higher ratio indicates the company can fund its operations using its earnings rather than borrowings.

X3 = EBIT ÷ Total Assets

EBIT, a measure of a company's profitability, refers to the ability of a company to generate profits solely from its operations. The EBIT/Total Assets ratio demonstrates a company's ability to generate enough revenues to stay profitable and fund ongoing operations and make debt payments.

The operating income to total assets ratio measures a company's ability to generate operating profits using its assets, meaning that a higher ratio indicates greater profits and asset-utilization efficiency.

X4 = Market Capitalization ÷ Total Liabilities

The market value, also known as market capitalization, is the value of a company's equity. It is obtained by multiplying the number of outstanding shares by the current price of stocks. The market value of the equity/total liabilities ratio shows the degree to which a company's market value would decline when it declares bankruptcy before the value of liabilities exceeds the value of assets on the balance sheet. A high market value of equity to total liabilities ratio can be interpreted to mean high investor confidence in the company's financial strength. The market cap to total liabilities ratio measures the potential downside in the market value of equity given the risk of insolvency. Hence, a low market cap relative to its liabilities reflects weak market sentiment regarding the company's outlook.

X5 = Sales ÷ Total Assets

The sales to total assets ratio shows how efficiently the management uses assets to generate revenues vis-à-vis the competition. A high sales to total assets ratio is translated to mean that the management requires a small investment to generate sales, which increases the overall profitability of the company.

In contrast, a low or falling sales to total assets ratio means that the management will need to use more resources to generate enough sales, which will reduce the company's profitability. The sales to total assets ratio measure the sales generated compared to a company's asset base. Thus, a higher percentage means more efficiency in producing revenue.

X_1 : 순운전자본/총자산

순운전자본을 총자산으로 나눈 비율은 기업의 단기채무상환능력인 유동성을 측정하는 비율이다.

X_3 : 영업이익/총자산

영업이익을 총자산으로 나눈 비율은 기업자산의 생산성을 측정하는 비율이다.

X_5 : 매출액/총자산

매출액을 총자산으로 나눈 총자산회전율은 기업자산의 매출창출능력을 측정하는 비율이다.

Altman의 신용평점모형에 따르면, Z값이 크면 클수록, 차입자의 채무불이행위험은 낮아진다. Z값이 1.81 미만인 기업은 높은 채무불이행위험을 가지고 있는 것으로 본다.

The lower the score, the higher the odds of bankruptcy. Companies with Z-Scores above 3 are considering to be healthy and, therefore, unlikely to enter bankruptcy. Scores in between 1.8 and 3 lie in a grey area.

$Z > 3$ → very low probability of bankruptcy

$Z < 1.8$ → significant probability of bankruptcy

Credit Risk

DD

부도거리(Distance to Default)

$$DD = \frac{A - D}{\sigma_A}$$

A is the market value of a company's assets.

D is the book value of a company's debt.

σ_A is the volatility of the company's asset value.

A: 자산의 시장가치

D: 부채의 장부가치

σ_A: 자산가치의 변동성

Example

Let's consider an imaginary company called ABC Corporation and calculate the distance to default (DD).

Assumptions:

ABC Corporation's assets market value: $100 million.

ABC Corporation's debt book value is $70 million.

The volatility of ABC Corporation's asset value : $10 million.

Solution

$$DD = \frac{A - D}{\sigma_A} = \frac{100 - 70}{10} = 3$$

Example

서울기업의 1년 후 기대 기업가치가 100억원이고, 표준편차는 10억원이며, 부채가치는 70억원이다. 부도거리를 계산하라.

Solution

$$DD = \frac{A - D}{\sigma_A} = \frac{100 - 70}{10} = 3$$

EL

예상손실(Expected Loss)

A bank may calculate its expected loss by multiplying the variable, EAD, with the DP and the LGD:

$EL = EAD \times DP \times LGD$

EAD: Exposure at default

DP: Default probability

LGD: Loss Given Default

Exposure at default is the total value a bank is exposed to when a loan defaults.

Exposure at Default is the predicted amount of loss a bank may face in the event of, and at the time of, the borrower's default.

Exposure at default, loss given default, and the probability of default is used to calculate the total credit risk capital of financial institutions.

Example

Let us assume that a bank lends $1000,000 to XYZ Ltd.

The default probability is 100%.

The loss given default is 38%.

Calculate EL.

Solution

The bank expects a loss of $380,000.

Example

EAD = $100 million

DP = 1%

LGD = 30%

Calculate EL.

Solution

$EL = EAD \times DP \times LGD = 100 \times 1\% \times 30\% = 0.3$ million

Example

국민은행이 100억원의 대출을 하고 있다. 대출의 부도율은 1%이고, 손실률은 30%이다. 예상손실을 계산하라.

Solution

$EL = EAD \times DP \times LGD = 100 \times 1\% \times 30\% = 0.3$억

chapter

10

The value of the firm

Working capital

Working capital, sometimes called gross working capital, simply refers to current assets used in operations.

A firm's investments in short-term assets — cash, marketable securities, inventory, and accounts receivable.

Net working capital

순운전자본

Net working capital is defined as current assets minus current liabilities.

Net working capital is positive when current assets are greater than current liabilities. This means the cash that will become available over the next 12 months will be greater than the cash that must be paid out.

Example

(million won)

	Y1	Y2
Current Assets	707	761
Current liabilities	455	486

Calculate the change in the net working capital.

Solution

(million won)

	Y1	Y2
Current Assets	707	761
Current liabilities	455	486
Net working capital	252	275

The change in net working capital in Y2 is the difference between the net working capital in Y2 and Y1; that is, 275 − 252 = 23(million won).

The change in net working capital is usually positivc in a growing firm.

Current assets increased from 707 in Y1 to 761 in Y2.

Current liabilities increased from 455 in Y1 to 486 in Y2.

Calculate the change in the net working capital.

Solution

	Y1	Y2
Current Assets	707	761
Current liabilities	455	486
Net working capital	252	275

The change in net working capital in Y2 is the difference between the net working capital in Y2 and Y1; that is, 275 − 252 = 23.

Example

(million won)

	Y1	Y2
Current Assets	700	800
Current liabilities	400	450

Calculate the change in the net working capital.

Solution

(million won)

	Y1	Y2
Current Assets	700	800
Current liabilities	400	450
Net working capital	300	350

350−300=50

Example

At the beginning of the year, a firm had current assets of $121,306 and current liabilities of $124,509. At the end of the year, the current assets were $122,418 and the current liabilities were $103,718. What is the change in net working capital?

Solution

Change in net working capital = ($122,418 − $103,718) − ($121,306 − $124,509) = $21,903

운전자본관리

운전자본관리는 현금관리, 유가증권관리, 매출채권관리, 재고자산관리 등 유동자산의 관리는 물론 외상매입금·단기부채·미지급비용 등 유동부채관리도 포함한다.

Accounts receivable

매출채권(accounts receivable)은 일반적인 상거래에 따라 발생하는 것으로, 매출액 중에서 아직 회수되지 않은 부분을 말한다.

현금보유동기

거래동기(transaction motive)란 영업활동을 원활히 하기 위해 거래에 필요한 현금을 충분히 보유하는 것을 말한다.

예비동기(precautionary motive)는 비상사태나 우발적인 사태에 대비하기 위하여 현금을 보유하는 것을 말한다.

투기동기(speculative motive)는 장래에 큰 이익을 얻을 수 있는 투자기회에 투자할 목적으로 현금을 보유하려는 것이다.

The value of the firm

Relative Valuation

One illustration of this approach is the use of an industry-average price/earnings ratio to value a firm, the assumption being that the other firms in the industry are comparable to the firm being valued and that the market, on average, prices these firms correctly.

EV/EBITDA multiple

기업의 가치가 영업활동을 통한 이익의 몇 배인가를 나타내는 지표.

EBITDA

Earnings Before Interest, Taxes, Depreciation, and Amortization
Estimated by adding depreciation and amortization back to operating income.

EBITDA는 현금지출이 없는 비용인 감가상각비를 비용에서 제거함으로써 영업활동을 통한 현금창출 능력을 보다 잘 알 수 있게 해준다. 또한 국가간 또는 기업간에 순이익이 상이하게 계산되는 요인(세제, 감가상각 방법의 차이)이 제거되므로, 기업의 수익창출 능력을 비교할 수 있는 지표로 널리 활용된다.

EBITDA는 수익성을 나타내는 지표로, 순이익 개념을 확장시킨 것이다. 순이익을 산출할 때, 회계처리 과정에서 이자비용과 세금, 감가상각비 등을 빼게 되는데, 이 중 감가상각비 관련 항목은 나라마다 회계기준이 달라 실제 수익 규모를 부풀리거나 줄여서 보여줄 수 있으며, 금융비용과 세금을 빼게 되면 그 회사가 순수하게 기본적인 영업 활동에서 수익을 지속적으로 창출할 수 있는 능력이 제대로 드러나지 않는 문제점이 생길 수 있다. 이런 관점에서, 일반적인 영업실적에 표시되는 순이익의 보조지표로 이자비용, 세금, 감가상각비를 빼지 않은 수익지표인 EBITDA를 활용하는 것이다.
EV는 타인자본까지 포함한 기업의 시장가치를, EBITDA는 기업의 실질적인 수익 창출 능력을 표시한다. 이 둘을 비교하면 기업의 시장가치가 순수한 영업활동을 통한 이익의 몇 배로 형성되어 있는지를 알 수 있다.
EV/EBITDA 비율은 EV를 EBITDA로 나눈 값으로 표시하며, 그 비율이 낮다면 회사의 주가가 기업가치에 비해 저평가되었다고 볼 수 있다.

EBITDA is commonly used in the telecommunications industry to analyze companies on the basis of operating performance, leverage and liquidity. Since the telecommunications business is a very capital intensive business, capital expenditures and level of debt and interest expenses may have a significant impact on net income for companies with similar operating results. Therefore, EBITDA provides a more accurate reflection of the company's operating results.

Depreciation and Amortization

While depreciation and amortization are treated as tax-deductible expenses in an income statement, they are different from other expenses because they are non-cash charges.

Goodwill

영업권

기업이 다른 동종의 기업들에 비하여 초과수익력을 가질 경우 그 배타적 영리기회를 가질 수 있는 권리. 영업권이 생기는 원인은 입지조건·생산기술·조직의 우수성, 상호·상표·상품에 대한 신용, 거래선이나 단골과의 특수관계, 제조·판매면에서의 법적·경제적 독점성, 고객 등 이해자 집단의 호의, 기업의 역사 등이 있는데, 이것들이 결합하여 초과수익력이 되는 것이 보통이다.

Amortization of goodwill

영업권의 상각

Intangible asset

A legal claim to some future benefit, typically a claim to future cash. Goodwill, intellectual property, patents, copyrights, and trademarks are examples of intangible assets.

Tangible asset

An asset whose value depends on particular physical properties. These include reproducible assets such as buildings or machinery and non-reproducible assets such as land, a mine, or a work of art. Also called real assets.

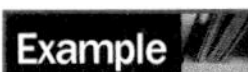

MBC와 SBS 두 기업이 비교가능할 때, 다음 빈 칸을 채우시오. SBS는 5년 감가상각이고, MBC는 10년 감가상각을 한다.

	SBS	MBC
Current Assets	3,000	4,500
Fixed Assets	5,000	
Revenues	10,000	
Cost of Goods Sold	6,000	
Depreciation		
EBIT		
EV/EBIT		
EBITDA		
EV/EBITDA		

Solution

$$\frac{Current\ Assets}{Fixed\ Assets}=\frac{3}{5}$$

$$\frac{Cost\ of\ Goods\ Sold}{Revenues}=\frac{6}{10}$$

$$\frac{Sales-Cost\ of\ goods\ sold}{net\ sales}=\frac{4}{10}$$, Gross Profit Margin=40%

$$\frac{Reveunes}{Assets}=\frac{10,000}{8,000}$$

	SBS	MBC
Current Assets	3,000	4,500
Fixed Assets	5,000	7,500
Revenues	10,000	15,000
Cost of Goods Sold	6,000	9,000
Depreciation	1,000	750
EBIT	3,000	5,250
EV/EBIT	2.67	2.29
EBITDA	4,000	6,000
EV/EBITDA	2	2

Example

Assume that an analyst is valuing K company. The EV/EBITDA multiples for comparable firms are as follows:

Firm	EV/EBITDA
1	8.1
2	11.5
3	5.7
4	7.6
5	9.8

Average: 8.5

While the average EV/EBITDA for comparable firms is 8.5, an analyst can believe K company should trade at 5.0 EV/EBITDA. The rationale behind 5.0 EV/EBITDA can be due to high sovereign risk and unfriendly regulatory environment.

Given that no two firms are exactly similar in terms of risk and growth, the definition of comparable firms is a subjective one.

Analyst

Employee of a brokerage or fund management house who studies companies and makes buy-and-sell recommendations on their stocks. Most specialize in a specific industry.

In the financial industry, an analyst, often known as a financial or equity analyst, is a professional who evaluates and analyzes financial data, market trends, and the performance of companies. Their primary responsibility is to provide insights and recommendations on stocks to assist investors, fund managers, and clients in making informed investment decisions. Here are key points about this role:

Job Description:

Analysts work for brokerages, investment banks, or fund management companies.

They study financial statements, market trends, economic indicators, and industry-specific factors to assess the performance of companies.

Buy-and-Sell Recommendations:

Based on their analysis, analysts make buy, sell, or hold recommendations for stocks. These recommendations are crucial for investors looking for guidance on which stocks to include or exclude from their portfolios.

Specialization:

Many analysts specialize in a specific industry or sector, becoming experts in understanding the nuances and dynamics of that particular market.

Research Reports:

Analysts compile their findings into research reports, presenting a detailed analysis of a company's financial health, growth prospects, and risks.

These reports often include earnings forecasts, valuation metrics, and a rationale for the buy or sell recommendation.

Client Interaction:

Analysts may interact with clients, fund managers, and other professionals, providing explanations and insights into their recommendations.

Market Insight:

Analysts contribute to the overall market understanding by sharing insights on industry trends, economic factors, and potential investment opportunities or risks.

Continuous Monitoring:

Analysts continuously monitor the companies and industries they cover, staying informed about any developments that could impact stock performance.

Regulatory Compliance:

They must adhere to financial regulations and ethical standards, ensuring the accuracy and fairness of their analyses.

The role of an analyst is crucial in helping market participants make well-informed investment decisions. Their insights and recommendations influence the buying and selling activities in the stock market.

Example

Assume that an analyst is valuing J company.

J Company has 50 shares of common stock outstanding, EBITDA of 2,000,000 won and Net Debt of 3,000,000 won.

The EV/EBITDA multiples for comparable firms are as follows:

Firm	EV/EBITDA
1	5.2
2	3.4
3	5.7
4	7.6
5	9.8

What's the target price of J Company?

Solution

Average: 6.3

$$6.3 = \frac{EV}{2{,}000{,}000}$$

Value per Share: $\frac{2{,}000{,}000 \times 6.3 - 3{,}000{,}000}{50} = 192{,}000$ won

EPS

$$\frac{(Net\ profit\ after\ taxes) - (Preferred\ stock\ dividends)}{Average\ number\ of\ common\ shares}$$

Earnings Per Share (EPS) shows the after-tax earnings generated for each share of common stock.

PER

$$PER = \frac{Price}{EPS}$$

주가수익비율(Price Earnings Ratio)은 주식시장 투자지표 중에서 가장 대표적으로 활용되고 있는 지표 중 하나이다. PER는 현재주가를 1주당순이익으로 나눈 비율로써 주가가 1주당순이익의 몇 배가 되는가를 측정하는 지표이다. 기업의 단위당 수익력(수익가치)에 대한 투자자들의 질적 평가로서 상대적인 주가수준을 평가하는데 활용되고 있다. 일반적으로 PER수준을 측정하여 과거와 비교함으로써 과거보다 높고 낮음에 따라 주가수준의 고평가 또는 저평가 정도를 판단하는데 활용되고 있다. 만일 과거에 비해 PER가 낮을 경우 현재주가는 주당이익 1원에 대해 시장에서 저평가되고 있다는 것으로 주가가 상승할 가능성이 높다고 판단할 수 있다. 이는 향후 주가가 적정하게 평가될 경우 주가가 상승하리라는 믿음에서 비롯된 것이다. 즉, 투자자들은 기업의 수익력에 근본적인 변화가 없다고 할 경우 PER가 과거평균수준으로 회귀할 것으로 예측한다는 것이다. 과거 PER수준과 비교하는데 활용되는 것 외에도 어느 한 시점에서 산업 또는 시장평균 PER수준과 비교하여 해당기업의 주가수준의 고평가 또는 저평가정도를 판단하는데 활용되기도 한다. 최근에는 주식투자가 글로벌화 되면서 국가 또는 거래소시장 평균 PER를 비교함으로써 국가 또는 거래소시장 전체의 상대적 주가수준을 평가하기도 한다.

If a company is making losses, it will not have a P/E ratio that makes any sense, as the earnings figure is negative.

PBR

$$PBR = \frac{Price}{BPS}$$

Price Book Value Ratio

현재의 주가를 주당순자산으로 나눈 것으로 현주가가 1주당 순자산의 몇 배인가를 나타낸다. PER가 기업의 수익성측면에서 주가를 판단하는 지표인데 비해 PBR은 재무상태 또는 재산상태 면에서 주가를 판단하는 지표라고 할 수 있다.

Example

Assets	Debt	20,000,000
	Equity	50,000,000
70,000,000		70,000,000

K Corporation has 2,000 shares of common stock outstanding that are currently being sold for 30,000 won per share. The firm's debt is 20 million won.

$$BPS = \frac{50,000,000}{2,000} = 25,000$$

$$PBR = \frac{Price}{BPS} = \frac{30,000}{25,000} = 1.2$$

Example

Given the financial information for ABC Inc. where the total shareholder's equity is W50 million, and the number of outstanding shares is 2,000, calculate the Book Value per Share for ABC Inc.

Solution

Book Value per Share = 25,000

Example

Consider a company, ABC Corporation, with a current market price of 30,000 won per share and a book value of 25,000 won per share. Calculate the Price-to-Book Ratio.

Solution

PBR = 1.2

Assume that an analyst is valuing K company.

K Company has 5 million shares of common stock outstanding and Net Income of 30,000 million won.

The PE multiples for comparable firms are as follows:

Firm	PE
1	8.1
2	11.5
3	5.7
4	7.6
5	9.8

What's the target price of K Company?

Solution

Average: 8.5

EPS: 6,000 won

Target price: $8.5 \times 6,000 = 51,000$ won

Tobin's q-ratio

$$\frac{The\,market\,value\,of\,assets}{The\,replacement\,value\,of\,assets}$$

기업의 자산에 대한 시장가치를 그 자산의 대체원가(replacement cost of its physical capital) 나눈 값이다.

The ratio of the market value of assets to their replacement value at the end of the most recent fiscal year. The market value of assets is proxied by the book value of assets minus the book value of equity minus deferred taxes plus the market value of common stock. The replacement value of assets is proxied by the book value of assets.

일반적으로 q비율이 1보다 큰 경우에는 자본설비(capital equipment)의 시장가치가 대체원가보다 큰 가치를 가지므로 기업이 투자하려는 유인(incentive)을 갖게 되며, q비율이 1보다 적으면 투자유인이 없다고 할 수 있다.

Example

다음 괄호 안에 들어갈 적절한 말을 쓰시오.

(　　　)는 기업의 부채 및 자기자본의 시장가치를 보유자산의 대체비용으로 나눈 비율이다.

Solution

Tobin's q

Example

서울기업의 내년도 예상주당순이익은 12,000원으로 예측된다. 이 기업의 평균 PER은 약 10배~15배 사이로 형성되고 있다. PER모형에 의하여 서울기업의 주가를 추정하면?

Solution

120,000원~180,000원

Example

피자헛은 EBITDA가 5,000원이고, 순이익이 4,000원이다. 순부채가 1,000원이고, 주식수가 20주이다. 부채는 2,000원이고, 자본은 6,000원이다.

	EV/EBITDA	PER	PBR	Tobin's Q
미스터피자	2	3	3	3
도미노피자	1	4	5	1
파파존스	3	5	7	5

1) EV/EBITDA에 따른 피자헛의 주당 주식가치는?
2) PER에 따른 피자헛의 주당 주식가치는?
3) PBR에 따른 피자헛의 주당 주식가치는?
4) Tobin's Q에 따른 피자헛의 주당 주식가치는?

Solution

1) $Average = 2 = \frac{EV}{5,000}$

$EV = 10,000$

Equity Value: 9,000원, Value per Share: 450원

2) Average:4, EPS: 200원,

$4 = \frac{Price}{200}$

Value per Share: 800원

3) Average: 5, BPS: 300원,

$5 = \frac{Price}{300}$

Value per Share: 1,500원

4) Average: 3,

$3 = \frac{8,000 - 6,000 + Equity\ Value}{8,000}$

Equity Value: 22,000원, Value per Share: 1,100원

Absolute Valuation Vs Relative Valuation

Analysts use valuation to establish the intrinsic value of a stock, business, or asset. Calculating an asset's intrinsic value is known as valuation in finance. Absolute valuation and relative valuation are the two main categories of valuation models.

Absolute valuation ignores the market value of other comparable assets in favor of focusing solely on the features of the support that has to be valued, such as free cash flow, to estimate its intrinsic worth.

Relative valuation is the antithesis of absolute valuation. Relative valuation assesses the value of a corporation based on the value of other comparable assets or businesses rather than the company's intrinsic value.

The defining characteristic of an absolute valuation model is that in this model the value of the asset is derived only on the basis of characteristics of that asset. There is no consideration regarding the valuation of other comparable assets that are trading in the marketplace. These models are basically known as the "discounted cash flow" of the DCF models.

Relative valuation models are different from discounted cash flow models. They are different in the sense that they do not value a firm or an asset based on what its intrinsic value is.

The term "absolute valuation" refers to the business valuation method that utilizes DCF analysis to determine the firm's fair value. This method helps determine a company's financial worth based on its projected cash flows. The absolute valuation model helps determine the fair market value of a business, security, or asset.

The absolute value method differs from the relative value models that examine what a company is worth compared to its competitors. Absolute value models try to determine a company's intrinsic worth based on its projected cash flows.

Relative value is the opposite of absolute value. While absolute value examines the intrinsic value of an asset or company without comparing it to any others, relative value is based on the value of similar assets or companies. Analysts and investors who use relative value analysis for stocks look at financial statements and other multiples of the companies they're interested in and compare it to other, similar firms to determine if those potential companies are over or undervalued.

Absolute Valuation

FCF

$EBIT(1-t)$

$+Depreciation$

$-Capital\ \ Expenditures$

$-Working\ Capital\ Change$

$=FCF$

The Free Cash Flow is calculated by multiplying the Earnings Before Interest and Taxes by 1 minus the tax rate and then adding Depreciation, while subtracting Capital Expenditures and the change in Working Capital.

Example

L company reported earnings before interest and taxes of 3,482 won in Y_0. It had depreciation of 4,613 won and capital expenditures of 5,560 won in Y_0. In addition, the working capital increased from 14,306 won in Y_{-1} to 15,405 won in Y_0. The earnings before interest and taxes is expected to increase to 3,967 won in Y_1. Capital expenditures, depreciation, and working capital are all expected to increase by 5% in Y_1. The firm had a tax rate of 38% in Y_0. Calculate the free cash flows to the firm for Y_0 and Y_1.

Solution

$Working\ Capital\ Change_0 = 15{,}405 - 14{,}306 = 1{,}099$

$Working\ Capital\ Change_1 = 15{,}405 \times 0.05 = 770$

	Y0	Project Y1
EBIT(1-t)	2,159	2,460
Depreciation	4,613	4,844
Capital Expenditures	5,560	5,838
Working Capital Change	1,099	770
FCF	114	696

Economic Value Added

경제적 부가가치

Value added to shareholders by management during a given year.
기업이 영업활동을 통하여 새로이 창출한 부가가치

EVA = EBIT(1 − Corporate tax rate) − (Total capital)(After-tax cost of capital)

Total capital includes long-term debt, preferred stock, and common equity.
EVA is an estimate of a business's true economic profit for the year.
EVA represents the residual income that remains after the cost of all capital has been deducted.

EVA는 타인자본은 물론 자기자본에 대한 자본비용을 차감한 이익이다.

기업이 양(+)의 EVA를 창출한다는 것은 영업용 투자자본을 가지고 영업활동을 통해 발생한 이익이 자본조달비용을 지불하고도 기업이 부가적인 이익이 창출되었다는 것이다.
EVA가 다른 경영성과지표와 비교하여 보다 우월하게 평가받고 있는 이유는 기업 고유의 영업활동에 투자된 자산과 영업성과를 통해 창출된 이익으로 평가한다는 점과 주주의 기회비용인 자기자본비용을 고려한다는 점이다.

손익계산서의 당기순이익은 자본비용 중 타인자본에 대한 이자비용만을 차감한 이익인데 반하여 EVA는 자기자본비용도 차감하기 때문에 경영의사결정 시 투하자기자본을 고려하게 한다.

NOPAT

Net Operating Profit After Tax

세후순영업이익

기업이 순수영업으로부터 창출한 이익에서 법인세를 차감한 이익

NOPAT = Operating Income × (1 − Tax Rate)

Net operating profit after tax is a financial measure that shows how well a company performed through its core operations, net of taxes.

Example

Last year K Inc. reported the following income statement:

Sales	2,000,000
Cost of goods sold	1,200,000
Depreciation	500,000
Operating income(EBIT)	300,000
Interest expense	100,000
EBT	200,000
Taxes (40%)	80,000
Net income	120,000

The company had a total of $250,000 of capital, and it estimates that its after-tax cost of capital is 10 percent. Assume that K's only noncash item was depreciation.

What was the company's EVA?

Solution

EVA

=EBIT(1 − Corporate tax rate) − (Total capital)(After-tax cost of capital)

= $300,000(1 − 0.4) − ($250,000)(0.1) = $155,000

Example

괄호 안을 채우시오.

EVA는 ( )에서 투하자본에 대한 자본비용을 차감하여 계산된다.

Solution

세후순영업이익

Example

Last year J Inc. had $5,000,000 in operating income(EBIT). The company had a depreciation expense of $1,000,000 and an interest expense of $1,000,000; its corporate tax rate was 40 percent. The company had a total of $25,000,000 of capital, and it estimates that its after-tax cost of capital is 10 percent. Assume that R's only noncash item was depreciation.

1. What was the company's net income for the year?
2. What was the company's EVA?

Solution

1.

EBIT	5,000,000
Interest	1,000,000
EBT	4,000,000
Taxes (40%)	1,600,000
Net income	2,400,000

2. EVA

$$=\text{EBIT}(1-\text{Corporate tax rate})-(\text{Total capital})(\text{After-tax cost of capital})$$

$$=\$5{,}000{,}000(1-0.4)-(\$25{,}000{,}000)(0.1)=\$500{,}000$$

Agency Theory

The theory of the relationship between principals and agents. It involves the nature of the costs of resolving conflicts of interest between principals and agents.
Shareholders are the Principals.
Managers are the Agents.

Agency problem

An agency problem arises when managers own only a fraction of the ownership shares of the firm. This partial ownership may cause managers to work less vigorously than otherwise and to consume more perquisites because the majority owners bear most of the cost.
Agency problems may arise if managers and shareholders have different objectives.

Perquisites

Luxurious offices, company car, membership in clubs

Agency relationship

We define an agency relationship as a contract under which the principals engage the agent to perform some service on their behalf which involves delegating some decision making authority to the agent.
1인 이상의 사람(주인: principal)이 다른 사람(대리인: agent)에게 자신을 대신하여 의사결정을 할 수 있도록 의사결정권한을 위임한 계약관계

Agency costs

We define agency costs as the sum of:

① the monitoring expenditures by the principal,

The principal can limit divergences from his interest by establishing appropriate incentives for the agent and by incurring monitoring costs designed to limit the aberrant activities of the agent.

② the bonding expenditures by the agent,

It will pay the agent to expend resources to guarantee that he will not take certain actions which would harm the principal.

③ the residual loss.

There will be some divergence between the agent's decisions and those decisions which would maximize the welfare of the principal.

기업을 둘러싸고 있는 이해관계자들이 자신들의 이익을 극대화하기 위해 노력하는 과정에서 나타나는 이해다툼으로 인해 발생하는 비용을 대리비용(agency cost)이라 한다.

Monitoring cost

감시비용(monitoring cost)는 대리인의 행위가 주인의 이익으로부터 이탈하는 것을 감시하는 데 드는 비용을 말한다.

Bonding cost

확증비용(bonding cost)은 대리인이 주인에게 해가 되는 행위를 하고 있지 않음을 보증하는 과정에서 발생하는 비용을 말한다.

Residual loss

잔여손실(residual loss)은 대리인의 의사결정과 주인의 입장에서 본 최적의사결정 사이에 존재하는 차이로 말미암아 나타나는 부의 감소를 의미한다.

M&A

mergers and acquisitions

합병은 규모의 경제, 시장경쟁력의 강화, 경영상의 비효율성 제거, 시너지효과, 제품의 다양화, 위험분산, 재무구조의 개선 및 조세효과 등을 목적으로 둘 이상의 기업이 일정한 법률적 절차에 따라 하나의 기업을 형성하는 것이다.

Merger

Merger means any transaction that forms one economic unit from two or more previous ones.

The combination of two firms to form a single firm.

Acquiring Company

A company that seeks to acquire another firm.

Target Company

Target firm

A firm that another company seeks to acquire.

A firm that is the object of a takeover by another firm.

Tender offer

주식의 공개매수제의

Horizontal merger

A horizontal merger involves two firms operating in the same kind of business activity.

Vertical mergers

Vertical mergers involve different stages of production operations.

Conglomerate mergers

Conglomerate mergers involve firms engaged in unrelated types of business activity.

Theories of M&A activity

Efficiency Explanations

If the management of firm X is more efficient than the management of firm Y, and if after firm X acquires firm Y, the efficiency of firm Y is brought up to the level of efficiency of firm X, efficiency is increased by merger.
기업 Y의 효율성이 기업 X의 효율성 보다 낮을 경우, 두 기업이 합병하면 기업 Y의 효율성이 기업 X의 수준으로 향상될 것이기 때문에 합병이 발생한다는 이론이다.

Efficiency theories also include the possibility of achieving some form of synergy.
If synergy occurs the value of the combined firm exceeds the value of the individual firms brought together by the mergers.

$$V_{XY} > V_X + V_Y$$

합병 후의 기업가치가 합병 전의 개별기업의 가치를 합한 것보다 클 것이라는 이론이다.

$$synergy = V_{XY} - (V_X + V_Y)$$

$$premium = C_0 - V_Y$$

C_0: 인수가격

An acquisition premium is the difference between the actual price paid to acquire a company and the estimated value of the acquired company before the acquisition.

Let's assume Company X wants to acquire Company Y. If Company Y is worth $20 per share but Company Y offers $25 per share, this means Company X is willing to pay a 25% acquisition premium.

합병의 NPV $= synergy - premium$

$$= V_{XY} - V_X - C_0$$

Example

Let's assume Company X wants to acquire Company Y.

If Company Y is worth $20 per share but Company Y offers $24 per share, this means Company X is willing to pay a (   ) acquisition premium.

Solution

20%

Example

Let's assume Company S wants to acquire Company K.

If Company K is worth 10,000 won per share but Company K offers 14,000 won per share, this means Company S is willing to pay a (   ) acquisition premium.

Solution

40%

Example

서울기업은 관악기업을 흡수합병하려고 한다. 합병 후 기업가치는 70억원이 될 것으로 예상되는데, 관악기업의 주주들은 현재 주가보다 40% 높은 인수가격을 요구하고 있다. 두 기업의 재무자료는 다음과 같다.

	서울기업	관악기업
기업가치	40억원	10억원
발행주식수	20만 주	10만 주
주가	2만원	1만원

1) 인수대금을 현금으로 지급하는 경우, 합병의 NPV는?

2) 인수대금을 주식으로 교부하는 경우, 합병의 NPV는?

Solution

1) $synergy = 70 - 50 = 20$

$premium = 14 - 10 = 4$

$NPV = 16$

2) $\text{교부주식수} = \dfrac{1{,}400{,}000{,}000}{20{,}000} = 70{,}000\text{주}$

합병 후 기업가치는 70억원이고, 발행주식수는 27만 주가 된다.

7만 주의 가치는 다음과 같다.

$70 \times \dfrac{7}{27} = 18.15\text{억원}$

$premium = 18.15 - 10 = 8.15$

$NPV = 11.85\text{억원}$

Going Public

기업공개(going public)란 일정한 요건을 갖춘 기업이 새로운 주식을 발행하여 일반투자자들에게 균일한 조건으로 공모하거나, 개인이나 소수의 주주에게 집중되어 있는 주식을 일반투자자에게 널리 분산시키기 위하여 매출하는 것을 말한다.
The act of selling stock to the public at large by a closely held corporation or its principal stockholders.

Going Private

공개된 주식을 매수하여 개인기업화하는 것.

Initial Public Offering (IPO) Market

The market consisting of stocks of companies that are in the process of going public.

상장

증권거래소는 상장요건을 충족한 기업들이 발행한 유가증권을 매매거래될 수 있는 대상물로 인정하고 있다. 이와 같이 증권거래소가 유가증권을 매매거래의 대상으로 인정하는 행위를 상장이라 한다.

Benefits of Listing

필요자금 조달의 용이.
기업인지도 제고.

Exemption of tax on capital gains - In case of listed stocks, tax on capital gains of ordinary investors (excluding majority shareholders who hold more that 3% of shares or more than KRW 10 billion, or a person who has special relationship with the companies) is exempted.
Application of elastic tax rate on the securities transaction - Securities transaction tax for unlisted stocks is at the rate of 0.5%, but for the listed stocks, it is 0.15%.

상장주식의 경우 일반투자자(지분율 3% 이상 또는 시가총액 100억원 이상 대주주 및 특수관계자 제외)의 주식 양도에 따른 양도소득세는 면제된다.
비상장기업의 주식양도는 0.5%의 증권거래세율이 적용되지만 증권거래소를 통해 양도되는 주식은 0.15%의 증권거래세가 적용된다.

주간사회사

유가증권 발행업무 총괄대행 회사. 주식 채권 등 유가증권 발행업무를 총괄하는 회사를 뜻한다. 발행사와 협의를 거쳐 유가증권의 모집주선 및 인수에 따른 모든 업무를 대행해 주는 역할을 한다.
주간사회사는 유가증권 인수가능여부에 대한 예비분석을 비롯하여 청약사무와 발행관련 공시 등 인수업무에 대해 총괄적인 책임을 진다.
발행규모가 방대하면 간사회사들이 간사단을 구성, 공동으로 간사업무를 수행하기도 한다. 이 경우 간사업무의 핵심역할을 하는 회사를 주간사회사, 다른 간사업체들은 공동간사회사라고 한다. 간사회사와 협의해 발행되는 유가증권을 인수하는 기관은 인수기관이라 부른다.

공모(public offering)는 증권의 인수자로 하여금 인수증권을 불특정다수인에게 공개매매하게 하는 방식이고, 사모(private placement)는 증권발행자가 직접 특정 소수의 인수인과의 교섭을 통하여 증권을 발행하는 방식이다. 공모는 일반투자자를 대상으로 주주를 모집하므로 일시에 거액의 자금조달이 가능하고 선전효과를 얻을 수도 있다. 반면 사모는 발행절차가 간편하고 발행자와 인수자간의 긴밀하고 신축적인 교섭이 가능하며 발행비용도 공모에 비해 저렴하고, 공모시 요구되는 재무상태의 공개의무가 부과되지 않는 이점이 있다.

IR

기업과 주주 및 투자자간의 적극적인 Communication을 통하여 기업의 내용과 경영방침 등에 관한 정보를 현재 또는 잠재적 투자자에게 제공함으로써 기업에 대한 이해를 증진시키고, 신뢰관계를 구축하려는데 그 목적이 있으며, 증권시장에서 안정주주의 확대와 함께 자금조달의 원활화를 도모함으로써 기업의 지속적인 성장 · 발전에 기여하도록 하는 전략적 Marketing 활동이다.

장기적인 증권시장 홍보전략의 일환이므로 주가에 긍정적인 영향을 주게 되어 주가의 상승이나 안정적인 주가유지에 기여한다.

기업정보를 자발적으로 신속하게 투자자들에게 전달함으로써 기업에 대한 신뢰성을 증대한다.

Securities market

증권시장

The financial market may be divided into the money market and capital market. Securities market is an important, organized capital market where transaction of capital is facilitated by means of direct financing using securities as a commodity. Securities market can be divided into a primary market and secondary market. The securities market includes both primary markets, where new securities are issued and sold to investors, and secondary markets, where existing securities are traded among investors.

The stock market is a type of capital market where investors buy and sell shares of publicly traded companies. It provides a platform for companies to raise capital by issuing stocks and for investors to invest in these stocks. The stock market plays a crucial role in the economy by facilitating the transfer of funds between savers and companies in need of capital.

금융시장은 금융자산의 만기에 따라 화폐시장(money market)과 자본시장(capital market)으로 구분된다. 화폐시장에서는 만기가 1년 미만인 증권이 거래가 되는데 여기에 참가하는 주체들은 이러한 단기증권을 매매함으로써 유동성을 조절하고 있다. 자본시장은 기업이나 정부가 1년 이상의 장기자금을 조달하기 위해 참가하는 시장인데, 주식, 회사채, 국공채 등 여러 종류의 장기증권이 거래된다.

화폐시장(money market)에는 콜시장, 기업어음시장, 양도성 예금증서시장 등이 있다.

Money markets are the financial markets in which funds are borrowed or loaned for short periods.

콜시장

금융기관 상호간에 일시적인 자금과부족 조절을 위해 초단기로 자금을 차입하거나 대여하는 시장

Direct financing

직접금융

자금의 수요자가 발행한 주식과 채권 등의 증권을 자금투자자인 투자자가 매입함으로써 자금이 투자자로부터 수요자에게로 직접 들어가는 금융거래를 직접금융이라 한다.

Direct finance is a method of financing where borrowers borrow funds directly from the financial market without using a third party service, such as a financial intermediary.

Indirect financing

Indirect finance is where borrowers borrow funds from the financial market through indirect means, such as through a financial intermediary. This is different from direct financing where there is a direct connection to the financial markets as indicated by the borrower issuing securities directly on the market.

간접금융

자금의 수요자와 공급자가 거래상대방을 직접 찾는다는 것은 매우 어려운 일이며 많은 시간과 비용이 든다. 이에 따라 금융기관이 자금의 공급자로부터 자금을 예치받아 이를 자금 수요자에게 공급해 주게 되는데, 이러한 금융방식을 간접금융이라 한다.

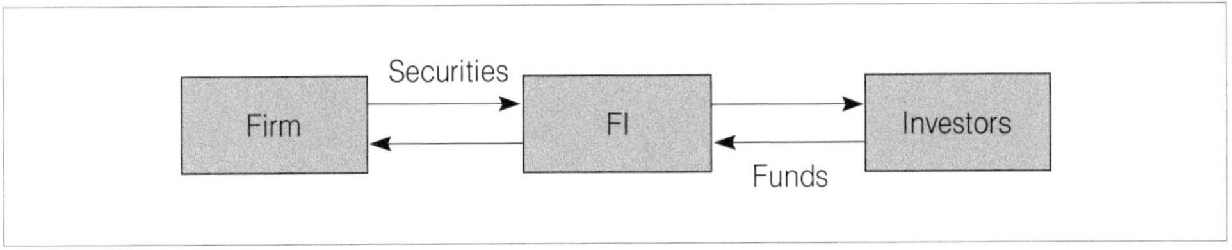

Primary markets

발행시장

New issues market

Primary markets are the markets in which corporations raise capital by issuing new securities. Primary markets are the markets in which corporations raise new capital.

증권을 발행하는 시장을 발행시장이라 하고, 발행된 증권이 거래되는 시장을 유통시장이라 한다.

The primary market is an intermittent and discrete market where the initially listed shares are traded first time, changing hands from the listed company to the investors. It refers to the process through which the companies, the issuers of stocks, acquire capital by offering their stocks to investors who supply the capital.

Secondary markets

유통시장

Secondary markets are the markets in which securities and other financial assets are traded among investors after they have been issued by corporations.

Secondary markets are markets in which existing securities are traded among investors.

Investment Banking House

Investment banking house is an organization that underwrites and distributes new investment securities and helps businesses obtain financing. Merrill Lynch, Dean Witter and Goldman Sachs are examples of financial service corporations which offer investment banking services.

"To underwrite" in finance refers to the process where a financial institution, typically an investment bank, guarantees to buy unsold shares or bonds from a company issuing them. This guarantees the issuing company that it will receive the necessary funds even if all the securities are not sold to investors during the initial public offering or bond issuance.

Underwriting involves assessing the risk associated with the securities being issued and setting the terms and conditions of the offering, including the price at which the securities will be sold. The underwriter may then purchase the securities from the issuing company at a predetermined price and resell them to investors, typically at a higher price, to make a profit.

직접발행과 간접발행

증권의 발행은 발행위험을 발행자와 인수자(underwriter) 사이에 누가 부담하느냐에 따라 직접발행과 간접발행으로 나누어진다.

직접발행은 증권발행자 자신이 증권발행에 따른 위험, 즉 공모발행시 미인수 잔여분이 발생하였을 경우 이를 인수해야 하는 위험을 직접 부담하는 발행방식이며, 간접발행은 인수자가 증권발행자로부터 발행증권을 인수하는 방식이다.

직접발행은 발행회사가 일반 공중에게 직접 증권을 발행하고 발행예정액이 전액 소화될 수 없을 때 야기되는 자금조달계획의 차질이라는 위험을 자신이 부담하는 방법이다. 반면에 간접발행은 증권의 발행위험이나 발행사무를 계약에 의해 제3의 인수기관이 맡는 방법이다.

인수는 유가증권의 매매차익을 목적으로 단순이 취득하는 것이 아니라 인수자가 유가증권이 공정한 가격에 거래가 이루어질 수 있도록 하기 위해 일단 자기계산으로 취득하였다가 분매하는 행위를 말한다.

간접발행은 증권인수방식에 따라 총액인수방식(firm commitment underwriting), 잔액인수방식(stand-by underwriting), 전부 아니면 무효방식(AON : all or none)으로 구분된다.

총액인수방식은 인수인이 사전에 발행자와 약정한 가액으로 증권발행 총액을 인수하여 이에 소정의 이익을 붙여 일반대중에게 판매하는 방식이다. 인수기관이 증권발행에 대한 모든 위험을 부담하고 증권발행 총액을 인수하여 인수회사의 자기책임하에 이를 투자자에게 매출하는 방법이다.
잔액인수방식은 인수인이 일차적으로 발행증권을 발행인과 사전에 약정한 가격으로 일반대중에게 매각한 다음 미소화분이 있을 경우 이를 인수하는 방식이다. 일정기간 동안은 발행자를 대신하여 신규로 발행되는 증권의 모집 또는 매출을 위탁판매하지만, 일정기간이 경과한 후 발행증권의 미매각분이 있을 경우 이를 발행자로부터 미리 정해진 발행가액으로 인수하여 자기책임하에 투자자에게 매각하는 방법이다.
전부 아니면 무효방식은 인수자가 일단 발행증권 특정량을 모두 맡아 분매하되, 일정기간 내에 인수전량을 분매하지 못할 경우 인수제의 자체가 무효가 되는 계약이다.

장외시장

장외시장(off-board market)이란 거래소 밖에서 증권의 매매가 이루어지는 시장을 말한다. 장외시장은 증권회사의 점두에서 증권회사와 고객 간에 거래가 이루어지는 점두시장(over-the-counter market)과 증권회사를 거치지 않고 거래당사자 간에 직접 증권을 매매하는 직접거래시장으로 분류할 수 있다.

MA

moving average

이동평균

2-day moving average

2일 이동평균: $MA_t = \dfrac{P_t + P_{t-1}}{2}$

3-day moving average

3일 이동평균: $MA_t = \dfrac{P_t + P_{t-1} + P_{t-2}}{3}$

Example

Draw 2-day MA line and 3-day MA line.

	Day 1	Day 2	Day 3	Day 4	Day 5	Day 6	Day 7
Price	1,000	1,500	2,000	2,500	2,100	1,700	3,100

Solution

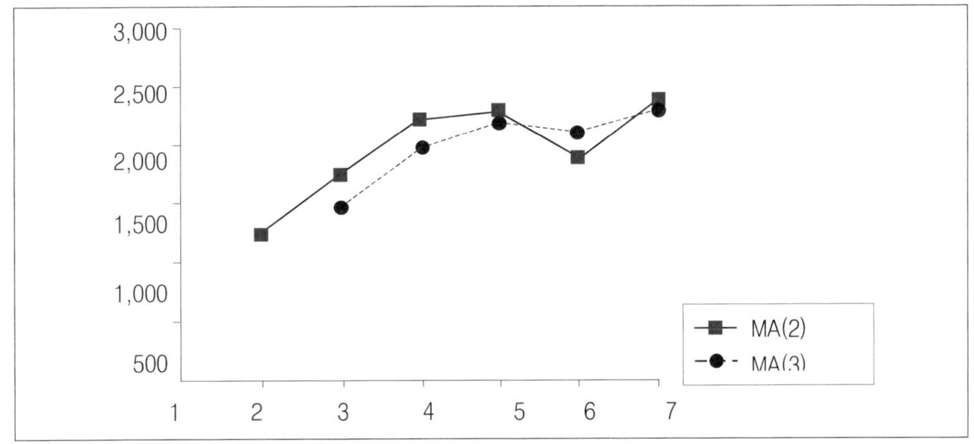

Example

주가가 다음과 같을 때, 2일 이동평균선과 3일 이동평균선을 그리시오.

	1일	2일	3일	4일	5일	6일	7일
주가	1,000	1,500	2,000	2,500	2,100	1,700	3,100

Solution

	1일	2일	3일	4일	5일	6일	7일
주가	1,000	1,500	2,000	2,500	2,100	1,700	3,100
2일 이동평균		1,250	1,750	2,250	2,300	1,900	2,400
3일 이동평균			1,500	2,000	2,200	2,100	2,300

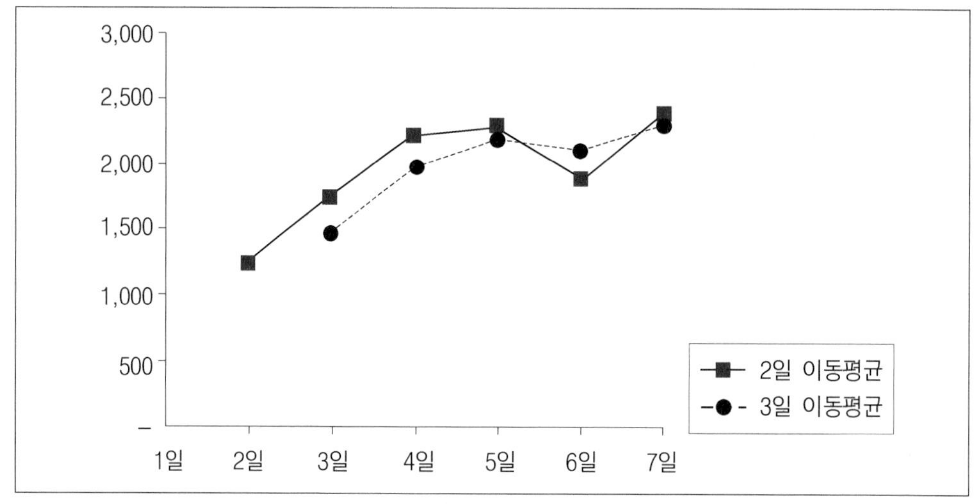

Calculate a two-day moving average from the following data set:

	Day 1	Day 2	Day 3	Day 4	Day 5	Day 6	Day 7
Price	1,000	1,500	2,000	2,500	2,100	1,700	3,100

Solution

	Day 1	Day 2	Day 3	Day 4	Day 5	Day 6	Day 7
Price	1,000	1,500	2,000	2,500	2,100	1,700	3,100
MA(2)		1,250	1,750	2,250	2,300	1,900	2,400

Example

Daily Closing Prices: 1000, 1500, 2000, 2500

Calculate a two-day moving average.

Solution

First day of 2-day MA: 1,250

Second day of 2-day MA: 1,750

Third day of 2-day MA: 2,250

Example

Daily Closing Prices: 1000, 1500, 2000, 2500

Calculate a three-day moving average.

Solution

First day of 3-day MA: 1,500

Second day of 3-day MA: 2,000

Golden cross

단기이동선이 중장기이동선을 아래로부터 상향 돌파할 때 골든크로스가 발생하였다고 한다. 골든크로스가 발생하였을 경우, 강세시장으로의 전환신호로 해석되어 매수신호로 받아들여진다. 그러나 주가는 이보다 먼저 상승하는 경우가 많으며, 때로는 골든크로스가 발생한 이후에 하락하는 경우도 있음에 유의해야 한다.

Bull market

강세시장

기술적 분석을 통한 매매전략은 추세추종거래(momentum trade)와 추세반대거래(contrarian trade)로 나뉜다. 추세추종거래는 일단 추세가 형성되면 관성에 의해 추세가 지속되는 경우에 유용하다. 추세반대거래는 추세가 붕괴되는 시점을 포착하여 이루어진다.

Candle-stick chart

봉차트

봉의 끝은 시가와 종가를 의미하고, 수직선의 끝은 고가와 저가를 의미한다. 종가가 시가보다 높은 경우에는 봉을 적색 또는 흰색으로 표시하고 양봉이라고 부른다. 반대의 경우에는 봉을 청색 또는 흑색으로 표시하고 음봉이라고 부른다. 따라서 양봉이 나타나면 하루 중 강세를 보였음을 알 수 있고, 음봉이 나타나면 하루 중 약세를 보였음을 알 수 있다.

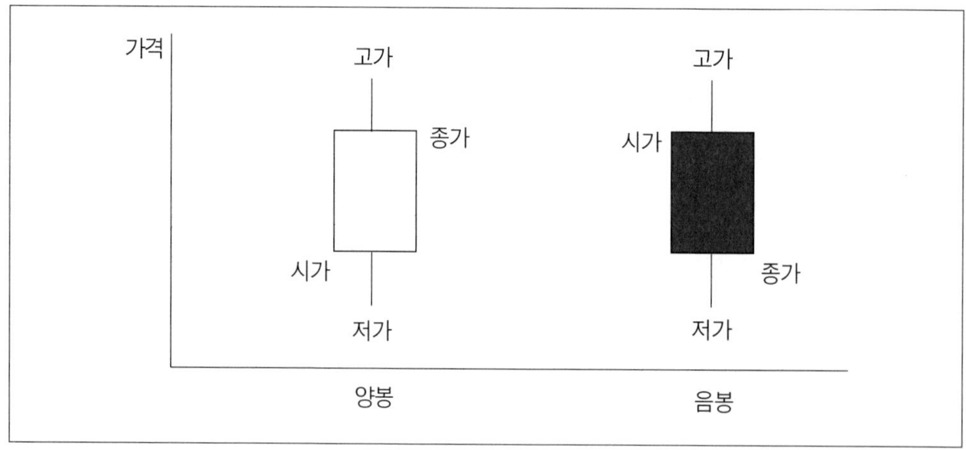

Candlestick charts display the high, low, open, and closing prices of a security for a specific period.

The wick illustrates the highest and lowest traded prices of a security during the time interval represented. The body illustrates the opening and closing trades. If the security closed higher than it opened, the body is white, with the opening price at the bottom of the body and the closing price at the top. If the security closed lower than it opened, the body is black, with the opening price at the top and the closing price at the bottom.

There are key components of a candle traders should be aware of to read candlestick charts:

Body: This is the thick bar section of a candlestick and it shows the difference between the opening and a closing price over the trading session.

Top wick: This is the line extending above a body and it shows the highest point the price reached over a trading session.

Bottom wick: This is the line extending below a body, and it shows the lowest price point over a trading session.

Color: The color of a candlestick is important as it defines whether the price has overall increased or decreased.

Example

Make a candlestick chart representing open, high, low, close prices.

Opening Price: 5,200 won

Low Price: 4,700 won

High Price: 5,500 won

Closing Price: 5,300 won

Solution

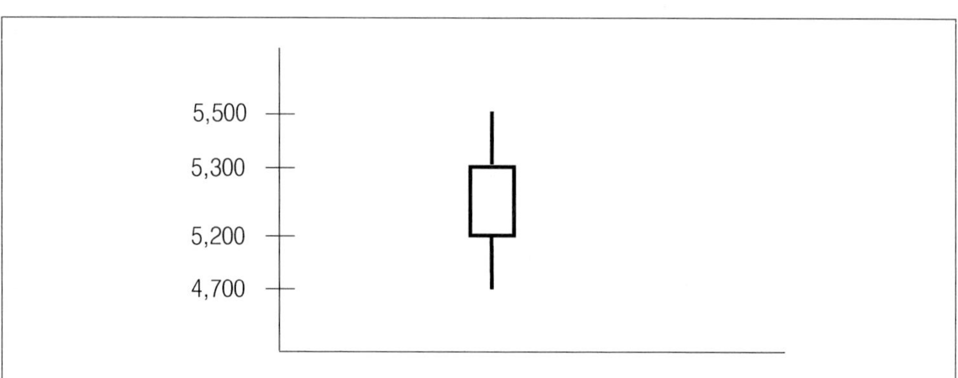

Example

서울기업 주가가 하루 중 시가 5,200원, 저가 4,700원, 고가 5,500원, 종가 5,300원인 경우, 봉차트를 그리시오.

Solution

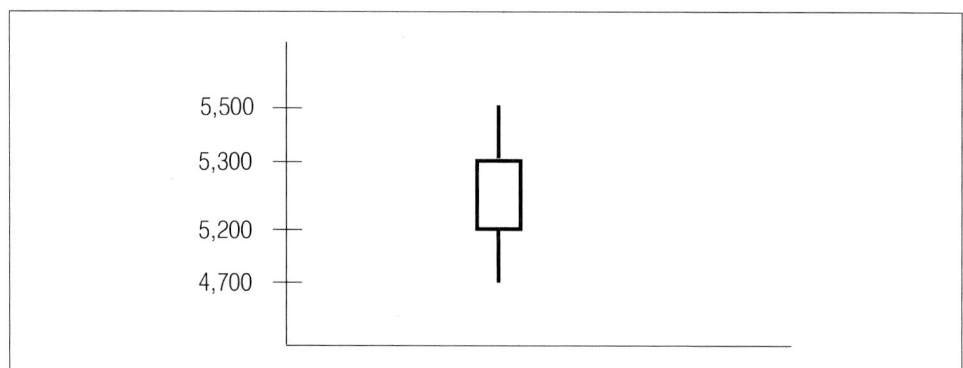

Example

Make a candlestick chart representing open, high, low, close prices.

Opening Price: 5,300 won

Low Price: 4,700 won

High Price: 5,500 won

Closing Price: 5,200 won

Solution

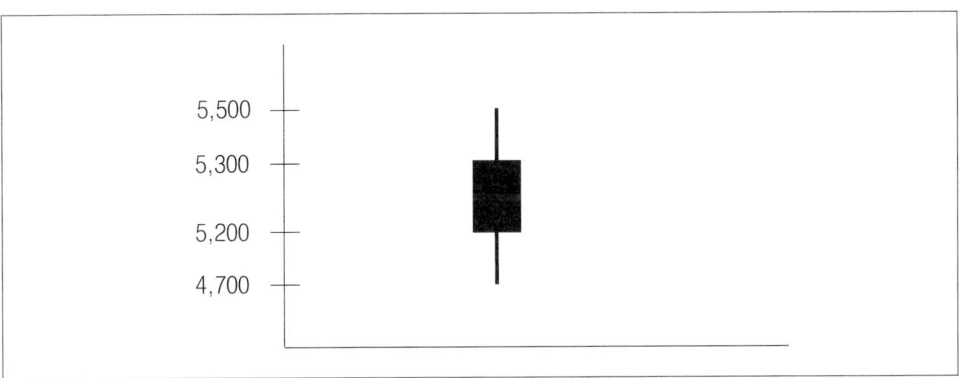

Example

서울기업 주가가 하루 중 시가 5,300원, 저가 4,700원, 고가 5,500원, 종가 5,200원인 경우, 봉차트를 그리시오.

Disparity

$$이격도 = \frac{당일의 주가}{당일의 이동평균주가} \times 100$$

이격도가 100% 이상이라는 것은 당일의 주가가 이동평균선보다 위에 있는 상태이고, 반대로 100% 이하는 당일주가가 이동평균선 아래에 있는 상태를 말한다.

VR

Volume Ratio

VR은 일정기간 동안의 주가상승일의 거래량과 주가하락일의 거래량과의 비율을 백분비로 나타낸 것이다. VR이 200%라면 대체로 주가상승시의 거래량이 주가하락시의 거래량의 2배라는 것을 나타낸다.

$$VR = \frac{\text{주가상승일의 거래량합계} + \text{변동이 없는 날의 거래량합계} \times 1/2}{\text{주가하락일의 거래량합계} + \text{변동이 없는 날의 거래량합계} \times 1/2} \times 100$$

일반적으로 VR은 150%가 보통 수준이며 450%를 초과하면 단기적으로 주가의 경계신호가 되고, 70% 이하이면 단기매입시점으로 본다.

ADR

Advance Decline Ratio

등락비율

$$ADR = \frac{\text{분석대상기간 동안의 상승종목수}}{\text{분석대상기간 동안의 하락종목수} } \times 100$$

등락비율이 120~125%에 속할 때 과열양상, 경계지대, 매도신호로 간주하며, 70~75% 범위 내에서는 침체양상, 안정지대, 매수신호로 파악한다.

PL

psychological line

투자심리선

$$PL = \frac{\text{10일 동안 주가 상승일수}}{10} \times 100$$

투자심리선의 값이 75% 이상이면 과열상태로 경계지대이며, 25% 이하이면 침체상태로 안전지대에 속하고, 25~75% 사이는 중립지대이다.

Given the function $y = 100 - \frac{100}{1+x}$, and x=1.

Find the value of y.

y=50

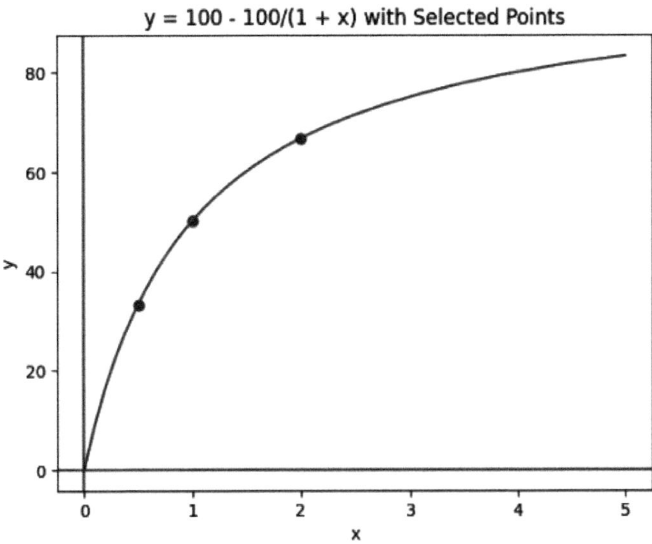

These three points are marked on the first-quadrant graph above: (0.5,33.33),(1,50),(2,66.67).

Efficient Market Hypothesis: EMH

An efficient capital market is one in which the current price of a security fully reflects all the information currently available about that security. An informationally efficient capital market is one in which security prices adjust rapidly and completely to new information.

시장이 효율적이라 함은 시장에서 거래되는 자산과 관련된 모든 정보가 신속하고 충분히 그 자산의 가격에 반영하고 있는 상태를 말한다.

There are three major versions of the hypothesis: "weak", "semi-strong", and "strong". The weak-form EMH claims that prices on traded assets already reflect all past publicly available information. The semi-strong-form EMH claims both that prices reflect all publicly available information and that prices instantly change to reflect new public information. The strong-form EMH additionally claims that prices instantly reflect even hidden or "insider" information.

In an influential academic paper, Eugene Fama divided the efficient market hypothesis into three categories.

Weak-form of EMH

The weak form of the EMH states that all information contained in past price movements is fully reflected in current market prices.
No investor can earn excess returns by developing trading rules based on historical price or return information.
현재의 주가는 과거의 주가가 지니는 정보를 모두 반영하고 있다는 가설이다. 따라서 과거의 정보를 이용하여 초과수익을 얻을 수 없다.

Semistrong-form of EMH

The semistrong form of the EMH states that current market prices reflect all publicly available information.
No investor can earn excess returns from trading rules based on any publicly available information.

현재의 주가는 공식적으로 이용 가능한(publicly available) 정보를 모두 반영하고 있다는 가설이다. 즉, 일반에게 공개되는 모든 정보가 신속하고 정확하게 주가에 반영된다는 것이다. 따라서 공식적으로 이용 가능한 정보를 이용하더라도 초과수익을 얻을 수 없다.

Strong–form of EMH

The strong form of the EMH states that current market prices reflect all pertinent information, whether publicly available or privately held.

No investor can earn excess returns using any information, whether publicly available or not.

현재의 주가는 이용 가능한 모든 정보를 반영하고 있다는 가설이다. 즉, 공개된 정보 뿐만 아니라 비공개된 내부정보까지도 주가에 완전히 반영되어 있다는 것이다. 따라서 어떤 투자자라도 초과수익을 얻을 수 없다.

Many empirical studies have been conducted to test for the three forms of market efficiency. Most of these studies suggest that the stock market is indeed highly efficient in the weak form and reasonably efficient in the semistrong form, at least for the larger and more widely followed stocks. However, the strong-form EMH does not hold, so abnormal profits can be made by those who possess inside information.

Chartist

Chartists plot past patterns of stock price movements.

A chartist might discover the following pattern: If a stock falls three consecutive days, its price typically rises 10 percent the following day.

People who believe that weak-form efficiency exists believe that chartists are wasting their time.

Event study

사건연구

사건연구는 배당, 유상증자, 합병 및 인수, 이익공시 등과 같은 기업의 고유한 사건들(firm-specific events)이 해당기업의 주식가격에 미치는 영향을 평가하는 연구방법론이다. An event study describes a technique of empirical financial research that enables an observer to assess the impact of a particular event on a firm's stock price.

사건연구를 하기 위해서는 모형추정기간(estimation period)과 검증기간(test period)이 필요하다. 모형추정기간은 정상수익률을 추정하기 위한 기간으로서, 보통 해당 사건의 영향을 받지 않을 것으로 판단되는 기간을 모형추정기간으로 정하게 된다.
추정기간(estimation window)은 사건과 무관한 정상수익률에 대한 모형을 추정하는데 사용되는 기간이고, 사건기간(event window)은 표본회사의 시장가격이 사건의 공표에 반응하는 것으로 판단되는 기간이다.

비정상수익률(abnormal return)을 측정하는 방법에는 시장모형(market model), 평균조정모형(mean-adjusted model) 및 시장조정모형(market-adjusted model)이 있다.

market model

$AR_{it} = r_{it} - \alpha_i - \beta_i r_{Mt}$

α_i, β_i : 모형추정기간 동안의 일별수익률 자료를 이용하여 구한 추정치

mean-adjusted model

$AR_{it} = r_{it} - \overline{r_i}$

$\overline{r_i}$: 모형추정기간 동안의 일별수익률의 평균값

market-adjusted model

$AR_{it} = r_{it} - r_{Mt}$

What Is a Prospectus?

A prospectus is a formal document required by and filed with the Securities and Exchange Commission that provides details about an investment offering to the public.

The prospectus can help investors make more informed investment decisions because it contains a host of relevant information about the investment or security.

The Securities and Exchange Commission requires that security issuers file a prospectus when offering investment securities to the public.

The prospectus provides details about the investment/security and the offering.

Companies that wish to offer bonds or stock for sale to the public must file a prospectus with the Securities and Exchange Commission as part of the registration process. Companies must file a preliminary and a final prospectus, and the SEC has specific guidelines as to what's listed in the prospectus for various securities.

A prospectus includes some of the following information:

A brief summary of the company's background and financial information

The name of the company issuing the stock

The number of shares

The type of securities being offered

Whether an offering is public or private

Names of the company's principals

Names of the banks or financial companies performing the underwriting

Underwriting is the process through which an individual or institution takes on financial risk for a fee. This risk most typically involves loans, insurance, or investments. The term underwriter originated from the practice of having each risk-taker write their name under the total amount of risk they were willing to accept for a specified premium.

What Is a Mutual Fund?

A mutual fund is a financial vehicle that pools assets from shareholders to invest in securities like stocks, bonds, money market instruments, and other assets. Mutual funds are operated by professional money managers, who allocate the fund's assets and attempt to produce capital gains or income for the fund's investors. A mutual fund's portfolio is structured and maintained to match the investment objectives stated in its prospectus.

Mutual funds give small or individual investors access to professionally managed portfolios of equities, bonds, and other securities. Each shareholder, therefore, participates proportionally in the gains or losses of the fund. Mutual funds invest in a vast number of securities, and performance is usually tracked as the change in the total market cap of the fund—derived by the aggregating performance of the underlying investments.

What Is an Exchange-Traded Fund?

An exchange traded fund is a basket of securities that can be bought and sold in a single trade on an exchange.

An ETF, or Exchange-Traded Fund, is a type of investment fund and exchange-traded product that is traded on stock exchanges, much like stocks.

An ETF is called an exchange-traded fund because it's traded on an exchange just like stocks are. The price of an ETF's shares will change throughout the trading day as the shares are bought and sold on the market.

An ETF is a type of fund that holds multiple underlying assets, rather than only one like a stock does. Because there are multiple assets within an ETF, they can be a popular choice for diversification. ETFs can thus contain many types of investments, including stocks, commodities, bonds, or a mixture of investment types.

An exchange-traded fund is a type of pooled investment security that operates much like a mutual fund. Typically, ETFs will track a particular index, sector, commodity, or other assets, but unlike mutual funds, ETFs can be purchased or sold on a stock exchange the same way that a regular stock can. An ETF can be structured to track anything from the price of an individual commodity to a large and diverse collection of securities. ETFs can even be structured to track specific investment strategies.

What Is a Public Offering?

A public offering is the sale of equity shares or other financial instruments such as bonds to the public in order to raise capital. The capital raised may be intended to cover operational shortfalls, fund business expansion, or make strategic investments. The financial instruments offered to the public may include equity stakes, such as common or preferred shares, or other assets that can be traded like bonds.

The SEC must approve all registrations for public offerings of corporate securities in the United States. An investment underwriter usually manages or facilitates public offerings.

A public offering is when an issuer, such as a firm, offers securities such as bonds or equity shares to investors in the open market.

Initial public offerings occur when a company sells shares on listed exchanges for the first time.

Generally, any sale of securities to more than 35 people is deemed to be a public offering, and thus requires the filing of registration statements with the appropriate regulatory authorities.

The issuing company and the investment bankers handling the transaction predetermine an offering price that the issue will be sold at.

Consumer Behavior

We will let $>$ denote this ordering and write $A > B$ whenever the consumer prefers bundle A to bundle B.

선호체계의 공리

Completeness

완전성

Any two bundles can be compared.

어떠한 두 개의 상품묶음을 비교한다 하더라도 하나가 다른 것보다 선호된다든가 아니면 양자 사이에 차이를 느끼지 못 한다는 판단을 내릴 수 있다.

Transitivity

이행성

If $x > y$ and $y > z$, then $x > z$.

If an individual prefers x to y and y to z, then x is preferred to z.

Continuity

연속성

Strong monotonicity

강단조성

The more, the better.

Convexity

볼록성

Law of decreasing marginal utility

Utility function

효용함수란 특정한 상품묶음 X가 주어졌을 때 이것이 소비자에게 주는 만족감의 정도를 하나의 실수(real number)로 나타내 주는 함수이다.

Utility is a measure of satisfaction.

Utility function is an important concept that measures preferences over a set of goods and services.

Utility represents the satisfaction that consumers receive for choosing and consuming a product or service.

Utility function measures the welfare or satisfaction of a consumer as a function of consumption of real goods such as food or clothing.

Utility is a function of the total quantity of goods consumes. If only one good is consumed, then the utility function is written as U(x).

Marginal Utility is the slope or first derivative of the utility function. Marginal Utility is positive, but decreasing.

The first derivative of the utility function is positive, while the second derivative is negative.

Example

Find the derivative of ln(x).

Solution

$$\frac{d}{dx} ln(x) = \frac{1}{x}$$

Example

Suppose y=ln(x). Determine the slope of the tangent line at $x = 3$.

Solution

$$y' = \frac{1}{x}$$

The derivative at $x = 3$ is $y' = \frac{1}{3}$.

Example

Find the derivative of 2ln(x/3).

Solution

$$y' = \frac{2}{x}$$

Bernoulli's utility function

$$U(x) = b \log \frac{x}{a}$$

$U(x)$ is the utility derived from an amount of money x, and a and b are positive coefficients.

$$U(x) = b \log x - b \log a$$

We obtain for the first derivative $U'(x) = \frac{b}{x} > 0$

$$U''(x) = -\frac{b}{x^2} < 0$$

The marginal utility of money decreases as wealth is increased.

Cramer's utility function

$U(x) = \sqrt{x}$

$U'(x) = \frac{1}{2}x^{-\frac{1}{2}} > 0$

$U''(x) = -\frac{1}{4}x^{-\frac{3}{2}} < 0$

Example

Given the function $y = \sqrt{x}$, find the derivative at x=4.

$y' = \frac{1}{2}x^{-\frac{1}{2}}$

The derivative at x=4 is $\frac{1}{4}$.

Example

Given the function $y = \sqrt{x}$, find the second derivative at x=4.

$y' = \frac{1}{2}x^{-\frac{1}{2}}$

$y'' = -\frac{1}{4}x^{-\frac{3}{2}}$

The second derivative at x=4 is $-\frac{1}{32}$.

Example

X 財의 효용함수가 $U(X) = 8X - X^2$ 일 때 X 財의 한계효용함수는?

Solution

$U'(X) = 8 - 2X$

Alternative Attitudes Toward Risk

An individual whose utility function is concave will be called a risk averter.

$$U[E(W)] > E[U(W)]$$

The utility of the expected value of wealth is greater than the expected utility of wealth.

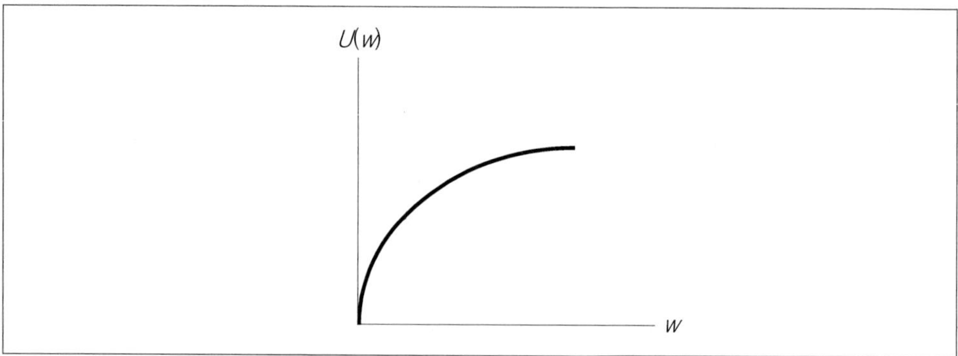

An individual whose utility function is convex will be called a risk lover.

$$U[E(W)] < E[U(W)]$$

An individual whose utility function is linear will be called a risk-neutral individual.

$$U[E(W)] = E[U(W)]$$

CE

확실성등가

Certainty Equivalence

불확실한 상태에서 기대되는 효용의 크기인 기대효용과 동일한 효용을 주는 확실한 현금의 크기

위험프리미엄

Risk premium

불확실한 자산을 확실한 자산으로 교환하기 위하여 지불할 용의가 있는 금액

Certainty Equivalence

The certainty equivalent is the amount of a certain wealth that has the same utility as the expected utility of the wealth x.

Certainty equivalent

The certainty equivalent is an amount of money that provides equal utility to the random payoff of the gamble.

$U(CE)=E[U(X)]$

Where U is the individual's utility function, X is the uncertain outcome (the "gamble" or risky asset), and E[U(X)] is the expected utility of the risky prospect.

Risk premium

The risk premium is defined to be the difference between the expected payoff and the certainty equivalent.

Risk Premium: The difference between the expected value of the risky asset (E[X]) and the certainty equivalent is called the risk premium (RP):

$RP=E[X]-CE$

Certainty Equivalent

Sure amount that makes the individual indifferent between accepting a lottery or not.

How much money would I need to have with certainty to be exactly as well as if I had this lottery.

The risk premium for a gamble is defined as the difference between the expected return of the gamble and the certainty equivalent of the gamble.

The Risk premium is the difference between the individual’s expected wealth, given the gamble, and the level of wealth the individual would accept with certainty if the gamble were removed, i.e., his or her certainty equivalent wealth.

The smallest dollar amount that the individual would accept instead of the bet is called the certainty equivalent, and the difference between the expected value and the certainty equivalent is called the risk premium.

Example

Imagine an investor is presented with a risky investment (a "gamble") with two possible outcomes:

The gamble offers a 50% chance of receiving \$64 and a 50% chance of receiving \$16.

$U(x) = \sqrt{x}$

Calculate the Expected Utility.

Solution

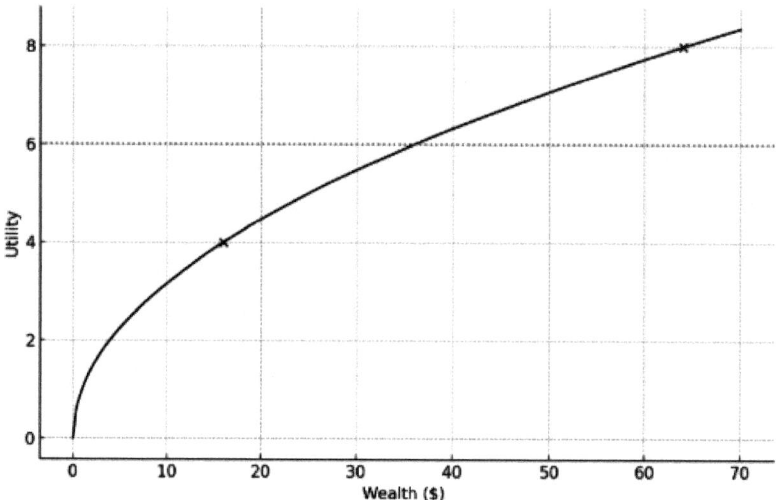

Example

Imagine an investor is presented with a risky investment (a "gamble") with two possible outcomes:

The gamble offers a 50% chance of receiving \$64 and a 50% chance of receiving \$16.

$U(x) = \sqrt{x}$

Calculate CE.

Solution

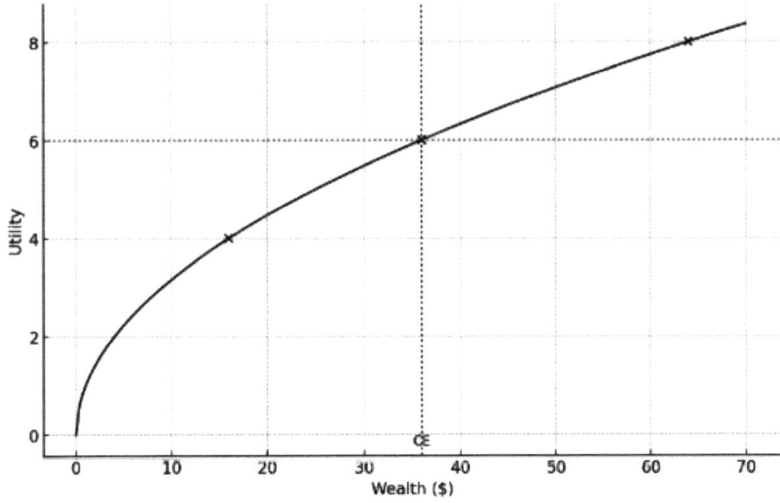

Example

Consider a lottery with two possible outcomes: $100 will be received with probability 0.5, and $300 with probability 0.5.

Let us assume that the utility function is $U(W) = \sqrt{W}$.

What is the certainty equivalent? What is the risk premium?

Solution

$E(W) = 200$

$U[E(W)] = 14.1$

$U(100) = 10, \quad U(300) = 17.3$

$E[U(W)] = 13.65$

$U[E(W)] > E[U(W)]$

Certainty equivalent: $13.65^2 = 186.3$

Risk premium: 13.7

Example

Consider a lottery with two possible outcomes: $100 will be received with probability 0.5, and $300 with probability 0.5.

Let us assume that the utility function is U(W) = SQRT(W).

What is the certainty equivalent? What is the risk premium?

Solution

$E(W) = 200$

$U[E(W)] = 14.1$

$U(100) = 10, \quad U(300) = 17.3$

$E[U(W)] = 13.65$

$U[E(W)] > E[U(W)]$

Certainty equivalent: $13.65^2 = 186.3$

Risk premium: 13.7

Example

상금 100원에 당첨될 확률이 0.5, 상금 300원에 당첨될 확률이 0.5인 복권이 있다. 효용함수는 $U(W)=\sqrt{W}$ 이다.

확실성등가와 위험 프리미엄은 얼마인가?

Solution

$E(W)=200$

$U[E(W)]=14.1$

$U(100)=10,\quad U(300)=17.3$

$E[U(W)]=13.65$

$U[E(W)]>E[U(W)]$

위험기피자는 기대값이 200원인 불확실한 복권보다 확실한 현금 200원을 더 선호한다.

확실성등가는 $13.65^2=186.3$ 이다.

위험프리미엄은 13.7원이다.

Example

Consider a lottery with two possible outcomes: $100 will be received with probability 0.5, and $400 with probability 0.5.

Let us assume that the utility function is $U(W)=\sqrt{W}$.

What is the certainty equivalent?

What is the risk premium?

Solution

$E(W)=250$

$U(100)=10,\quad U(400)=20$

$E[U(W)]=15$

Certainty equivalent: $15^2=225$

Risk premium: 25

Example

철수의 소득이 100원이 될 확률이 0.5, 400원이 될 확률이 0.5이다. 효용함수는 $U(W)=\sqrt{W}$이다. 소득의 불확실성을 피하기 위해 지불할 용의가 있는 금액은 얼마인가?

Solution

$E(W)=250$

$U(100)=10, \quad U(400)=20$

$E[U(W)]=15$

확실성등가는 $15^2=225$ 이다.
위험프리미엄은 25원이다.

Example

Consider a lottery with two possible outcomes: $100 will be received with probability 0.5, and $400 with probability 0.5.
Let us assume that the utility function is $U(W)=\sqrt{W}$.
Find U[E(W)] and E[U(W)].

Solution

$E(W)=250$

$U[E(W)]=15.8$

$U(100)=10, \quad U(400)=20$

$E[U(W)]=15$

Example

철수의 소득이 100원이 될 확률이 0.5, 400원이 될 확률이 0.5이다. 효용함수는 $U(W)=\sqrt{W}$ 이다. $U[E(W)]$과 $E[U(W)]$은 얼마인가? 철수는 위험회피자인가, 위험선호자인가?

Solution

$E(W)=250$

$U[E(W)]=15.8$

$U(100)=10,\quad U(400)=20$

$E[U(W)]=15$

위험회피자

Example

Translate the sentence into an equation: The *risk premium* is defined to be the difference between the expected payoff and the certainty equivalent.

Solution

$y=E(W)-x$ where $U(x)=E[U(W)]$.

Example

Consider a lottery with two possible outcomes: \$100 will be received with probability 0.5, and \$900 with probability 0.5.

Let us assume that the utility function is $U(W)=\sqrt{W}$.

What is the certainty equivalent?

What is the risk premium?

Solution

Certainty equivalent: 400

Risk premium: 100

Example

Consider a lottery with two possible outcomes: $10 will be received with probability 0.5, and $20 with probability 0.5.

Let us assume that the utility function is $U(W) = W^2$.

Find U[E(W)] and E[U(W)].

Solution

$E(W) = 15$

$U[E(W)] = 225$

$U(10) = 100, \quad U(20) = 400$

$E[U(W)] = 250$

Example

철수의 소득이 10원이 될 확률이 0.5, 20원이 될 확률이 0.5이다. 효용함수는 $U(W) = W^2$ 이다.

Solution

$E(W) = 15$

$U[E(W)] = 225$

$U(10) = 100, \quad U(20) = 400$

$E[U(W)] = 250$

$U[E(W)] < E[U(W)]$

위험선호자는 확실한 현금 15원보다 기대값이 15원인 불확실한 경우를 더 선호한다.

Example

Consider a lottery with two possible outcomes: $100 will be received with probability 0.5, and $400 with probability 0.5.

Let us assume that the utility function is $U(W) = W^2$.

Find U[E(W)] and E[U(W)].

Solution

$E(W) = 250$

$U[E(W)] = 62{,}500$

$U(100) = 100{,}000$, $U(400) = 160{,}000$

$E[U(W)] = 85{,}000$

Example

민수의 소득이 100원이 될 확률이 0.5, 400원이 될 확률이 0.5이다. 효용함수는 $U(W) = W^2$이다. $U[E(W)]$과 $E[U(W)]$은 얼마인가? 민수는 위험회피자인가, 위험선호자인가?

Solution

$E(W) = 250$

$U[E(W)] = 62{,}500$

$U(100) = 100{,}000$, $U(400) = 160{,}000$

$E[U(W)] = 85{,}000$

위험선호자

Insurance vs gamble decision

Example

A person is given the choice between two scenarios, one with a guaranteed payoff and one without. In the guaranteed scenario, the person receives $50. In the uncertain scenario, a coin is flipped to decide whether the person receives $100 or nothing.

The utility function is $U(W) = \sqrt{W}$.

Find E[U(W)].

Solution

E[U(W)]=5

Example

철수의 효용함수가 $U(W) = \sqrt{W}$ 이다. 철수의 현재 보유액은 250원이고 150원을 벌 확률이 0.5이고 150원을 잃을 확률이 0.5인 게임에 놓여 있고, 게임의 위험을 제거하는 보험의 수수료는 30원일 때, 보험에 가입하겠는가, 아니면 게임에 임하겠는가?

Solution

$E(W) = 250$

$U(100) = 10, \quad U(400) = 20$

$E[U(W)] = 15$

확실성등가는 $15^2 = 225$ 이다.

위험프리미엄은 25원이다.

게임에 임한다.

Example

You have a utility function $U(W) = \sqrt{W}$, and your current level of wealth is 250 won. Suppose you are exposed to a situation that results in a 50/50 chance of winning or losing 150 won. If you can buy insurance that completely removes the risk for a fee of 30 won, will you buy it or take the gamble?

Solution

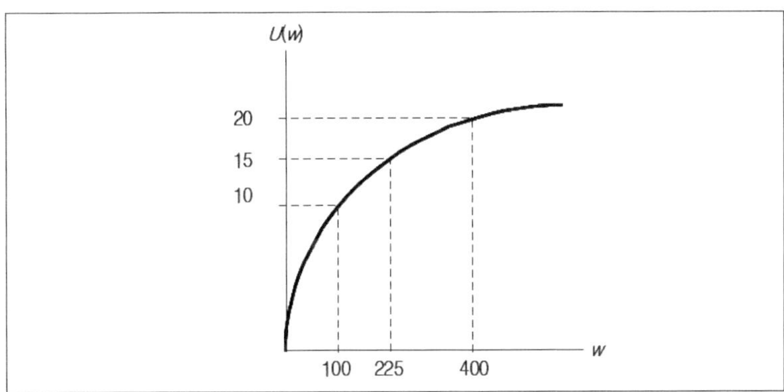

$E(W) = 250$

$U(100) = 10, \quad U(400) = 20$

$E[U(W)] = 15$

Certainty Equivalence: $U(x) = E[U(W)]$

$\sqrt{x} = 15$

$x = 225$

Risk premium: $y = E(W) - x$

$y = 25$

I will take the gamble.

Example

You have a utility function U(W)=SQRT(W), and your current level of wealth is 25,000 won. Suppose you are exposed to a situation that results in a 50/50 chance of winning or losing 15,000 won. If you can buy insurance that completely removes the risk for a fee of 2,000 won, will you buy it or take the gamble?

Solution

E[U(W)] = 150

U(CE)=150

CE: 22,500

E(W): 25,000

RP: 2,500

The insurance fee of 2,000 won is less than your maximum willingness to pay to eliminate the risk.

I will buy the insurance.

Example

You have a utility function $U(W) = \sqrt{W}$, and your current level of wealth is 800 won. Suppose you are exposed to a situation that results in a 50/50 chance of winning or losing 100 won. If you can buy insurance that completely removes the risk for a fee of 20 won, will you buy it or take the gamble?

Solution

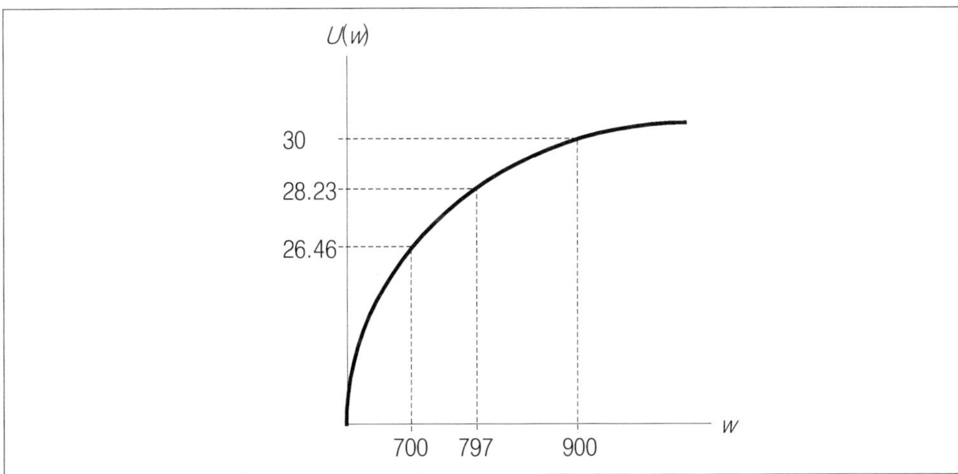

CE: $28.23^2 = 797$

RP: 3

I will take the gamble.

Example

효용함수가 $U(W)=\sqrt{W}$ 인 투자자가 있다. 이 투자자의 현재 보유액은 800원이고 100원을 벌 확률이 0.5이고 100원을 잃을 확률이 0.5인 게임에 놓여 있고, 게임의 위험을 제거하는 보험의 수수료는 20원일 때, 보험에 가입하겠는가, 아니면 게임에 임하겠는가?

Solution

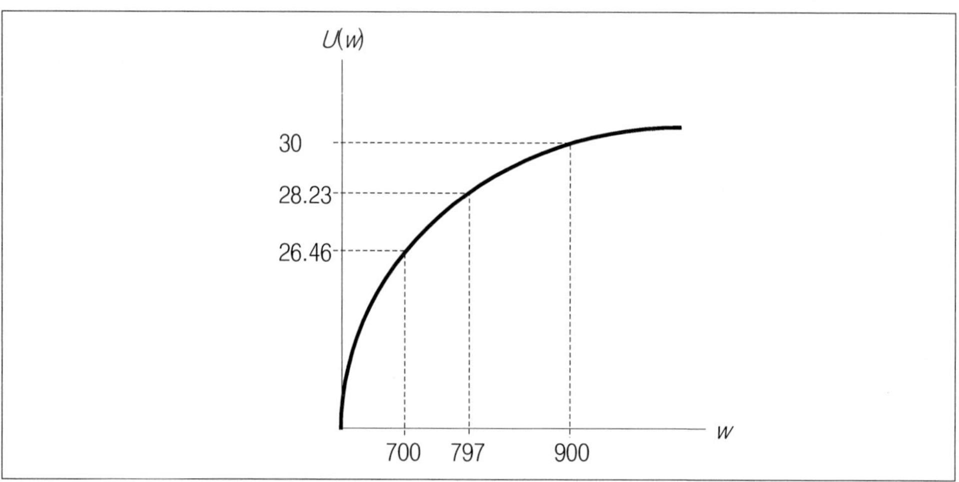

확실성등가는 $28.23^2 = 797$ 이다.
위험프리미엄은 3원이다.

게임에 임한다.

Example

You have a utility function $U(W) = \sqrt{W}$, and your current level of wealth is 650 won. Suppose you are exposed to a situation that results in a 50/50 chance of winning or losing 250 won. If you can buy insurance that completely removes the risk for a fee of 20 won, will you buy it or take the gamble?

Solution

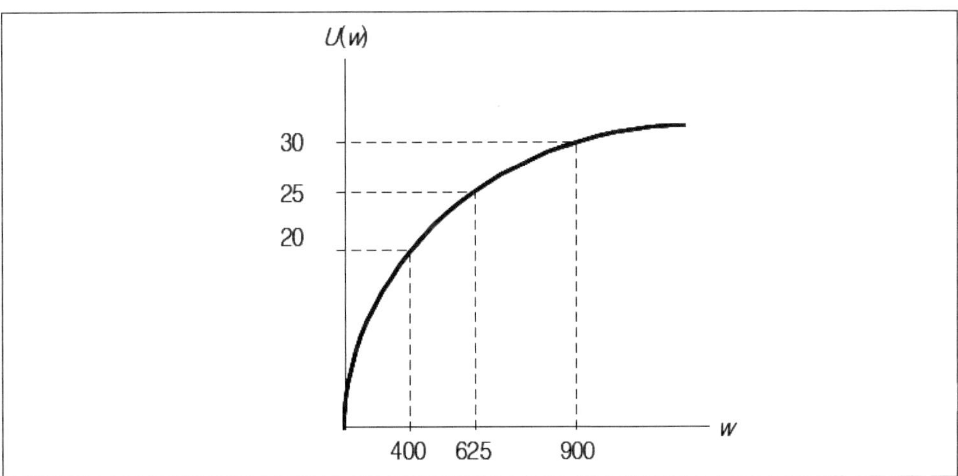

$E(W) = 650$

$E[U(W)] = 25$

Certainty Equivalence: $U(x) = E[U(W)]$

$\sqrt{x} = 25$

$x = 625$

Risk premium: $y = E(W) - x$

$y = 25$

I will buy it.

Example

효용함수가 $U(W)=\sqrt{W}$인 투자자가 있다. 이 투자자의 현재 보유액은 650만원이고 250만원을 벌 확률이 0.5이고 250만원을 잃을 확률이 0.5인 게임에 놓여 있고, 게임의 위험을 제거하는 보험의 가입수수료는 20만원일 때, 보험에 가입하겠는가, 아니면 게임에 임하겠는가?

Solution

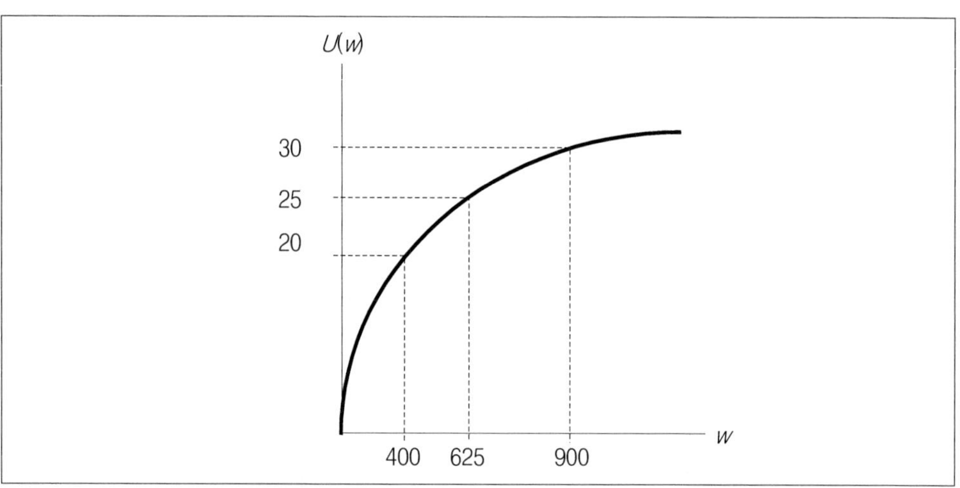

위험프리미엄: 25만원

보험에 가입한다.

Cf.

게임에 임했을 때의 기대효용은 25.

보험에 가입했을 때의 효용은 $U(630)=\sqrt{630}=25.1$

Example

You have a utility function $U(W) = \sqrt{W}$, and your current level of wealth is 1,650 won. Suppose you are exposed to a situation that results in a 50/50 chance of winning or losing 250 won. If you can buy insurance that completely removes the risk for a fee of 20 won, will you buy it or take the gamble?

Solution

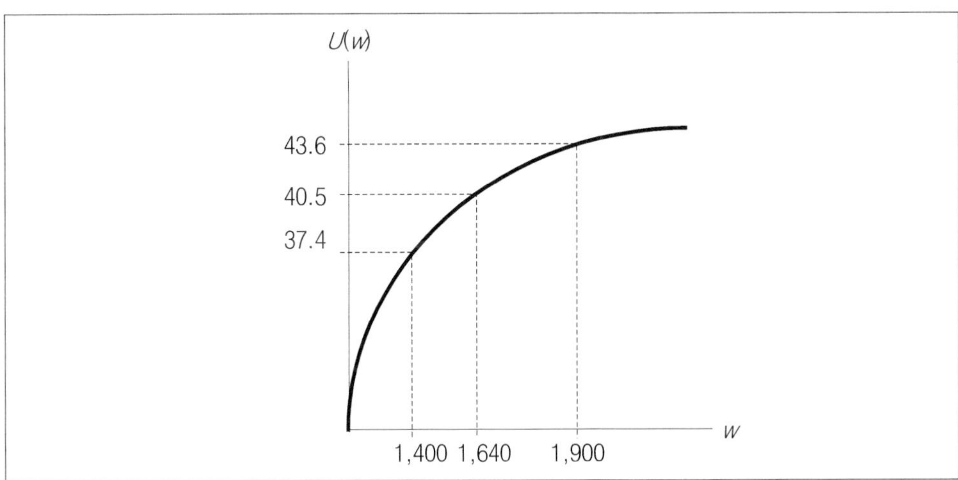

RP: 10

I will take the gamble.

Example

효용함수가 $U(W)=\sqrt{W}$ 인 투자자가 있다. 이 투자자의 현재 보유액은 1,650만원이고 250만원을 벌 확률이 0.5이고 250만원을 잃을 확률이 0.5인 게임에 놓여 있고, 게임의 위험을 제거하는 보험의 가입수수료는 20만원일 때, 보험에 가입하겠는가, 아니면 게임에 임하겠는가?

Solution

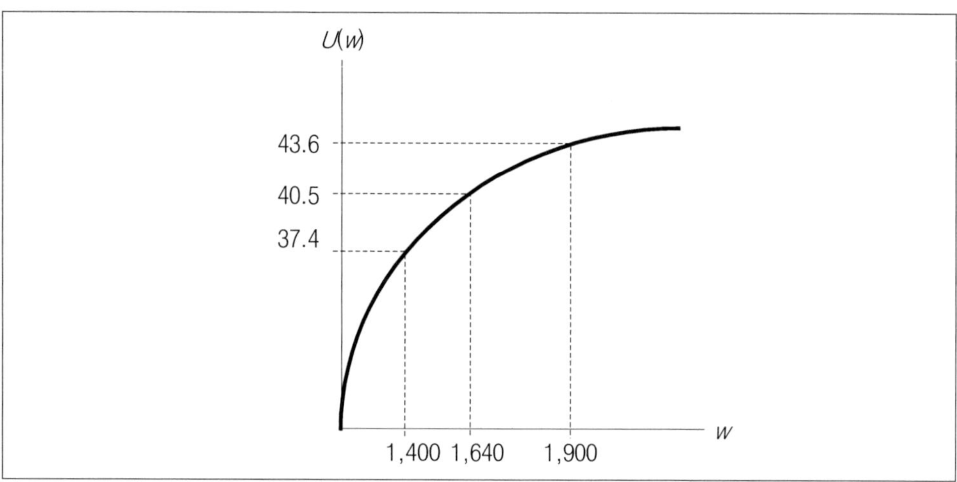

위험프리미엄: 10만원
게임에 임한다.

Cf.

게임에 임했을 때의 기대효용은 40.5.

보험에 가입했을 때의 효용은 $U(1{,}630)=\sqrt{1{,}630}=40.4$

Example

You have a utility function $U(W) = \sqrt{W}$, and your current level of wealth is 200 won. Suppose you are exposed to a situation that results in a 50/50 chance of winning or losing 100 won. If you can buy insurance that completely removes the risk for a fee of 10 won, will you buy it or take the gamble?

Solution

$E(W) = 200$

$E[U(W)] = 13.65$

Certainty Equivalence: $U(x) = E[U(W)]$

$x = 186.3$

Risk premium: $y = E(W) - x$

$y = 13.7$

I will buy it.

Example

You have a utility function $U(W) = \sqrt{W}$, and your current level of wealth is 500 won. Suppose you are exposed to a situation that results in a 50/50 chance of winning or losing 400 won. If you can buy insurance that completely removes the risk for a fee of 80 won, will you buy it or take the gamble?

Solution

$E(W) = 500$

$E[U(W)] = 20$

Certainty Equivalence: $U(x) = E[U(W)]$

$x = 400$

Risk premium: $y = E(W) - x$

$y = 100$

I will buy it.

Example

You have a utility function U(W)=SQRT(W), and your current level of wealth is 500 won. Suppose you are exposed to a situation that results in a 50/50 chance of winning or losing 400 won. If you can buy insurance that completely removes the risk for a fee of 80 won, will you buy it or take the gamble?

Solution

$E(W)=500$

$E[U(W)]=20$

Certainty Equivalence: $U(x)=E[U(W)]$

$x=400$

Risk premium: $y=E(W)-x$

$y=100$

I will buy it.

Example

You have a utility function $U(W)=\sqrt{W}$, and your current level of wealth is 1,250 won. Suppose you are exposed to a situation that results in a 50/50 chance of winning or losing 350 won. If you can buy insurance that completely removes the risk for a fee of 20 won, will you buy it or take the gamble?

Solution

$E(W)=1,250$

$E[U(W)]=35$

Certainty Equivalence: $U(x)=E[U(W)]$

$x=1,225$

Risk premium: $y=E(W)-x$

$y=25$

I will buy it.

Example

You have a utility function U(W)=SQRT(W), and your current level of wealth is 1,250 won. Suppose you are exposed to a situation that results in a 50/50 chance of winning or losing 350 won. If you can buy insurance that completely removes the risk for a fee of 20 won, will you buy it or take the gamble?

Solution

$E(W) = 1,250$

$E[U(W)] = 35$

Certainty Equivalence: $U(x) = E[U(W)]$

$x = 1,225$

Risk premium: $y = E(W) - x$

$y = 25$

I will buy it.

Indifference Curve

무차별곡선

A curve that defines the combinations of two or more goods that give a consumer the same level of satisfaction.

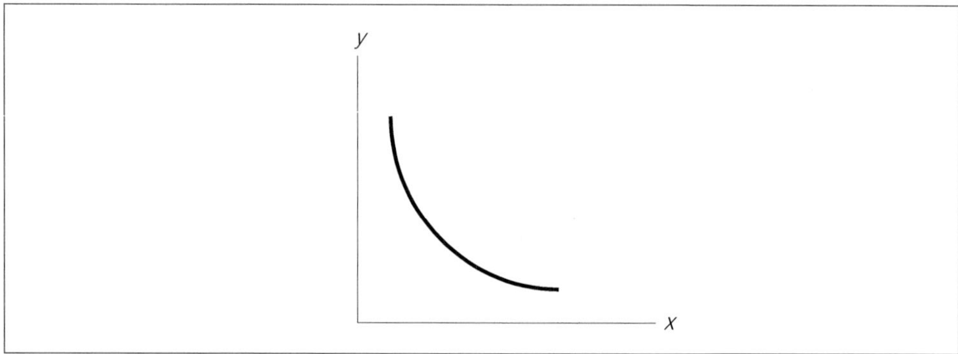

An indifference curve is a graph showing combination of two goods that give the consumer equal satisfaction and utility. Each point on an indifference curve indicates that a consumer is indifferent between the two and all points give him the same utility.

An indifference curve connects points on a graph representing different quantities of two goods, points between which a consumer is indifferent. That is, any combinations of two products indicated by the curve will provide the consumer with equal levels of utility, and the consumer has no preference for one combination or bundle of goods over a different combination on the same curve.

An indifference curve is a chart showing various combinations of two goods or commodities that consumers can choose. At any point on the curve, the combination of the two will leave the consumer equally well off or equally satisfied—hence indifferent.

Utility function

$U(x, y)$

An indifference curve is defined as the locus of the combinations of x and y that will yield a constant level of U. This means that on an indifference curve we must find

$dU = U_x dx + U_y dy = 0$

$\frac{dy}{dx}$: derivative of y with respect to x

$$\frac{dy}{dx} = -\frac{U_x}{U_y}$$

Example

Suppose $xy = 6$. Determine the slope of the tangent line at $x = 2$ and $y = 3$.

Solution

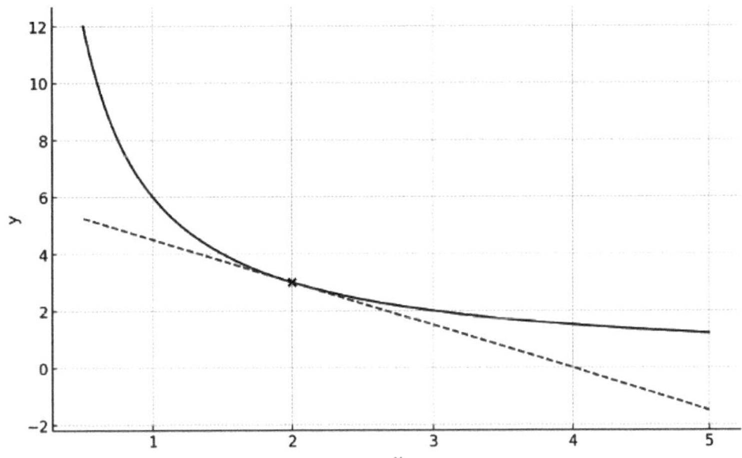

$$\frac{dy}{dx} = -\frac{3}{2}$$

Example

Given $z = xy$, find dz at the point $x = 2$ and $y = 3$.

Example

$U(x,y)=xy$

$dU=U_x dx+U_y dy=0=ydx+xdy$

$\frac{dy}{dx}=-\frac{y}{x}$

Example

효용함수가 $U(x,y)=\sqrt{xy}$ 인 경우, 무차별곡선은 다음과 같다.

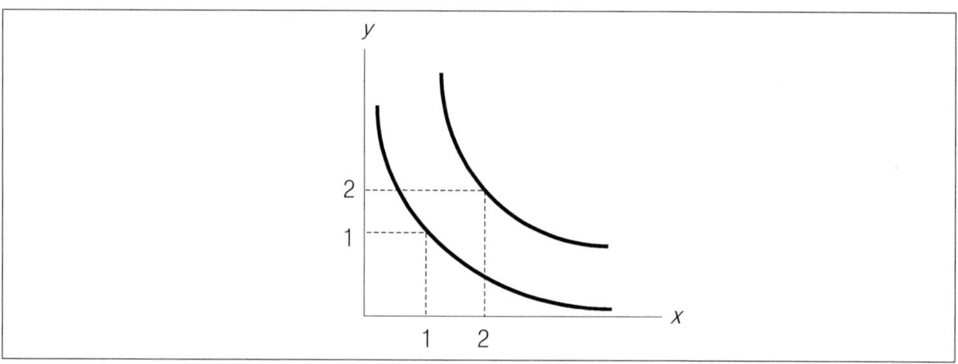

추가적인 재화의 소비가 소비자의 만족수준을 감소시키지 않는 한 B점은 A점보다 더 큰 만족을 준다.

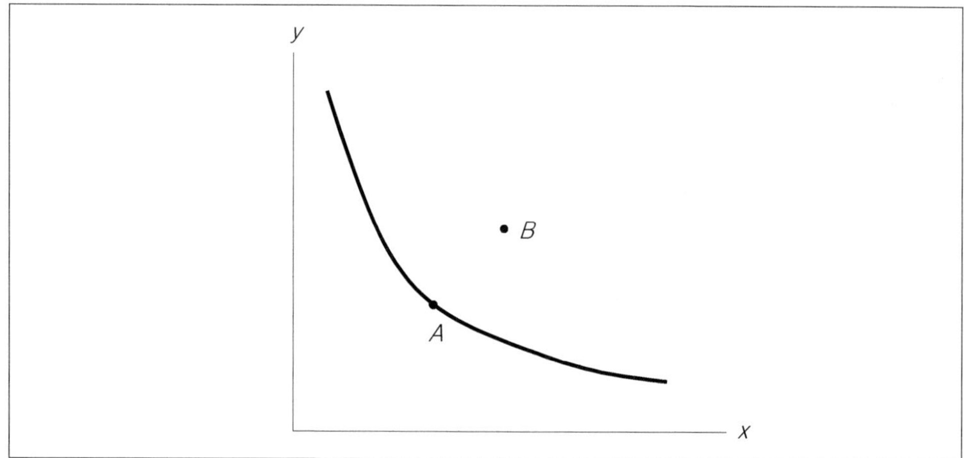

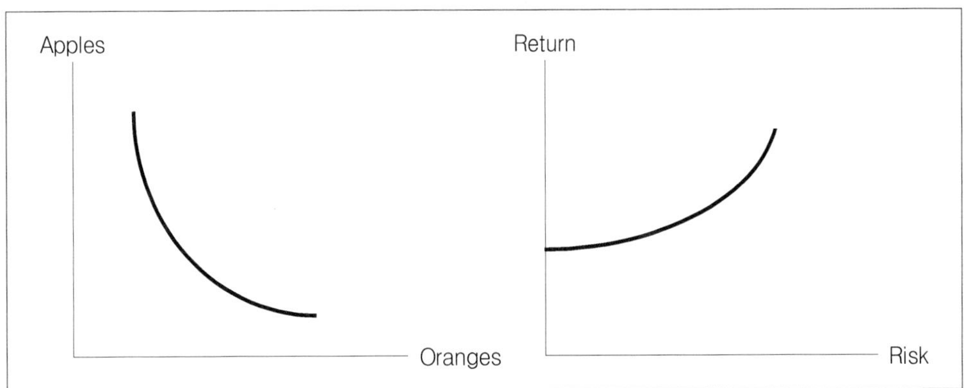

두 재화 중 하나가 음의 효용을 주는 비재화(bads)라면 무차별곡선은 우상향한다.

Bads vs. Goods

A bad is a commodity that the consumer doesn't like.

A good refers to a commodity that provides utility or satisfaction to individuals.

Perfect Complements

Perfect complements are goods that are always consumed together in fixed proportions.

효용함수가 $U(x, y) = Min(x, y)$인 경우, 무차별곡선은 다음과 같다.

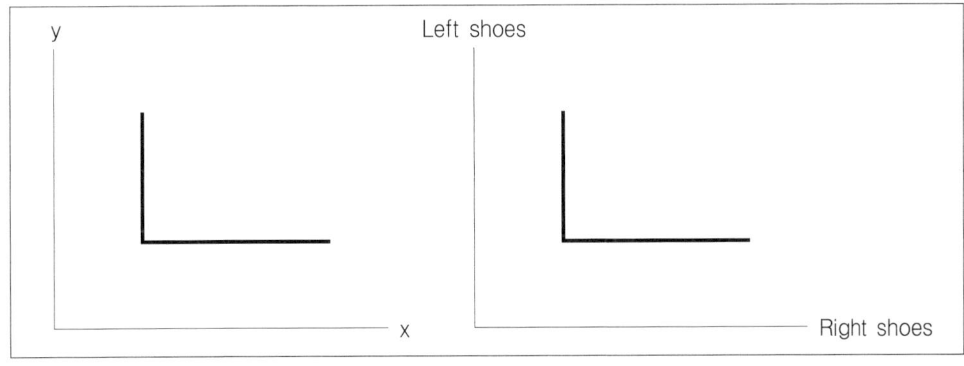

Example

$U(x,y) = \sqrt{xy}$

To the consumer, bundle A and B are the same as both of them give him the equal satisfaction. In other words, point A(2,8) gives as much utility as point B(3,b) to the individual. The consumer will be satisfied at any point along the curve assuming that other things are constant. Find b.

Solution

$b = \frac{16}{3}$

Example

$U(x,y) = \sqrt{xy}$

A(2,8), B(3,b), C(c,5) are on the same indifference curve.

Find b and c.

Solution

$b = \frac{16}{3}, \; c = \frac{16}{5}$

Example

효용함수는 $U(x,y) = \sqrt{xy}$ 이다. 세 개의 점 A(2,8), B(3,b), C(c,5)가 동일한 무차별곡선에 있을 때, b와 c는 얼마인가?

점A에서 점B로 이동할 때, $\triangle U$는 얼마인가?

Solution

$b = \frac{16}{3}, \; c = \frac{16}{5}$

$\triangle U = 0$

Example

$U(x,y) = xy$

A(3,2), B(1,b), C(c,5) are on the same indifference curve.

Find b and c.

Solution

$b = 6,\ c = \frac{6}{5}$

Example

Given three points (3,2),(1,b),(c,5) lying on $U(x,y) = xy$, find the value of b and c.

Solution

$b = 6,\ c = \frac{6}{5}$

Example

Given three points (1, 5), (2, 8), and (3, a) lying on the same line, find the value of a.

Solution

y=3x+2

a=11

MRS

한계대체율

Marginal Rate of Substitution

$$\frac{U_x}{U_y}$$

The rate at which a consumer is willing to substitute one good for another good and still maintain the same level of satisfaction.

The marginal rate of substitution is the amount of a good that a consumer is willing to consume in relation to another good, as long as the comparable good is equally satisfying.

The Marginal Rate of Substitution is the rate at which a consumer would be willing to give up a very small amount of good 2 for some of good 1 in order to be exactly as happy after the trade as before the trade.

The marginal rate of substitution is the rate of exchange between some units of goods X and Y which are equally preferred.

Utility function

$U(x, y)$

If we plot an indifference curve in the xy plane, its slope must be equal to the negative of the marginal-utility ratio.

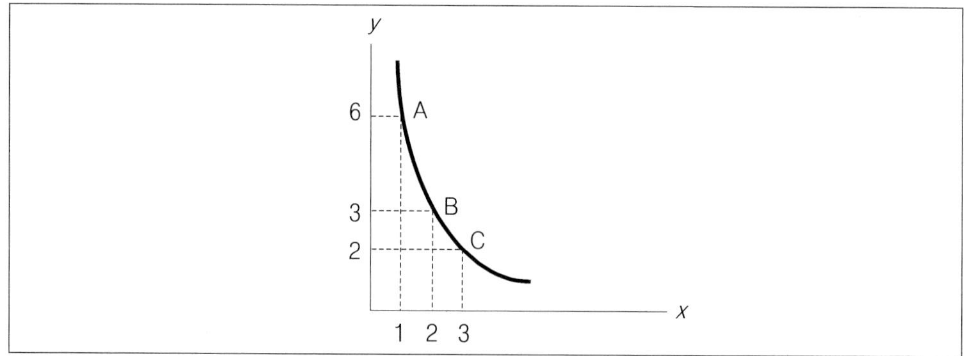

어떤 재화의 소비량이 많아질수록 그 재화의 상대적 중요성은 감소한다.

Convexity

볼록성

극단적인 상품묶음보다는 고루 섞여 있는 상품묶음을 더 선호한다.

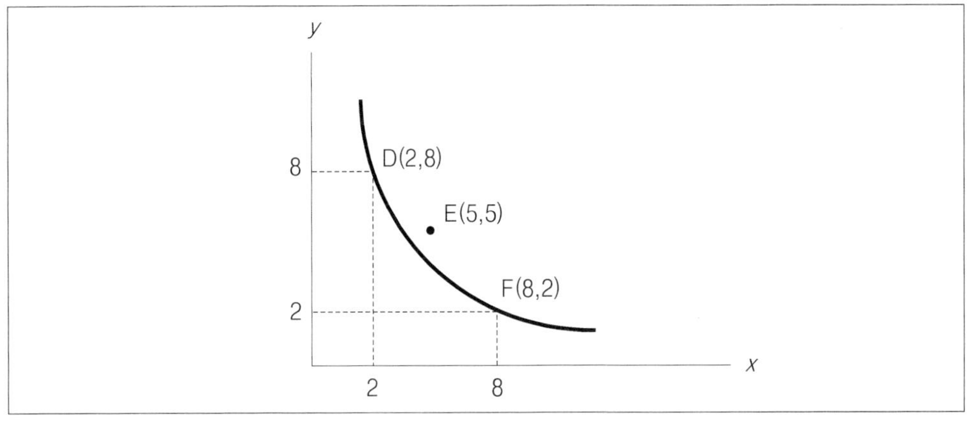

E(5,5): Averaged bundle

상품묶음 D, F보다 고루 섞여 있는 E를 선호한다.

Example

Given $U(x, y) = xy$, find MRS at the point $x = 2$ and $y = 3$.

Solution

$$MRS_{xy} = \frac{U_x}{U_y} = \frac{y}{x} = \frac{3}{2}$$

Example

효용함수는 $U(x, y) = xy$ 이고, $(x, y) = (2,3)$ 인 경우의 한계대체율은?

Solution

$$MRS_{xy} = \frac{U_x}{U_y} = \frac{y}{x} = \frac{3}{2}$$

Example

철수의 효용함수는 $U(x,y)=(x+2)(y+1)$이고, 한계대체율은 3이다. 철수의 x재의 소비량이 10이라면 y재 소비량은 얼마인가?

Solution

$$MRS_{xy}=\frac{U_x}{U_y}=\frac{y+1}{x+2}$$

$$MRS_{xy}=\frac{U_x}{U_y}=\frac{y+1}{10+2}=3$$

$$y=35$$

Example

효용함수는 $U(x,y)=xy$이고, $(x,y)=(1,3)$인 경우의 한계대체율은?

Solution

$$MRS_{xy}=\frac{U_x}{U_y}=\frac{y}{x}=3$$

Example

Given $U(x,y)=\sqrt{xy}$, find MRS at the point $x=2$ and $y=8$.

Solution

$$U_x=\frac{1}{2}x^{-\frac{1}{2}}y^{\frac{1}{2}}$$

$$U_y=\frac{1}{2}x^{\frac{1}{2}}y^{-\frac{1}{2}}$$

$$MRS_{xy}=\frac{U_x}{U_y}=\frac{y}{x}=4$$

Example

효용함수는 $U(x,y)=\sqrt{xy}$ 이고, $(x,y)=(2,8)$인 경우의 한계대체율은?

Solution

$$U_x=\frac{1}{2}x^{-\frac{1}{2}}y^{\frac{1}{2}}$$

$$U_y=\frac{1}{2}x^{\frac{1}{2}}y^{-\frac{1}{2}}$$

$$MRS_{xy}=\frac{U_x}{U_y}=\frac{y}{x}=4$$

Example

효용함수는 $U(x,y)=\sqrt{xy}$ 이고, $(x,y)=\left(3,\frac{16}{3}\right)$인 경우의 한계대체율은?

Solution

$$U_x=\frac{1}{2}x^{-\frac{1}{2}}y^{\frac{1}{2}}$$

$$U_y=\frac{1}{2}x^{\frac{1}{2}}y^{-\frac{1}{2}}$$

$$MRS_{xy}=\frac{U_x}{U_y}=\frac{y}{x}=\frac{16}{9}$$

Budget Line

예산선

주어진 소득을 전부 사용했을 때 구입할 수 있는 상품묶음의 집합을 그림으로 나타낸 것이다.

A graphical depiction of the various combinations of two selected products that a consumer can afford at specified prices for the products given their particular income level.

$P_X x + P_Y y = I$

I: income

$M = P_x x + P_y y$

M: income

x: quantity of x

y: quantity of y

M : 소득

x : x재 구입량

y : y재 구입량

Example

$U(x, y) = \frac{1}{2}xy$

income: 120 won, Price of X: 4 won, Price of Y: 2 won

Find (x, y) to maximize the utility.

Solution

$y = -2x + 60$

$\frac{U_x}{U_y} = \frac{y}{x} = 2$

$2x = -2x + 60$

$x = 15, \ y = 30$

Example

소득이 120원, x재 가격이 4원, y재 가격이 2원이고, 효용함수는 $U(x,y)=\frac{1}{2}xy$이다. 소비자 균형점을 구하라.

Solution

$y=-2x+60$

$\frac{U_x}{U_y}=\frac{y}{x}=2$

$2x=-2x+60$

$x=15,\ \ y=30$

Example

Find the extremum of

$U=\frac{1}{2}xy$ subject to $2x+y=60$

Solution

$y=-2x+60$

$\frac{U_x}{U_y}=\frac{y}{x}=2$

$2x=-2x+60$

$x=15,\ \ y=30$

Example

장동건의 효용함수는 $U(x,y)=xy$ 이다. 그는 60의 소득을 가지고 전액을 x, y재의 구입에 사용한다. x재 가격이 1, y재 가격이 2라고 할 때, 장동건의 효용을 극대화하기 위한 x, y재의 양은?

Solution

$$y=-\frac{1}{2}x+30$$

$$\frac{U_x}{U_y}=\frac{y}{x}=\frac{1}{2}$$

$$\frac{1}{2}x=-\frac{1}{2}x+30$$

$$x=30,\ \ y=15$$

Example

Find the extremum of

$U=xy$ subject to $x+2y=60$

Solution

$$y=-\frac{1}{2}x+30$$

$$\frac{U_x}{U_y}=\frac{y}{x}=\frac{1}{2}$$

$$\frac{1}{2}x=-\frac{1}{2}x+30$$

$$x=30,\ \ y=15$$

Example

장동건의 효용함수는 $U(x,y)= xy$ 이다. 그는 60의 소득을 가지고 전액을 x, y財의 구입에 사용한다. x재 가격이 2, y재 가격이 3라고 할 때, 장동건의 효용을 극대화하기 위한 x, y財의 양은?

Example

$U(x,y) = xy$

income: 60 won, Price of X: 2 won, Price of Y: 3 won

Find (x,y) to maximize the utility.

Solution

$$y = -\frac{2}{3}x + 20$$

$$\frac{U_x}{U_y} = \frac{y}{x} = \frac{2}{3}$$

$$\frac{2}{3}x = -\frac{2}{3}x + 20$$

$$x = 15,\ y = 10$$

Example

지은이의 효용함수는 $U(x,y)=xy$이다. 지은이는 120의 소득을 가지고 전액을 x, y財의 구입에 사용한다. x재 가격이 2, y재 가격이 3라고 할 때, 지은의 효용을 극대화하기 위한 x, y財의 양은?

Example

$U(x,y)=xy$

income: 120 won, Price of X: 2 won, Price of Y: 3 won

Find (x,y) to maximize the utility.

Solution

$2x+3y=120$

$\frac{U_x}{U_y}=\frac{y}{x}=\frac{2}{3}$

$\frac{2}{3}x=-\frac{2}{3}x+40$

$x=30,\ y=20$

Example

소비자의 효용함수는 $U(x,y)= x^{0.7}y^{0.3}$이다. 그는 1,000,000원의 소득을 가지고 전액을 x,y 財의 구입에 사용한다. x재 가격이 1,000원, y재 가격이 5,000원이라고 할 때, 효용을 극대화하기 위한 x,y 財의 양은?

Example

$U(x,y)= x^{0.7}y^{0.3}$

income: 1,000,000 won, Price of X: 1,000 won, Price of Y: 5,000 won

Find (x,y) to maximize the utility.

Solution

$$dU = U_x dx + U_y dy = 0$$

$$U_x = 0.7x^{-0.3}y^{0.3},\ U_y = 0.3x^{0.7}y^{-0.7}$$

$$\frac{dy}{dx} = -\frac{U_x}{U_y} = -\frac{7y}{3x}$$

$$x + 5y = 1{,}000$$

$$y = -\frac{1}{5}x + 200$$

$$\frac{dy}{dx} = -\frac{U_x}{U_y} = -\frac{7y}{3x} = -\frac{1}{5}$$

$$35y = 3x$$

$$x + 5y = 1{,}000$$

$$35y = 3x$$

$$x = 700,\ \ y = 60$$

Example

$U(x,y)= x^{0.6}y^{0.4}$

income: 1,000,000 won, Price of X: 1,000 won, Price of Y: 5,000 won

Find (x,y) to maximize the utility.

Solution

$1,000 = x + 5y$

$x = 600, y = 80$

Example

소비자의 효용함수는 $U(x,y)= x^{0.6}y^{0.4}$ 이다. 그는 100,000원의 소득을 가지고 전액을 x,y財의 구입에 사용한다. x재 가격이 1,000원, y재 가격이 5,000원이라고 할 때, 효용을 극대화하기 위한 x,y 財의 양은?

Example

$U(x,y)= x^{0.6}y^{0.4}$

income: 100,000 won, Price of X: 1,000 won, Price of Y: 5,000 won

Find (x,y) to maximize the utility.

Solution

$1,000 = x + 5y$

$x = 60, y = 8$

Investment Decisions Under Certainty

Intertemporal choice is an economic term describing how current decisions affect what options become available in the future. Theoretically, by not consuming today, consumption levels could increase significantly in the future, and vice versa.

An individual who saves today consumes less, causing their current utility to decline. Over time, the savings grow, increasing the number of goods the individual can consume and, therefore, the person's future utility.

Intertemporal Choice Model

Consider a simple two-period world in which a single consumer must decide between consumption c_0 today and consumption c_1 tomorrow.

c_0: consumption today

c_1: consumption tomorrow

or c_0: consumption in the first period

c_1: consumption in the second period

Intertemporal choice model refers to the decision-making process that involves choosing between outcomes that occur at different points in time. It examines how individuals make decisions when considering trade-offs between present and future consumption or outcomes.

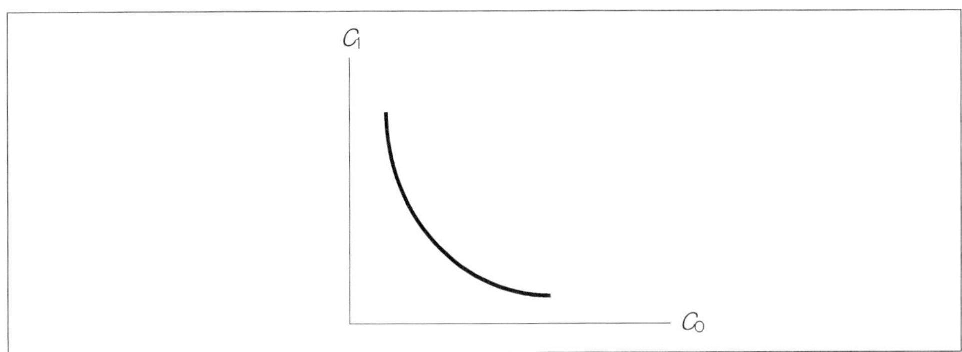

The curve has been drawn convex to the origin on the assumption that each additional decrease in current consumption requires increasingly larger increments of future consumption if the individual is to remain indifferent to the change.

Example

The investor's utility function is defined as: $U(c_o, c_1) = c_0 \times c_1^2$

To the investor, bundle A and B are the same as both of them give him the equal satisfaction. In other words, point A(2,3) gives as much utility as point B(3,b) to the individual. Find b.

Solution

$$3b^2 = 18$$

$$b = \sqrt{6} = 2.45$$

Example

The investor's utility function is defined as: $U(c_o, c_1) = c_0 \times c_1^2$

To the investor, bundle A and D are the same as both of them give him the equal satisfaction. In other words, point A(2,3) gives as much utility as point D(4,d) to the individual. Find d.

Solution

$$4d^2 = 18$$

$$d = \sqrt{4.5} = 2.12$$

Example

Given $U(c_o, c_1) = c_0 \times c_1^2$, find MRS at the point C0=2 and C1=3.

Solution

$$U_{C0} = c_1^2$$

$$U_{C1} = 2c_0c_1$$

$$MRS = \frac{c_1}{2c_0} = \frac{3}{4}$$

PPF

The production possibility frontier, also known as the production possibility curve, is a graphical representation of the maximum output combinations of two goods or services that an economy can produce with its given resources and technology, assuming full and efficient utilization of those resources. It illustrates the trade-offs an economy faces when allocating resources between the production of two different goods or services.

Example

Suppose the economy has a fixed amount of resources, such as labor, capital, and technology. These resources can be allocated to produce either computers or smartphones, or a combination of both. The following table shows different production combinations of computers and smartphones that this economy can produce:

Production Combination	Computers (units)	Smartphones (units)
A	0	20
B	10	18
C	20	14
D	30	8
E	40	0

Now, let's plot these production combinations on a graph, where the x-axis represents the quantity of computers produced, and the y-axis represents the quantity of smartphones produced. By connecting these points, we can draw the production possibility frontier. The PPF represents the maximum possible combinations of computers and smartphones that the economy can produce given its resources and technology.

MRT

Marginal Rate of Transformation

한계변환율

$$MRT_{XY} = -\frac{\Delta Y}{\Delta X}$$

X재 생산량을 1단위 증가시키기 위하여 감소시켜야 하는 Y재의 수량

The marginal rate of transformation is the number of units or amount of a good that must be forgone to create or attain one unit of another good. It is the number of units of good Y that will be foregone to produce an extra unit of good X while keeping the factors of production and technology constant.

MRT is also considered the absolute value of the slope of the production possibilities frontier. The marginal rate of transformation allows economists to analyze the opportunity costs to produce one extra unit of something. In this case, the opportunity cost is represented in the lost production of another specific good. The marginal rate of transformation is tied to the production possibility frontier, which displays the output potential for two goods using the same resources.

The marginal rate of substitution focuses on demand, while MRT focuses on supply.

Example

If baking one less cake frees up enough resources to bake three more loaves of bread, the rate of transformation is 3 to 1 at the margin. Or consider that it costs $3 to make a cake. Meanwhile, $1 can be saved by not making a loaf of bread. Thus, the MRT is 3, or $3 divided by $1.

Example

Consider a student who faces a tradeoff that involves giving up some free time to get better grades in a particular class by studying more. The MRT is the rate at which the student's grade increases as free time is given up for studying, which is given by the absolute value of the slope of the production possibility frontier curve.

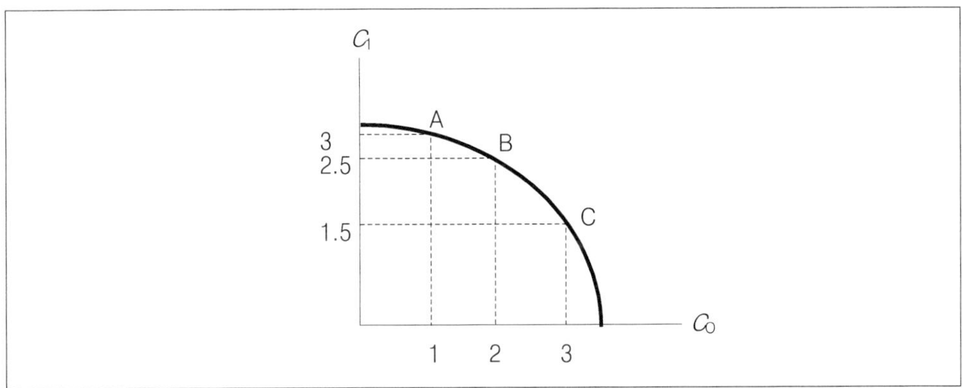

The production opportunity set

This implies diminishing marginal returns to investment because the more an individual invests, the lower the rate of return on the marginal investment.

규모에 대한 수익체감을 가정한다.

생산의 기회가 있다고 함은 주어진 소득을 사용하여 다른 형태의 자원을 생산할 수 있음을 뜻한다. 이렇게 생산의 기회가 있을 경우, 주어진 소득의 일부를 생산활동에 투자하여 원하는 시점에서의 소비의 양을 조절할 수 있다.

실물투자안에 투자하는 경우 현재소득은 투자금액만큼 감소하나 투자수익만큼 미래소득이 증가한다. 실물투자기회를 이용하는 경우 현재소득이 감소하면서 미래소득이 증가하는데, 이러한 소득의 가능한 조합들을 연결한 궤적이 생산기회선이다.

Example

An investor is confronted with the productivity curve defined as follows:

$$c_1 = 90 - \frac{1}{90}c_0^2$$

Find the consumption in the future when the consumption at present is 30.

Solution

the consumption in the future: 80

Example

An investor is confronted with the productivity curve defined as follows:

$$c_1 = 90 - \frac{1}{90}c_0^2$$

Find the consumption in the future when the consumption at present is 60.

Solution

the consumption in the future: 50

Example

An investor is confronted with the productivity curve defined as follows:

$$c_1 = 90 - \frac{1}{90}c_0^2$$

Find MRT when the consumption at present is 30.

Solution

$$\frac{dc_1}{dc_0} = -\frac{1}{45}c_0$$

$$\text{MRT} = \frac{2}{3}$$

Consumption and investment without capital markets

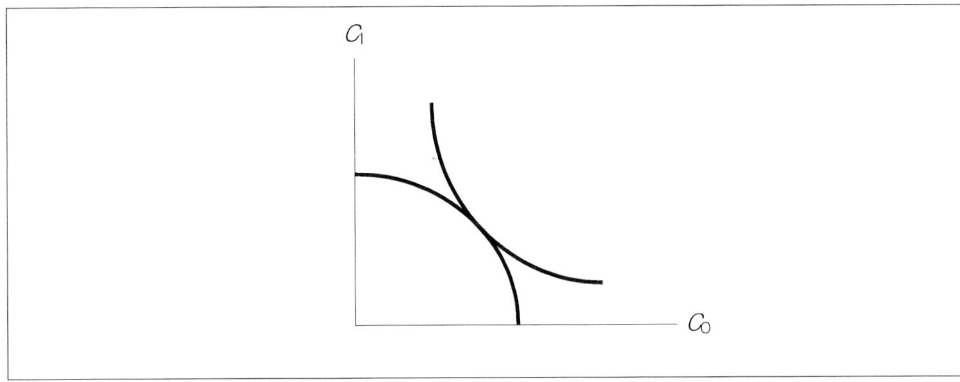

$MRS = MRT$

Example

An investor is confronted with the productivity curve defined as follows:

$$c_1 = 90 - \frac{1}{90}c_0^2$$

where c_0 indicates consumption at present and c_1 is the consumption in the future.

The investor's utility function is defined as: $U(c_o, c_1) = c_0 \times c_1^2$

How much will the investor invest in production?

Solution

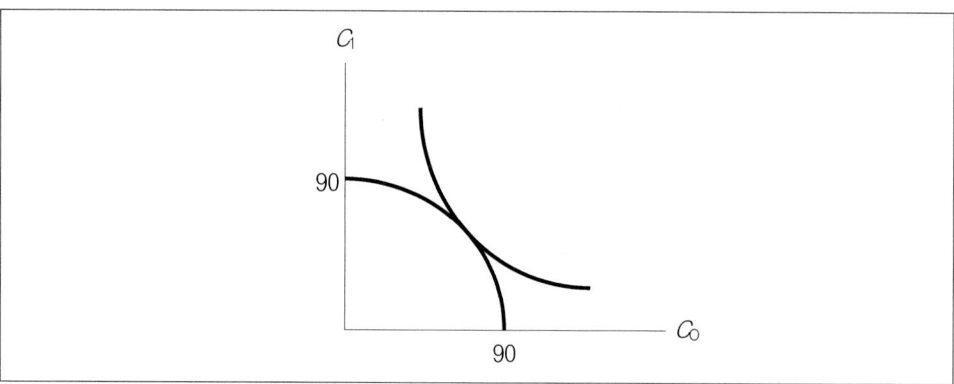

$$dU = c_1^2 dc_0 + 2c_0 c_1 dc_1 = 0$$

$$\frac{dc_1}{dc_0} = -\frac{c_1}{2c_0}$$

$$\frac{dc_1}{dc_0} = -\frac{1}{45}c_0$$

$$\frac{c_1}{2c_0} = \frac{1}{45}c_0$$

$$c_1 = \frac{2}{45}c_0^2$$

$$c_1 = 90 - \frac{1}{90}c_0^2$$

$$c_0 = 18\sqrt{5} = 40.249 = 40.25, \; c_1 = 72$$

The investor will invest 49.75 in production.

Example

효용함수는 $U(c_0, c_1) = c_0 \times c_1^2$ 이고, 생산기회선은 $c_1 = 90 - \frac{1}{90}c_0^2$ 이다. 효용을 극대화하기 위해 어떤 의사결정을 해야 하는가?

Solution

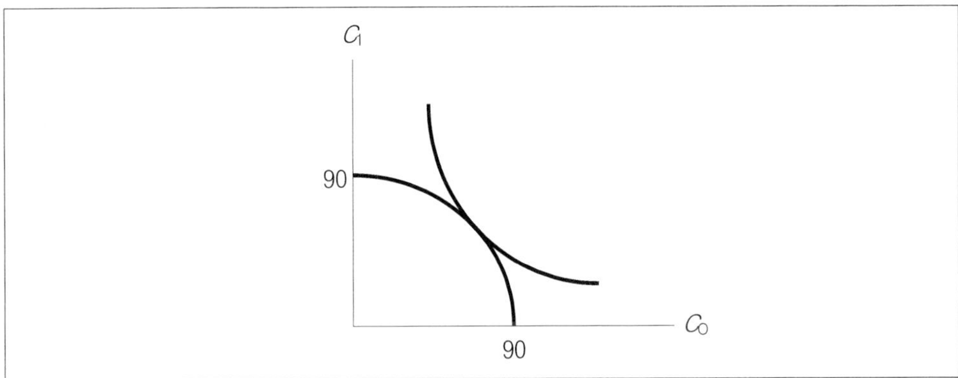

MRS와 관련된 식은 다음과 같다.

$dU = c_1^2 dc_0 + 2c_0 c_1 dc_1 = 0$

$\frac{dc_1}{dc_0} = -\frac{c_1}{2c_0}$

MRT와 관련된 식은 다음과 같다.

$\frac{dc_1}{dc_0} = -\frac{1}{45}c_0$

$\frac{c_1}{2c_0} = \frac{1}{45}c_0$

$c_1 = \frac{2}{45}c_0^2$

$c_1 = 90 - \frac{1}{90}c_0^2$

$c_0 = \sqrt{1,620} = 40.249 = 40.25$

$c_0 = 40.25,\ c_1 = 72$

40.25를 현재소비하고, 72를 미래소비한다.

49.75를 투자한다.

Example

효용함수는 $U(c_o, c_1) = c_0 \times c_1^2$이고, 생산기회선은 $c_1 = 100 - \frac{1}{9}c_0^2$이다. 효용을 극대화하기 위해 얼마를 현재소비하고, 투자를 얼마하며, 미래소비를 얼마하는 선택을 하겠는가?

Solution

$$U(c_o, c_1) = c_0 \times c_1^2$$

$$dU = c_1^2 dc_0 + 2c_0 c_1 dc_1 = 0$$

$$\frac{dc_1}{dc_0} = -\frac{c_1}{2c_0}$$

$$c_1 = 100 - \frac{1}{9}c_0^2$$

$$\frac{dc_1}{dc_0} = -\frac{2}{9}c_0$$

$$\frac{2}{9}c_0 = \frac{c_1}{2c_0}$$

$$c_1 = \frac{4}{9}c_0^2$$

$$c_0 = 13.4$$

현재소비: $\sqrt{180} = 13.416 = 13.4$,

투자: 16.6, 미래소비: 80

Example

효용함수는 $U(c_0, c_1) = c_0 \times c_1^2$ 이고, 생산기회선은 $c_1 = 100 - \frac{1}{4}c_0^2$ 이다. 효용을 극대화하기 위해 얼마를 현재소비하고, 투자를 얼마하며, 미래소비를 얼마하는 선택을 하겠는가?

Solution

$$U(c_o, c_1) = c_0 \times c_1^2$$

$$dU = c_1^2 dc_0 + 2c_0 c_1 dc_1 = 0$$

$$\frac{dc_1}{dc_0} = -\frac{c_1}{2c_0}$$

$$c_1 = 100 - \frac{1}{4}c_0^2$$

$$\frac{dc_1}{dc_0} = -\frac{1}{2}c_0$$

$$\frac{1}{2}c_0 = \frac{c_1}{2c_0}$$

$$c_1 = c_0^2$$

$$c_0 = \sqrt{80} = 8.944 = 8.94$$

The investor will invest 11.06 in production.

Consumption and investment with capital markets

The Money Market Line

$c_1 = W_1 - (1+r)c_0$

r: market rate

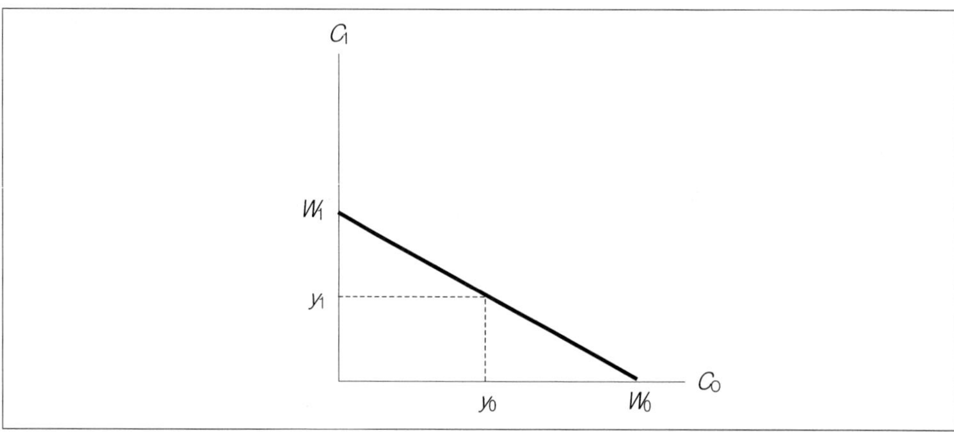

(y_0, y_1): initial endowment

$W_0 = y_0 + \frac{y_1}{1+r}$

$W_1 = W_0(1+r)$

Example

Suppose $(y_0, y_1) = (20000, 15000)$ and market rate: 25%.

Find W_0 and W_1.

Solution

$W_0 = y_0 + \frac{y_1}{1+r} = 20{,}000 + \frac{15{,}000}{1.25} = 32{,}000$

$W_1 = W_0(1+r) = 32{,}000 \times 1.25 = 40{,}000$

Example

오늘 소득이 20,000원이고, 내일 소득이 15,000원으로 주어지고 시장이자율이 25%인 경우, 최대로 가능한 오늘 소비와 내일 소비는 각각 얼마인가?

Solution

$$W_0 = y_0 + \frac{y_1}{1+r} = 20{,}000 + \frac{15{,}000}{1.25} = 32{,}000$$

$$W_1 = W_0(1+r) = 32{,}000 \times 1.25 = 40{,}000$$

Example

Suppose $(y_0, y_1) = (20000, 15000)$ and market rate: 25%.

Solve for c_1 when $c_0 = 25{,}000$.

Solution

$$c_1 = -1.25(c_0 - 20{,}000) + 15{,}000$$

$$c_1 = 8{,}750$$

Example

Suppose $(y_0, y_1) = (20000, 15000)$ and market rate: 25%.

The consumption plan $(c_0, c_1) = (25000, 8750)$ satisfies the budget constraint. To achieve this consumption plan, then consumer borrows 5,000 in period 0 and pays back 6,250 in period 1.

Example

오늘 소득이 20,000원이고, 내일 소득이 15,000원으로 주어지고 시장이자율이 25%인 경우, 오늘 소비를 25,000원 하기 위해 5,000원을 차입하면, 내일 소비할 수 있는 금액은?

Solution

$$c_1 = -1.25(c_0 - 20{,}000) + 15{,}000$$

$$c_1 = 8{,}750$$

Example

Suppose $(y_0, y_1) = (2000, 3000)$ and market rate: 20%.

Solve for c_1 when $c_0 = 3,500$.

Solution

The Money Market Line

$$c_1 = -1.2(c_0 - 2,000) + 3,000$$

$$c_0 = 3,500 \quad c_1 = 1,200$$

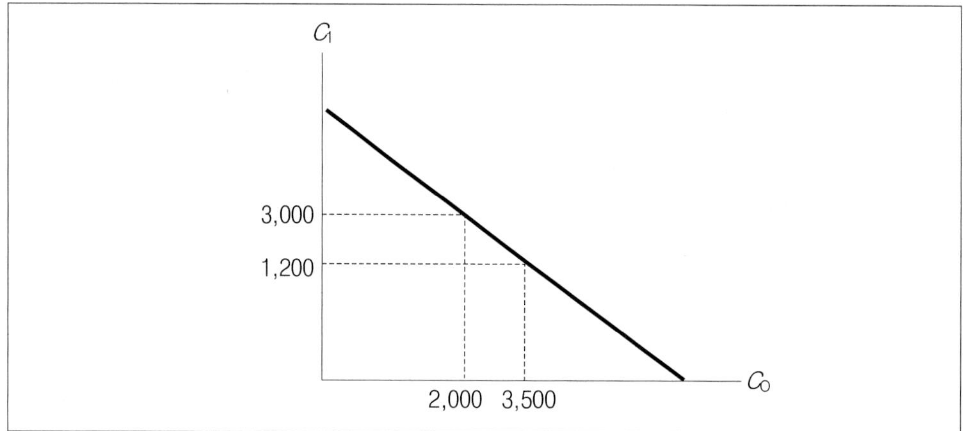

Example

오늘 소득이 2,000원이고, 내일 소득이 3,000원으로 주어지고 시장이자율이 20%인 경우, 오늘 소비를 3,500원 하기 위해 1,500원을 차입하면, 내일 소비할 수 있는 금액은?

Solution

The Money Market Line

$c_1 = -1.2(c_0 - 2,000) + 3,000$
$c_0 = 3,500$이면 $c_1 = 1,200$

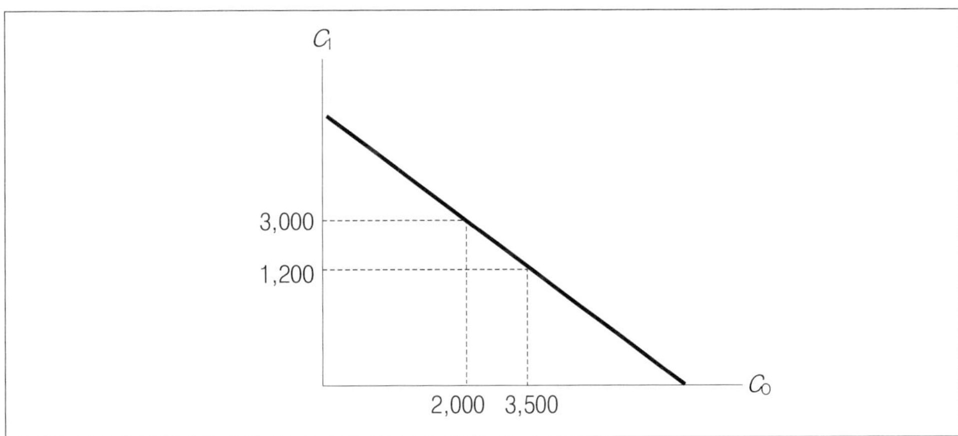

Example

Suppose $(y_0, y_1) = (2000, 3000)$ and market rate: 20%.

Find W_0 and W_1.

Solution

$W_0 = 4,500$

$W_1 = 5,400$

Example

오늘 소득이 2,000원이고, 내일 소득이 3,000원으로 주어지고 시장이자율이 20%인 경우, 최대로 가능한 오늘 소비와 내일 소비는 각각 얼마인가?

Solution

$W_0 = 4,500$

$W_1 = 5,400$

Example

Suppose $(y_0, y_1) = (2000, 3000)$ and market rate: 20%.

Solve for c_1 when $c_0 = 1,000$.

Solution

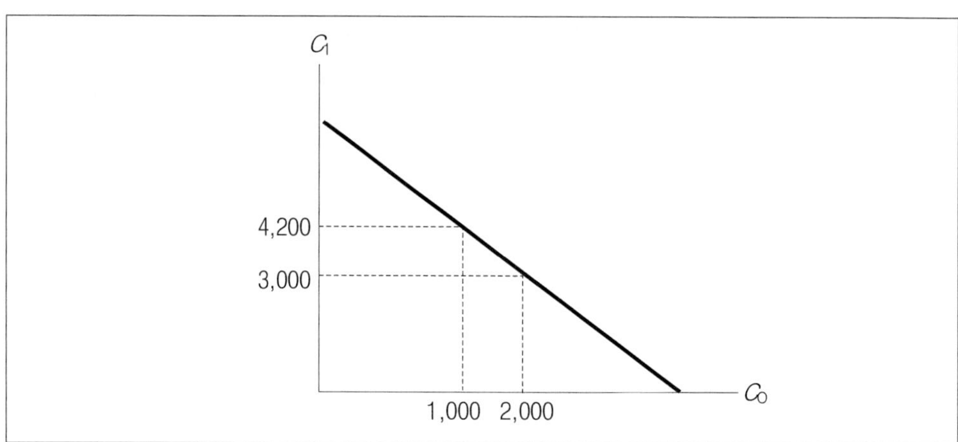

$c_1 = -1.2(c_0 - 2,000) + 3,000$

$c_0 = 1,000 \quad c_1 = 4,200$

Example

오늘 소득이 2,000원이고, 내일 소득이 3,000원으로 주어지고 시장이자율이 20%인 경우, 오늘 소비를 1,000원 하고 1,000원을 대출하면, 내일 소비할 수 있는 금액은?

Solution

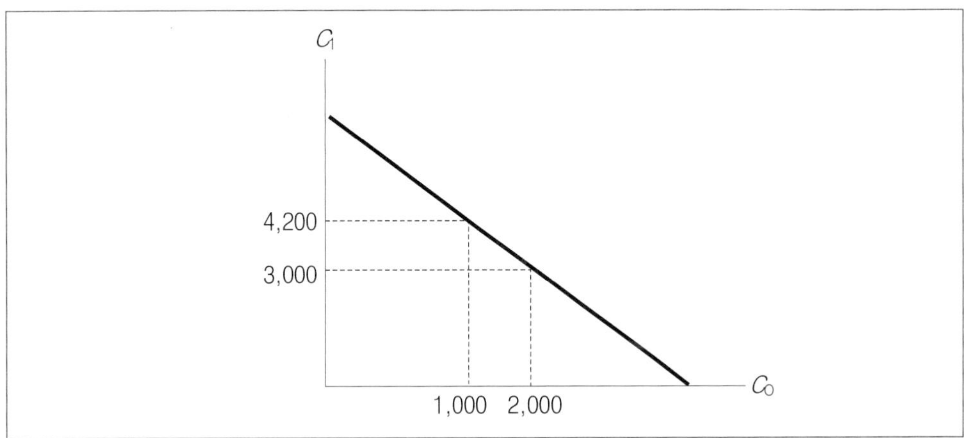

$c_1 = -1.2(c_0 - 2,000) + 3,000$

$c_0 = 1,000$이면 $c_1 = 4,200$

Fisher's separation theorem

Given perfect and complete capital markets, the production decision is governed by an objective market criterion without regard to individuals' subjective preferences that enter into their consumption decisions.

개인의 소비투자결정에 있어 그 과정이 분리된 두 단계로 이루어진다는 것이다. 즉 ① 우선 투자로부터의 현금흐름의 현가가 가장 크도록 실물투자에 대한 결정을 하여 개인의 소비기회집합을 최대로 한 후 ② 소비에 대한 개인의 시간선호에 따라 차입 내지 대출을 통하여 최적의 소비조합을 선택하게 된다. 이와 같이 투자결정과 소비결성이 분리되어 이루어진다는 것이 피셔의 분리이론(Fisher's separation theorem)이다.

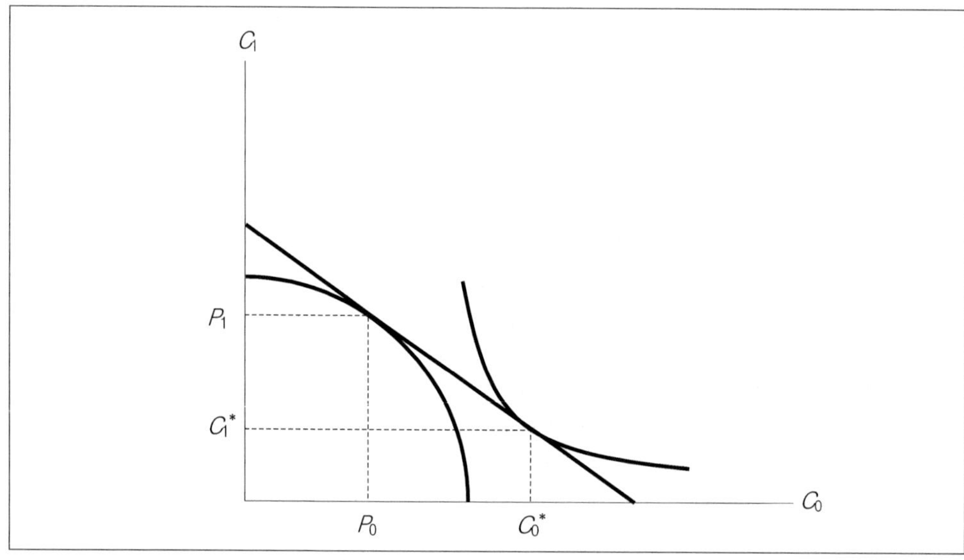
C_1
P_1
C_1^*
P_0
C_0^*
C_0

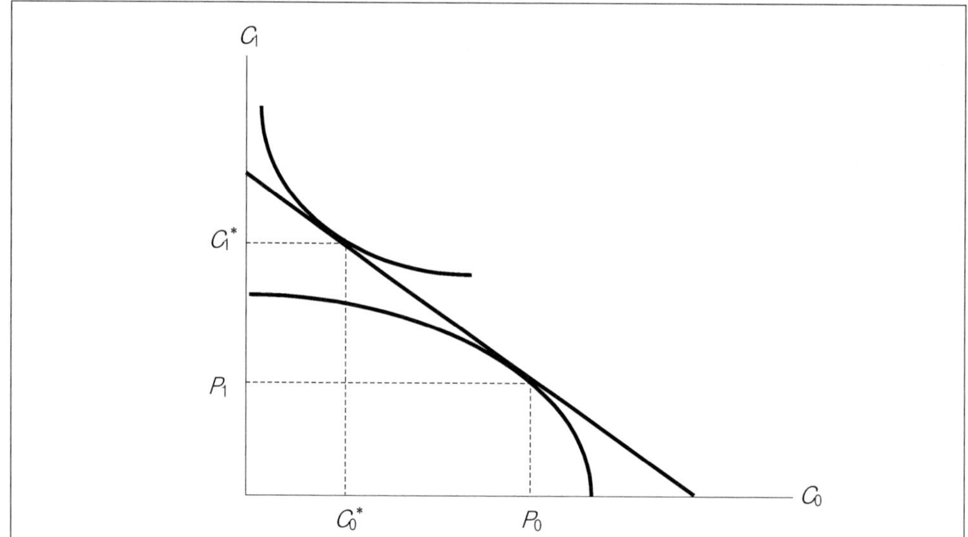
C_1
C_1^*
P_1
C_0^*
P_0
C_0

Perfect and complete capital markets

Perfect market에서는 transaction cost가 0이다.
시장이 complete하다는 것은 시장에서 증권의 수와 미래상황의 수가 일치하는 것을 의미한다.

Example

1) Find the interest rate.
2) How much will the investor invest in production?
3) Does the investor borrow or lend in the capital market?

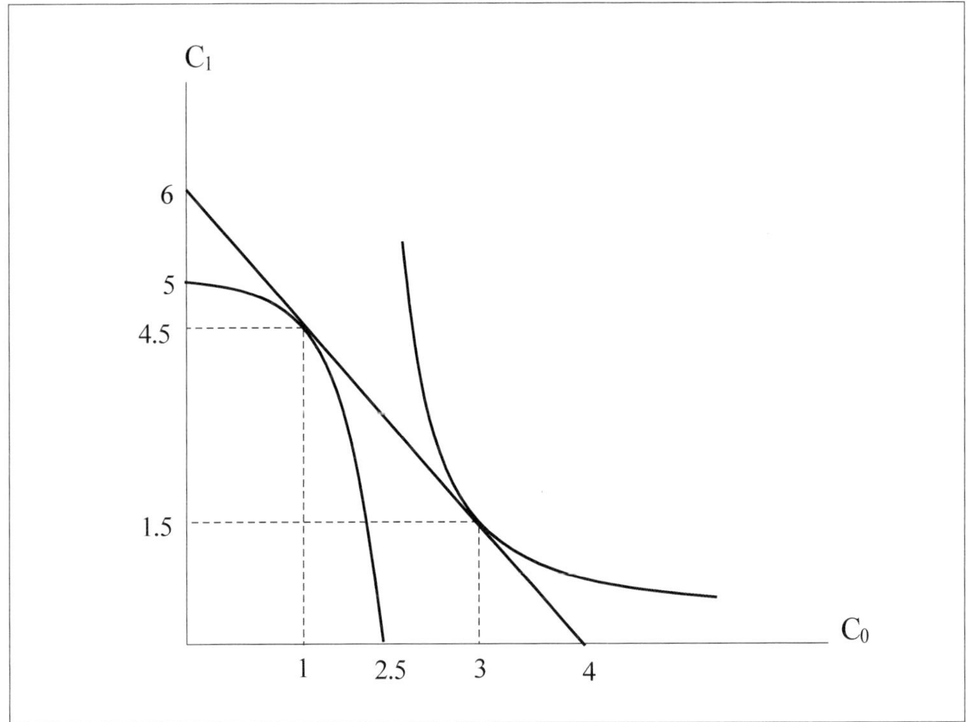

Solution

1) 0.5
2) 1.5
3) The investor borrows 2.

Example

1) 시장이자율은 얼마인가?

2) 생산활동에 얼마를 투자하는가?

3) 최적소비를 위하여 얼마를 차입 또는 대출하는가?

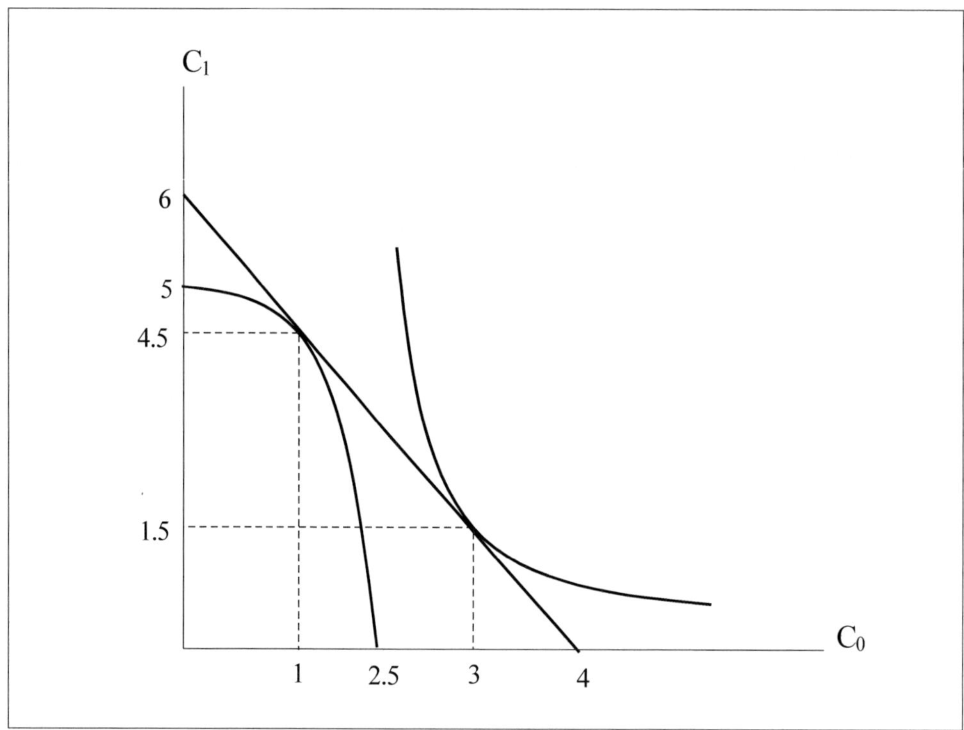

Solution

1) 0.5

2) 1.5원

3) 2원 차입

Example

1) Find the interest rate.

2) How much will the investor invest in production?

3) Does the investor borrow or lend in the capital market?

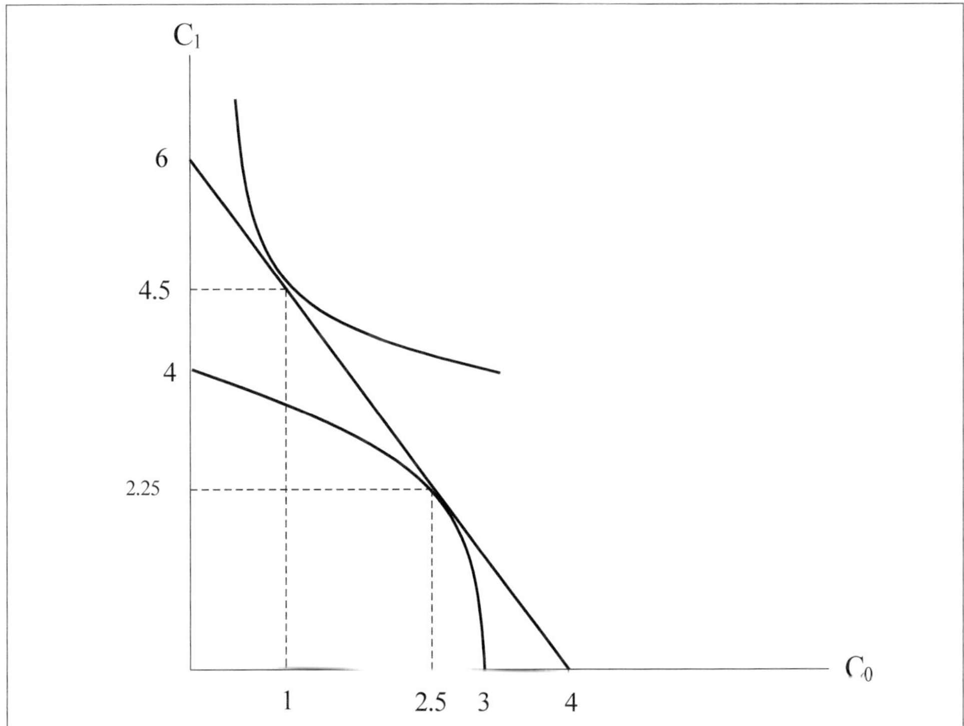

Solution

1) 0.5

2) 0.5

3) The investor lends 1.5.

Example

1) 시장이자율은 얼마인가?

2) 생산활동에 얼마를 투자하는가?

3) 최적소비를 위하여 얼마를 차입 또는 대출하는가?

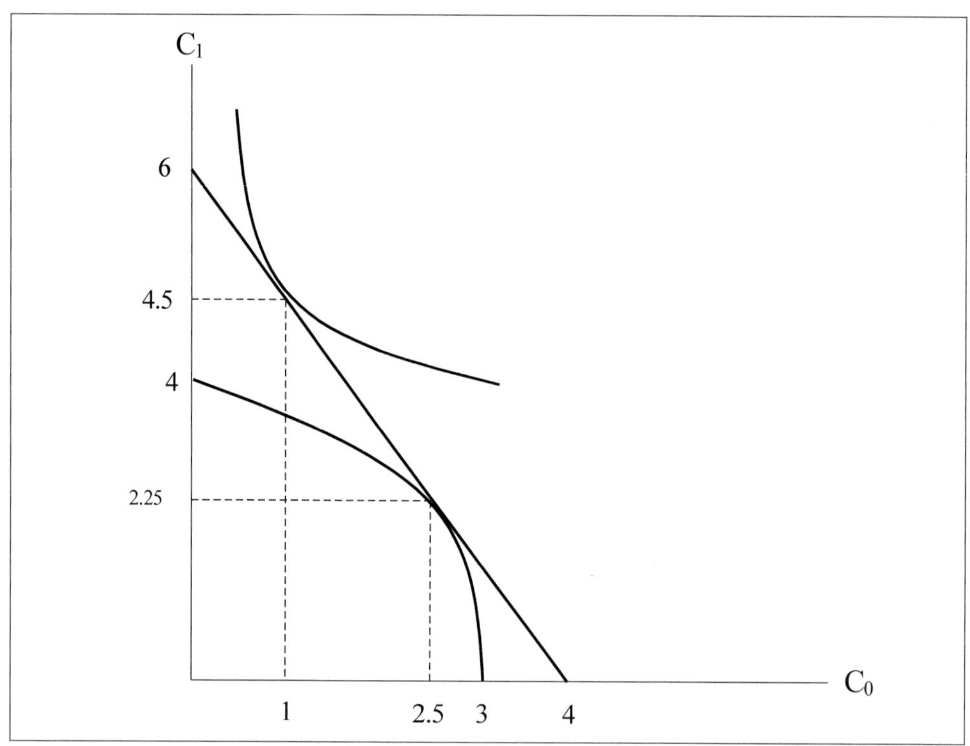

Solution

1) 0.5

2) 0.5원

3) 1.5원 대출

Example

An investor with an initial endowment of 16,000 won is confronted with the productivity curve defined as follows: $c_1 = 240(16{,}000 - c_0)^{\frac{1}{2}}$

where c_0 indicates consumption at present and c_1 is the consumption in the future. Assume that the interest rate is equal to 20%.

The investor's utility function is defined as: $U(c_0, c_1) = c_0 c_1$

1) How much will the investor invest in production?

2) Does the investor borrow or lend in the capital market? Give a numerical answer.

Solution

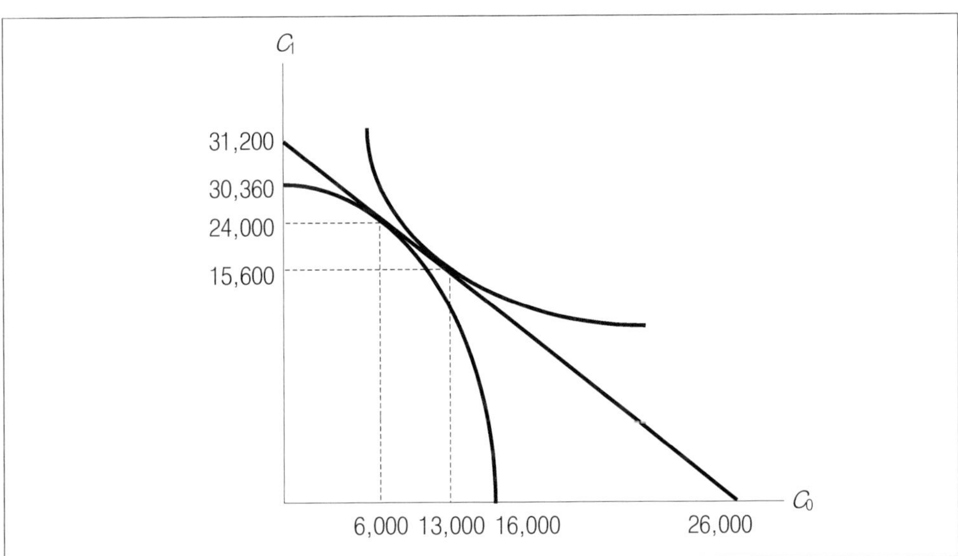

1)

$$\frac{dc_1}{dc_0} = -\frac{120}{(16{,}000 - c_0)^{\frac{1}{2}}} = -1.2$$

$c_0^* = 6{,}000$

The investor invests 10,000 won in production.

2)

$$U(c_0, c_1) = c_0 c_1$$

$$dU = c_1 dc_0 + c_0 dc_1 = 0$$

$$\frac{dc_1}{dc_0} = -\frac{c_1}{c_0} = -1.2$$

$$c_0^* = 6{,}000$$

$$c_1^* = 240 \times (10{,}000)^{\frac{1}{2}} = 24{,}000$$

The money market line is $c_1 = -1.2(c_0 - 6{,}000) + 24{,}000$

$$1.2c_0 = -1.2(c_0 - 6{,}000) + 24{,}000$$

$$c_0^{**} = 13{,}000$$

The investor borrows 7,000 won.

Example

An investor with an initial endowment of 16,000 won is confronted with the productivity curve defined as follows: $c_1 = 90 - \frac{1}{90}c_0^2$

where c_0 indicates consumption at present and c_1 is the consumption in the future. Assume that the interest rate is equal to 20%.

The investor's utility function is defined as: $U(c_o, c_1) = c_0 \times c_1^2$

1) How much will the investor invest in production?

2) Does the investor borrow or lend in the capital market? Give a numerical answer.

Solution

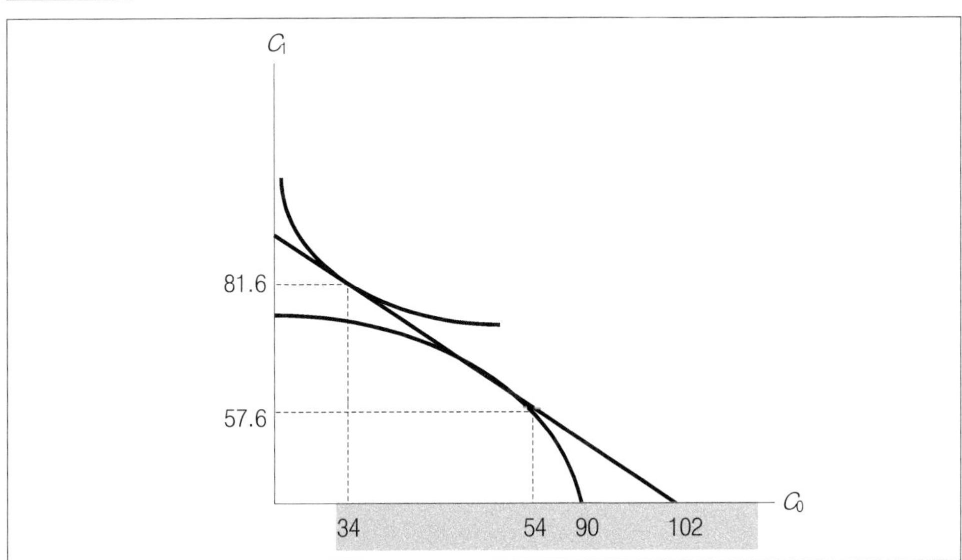

MRT와 관련된 식은 다음과 같다.

$$\frac{dc_1}{dc_0} = -\frac{1}{45}c_0$$

$$\frac{1}{45}c_0 = 1.2$$

$c_0 = 54,\ c_1 = 57.6$

36을 투자한다.

Money Market line: $c_1 = -1.2(c_0 - 54) + 57.6$

MRS와 관련된 식은 다음과 같다.

$$dU = c_1^2 dc_0 + 2c_0 c_1 dc_1 = 0$$

$$\frac{dc_1}{dc_0} = -\frac{c_1}{2c_0}$$

$$\frac{c_1}{2c_0} = 1.2$$

$$c_0 = 34,\ c_1 = 81.6$$

34를 현재소비하고, 20을 예금하며, 81.6을 미래소비한다.

Example

효용함수는 $U(c_o, c_1) = c_0 \times c_1^2$이고, 생산기회선은 $c_1 = 90 - \frac{1}{90}c_0^2$이다. 시장이자율이 20%일 때, 효용을 극대화하기 위해 어떤 의사결정을 해야 하는가?

Solution

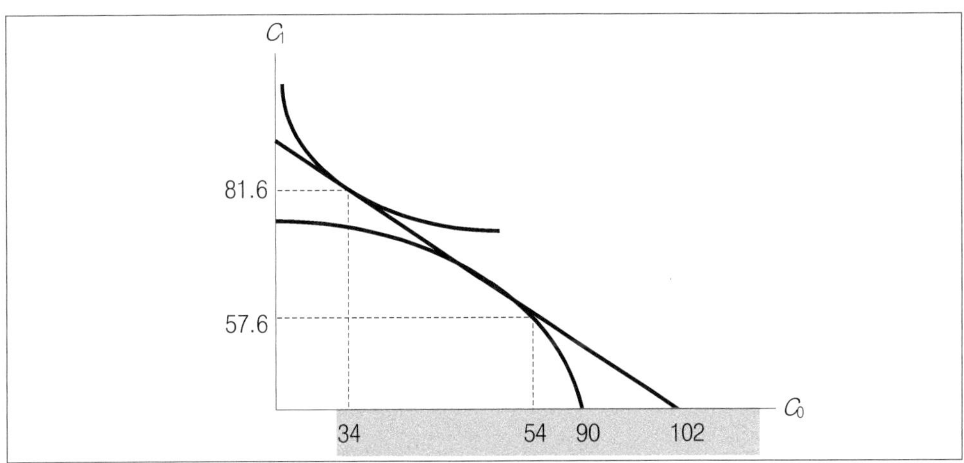

MRT와 관련된 식은 다음과 같다.

$$\frac{dc_1}{dc_0} = -\frac{1}{45}c_0$$

$$\frac{1}{45}c_0 = 1.2$$

$c_0 = 54, c_1 = 57.6$

36을 투자한다.

Money Market line: $c_1 = -1.2(c_0 - 54) + 57.6$

MRS와 관련된 식은 다음과 같다.

$$dU = c_1^2 dc_0 + 2c_0 c_1 dc_1 = 0$$

$$\frac{dc_1}{dc_0} = -\frac{c_1}{2c_0}$$

$$\frac{c_1}{2c_0} = 1.2$$

$c_0 = 34,\ c_1 = 81.6$

34를 현재소비하고, 20을 예금하며, 81.6을 미래소비한다.

$U(34, 81.6) = 226,391$

Example

효용함수는 $U(c_o, c_1) = c_0^2 \times c_1$이고, 생산기회선은 $c_1 = 100 - \frac{1}{4}c_0^2$이다. 시장이자율이 50%일 때, 효용을 극대화하기 위해 현재소비, 미래소비, 차입 또는 대출, 투자를 어떻게 해야 하는가?

Solution

MRT와 관련된 식은 다음과 같다.

$$\frac{dc_1}{dc_0} = -\frac{1}{2}c_0$$

$$\frac{1}{2}c_0 = 1.5$$

$$c_0 = 3, \quad c_1 = 97.75$$

17을 투자한다.

Money Market line: $c_1 = -1.5(c_0 - 3) + 97.75$

MRS와 관련된 식은 다음과 같다.

$$dU = 2c_0c_1dc_0 + c_0^2dc_1 = 0$$

$$\frac{dc_1}{dc_0} = -\frac{2c_1}{c_0}$$

$$\frac{2c_1}{c_0} = 1.5$$

$$c_1 = -1.5\left(\frac{2}{1.5}c_1 - 3\right) + 97.75$$

$$3c_1 = 102.25$$

$$c_1 = 34.083 = 34.1$$

$$c_0 = 45.5$$

45.5를 현재소비하고, 42.5를 차입하며, 34.1을 미래소비한다.

The concept of derivative

Instantaneous Rate of Change

순간변화율

A derivative, in mathematics, represents the rate at which a function is changing at any given point.

It tells you how fast the function is increasing or decreasing at a particular point.

When x changes from an initial value x_0 to a new value $(x_0 + \triangle x)$, the value of function $y = f(x)$ changes from $f(x_0)$ to $f(x_0 + \Delta x)$.

$$\frac{\Delta y}{\Delta x} = \frac{f(x_0 + \Delta x) - f(x_0)}{\Delta x}$$

$$\frac{dy}{dx} \equiv f'(x) \equiv \lim_{\Delta x \to 0} \frac{\Delta y}{\Delta x}$$

$$f'(x) = \lim_{h \to 0} \frac{f(x+h) - f(x)}{h}$$

In calculus, a branch of mathematics, the derivative is a measure of how a function changes as its input changes.

Geometrically, the derivative of a function can be interpreted as the slope of the graph of the function or, more precisely, as the slope of the tangent line at a point.

$y = f(x)$

y' is the rate of change of y with respect to x.

Rules of Differentiation

The derivative of $y = ax^n$ is $y' = anx^{n-1}$.

Example

Find the derivative of $y = 7x^6$.

Solution

$y' = 42x^5$

Example

Find $\frac{d}{dx}(x^n)$.

Solution

When we differentiate $y = x^n$, the power on x becomes the coefficient of x^{n-1} in the derivative and the power on x in the derivative decreases by 1.

$$\frac{d}{dx}(x^n) = nx^{n-1}$$

Example

If $y = x^2 - 4x + 5$, find $f(x+h)$.

Solution

$f(x+h) = (x+h)^2 - 4(x+h) + 5$

The tangent line of a curve at a given point is a line that just touches the curve at that point.

The point at which the tangent is drawn is known as the "point of tangency".

Example

The function given by $y = x^2 - 4x + 5$ is differentiable at $x = 3$, and its derivative there is (   ).

Solution

$y' = 2x - 4$

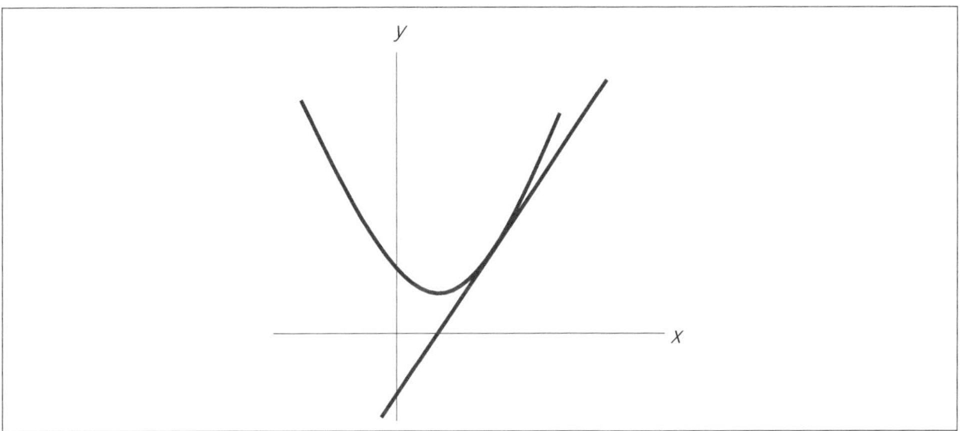

The derivative at $x = 3$ is $y' = 2$.

Example

다음 함수에서 $x = 3$에서의 접선의 기울기는 얼마인가?

$y = x^2 - 4x + 5$.

Example

Suppose $y = x^2 - 4x + 5$. Determine the slope of the tangent line at x=3.

Solution

$y' = 2x - 4$

The derivative at $x = 3$ is $y' = 2$.

Example

For the function $y = x^2 - x + 4$, suppose x changes from 0 to 3.

Find change in x and change in y.

Solution

When x changes from an initial value of 0 to a new value of 3, the value of function $y = x^2 - x + 4$ changes from 4 to 10.

$\Delta x = 3$ and $\Delta y = 6$

Example

For the function $y = 3x^2$, suppose x changes from 0 to 2.

Find change in x and change in y.

Solution

When x changes from an initial value of 0 to a new value of 2, the value of function $y = 3x^2$ changes from 0 to 12.

$\Delta x = 2$ and $\Delta y = 12$

Example

For the function $y = x^2 - 2x + 6$, find the derivative at x=3.

Solution

$y' = 2x - 2$

The derivative at $x = 3$ is $y' = 4$.

Example

For the function $y = 3x^2 + 5$, find the derivative at $x = 3$.

Solution

$f'(x) = 6x$

$f'(3) = 18$

The function given by $y = 3x^2 + 5$ is differentiable at $x = 3$, and its derivative there is 18.

Example

Evaluate the following limit.

$$\lim_{h\to 0}\frac{2xh + h^2 - 4h}{h}$$

Solution

We can factor out the common factor (h) from the numerator.

$$\lim_{h\to 0}\frac{2xh + h^2 - 4h}{h} = \lim_{h\to 0}\frac{h(2x + h - 4)}{h}$$

We can cancel out the common factor (h) from the numerator and denominator.

$$\lim_{h\to 0}\frac{h(2x + h - 4)}{h} = \lim_{h\to 0}(2x + h - 4) = 2x - 4$$

Example

$y = 3x^2 - 9x + 7$를 미분하면 $y' = 6x - 9$가 됨을 미분의 정의를 이용하여 증명하시오.

Solution

$$y' = \lim_{h\to 0}\frac{f(x+h) - f(x)}{h} = \lim_{h\to 0}\frac{3(x+h)^2 - 9(x+h) + 7 - (3x^2 - 9x + 7)}{h}$$

$$= \lim_{h\to 0}\frac{6xh + 3h^2 - 9h}{h} = \lim_{h\to 0}(6x + 3h - 9) = 6x - 9$$

Example

Translate the sentence into an equation: As the variable x approaches the value a, the function f(x) approaches the value k.

Solution

$$\lim_{x \to a} f(x) = k$$

Example

Find the limit of the function $f(x) = \frac{x^2 - 4}{x - 2}$ as x approaches 2.

Solution

We can simplify the function by factoring the numerator:

$$f(x) = \frac{x^2 - 4}{x - 2} = \frac{(x+2)(x-2)}{x-2} = x + 2$$

The limit of f(x) as x approached 2 is 4.

Example

Find the derivative of $y = \sqrt{x^2 + x + 3}$.

Solution

$$y' = \frac{1}{2}(x^2 + x + 3)^{-\frac{1}{2}}(2x + 1)$$

The Product Rule

The Product Rule says that the derivative of a product of two functions is the first function times the derivative of the second function plus the second function times the derivative of the first function.

$$\frac{d}{dx}(f(x)g(x)) = f'(x)g(x) + f(x)g'(x)$$

Example

Find the derivative of y=(2x−1)(3x−2).

Solution

$$y' = 2(3x-2) + 3(2x-1) = 12x - 7$$

Quotient Rule

The derivative of the quotient of two functions, $\frac{f(x)}{g(x)}$, is

$$\frac{d}{dx}\frac{f(x)}{g(x)} = \frac{f'(x)g(x) - f(x)g'(x)}{g^2(x)}$$

The Quotient Rule says that the derivative of a quotient is the denominator times the derivative of the numerator minus the numerator times the derivative of the denominator, all divided by the square of the denominator.

In calculus, the quotient rule is a method of finding the derivative of a function that is the ratio of two differentiable functions.

Example

Find the derivative of $\frac{2x-3}{x+1}$.

Solution

$$\frac{d}{dx}\left(\frac{2x-3}{x+1}\right) = \frac{5}{(x+1)^2}$$

Interpretation of the Derivative

$f'(x_0) > 0$ means that the value of the function tends to increase.

$f''(x_0) > 0$ means that the slope of the curve tends to increase.

If the first derivative is positive at a point, the value of the function tends to increase. If the second derivative is positive at a point, the slope of the curve tends to increase. The first derivative primarily tells us about the direction the function is going. That is, it tells us if the function is increasing or decreasing.

The second-order derivative is nothing but the derivative of the first derivative of the given function.

The second derivative of a function is simply the derivative of the derivative.

In calculus, the second derivative, or the second order derivative, of a function f is the derivative of the derivative of f.

Graphically the first derivative represents the slope of the function at a point, and the second derivative describes how the slope changes over the independent variable in the graph.

Example

Find the second derivative of $f(x) = x^2$.

Solution

$f''(x) = 2$

Example

The second derivative primarily tells us if the (   ) is increasing or decreasing.

Solution

The second derivative primarily tells us if the slope is increasing or decreasing.

편미분

하나의 변수에 대해 미분하며 다른 변수는 상수로 취급한다.

Example

Suppose we have a function $f(x,y)=x^2+2xy+3y^2$.

The partial derivative of f with respect to x is 2x+2y.

Example

Find the first and second partial derivatives of

$z=x^3+5xy-y^2$

Solution

$f_x=3x^2+5y \qquad f_y=5x-2y$

$f_{xx}=6x \qquad f_{xy}=5 \qquad f_{yy}=-2$

Example

Find the first and second partial derivatives of

$z=8x^3+2xy-3x^2+y^2+1$

Solution

$f_x=24x^2+2y-6x \qquad f_y=2x+2y$

$f_{xx}=48x-6 \qquad f_{xy}=2 \qquad f_{yy}=2$

Example

Find the first and second partial derivatives of

$z = (x-2)^3 + (y-3)^5$

Solution

$f_x = 3(x-2)^2 \qquad f_y = 5(y-3)^4$

$f_{xx} = 6(x-2) \qquad f_{xy} = 0 \qquad f_{yy} = 20(y-3)^3$

Example

Let $f(x,y) = y^3x^2$. Calculate $\dfrac{\partial f}{\partial x}(x,y)$.

Solution

$\dfrac{\partial f}{\partial x}(x,y) = 2y^3x$

Example

Let $f(x,y) = y^3x^2$. Calculate $\dfrac{\partial f}{\partial x}(1,2)$.

Solution

$\dfrac{\partial f}{\partial x}(x,y) = 2y^3x$

$\dfrac{\partial f}{\partial x}(1,2) = 16$

Example

Suppose that f is a function of more than one variable. For instance,

$$z = f(x, y) = x^2 + xy + y^2$$

Find the partial derivative of z with respect to x at the point (1,1).

Solution

$$\frac{\partial z}{\partial x} = 2x + y$$

$$\frac{\partial z}{\partial x} = 3 \text{ at the point } (1,1)$$

A partial derivative of a function of several variables is its derivative with respect to one of those variables, with the others held constant.

Let f(x,y) be a function with two variables. If we keep y constant and differentiate f with respect to the variable x, we obtain what is called the partial derivative of f with respect to x which is denoted by $\frac{\partial f}{\partial x}$ or f_x.

When spoken, $\frac{\partial y}{\partial x}$, the partial derivative of y with respect to x is often shortened to partial y partial x, or del y del x.

Total differential

For the function

$z = f(x, y)$

$dz = f_x dx + f_y dy$

For a function of two or more independent variables, the total differential of the function is the sum over all of the independent variables of the partial derivative of the function with respect to a variable times the total differential of that variable.

It refers to the total change in a function resulting from changes in multiple variables. The total differential measures how much a function changes as each of its independent variables changes. It provides a way to estimate the change in the function's value when there are simultaneous changes in multiple variables.

Example

Given $z = x^3 + 5xy - y^2$, find dz

Solution

$dz = (3x^2 + 5y)dx + (5x - 2y)dy$

Example

Given $z = x^3 + 5xy - y^2$, find dz at the point $x = 1$ and $y = 2$

Solution

$dz = (3x^2 + 5y)dx + (5x - 2y)dy$

At the point $x = 1$ and $y = 2$, we have

$dz = 13dx + dy$

Find the total differential of $z = x^3 + 5xy - y^2$ at (1,2).

Solution

$$dz = (3x^2 + 5y)dx + (5x - 2y)dy$$

At the point $x = 1$ and $y = 2$, we have

$$dz = 13dx + dy$$

Demand

Quantity demanded is the amount of a good that buyers are willing and able to purchase.

Law of Demand

The law of demand states that, other things equal, the quantity demanded of a good falls when the price of the good rises.

Demand curve

A graph of the relationship between the price of a good and the quantity demanded

Market Demand Function

$Q_d = f(P, P_R, M, N, T)$

where:

P is the price of the product.

P_R is the level of prices of other goods.

M is the level of consumer income.

N is the number of consumers in the market.

T is the consumer desire or taste.

P : 상품의 가격

P_R : 다른 상품들의 가격

M : 소득수준

N : 인구의 크기

T : 기호

A demand function is a mathematical equation that expresses the relationship between the quantity demanded of a good and various factors that influence demand, such as the price of the good, the prices of related goods, consumer income, and preferences.
Rewrite the function so that the quantity demanded is explicitly expressed as a function of the price of the good, while keeping the other factors affecting demand constant.

Ceteris Paribus

Other things being equal
다른 모든 조건이 변하지 않는다면
$Q_d = f(P; P_R, M, N, T)$

Ceteris paribus is a Latin phrase meaning “other things being equal or held constant”.

Example

The demand for ice cream cones is $P = 800 - 2Q_D$.
The supply of ice cream cones is $P = 200 + Q_S$.
Find the equilibrium price and equilibrium quantity.

Solution

To find the equilibrium price and equilibrium quantity, substitute Q^* for Q_D and Q_S and P^* for P.
That is,

$$P^* = 800 - 2Q^*$$

$$P^* = 200 + Q^*$$

$$Q^* = 200$$

$$P^* = 400$$

Example

Let the demand and supply function be as follows:

$$Q_d = 40 - 3P$$

$$Q_s - 7P - 10$$

find $\overline{P}$ and $\overline{Q}$

Solution

$\overline{P} = 5$ and $\overline{Q} = 25$

Example

The demand for ice cream cones is $Q_d = 40 - 3P$
The supply of ice cream cones is $Q_s = 7P - 10$
Find the equilibrium price and equilibrium quantity.

Solution

$\overline{P} = 5$ and $\overline{Q} = 25$

Example

$Q_D = 4 - 3P,\ Q_S = 4P - 3$ 일 때 균형가격은?

Solution

$P^* = 1$

PED

Price elasticity of demand

수요의 가격탄력성

$$e_p = -\frac{\frac{\Delta Q_d}{Q_d}}{\frac{\Delta P}{P}} = -\frac{\Delta Q_d}{\Delta P}\frac{P}{Q_d}$$

$$e_p = -\frac{dQ_d}{dP}\frac{P}{Q_d}$$

The price elasticity of demand (PED) is the percentage change in the quantity demanded of a good or service divided by the percentage change in the price.

Elasticity of demand is the percentage change in the quantity demanded that results from a given percentage change in the price.

Example

The figure shows the demand for pens.

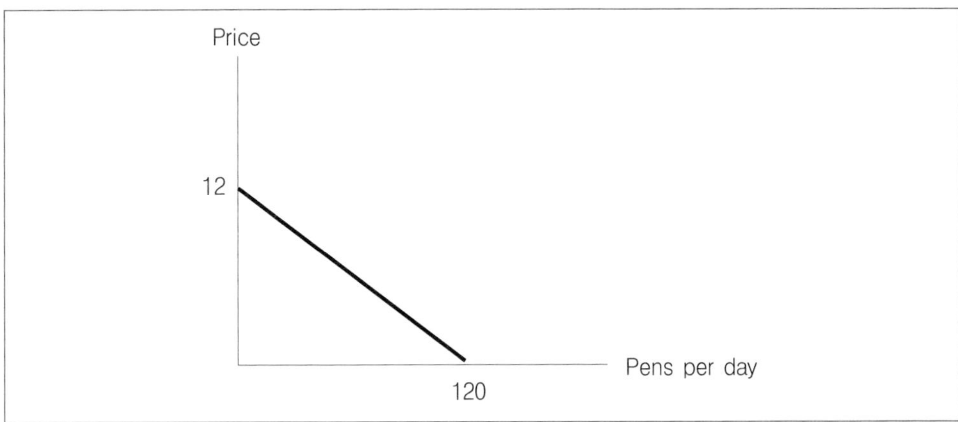

Calculate the elasticity of demand when the price is \$2.

Solution

$$P = -\frac{1}{10}Q + 12$$

$$2 = -\frac{1}{10}Q + 12$$

$$Q = 100$$

$$e_p = -\frac{dQ_d}{dP}\frac{P}{Q_d} = 10 \times \frac{2}{100} = 0.2$$

Example

Let the demand function be as follows:

$Q = 120 - 10P$

Calculate the elasticity of demand when the price is \$2.

Solution

$Q = 100$

$$e_p = -\frac{dQ_d}{dP}\frac{P}{Q_d} = 10 \times \frac{2}{100} = 0.2$$

Example

Let the demand function be as follows:

$P = 800 - 2Q$

Calculate the elasticity of demand when the price is \$600.

Solution

$$\frac{dP}{dQ} = -2$$

$Q = 100$

$$e_p = \frac{1}{2}\frac{600}{100} = 3$$

Example

Let the demand function be as follows:

$P = 800 - 2Q$

Calculate the elasticity of demand when the price is \$400.

Solution

$$e_p = -\frac{dQ_d}{dP}\frac{P}{Q_d}$$

$$\frac{dP}{dQ} = -2$$

$$Q = 200$$

$$e_p = 1$$

Example

Let the demand function be as follows:

$P = 800 - 4Q$

Calculate the elasticity of demand when the price is \$600.

Solution

$$\frac{dP}{dQ} = -4$$

$$Q = 50$$

$$e_p = \frac{1}{4}\frac{600}{50} = 3$$

Example

Let the demand function be as follows:

$$Q = \frac{100}{P^3}$$

1 percent change in price results in (　　) percent change in quantity demanded.

Solution

$$\frac{dQ_d}{dP} = -\frac{300}{P^4}$$

$$e_p = -\frac{dQ_d}{dP}\frac{P}{Q_d} = \frac{300}{P^4}\frac{P}{\frac{100}{P^3}} = 3$$

1 percent change in price results in 3 percent change in quantity demanded.

Example

어떤 사람의 맥주에 대한 수요함수가 $Q = \frac{100}{P^3}$ 으로 주어져 있다면 가격이 1% 상승할 때, 맥주 구입량은 몇% 감소하겠는가?

Solution

$$\frac{dQ_d}{dP} = -\frac{300}{P^4}$$

$$e_p = -\frac{dQ_d}{dP}\frac{P}{Q_d} = \frac{300}{P^4}\frac{P}{\frac{100}{P^3}} = 3$$

맥주가 가격이 1% 상승하면 맥주구입량은 3% 감소한다.

Example

Let the demand function be as follows:

$$Q = \frac{100}{P^2}$$

2 percent change in price results in (   ) percent change in quantity demanded.

Solution

$$\frac{dQ_d}{dP} = -\frac{200}{P^3}$$

$$e_p = -\frac{dQ_d}{dP}\frac{P}{Q_d} = \frac{200}{P^3}\frac{P}{\frac{100}{P^2}} = 2$$

$$\frac{4\%}{2\%} = 2$$

2 percent change in price results in 4 percent change in quantity demanded.

Example

어떤 사람의 맥주에 대한 수요함수가 $Q = \frac{100}{P^2}$ 으로 주어져 있다면 가격이 2% 상승할 때, 맥주 구입량은 몇% 감소하겠는가?

Solution

$$\frac{dQ_d}{dP} = -\frac{200}{P^3}$$

$$e_p = -\frac{dQ_d}{dP}\frac{P}{Q_d} = \frac{200}{P^3}\frac{P}{\frac{100}{P^2}} = 2$$

맥주가 가격이 2% 상승하면 맥주구입량은 4% 감소한다.

Price elasticity of supply

공급의 가격탄력성

$$e_p = \frac{\frac{\Delta Q_s}{Q_s}}{\frac{\Delta P}{P}} = \frac{\Delta Q_s}{\Delta P}\frac{P}{Q_s}$$

$$e_p = \frac{dQ_s}{dP}\frac{P}{Q_s}$$

Example

Let the supply function as follows:

$Q_s = 5P - 25$

Calculate the elasticity of supply when the quantity supplied is 100.

Solution

$100 = 5P - 25$

$P = 25$

$$e_p = \frac{dQ_s}{dP}\frac{P}{Q_s} = 5 \times \frac{25}{100} = 1.25$$

Example

공급곡선이 다음과 같다.

$Q_s = 5P - 25$

$Q_s = 100$ 인 점에서의 공급탄력성을 구하라.

Solution

$100 = 5P - 25$

$P = 25$

$$e_p = \frac{dQ_s}{dP}\frac{P}{Q_s} = 5 \times \frac{25}{100} = 1.25$$

Price elasticity of demand

The price elasticity of demand measures the change in the quantity demanded in response to a change in market price.

Production function

A function that defines the maximum amount of output that can be produced with a given set of inputs

$Q = f(K, L)$

We will let K denote the quantity of capital, L the quantity of labor, and Q the level of output produced in the production process.

생산함수는 주어진 시간 동안 사용된 여러 가지 생산요소의 양과 이를 통해 그 기간 동안 생산될 수 있는 최대한의 상품량과의 관계를 나타내는 함수이다.

Linear Production function

$Q = f(K, L) = aK + bL$

Example

A firm can manufacture a product according to the production function

$Q = f(K, L) = 2K + 3L$

How much output is produced when 2 units of labor and 5 units of capital are employed?

Solution

2 units of labor and 5 units of capital produce 16 units of output.

Leontief Production function

$Q = f(K,L) = Min\{aK, bL\}$

Example

A firm can manufacture a product according to the production function

$Q = f(K,L) = Min\{2K, 3L\}$

How much output is produced when 2 units of labor and 5 units of capital are employed?

Solution

$Q = f(K,L) = Min\{2K, 3L\} = Min\{10, 6\} = 6$

2 units of labor and 5 units of capital produce 6 units of output.

Cobb–Douglas Production function

$Q = f(K,L) = K^a L^b$

The function form of the CD production function:

$y = AL^{\alpha}K^{\beta}$

A is the total factor productivity.

Alpha represents the output elasticity of labor.

Beta represents the output elasticity of capital.

Example

A firm can manufacture a product according to the production function

$$Q = f(K, L) = K^{\frac{1}{2}} L^{\frac{1}{2}}$$

How much output is produced when 4 units of labor and 9 units of capital are employed?

Solution

4 units of labor and 9 units of capital produce 6 units of output.

Example

A firm can manufacture a product according to the CD production function.

The total factor productivity is 1.

The output elasticity of capital is 1/2.

The output elasticity of labor is 1/2.

How much output is produced when 4 units of labor and 9 units of capital are employed?

Solution

$$Q = f(K, L) = K^{\frac{1}{2}} L^{\frac{1}{2}}$$

4 units of labor and 9 units of capital produce 6 units of output.

Example

A firm can manufacture a product according to the production function

$$Q = f(K, L) = K^{\frac{1}{2}} L^{\frac{1}{2}}$$

How much output is produced when 16 units of labor and 9 units of capital are employed?

Solution

$$\sqrt{9}\,\sqrt{16} = 12$$

16 units of labor and 9 units of capital produce 12 units of output.

Example

A firm can manufacture a product according to the CD production function.

The total factor productivity is 1.

The output elasticity of capital is 1/2.

The output elasticity of labor is 1/2.

How much output is produced when 16 units of labor and 9 units of capital are employed?

Solution

$\sqrt{9}\,\sqrt{16}=12$

16 units of labor and 9 units of capital produce 12 units of output.

Returns to Scale

Constant Returns to Scale

If we scale all of the inputs up by some amount m, constant returns to scale implies that we should get m times as much output:

$f(mx, my) = mf(x, y)$

Increasing Returns to Scale

$f(mx, my) > mf(x, y)$

for all $m > 1$

Decreasing Returns to Scale

$f(mx, my) < mf(x, y)$

for all $m > 1$

Example

Consider the production function $f(x,y) = 4x + y$. Does this exhibit constant, increasing, or decreasing returns to scale?

Solution

$f(mx, my) = 4mx + my = m(4x + y)$

$mf(x, y) = m(4x + y)$

$f(mx, my) = mf(x, y)$

for all $m > 1$

Constant returns to scale

Example

Consider the production function $f(x,y) = x^2y^2$. Does this exhibit constant, increasing, or decreasing returns to scale?

Solution

$f(mx, my) = m^4x^2y^2$

$mf(x, y) = mx^2y^2$

$f(mx, my) > mf(x, y)$

for all $m > 1$

Increasing returns to scale

Example

When both inputs x and y are multiplied by a factor m, the resulting output f(mx,my) is greater than mf(x,y), indicating that the function $f(x,y) = x^2 + y^2$ exhibits increasing returns to scale.

Example

Consider the production function $f(x,y) = x^2y$. Does this exhibit constant, increasing, or decreasing returns to scale?

Solution

$f(2x,2y) = 2^3x^2y$

$2f(x,y) = 2x^2y$

$f(2x,2y) > 2f(x,y)$

Increasing returns to scale

Example

Consider the production function $f(x,y) = x^{\frac{1}{2}}y^{\frac{1}{3}}$. Does this exhibit constant, increasing, or decreasing returns to scale?

Solution

$f(mx,my) = m^{\frac{5}{6}}x^{\frac{1}{2}}y^{\frac{1}{3}}$

$mf(x,y) = mx^{\frac{1}{2}}y^{\frac{1}{3}}$

$f(mx,my) < mf(x,y)$

for all $m > 1$

Decreasing returns to scale

Measures of Productivity

Total Product

The maximum level of output that can be produced with a given amount of inputs.

Average Product

The average product is a measure of the output produced per unit of input. Mathematically, the average product can be calculated as the total output divided by the total units of the variable input.

Average Product of capital
자본의 평균생산

$$AP_K = \frac{Q}{K}$$

Average Product of labor
노동의 평균생산

$$AP_L = \frac{Q}{L}$$

Example

A firm can manufacture a product according to the production function

$$Q = f(K, L) = K^{\frac{3}{4}} L^{\frac{1}{4}}$$

Calculate the average product of labor when the level of capital is fixed at 16 units and the firm uses 16 units of labor.

Solution

$$AP_L = \frac{Q}{L} = \frac{16}{16} = 1$$

Example

A firm can manufacture a product according to the production function

$Q = f(K,L) = K^{\frac{3}{4}}L^{\frac{1}{4}}$

Calculate the average product of labor when the level of capital is fixed at 16 units and the firm uses 81 units of labor.

Solution

$$AP_L = \frac{Q}{L} = \frac{24}{81} = \frac{8}{27}$$

Marginal Product

The change in total output attributable to the last unit of an input.

Marginal product can be defined as the derivative of the total product function with respect to the input variable.

Example

A firm can manufacture a product according to the production function

$Q = f(K,L) = K^{\frac{3}{4}}L^{\frac{1}{4}}$

Calculate the marginal product of labor when the level of capital is fixed at 16 units and the firm uses 81 units of labor.

Solution

$$MP_L = \frac{1}{4}K^{\frac{3}{4}}L^{-\frac{3}{4}}$$

$$MP_L = \frac{1}{4}16^{\frac{3}{4}}81^{-\frac{3}{4}} = \frac{1}{4}2^3 3^{-3} = \frac{2}{27}$$

Example

A firm can manufacture a product according to the CD production function.

The total factor productivity is 1.

The output elasticity of capital is 3/4.

The output elasticity of labor is 1/4.

Calculate the marginal product of labor when the level of capital is fixed at 16 units and the firm uses 81 units of labor.

Solution

$$Q = f(K,L) = K^{\frac{3}{4}}L^{\frac{1}{4}}$$

$$MP_L = \frac{1}{4}K^{\frac{3}{4}}L^{-\frac{3}{4}}$$

$$MP_L = \frac{1}{4}16^{\frac{3}{4}}81^{-\frac{3}{4}} = \frac{1}{4}2^3 3^{-3} = \frac{2}{27}$$

Example

A firm can manufacture a product according to the production function

$$Q = f(K,L) = \frac{1}{2}K^{\frac{1}{3}}L^{\frac{2}{3}}$$

Calculate the marginal product of labor when the level of capital is fixed at 1 units and the firm uses 1 units of labor.

Solution

$$MP_L = \frac{1}{3}K^{\frac{1}{3}}L^{-\frac{1}{3}}$$

Suppose $K = 1$ and $L = 1$. Then

$$MP_L = \frac{1}{3}$$

Example

A firm can manufacture a product according to the production function

$Q = f(K,L) = K^{\frac{3}{4}}L^{\frac{1}{4}}$

Calculate the marginal product of capital when the level of capital is fixed at 16 units and the firm uses 81 units of labor.

Solution

$$MP_K = \frac{3}{4}K^{-\frac{1}{4}}L^{\frac{1}{4}}$$

$$MP_K = \frac{3}{4}16^{-\frac{1}{4}}81^{\frac{1}{4}} = \frac{3}{4}\times\frac{1}{2}\times 3 = \frac{9}{8}$$

Homogeneous function of degree k

In mathematics, a function $f(x,y)$ is said to be homogeneous of degree k if multiplying all of its arguments by a constant m results in multiplying the function itself by m^k.

$f(mx,my) = m^k f(x,y)$

Example

Suppose a firm's production function is given by:

$f(x,y) = x^2 + y^2$

Is this production function homogeneous? If so, what is its degree of homogeneity?

Solution

$f(x,y) = x^2 + y^2$

$f(mx,my) = (mx)^2 + (my)^2 = m^2 f(x,y)$

The function is homogeneous. It is homogeneous of degree 2.

The function $f(x,y) = x^2 + y^2$ is homogeneous of degree 2.

Example

The production function $Q=f(K,L)=K^{\frac{1}{3}}L^{\frac{2}{3}}$ is homogeneous of degree (   ).

Solution

$$f(mK,mL)=(mK)^{\frac{1}{3}}(mL)^{\frac{2}{3}}=mK^{\frac{1}{3}}L^{\frac{2}{3}}$$

The production function $Q=f(K,L)=K^{\frac{1}{3}}L^{\frac{2}{3}}$ is homogeneous of degree 1.

Example

A firm can manufacture a product according to the production function
$Q=f(K,L)=aK^{b}L^{c}$

The production function is homogeneous of degree 1.

$MP_L=\frac{1}{3}$ and $MP_K=\frac{1}{6}$ when the level of capital is fixed at 1 units and the firm uses 1 units of labor.

Find a, b and c.

Solution

$$MP_K=abK^{b-1}L^{c}=ab=\frac{1}{6}$$

$$MP_L=acK^{b}L^{c-1}=ac=\frac{1}{3}$$

$$\frac{b}{c}=\frac{1}{2}$$

$$f(mK,mL)=am^{b+c}K^{b}L^{c}$$

$$b+c=1$$

$$a=\frac{1}{2},b=\frac{1}{3},c=\frac{2}{3}$$

Example

어떤 기업의 생산함수는 $Q = f(K, L) = aK^bL^c$이며, 1차 동차함수이다. $L = 1$, $K = 1$에서 노동의 한계생산성은 $\frac{1}{3}$, 자본의 한계생산성은 $\frac{1}{6}$이다.

a, b, c의 값은?

Example

서울기업의 생산함수는 $Q = f(K, L) = aK^bL^c$이며, 1차 동차함수이다. $L = 1$, $K = 1$ 에서 노동의 한계생산성은 $\frac{1}{6}$, 자본의 한계생산성은 $\frac{1}{3}$이다. a,b,c의 값은?

Solution

$$ab = \frac{1}{3}$$

$$ac = \frac{1}{6}$$

$$\frac{b}{c} = 2$$

$$b + c = 1$$

$$a = \frac{1}{2},\ b = \frac{2}{3},\ c = \frac{1}{3}$$

Example

어떤 기업의 생산함수는 $Q = f(K, L) = aK^b L^c$이며, 1차 동차함수이다. $L = 1, K = 1$에서 노동의 한계생산성은 $\frac{1}{2}$, 자본의 한계생산성은 $\frac{1}{3}$이다. a,b,c의 값은?

Solution

$$ab = \frac{1}{3}$$

$$ac = \frac{1}{2}$$

$$\frac{b}{c} = \frac{2}{3}$$

$$f(mK, mL) = am^{b+c} K^b L^c$$

$$b + c = 1$$

$$a = \frac{5}{6},\ b = \frac{2}{5},\ c = \frac{3}{5}$$

Total Costs

Companies can have two types of costs, fixed costs or variable costs, which together result in their total costs.

$TC = FC + VC$

TC : Total Cost, 총비용

FC : Fixed Cost, 고정비용

생산량과 관계없이 항상 일정한 크기를 유지

VC : Variable Cost, 가변비용

생산량이 커짐에 따라 함께 커짐

Marginal Cost

The marginal cost of production measures the change in the total cost of a good that arises from producing on additional unit of that good.

Example

A firm can manufacture a product according to the cost function

$C = Q^3 - 10Q^2 + 40Q + 50$

Calculate AFC, AVC, AC and MC of producing 10 units.

Solution

$TVC = Q^3 - 10Q^2 + 40Q$

$TFC = 50$

$AFC = \frac{TFC}{Q} = 5$

$AVC = Q^2 - 10Q + 40 = 40$

$AC = \frac{TC}{Q} = 45$

$MC = 3Q^2 - 20Q + 40 = 140$

Example

강남기업의 비용함수가 $C = Q^3 - 10Q^2 + 40Q + 50$으로 주어져 있다. 생산량이 10단위일 때 평균고정비용, 평균가변비용, 평균비용, 한계비용은 각각 얼마인가?

Solution

$TVC = Q^3 - 10Q^2 + 40Q$

$TFC = 50$

$$AFC = \frac{TFC}{Q} = 5$$

$AVC = Q^2 - 10Q + 40 = 40$

$$AC = \frac{TC}{Q} = 45$$

$MC = 3Q^2 - 20Q + 40 = 140$

Example

어떤 기업의 비용함수가 $C = 35 + 6Q - 10Q^2 + 2Q^3$ 으로 주어져 있다. 생산량이 5단위일 때 평균고정비용, 평균가변비용, 평균비용, 한계비용은 각각 얼마인가?

Solution

$TVC = 2Q^3 - 10Q^2 + 6Q$

$TFC = 35$

$$AFC = \frac{TFC}{Q} = 7$$

$AVC = 2Q^2 - 10Q + 6 = 6$

$$AC = \frac{TC}{Q} = 13$$

$MC = 6Q^2 - 20Q + 6 = 56$

Example

어떤 기업의 비용함수가 $C=35+6Q-12Q^2+2Q^3$으로 주어져 있다면 평균가변비용이 최소가 되는 생산량은?

Solution

$TVC=6Q-12Q^2+2Q^3$

$AVC=6-12Q+2Q^2$

$$\frac{dAVC}{dQ}=-12+4Q=0$$

$Q=3$

Profit maximization

Profits are defined as the difference between total costs and total revenue.

TR = Price × Quantity

이윤극대화 생산량

$\pi=TR-TC$

π : 이윤
TR : 총수입
TC : 총비용

There are two approaches to explain the equilibrium or profit maximization by the firm;

(a) Total revenue and total cost approach, and

(b) MR and MC approach.

Example

Let the demand function and total costs be as follows:

$P = -Q + 30$

$TC = Q^2 + 10Q + 20$

Find Q and P that maximize profit and maximum profit.

Solution

$TR = P \times Q = -Q^2 + 30Q$

$TC = Q^2 + 10Q + 20$

$\pi = -2Q^2 + 20Q - 20$

$\frac{d\pi}{dQ} = -4Q + 20 = 0$

$Q = 5, P = 25, \pi = 30$

Example

수요함수가 $P = -Q + 30$, 총비용이 $TC = Q^2 + 10Q + 20$ 으로 주어져 있다면 이윤극대화 생산량, 가격, 그리고 이윤의 크기는?

Solution

$TR = P \times Q = -Q^2 + 30Q$

$TC = Q^2 + 10Q + 20$

$\pi = -2Q^2 + 20Q - 20$

$\frac{d\pi}{dQ} = -4Q + 20 = 0$

$Q = 5, P = 25, \pi = 30$

Example

Let the demand function and total costs be as follows:

$P = -3Q + 24$

$TC = 2Q^2 + 4Q + 1$

Find Q and P that maximize profit and maximum profit.

Solution

$$TR = P \times Q = -3Q^2 + 24Q$$

$$TC = 2Q^2 + 4Q + 1$$

$$\pi = -5Q^2 + 20Q - 1$$

$$\frac{d\pi}{dQ} = -10Q + 20 = 0$$

$$Q = 2, P = 18, \pi = 19$$

Example

수요함수가 $P = -3Q + 24$, 총비용이 $TC = 2Q^2 + 4Q + 1$으로 주어져 있다면 이윤극대화 생산량, 가격, 그리고 이윤의 크기는?

Solution

$$TR = P \times Q = -3Q^2 + 24Q$$

$$TC = 2Q^2 + 4Q + 1$$

$$\pi = -5Q^2 + 20Q - 1$$

$$\frac{d\pi}{dQ} = -10Q + 20 = 0$$

$$Q = 2, P = 18, \pi = 19$$

Example

Let the demand function and total costs be as follows:

$P = -2Q + 28$

$TC = 2Q^2 + 4Q + 1$

Find Q and P that maximize profit and maximum profit.

Solution

$TR = -2Q^2 + 28Q$

$TC = 2Q^2 + 4Q + 1$

$\pi = -4Q^2 + 24Q - 1$

$\frac{d\pi}{dQ} = -8Q + 24 = 0$

$Q = 3, P = 22$

$\pi = 35$

Example

수요함수가 $P = -2Q + 28$, 총비용이 $TC = 2Q^2 + 4Q + 1$으로 주어져 있다면 이윤극대화 생산량, 가격, 그리고 이윤의 크기는?

Solution

$TR = -2Q^2 + 28Q$

$TC = 2Q^2 + 4Q + 1$

$\pi = -4Q^2 + 24Q - 1$

$\frac{d\pi}{dQ} = -8Q + 24 = 0$

$Q = 3, P = 22$

$\pi = 35$

Example

수요함수가 $P=-Q+8$, 한계비용이 $MC=4$으로 주어져 있다면 이윤극대화 생산량은?

Solution

이윤극대화 조건은 $MR=MC$

$TR=-Q^2+8Q$

$MR=-2Q+8$

$MR=MC=-2Q+8=4$

$Q=2$

Example

Let the demand function and marginal cost be as follows:

$P=-Q+8$

$MC=4$

Find Q that maximize profit.

Solution

Marginal revenue equals marginal cost.

$MR=MC$

$TR=-Q^2+8Q$

$MR=-2Q+8$

$MR=MC=-2Q+8=4$

$Q=2$

What are the seven drivers of value?

Increase sales growth

Increase operating profit margin

Reduce cash tax rate

Reduce incremental investment in capital expenditure

Reduce investment in working capital

Increase time period of competitive advantage

Reduce cost of capital

Sales growth

Sales growth is the percent growth in the net sales of business from one fiscal period to another.

Example

The net sales for the former period were $200,000. The net sales for the latter period were $210,000. Calculate Sales growth.

Solution

5 percent

YoY

YoY typically stands for "Year over Year" and is used in business and finance to compare data from one year to the same period in the previous year. For example, a company might compare its sales figures from this year to the sales figures from the same period last year to see if there has been growth or decline.

Example

let's say a company wants to analyze its sales performance. If they made $100,000 in sales in January 2023 and $120,000 in January 2024. Calculate the YoY growth.

Solution

They would calculate the YoY growth by subtracting the sales from the previous year from the current year and then dividing by the sales from the previous year:

YoY Growth = ((Current Year Sales - Previous Year Sales) / Previous Year Sales)

YoY Growth = (($120,000 - $100,000) / $100,000)

= 20%

So, in this case, the YoY growth would be 20%, indicating that sales increased by 20% from January 2023 to January 2024.

Net sales

Net sales are total sales revenue less returns, allowances and discounts.

Net sales is the result of gross sales minus returns, allowances, and discounts.

Net sales is total revenue, less the cost of sales returns, allowances, and discounts.

Sales Returns

Customers are normally entitled to return the products they purchase from a company when they are not satisfied, usually within a specified duration after the sale. When a sales return occurs, the customer physically returns the product and receives his cash back.

Sales allowance

A sales allowance is a reduction in the selling price of goods or services offered by a company to compensate a customer for issues such as damaged goods, defects, or other problems encountered with the product or service.

Sales allowance is a reduction in the price of product charged by a seller, due to a problem with the product. The problem could be related to quality issues, delayed delivery, an incorrect price etc.

A sales allowance is recorded when a customer complains about the condition of received goods, and negotiates for a reduced price.

Sales returns are recorded when customers return defective or unwanted products for full refund. Sales allowances are recorded when customers are induced to keep defective or unwanted products for a price reduction.

Gross sales are the grand total of all sale transactions reported in a period, without any deductions included within the figure. Net sales are defined as gross sales minus the following three deductions:

Sales allowances. A reduction in the price paid by a customer, due to minor product defects. The seller grants a sales allowance after the buyer has purchased the items in question.

Sales discounts. An early payment discount, such as paying 2% less if the buyer pays within 10 days of the invoice date. The seller does not know which customers will take the discount at the time of sale, so the discount is typically applied upon the receipt of cash from customers.

Sales returns. A refund granted to customers if they return goods to the company (typically under a return merchandise authorization).

In total, these deductions are the difference between gross sales and net sales. If a company does not record sales allowances, sales discounts, or sales returns, there is no difference between gross sales and net sales.

Example

ABC company has gross sales of $1,000,000, sales returns of $10,000, sales allowances of $5,000, and discounts of $15,000. Calculate Net Sales.

Solution

1,000,000 − 10,000 − 5,000 − 15,000
= $970,000

Example

If the company refunds $35,000 and discounts $13,000 for the period and it has $210,000 in gross sales, this results in a net sales of $162,000.

Example

Let's say that a bakery sells $10,000 worth of baked goods to a customer, but upon delivery, the customer notices that some of the items are damaged. As a result, the bakery agrees to provide a sales allowance of $500 to compensate for the damaged goods.
The bakery would record a sales allowance of $500, which would be deducted from the gross sales of $10,000 to calculate the net sales of $9,500.

Example

ABC Bakery sold $10,000 worth of baked goods to a customer, but upon delivery, some items were damaged. As compensation, the bakery provided a sales allowance of $500 to the customer. Calculate the net sales for ABC Bakery after accounting for the sales allowance.

Solution

$9,500

OPM

Operating Profit Margin

$$Operating\ Profit\ Margin = \frac{Operating\ Income}{Revenue}$$

Operating Profit Margin is a profitability or performance ratio that reflects the percentage of profit a company produces from its operations before subtracting taxes and interest charges. It is calculated by dividing the operating profit by total revenue and expressing it as a percentage. The operating profit margin provides an insight into how well the target company performs in comparison to its peers, in particular, how efficiently a company manages its expenses so as to maximize profitability.

Example

K company had revenue of $2,000,000 and EBIT of $300,000. What is the operating profit margin?

Solution

15%

Cash tax

Differences between cash taxes and reported taxes typically result from timing differences between accounting and tax calculations and are reflected as a deferred tax asset or a deferred tax liability.

CapEx

CAPEX, short for Capital Expenditure, refers to the funds used by a company to acquire, upgrade, or maintain physical assets such as property, buildings, equipment, or technology. These expenditures are typically for long-term investments that will benefit the company over an extended period rather than being consumed immediately.

CAPEX is essential for businesses to maintain and expand their operations. By investing in capital assets, companies can improve efficiency, increase productivity, and stay competitive in the market.

Capital expenditures, commonly known as CapEx, are funds used by a company to acquire, upgrade, and maintain physical assets such as property, buildings, an industrial plant, technology, or equipment. CapEx is often used to undertake new projects or investments by a company. Making capital expenditures on fixed assets can include repairing a roof, purchasing a piece of equipment, or building a new factory.

CapEx spending is important for companies to maintain existing property and equipment, and invest in new technology and other assets for growth.

CAPEX is the money an organization spends to buy, maintain, or improve its fixed assets, such as buildings, vehicles, equipment, or land.

It is considered a capital expenditure when the asset is newly purchased or when money is used towards extending the useful life of an existing asset, such as repairing the roof.

Capital expenditures are the funds used to acquire or upgrade a company's fixed assets, such as expenditures towards property, plant, or equipment.

PP&E are long-term assets vital to business operations and not easily converted into cash.

Property, plant, and equipment are tangible assets, meaning they are physical in nature or can be touched.

Property, plant, and equipment are also called fixed assets, meaning they are physical assets that a company cannot easily liquidate or sell. PP&E fall under the category of noncurrent assets, which are the long-term investments or assets of a company.

Examples of PP&E include Machinery, Equipment, Vehicles, Buildings, Land, Office Equipment, Furniture, Fixtures, etc.

Example

Suppose a bakery decides to invest in a new industrial oven to increase production capacity. The cost of the new oven is $50,000. This expenditure is considered a capital expenditure because the oven is a long-term asset that will benefit the bakery for several years. After purchasing the oven, the bakery records the $50,000 as a capital expenditure on its balance sheet under the category of property, plant, and equipment.

OpEx

Operating expenses are shorter-term expenses required to meet the ongoing operational costs of running a business.
Capital expenditures contrast with opex, which are ongoing expenses that are inherent to the operation of the asset.

Competitive advantage

Competitive advantages are conditions that allow a company to produce a good of equal value at a lower price or in a more desirable fashion.

Cost of capital

The cost of capital is the cost of a company's funds (both debt and equity), or, from an investor's point of view the required rate of return on a portfolio company's existing securities. It is the minimum return that investors expect for providing capital to the company.

chapter

11

OPM

Derivative

A derivative is a financial instrument whose value depends on the values of other, more basic underlying variables.

A derivative is a financial instrument or security whose payoffs depend on a more primitive or fundamental good.

A financial derivative is a financial instrument or security whose payoffs depend on another financial instrument or security.

파생상품(derivatives)이란 다른 자산(underlying asset)의 가격에 따라 그 가격이 결정되는 증권이다. 즉, 다른 자산을 기초로 하여 생겨난 금융상품을 말한다. 파생상품은 다른 자산의 가격변동에 따라서 투자성과가 결정된다는 의미에서 조건부청구권(contingent claims)이라고도 불린다. 선물(futures)과 옵션(options)은 대표적인 파생상품이다.

Forward contracts

A forward contract is an agreement to buy or sell an asset at a certain future time for a certain price.

It can be contrasted with a spot contract, which is an agreement to buy or sell an asset today.

선도거래는 미래의 특정시점에 특정기초자산을 약정된 가격으로 거래하기로 현재시점에서 하는 계약을 말한다.

선도거래는 선도계약이라고도 불리는데, 정의를 다르게 표현하면 다음과 같다. 선도계약이란 특정한 자산을 미리 정해진 시기에 미리 정한 값으로 현재시점에 사거나 팔기로 약정한 계약을 말한다.

The buyer is said to have a long position, while the seller has a short position.

The act of buying is called going long, and the act of selling is called going short.

One of the parties to a forward contract assumes a long position and agrees to buy the underlying asset on a certain specified future date for a certain specified price.

The other party assumes a short position and agrees to sell the asset on the same date for the same price.

Payoffs from Forward Contracts

The payoff from a long position in a forward contract on one unit of an asset is $S_T - K$.

where

K : Delivery price

S_T : Price of asset at maturity.

Example

Consider a trader who enters into a long forward contract on September 2, 2022, to buy $ 1 million in three months at an exchange rate of 1,300.

The contract would obligate the trader to buy $ 1 million for 1,300 million won.

If the spot exchange rate rose to 1,350, at the end of three months, the trader would gain 50 million won.

If the spot exchange rate fell to 1,270 at the end of the 90 days, the trader would lose 30 million won.

Short position

The payoff from a short position in a forward contract on one unit of an asset is $K - S_T$.

Futures contracts

Like a forward contract, a futures contract is an agreement between two parties to buy or sell an asset at a certain time in the future for a certain price. Unlike forward contracts, futures contracts are normally traded on an exchange.

선물거래란 수량·규격·품질 등이 표준화되어 있는 상품 또는 금융자산을 현재시점에 정한 가격으로 장래의 일정시점에 인수·도할 것을 약속하는 거래로 조직화된 거래소에서 이루어지는 거래이다.

선물거래는 거래내용과 조건을 표준화하여 시장성을 높인 선도거래라고 할 수 있다.

현물거래(spot transaction)에서는 매매계약이 이루어지는 시점에서 거래대상물의 인수·도와 대금수수가 동시에 이루어지는 반면, 선물거래의 경우 인수·도와 대금수수 발생시점이 계약시점에서 이미 정해진 미래의 일정시점이다.

구분	현재시점	미래시점
현물거래	매도자 → 계약체결 → 매수자 대상물 결제 ⇄ 대금	
선물거래	매도자 ← 계약체결 → 매수자	매도자 매수자 대상물 결제 ⇄ 대금

	계약	실물인수도	대금결제
현물거래	현재	현재	현재
선물거래	현재	미래	미래

선물거래는 거래대상이 되는 기초자산에 따라 크게 상품선물(commodity futures)과 금융선물(financial futures)로 나뉜다.

선물거래의 매입(long futures)은 만기일에 기초자산을 선물가격으로 매입할 것을 계약한 것이며, 선물거래의 매도(short futures)는 만기일에 기초자산을 선물가격으로 매도할 것을 계약한 것이다.

선물거래의 결제방법은 선물만기일에 가서 현물을 인수도하는 실물인수도방식(physical delivery settlement)과 선물가격과 선물만기일의 현물가격과의 차이만큼을 정산하는 현금결제방식(cash settlement)으로 구분된다.

증거금 거래

선물거래는 현물거래와 달리 거래대금(약정금액)을 매매결제 시(현물주식의 경우 3일 결제) 납부하거나 지급받지 않고 거래소에서 정하는 증거금율 만큼의 금액만 납부하고 거래한다. 즉, 선물거래의 경우 거래개시 때 개시증거금(initial margin)을 납부하고 시세변동으로 손실발생시 유지증거금(maintenance margin)을 유지하도록 증거금 추가납부를 할 뿐이므로 실제 거래대금의 일부인 증거금으로만 거래한다.

결제소의 추가납부에 대한 요구를 margin call이라고 하며, 추가로 납부할 증거금을 변동증거금(variation margin)이라고 한다.

Initial margin

Initial Futures Margin is the amount of money that is required to open a buy or sell position on a futures contract.

Initial margin is calculated based on a percentage of the total value covered under the futures contracts. In single stock futures trading, the required initial margin is 20% of the value of the contract in the USA.

Maintenance margin

Margin Maintenance is the amount of money where a loss on your futures position requires you to allocate more funds to bring the margin back to the initial margin level.

Maintenance Margin is the minimum amount of margin balance that you need to have in your account in order to keep your futures position valid. Maintenance margin is the minimum amount of money which your broker or the exchange require you to have in your account so that losses can be deducted from it. Maintenance margin for trading Single Stock Futures in the US market is 20% of the cash value of the futures contract. Yes, it is the same level as the initial margin.

Margin Call

A margin call is a "call" from your broker requiring you to top up cash into your account when your margin balance for your futures position drops below the maintenance margin level.

Variation Margin

The additional amount of cash that is needed to bring your margin balance back up to the initial margin level from the maintenance margin level is known as the "Variation Margin". This means that you will receive a margin call to deposit variation margin into your account to bring it back up to the initial margin level when the margin balance drops below maintenance margin.

Example

Assume you go long on the futures contracts for Samsung stock trading at $100. Initial margin required?

Solution

Initial margin required $= 100 \times 0.2 = \$20$

일일정산

Marking to market

결제소(clearing house)는 매일매일 형성되는 정산가격(settlement price)을 기준으로 모든 거래참여자들의 미결제약정(open interest)에 대한 손익을 계산하여 반영하며, 이를 일일정산이라 한다.

Example

Assume you go long on the futures contracts for Samsung stock trading at $100.

Initial margin required?

Assuming at the end of the first trading day, Samsung stock drops to $99.

Total Loss?

Margin balance?

Variation Margin?

Solution

Assume you go long on the futures contracts for Samsung stock trading at $100.

Initial margin required $= 100 \times 0.2 = \$20$

Assuming at the end of the second trading day, Samsung stock drops to $99.

Total Loss = 1

Margin balance = 19

Variation Margin $= 20 - 19 = 1$

Example

Let's assume we have a speculator who has $10000 in his trading account. He decides to buy August Crude Oil at $40 per barrel. Each Crude Oil futures contract represents 1000 barrels and requires an initial margin of $9000 and has a maintenance margin level set at $6500.

Since his account is $10000, which is more than the initial margin requirement, he can therefore open up one August Crude Oil futures position.

One day later, the price of August Crude Oil drops to $38 a barrel. Our speculator has suffered an open position loss of $2000 and thus his account balance drops to $8000. Although his balance is now lower than the initial margin requirement, he did not get the margin call as it is still above the maintenance level of $6500.

Unfortunately, on the very next day, the price of August Crude Oil crashed further to $35, leading to an additional $3000 loss on his open Crude Oil position.

With only ( ) left in his trading account, which is below the maintenance level of $6500, he received a call from his broker asking him to top up his trading account back to the initial level of $9000 in order to maintain his open Crude Oil position.

Solution

$5,000

Comparison of Forward and Futures Contracts

Forwards	Futures
Private contract between two parties	Traded on an exchange
Not standardized	Standardized contract
Usually one specified delivery date	Range of delivery dates
Settled at end of contract	Settled daily
Delivery or final cash settlement usually takes place	Contract usually closed out prior to maturity

구분	선도거래	선물거래
거래장소	장외	거래소
계약의 표준화	계약상대방간의 합의에 의해 결정	상품의 규격, 품질, 수량 및 결제일 등
결제이행 보증장치	계약상대방의 신용에 의존	증거금, 일일정산, 결제기관 등의 장치가 있음
매매계약 체결방법	개인간 상대매매	완전경쟁매매
결제일전 계약해소	대부분 결제일에 계약이행	반대매매에 의해 언제든지 가능
거래상대방	계약조건이 합치하는 특정인 (거래성립이 어려움)	불특성다수 (거래용이)

Example

다음 내용이 맞으면 T, 틀리면 F를 하시오.

1) 선도계약은 계약당사자가 계약불이행에 관한 위험을 직접 부담한다.

2) 증거금제도와 일일정산제도를 통하여 선물거래의 신용위험은 선도계약보다 크다.

3) 선도거래에는 청산소가 존재하여 거래이행을 보증한다.

4) 선물거래를 위해 거래소는 일정한 증거금(margin)을 요구한다.

Solution

1) T, 2) F, 3)F, 4)T

선물거래의 이익

만기일에서의 선물 매입포지션의 이익

$Profit = S_T - F_0$

At maturity :

Profit to long = Spot price at maturity − Original futures price

Profit to short = Original futures price − Spot price at maturity

만기 이전에서의 선물 매입포지션의 이익

$Profit = F_t - F_0$

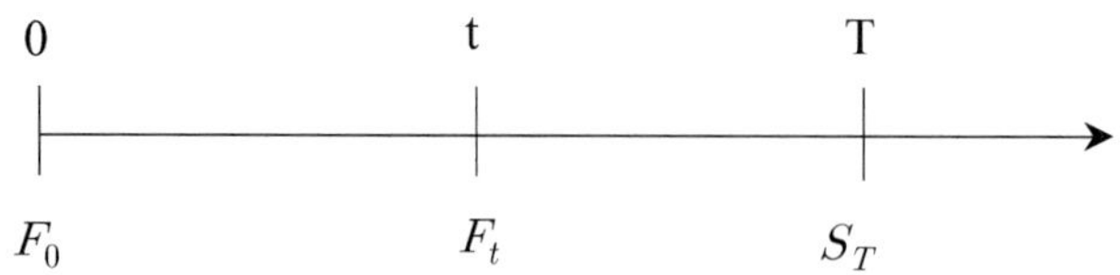

The Spot-Futures Parity Theorem

	Initial Cash Flow	Cash Flow in One Year
Borrow S_0 dollars	S_0	$-S_0(1+r)$
Buy stock for S_0	$-S_0$	S_T+D
Enter short futures position	0	F_0-S_T
	0	$F_0-S_0(1+r)+D$

$F_0=S_0(1+r)-D$

where D is the dividend payout.

A trader would borrow the money to buy the stock, buy the stock and concurrently short the futures.

Example

Construct a table to derive the spot-futures parity theorem.

Solution

The Spot-Futures Parity Theorem

	Initial Cash Flow	Cash Flow in One Year
Borrow S_0 dollars	S_0	$-S_0(1+r)$
Buy stock for S_0	$-S_0$	S_T+D
Enter short futures position	0	F_0-S_T
	0	$F_0-S_0(1+r)+D$

Example

A stock price has a current share price of 18,000 won and a dividend yield of 1 percent. The risk-free rate is 5 percent.

What is the futures price?

Solution

$F_0=S_0(1+r)-D=S_0(1+r-d)=18{,}000(1+0.05\quad 0.01)-18{,}720$

where d is the dividend yield.

Example

서울기업의 현재 주가가 18,000원이고, 연간 배당수익률이 1%로 예정되어 있으며, 무위험이자율은 5%이다. 현물-선물 패리티를 이용하여 이론선물가격을 계산하라.

Solution

$F_0 = S_0(1+r) - D = S_0(1+r-d) = 18{,}000(1+0.05-0.01) = 18{,}720$

where d is the dividend yield.

Options

An option is a contract giving its owner the right to buy or sell an asset at a fixed price on or before a given date.

옵션이란 특정한 자산을 미리 정해진 기한내에 미리 정한 가격에 사거나 팔 수 있는 권리를 말한다. 특정한 자산을 기초자산이라고 하며, 정해진 기한을 만기, 미리 정한 가격을 행사가격이라고 한다.

옵션은 정해진 시점에서 대상자산을 살 것인지 아니면 팔 것인지를 결정할 수 있는 선택권이다.

옵션가격은 프리미엄(premium)이라고 불린다. 옵션 매입자는 옵션의 권리 행사를 결정할 수 있는 권한을 대가로 옵션 매도자에게 프리미엄을 지급한다.

The buyer of an option contract pays an option premium in exchange for a right to buy or sell an underlying asset during a specified period of time.

Example

An option on a building might give the buyer the right to buy the building for 1 billion won on or anytime before the Saturday prior to the third Wednesday in January 2025.

Call option & Put option

A call option gives the holder the right to buy the underlying asset by a certain date for a certain price.

A put option gives the holder the right to sell the underlying asset by a certain date for a certain price.

The price in the contract is known as the exercise price or strike price.

The date in the contract is known as the expiration date or maturity.

American options can be exercised at any time up to the expiration date.

European options can be exercised only on the expiration date.

Bermuda option

옵션기간 중에 미리 정해둔 시점에 한해서 만기 이전에라도 권리를 행사할 수 있는 옵션이다.

Example

Consider the situation of a trader who buys one European call option contract on K stock with a strike price of 50,000 won.

Suppose that the current stock price is 48,000 won, the expiration date of the option is in two months, and the option price is 2,000 won.

If the stock price on the expiration date is less than 50,000 won, the trader will choose not to exercise. In these circumstances the trader loses the entire initial investment of 2,000 won.

If the stock price is above 50,000 won on the expiration date, the options will be exercised. Suppose that the stock price is 53,000 won. The trader makes a gain of 3,000 won per share. When the initial cost of the options is taken into account, the net profit to the trader is 1,000 won per option.

Example

You sell a two-month European call option on the stock with a strike price of W50,000 and an option price of W3,000. What will be your profit on this investment if the stock price at maturity is less than W50,000?

Solution

The call option provides no payoff.

Profit $= 3,000$

Example

You sell a two-month European call option on the stock with a strike price of W50,000 and an option price of W3,000. What will be your profit on this investment if the stock price at maturity is greater than W50,000?

Solution

Profit $= 50,000 - S_T + 3,000$

Profit $= 53,000 - S_T$

Example

Suppose that a European call option to buy a share for 50,000 won costs 3,000 won and is held until maturity. Draw a diagram illustrating how the profit from a long position in the option depends on the stock price at maturity of the option.

Solution

Stock Price	Payoff from Option	Profit from Option
47,000	0	−3,000
48,000	0	−3,000
49,000	0	−3,000
50,000	0	−3,000
51,000	1,000	−2,000
52,000	2,000	−1,000
53,000	3,000	0
54,000	4,000	1,000
55,000	5,000	2,000

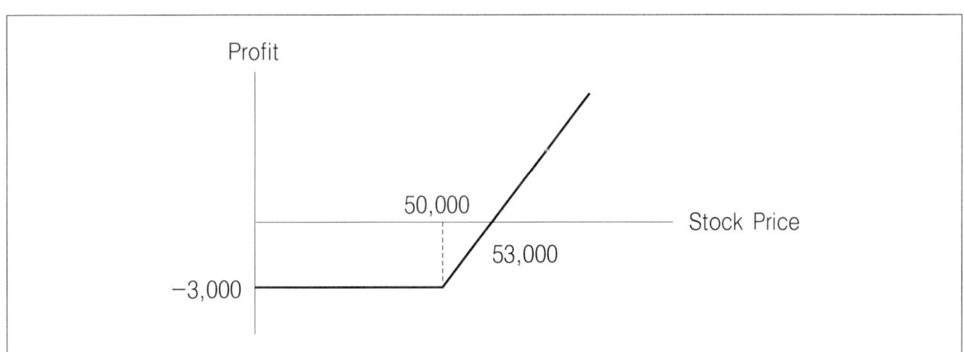

Example

A trader buys a European put option for 3,000 won. The strike price is 50,000 won. Draw a diagram showing the variation of the trader's profit with the stock price at maturity of the option.

Solution

Stock Price	Payoff from Option	Profit from Option
45,000	5,000	2,000
46,000	4,000	1,000
47,000	3,000	0
48,000	2,000	−1,000
49,000	1,000	−2,000
50,000	0	−3,000
51,000	0	−3,000
52,000	0	−3,000
53,000	0	−3,000
54,000	0	−3,000
55,000	0	−3,000

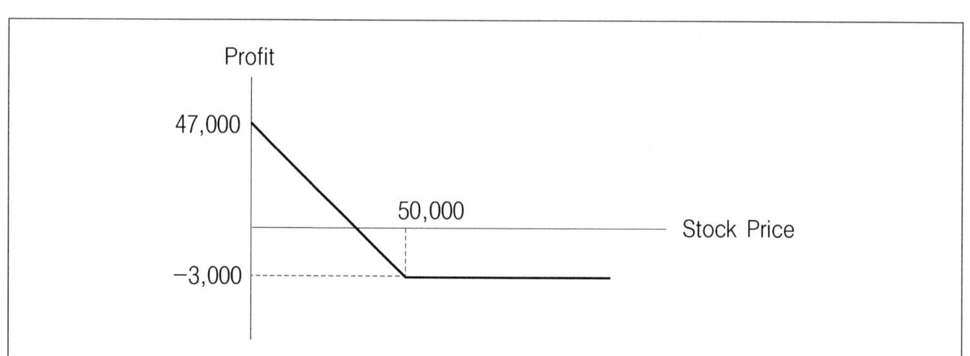

Swaps

A swap is an agreement between two companies to exchange cash flows in the future. The agreement defines the dates when the cash flows are to be paid and the way that they are to be calculated.
스왑이란 자신이 소유한 것을 서로 교환하는 거래를 말한다.

Whereas a forward contract leads to the exchange of cash flows on just one future date, swaps lead to cash flow exchanges on several future dates.

LIBOR

LIBOR is short for the London Interbank Offer Rate. It is the rate at which one large international bank is willing to lend money to another large international bank.
LIBOR is the world's most widely-used benchmark for short-term interest rates.
LIBOR는 런던은행간 대출금리를 의미한다.
The reference rate most commonly used globally is LIBOR.

Example

Consider a three-year swap initiated on March 1, 2015, in which company B agrees to pay to company A an interest rate of 5% per annum on a notional principal of $100 million and in return company A agrees to pay to company B the six-month LIBOR rate on the same notional principal. Find the net cash flows of Company B.

Date	LIBOR Rate(%)
March 1, 2015	4.2
September 1, 2015	4.8
March 1, 2016	5.3
September 1, 2016	5.5
March 1, 2017	5.6
September 1, 2017	5.9
March 1, 2018	6.4

Solution

On September 1, 2015, company A pays company B $2.1 million.

$$\frac{0.042}{2} \times 100 = 2.1$$

On March 1, 2016, company A pays company B $2.4 million.

$$\frac{0.048}{2} \times 100 = 2.4$$

Date	LIBOR Rate(%)	Floating Cash Flow Received	Fixed Cash Flow Paid	Net Cash Flow
March 1, 2015	4.2			
September 1, 2015	4.8	2.1	−2.5	−0.4
March 1, 2016	5.3	2.4	−2.5	−0.1
September 1, 2016	5.5	2.65	−2.5	0.15
March 1, 2017	5.6	2.75	−2.5	0.25
September 1, 2017	5.9	2.8	−2.5	0.3
March 1, 2018	6.4	2.95	−2.5	0.45

There are six exchanges of payment on the swap. The fixed payments are always $2.5 million.

Example

Consider a three-year swap initiated on March 1, 2018, in which company B agrees to pay to company A an interest rate of 4% per annum on a notional principal of $100 million and in return company A agrees to pay to company B the six-month LIBOR rate on the same notional principal. Find the net cash flows of Company B.

Date	LIBOR Rate(%)
March 1, 2018	5.2
September 1, 2018	4.8
March 1, 2019	5.3
September 1, 2019	4.5
March 1, 2020	5.6
September 1, 2020	3.9
March 1, 2021	6.4

Solution

On September 1, 2018, company A pays company B $2.6 million.

$$\frac{0.052}{2}\times 100 = 2.6$$

On March 1, 2019, company A pays company B $2.4 million.

$$\frac{0.048}{2}\times 100 = 2.4$$

Date	LIBOR Rate(%)	Floating Cash Flow Received	Fixed Cash Flow Paid	Net Cash Flow
March 1, 2018	5.2			
September 1, 2018	4.8	2.6	−2	0.6
March 1, 2019	5.3	2.4	−2	0.4
September 1, 2019	4.5	2.65	−2	0.65
March 1, 2020	5.6	2.25	−2	0.25
September 1, 2020	3.9	2.3	−2	0.3
March 1, 2021	6.4	1.95	−2	−0.05

There are six exchanges of payment on the swap. The fixed payments are always $2 million.

Example

Companies X and Y have been offered the following rates per annum on a $20 million five-year loan:

	Fixed rate	Floating rate
Company X	4%	LIBOR+0.5%
Company Y	7%	LIBOR+1%

Solution

기업X는 고정금리에서 기업Y에 비하여 3% 낮은 금리로 차입을 할 수 있고, 변동금리로는 0.5% 낮은 금리로 차입을 할 수 있다. 그러므로 기업X 입장에서는 고정금리와 변동금리 중에서 고정금리에 비교우위를 가진다.

기업Y 입장에서는 고정금리에서 기업X에 비하여 3% 높은 금리로 차입을 해야 하는 반면, 변동금리로는 0.5% 높은 금리로 차입을 할 수 있다. 그러므로 기업Y는 고정금리와 변동금리 중에서 변동금리에 비교우위를 가진다.

Company X appears to have a comparative advantage in fixed rate markets, whereas company Y appears to have a comparative advantage in floating rate markets.

They enter into a swap agreement.

만약 기업Y가 기업X에 지불하는 금리가 5%라면, X와 Y의 스왑으로 인한 이득은 다음과 같다.

Company X has three sets of interest rate cash flows:

1. It pays 4% to outside lenders.
2. It pays LIBOR to Y.
3. It receives 5% from Y.

The net effect of the three cash flows is that X pays $(LIBOR-1\%)$.

This is 1.5% less than it would pay if it went directly to floating rate markets.

Company Y has three sets of interest rate cash flows:

1. It pays LIBOR+1% to outside lenders.
2. It pays 5% to X.
3. It receives LIBOR from X.

The net effect of the three cash flows is that Y pays 6%.

This is 1% less than it would pay if it went directly to fixed rate markets.

The swap appears to improve the position of both X and Y.

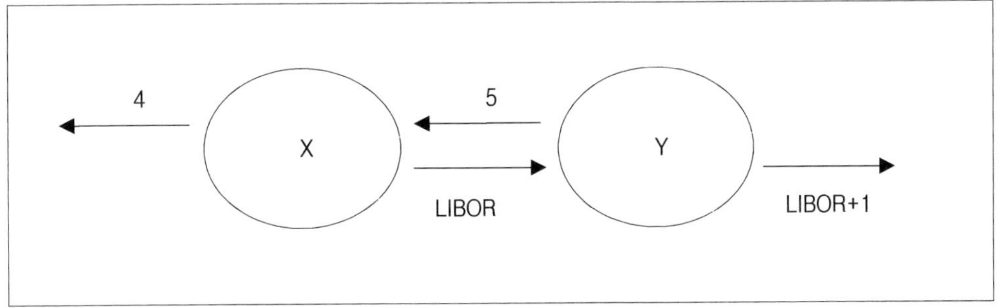

Example

Companies X and Y have been offered the following rates per annum on a $20 million five-year loan:

	Fixed rate	Floating rate
Company X	4%	LIBOR+0.5%
Company Y	7%	LIBOR+1%

Find the range of interest rate that company Y pays to company X and that will appear attractive to both companies.

Solution

Company X appears to have a comparative advantage in fixed rate markets, whereas company Y appears to have a comparative advantage in floating rate markets.

They enter into a swap agreement.

Company X has three sets of interest rate cash flows:

1. It pays 4% to outside lenders.
2. It pays LIBOR to Y.
3. It receives R% from Y.

Company Y has three sets of interest rate cash flows:

1. It pays LIBOR+1% to outside lenders.
2. It pays R% to X.
3. It receives LIBOR from X.

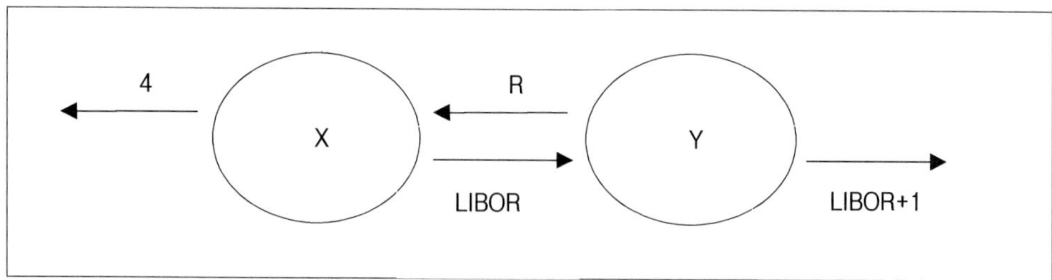

$$LIBOR + 4 - R < LIBOR + 0.5$$

$$(LIBOR + 1) + R - LIBOR < 7$$

$$3.5 < R < 6$$

Example

Companies X and Y have been offered the following rates per annum on a $20 million five-year loan:

	Fixed rate	Floating rate
Company X	4%	SOFR+0.5%
Company Y	7%	SOFR+1%

Design a swap that will appear equally attractive to both companies.

Solution

$(SOFR+0.5)-(SOFR+4-R)=7-\{(SOFR+1)+R-SOFR\}$

R=4.75%

Company X has three sets of interest rate cash flows:

1. It pays 4% to outside lenders.
2. It pays SOFR to Y.
3. It receives 4.75% from Y.

The net effect of the three cash flows is that X pays $(SOFR-0.75\%)$.

This is 1.25% less than it would pay if it went directly to floating rate markets.

Company Y has three sets of interest rate cash flows:

1. It pays SOFR+1% to outside lenders.
2. It pays 4.75% to X.
3. It receives SOFR from X.

The net effect of the three cash flows is that Y pays 5.75%.

This is 1.25% less than it would pay if it went directly to fixed rate markets.

Example

Companies X and Y have been offered the following rates per annum on a $20 million five-year loan:

	Fixed rate	Floating rate
Company X	8%	LIBOR+2%
Company Y	5%	LIBOR+1%

Design a swap that will appear equally attractive to both companies.

Solution

$$(LIBOR+1)-(LIBOR+5-R)=8-\{(LIBOR+2)+R-LIBOR\}$$

$$R=5$$

Example

X기업과 Y기업 각각의 고정금리와 변동금리에 대한 차입이자율이 다음과 같다.

	고정금리차입	변동금리차입
X기업	8.25%	LIBOR+0.25%
Y기업	9.00%	LIBOR+0.50%

스왑이 계약되기 위한 약정조건에 대해 설명하시오.

Solution

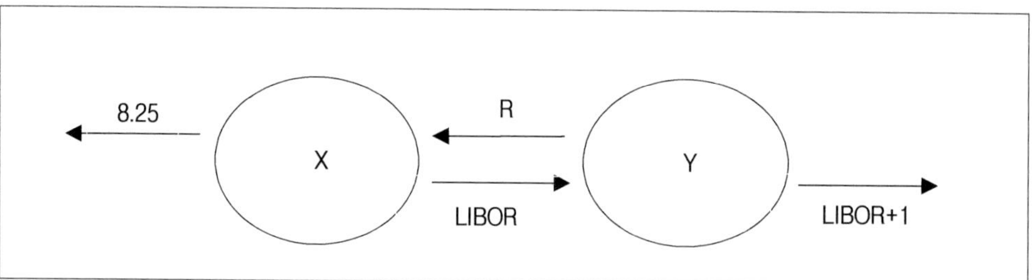

X기업이 계약하기 위한 조건은 다음과 같다.

$$LIBOR+8.25-R<LIBOR+0.25$$

Y기업이 계약하기 위한 조건은 다음과 같다.

$$LIBOR+0.5+R-LIBOR<9$$

$$8 < R < 8.5$$

Example

X기업과 Y기업 각각의 고정금리와 변동금리에 대한 차입이자율이 다음과 같다.

	고정금리차입	변동금리차입
X기업	8.25%	LIBOR+0.25%
Y기업	9.00%	LIBOR+0.50%

스왑으로 인해 X기업과 Y기업에 동등하게 이득을 가져오는 약정조건에 대해 설명하시오.

Solution

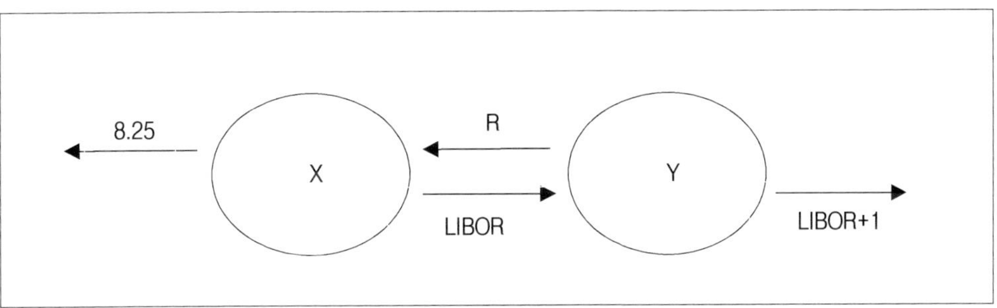

X기업과 Y기업에 동등하게 이득을 가져오는 약정조건은 다음과 같다.

$$LIBOR + 8.25 - R - (LIBOR + 0.25) = LIBOR + 0.5 + R - LIBOR - 9$$

$$R = 8.25\%$$

Example

Companies X and Y have been offered the following rates per annum on a $20 million five-year loan:

	Fixed rate	Floating rate
Company X	5%	SOFR+2%
Company Y	10%	SOFR+4%

Design a swap that will appear equally attractive to both companies.

Solution

$$(SOFR+2)-(SOFR+5-R)=10-\{(SOFR+4)+R-SOFR\}$$

$$R-3=6-R$$

$$R=4.5\%$$

Example

Company X can borrow at a fixed rate of 5% or at a floating rate of SOFR+2%. Company Y can borrow at a fixed rate of 10% or at a floating rate of SOFR+4%. Design a swap that will appear equally attractive to both companies.

Solution

	Fixed rate	Floating rate
Company X	5%	SOFR+2%
Company Y	10%	SOFR+4%

$$(SOFR+2)-(SOFR+5-R)=10-\{(SOFR+4)+R-SOFR\}$$

$$R-3=6-R$$

$$R=4.5\%$$

Example

Company X can borrow money at a fixed rate of 5 percent or a variable rate at SOFR plus 2 percent. Company Y can borrow money at a variable rate of SOFR plus 4 percent or a fixed rate of 10 percent.

Design a swap that will appear equally attractive to both companies.

Solution

	Fixed rate	Floating rate
Company X	5%	SOFR+2%
Company Y	10%	SOFR+4%

$(SOFR+2)-(SOFR+5-R)=10-\{(SOFR+4)+R-SOFR\}$

$R-3=6-R$

$R=4.5\%$

Example

Companies X and Y have been offered the following rates per annum on a $20 million five-year loan:

	Fixed rate	Floating rate
Company X	4%	SOFR+0.5%
Company Y	7%	SOFR+1%

Design a swap that will net a bank 0.02% per annum and that will appear equally attractive to both companies.

Solution

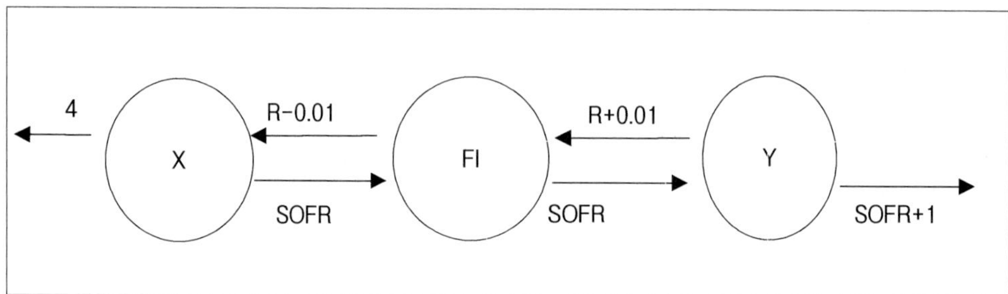

$$(SOFR+0.5)-\{SOFR+4-(R-0.01)\}=7-\{(SOFR+1)+(R+0.01)-SOFR\}$$
$$R=4.75\%$$

Company X has three sets of interest rate cash flows:

1. It pays 4% to outside lenders.
2. It pays SOFR to FI.
3. It receives 4.74% from FI.

The net effect of the three cash flows is that X pays $(SOFR-0.74\%)$.
This is 1.24% less than it would pay if it went directly to floating rate markets.

Company Y has three sets of interest rate cash flows:

1. It pays SOFR+1% to outside lenders.
2. It pays 4.76% to FI.
3. It receives SOFR from FI.

The net effect of the three cash flows is that Y pays 5.76%.
This is 1.24% less than it would pay if it went directly to fixed rate markets.

Example

Companies X and Y have been offered the following rates per annum on a $20 million five-year loan:

	Fixed rate	Floating rate
Company X	5%	LIBOR+2%
Company Y	10%	LIBOR+4%

Find the range of interest rate that company Y pays to company X and that will appear attractive to both companies.

Solution

$(LIBOR+2)>(LIBOR+5-R)$

$10>\{(LIBOR+4)+R-LIBOR\}$

$3\%<R<6\%$

Example

Companies X and Y have been offered the following rates per annum on a $20 million five-year loan:

	Fixed rate	Floating rate
Company X	5%	LIBOR+2%
Company Y	10%	LIBOR+4%

Design a swap that will net a bank 0.4% per annum and that will appear equally attractive to both companies.

Solution

$(LIBOR+2)-\{LIBOR+5-(R-0.2)\}=10-\{(LIBOR+4)+(R+0.2)-LIBOR\}$

$R-3=6-R$

$R=4.5\%$

Interest rate swap

금리스왑이란 두 당사자가 동일한 통화로 표시된 차입금을 부담하고 있을 때, 이에 대한 이자지급의무를 교환하여 미래 일정기간 동안 서로 상대방의 이자를 바꾸어 부담하는 것을 말한다.

금리스왑 중 가장 기본적인 형태는 고정금리와 변동금리간의 스왑(fixed-floating rate swap)이다. 이는 표준형 금리스왑(plain vanilla interest swap) 또는 쿠폰스왑(coupon swap)이라고도 부른다.

Comparative advantage

비교우위

한 경제주체가 수행하는 어떤 활동의 기회비용이 다른 주체들보다 쌀 때 그 주체는 그 활동에 비교우위가 있다고 말한다.

The term 'Comparative Advantage' refers to the ability of an individual, a company or a country to produce a particular product or to provide a particular service at a lower opportunity cost.

Absolute advantage

절대우위

한 경제주체가 어떤 활동을 다른 주체들보다 더 잘 할 때 그 주체는 그 활동에 절대우위가 있다고 말한다.

Principle of absolute advantage refers to the ability of a party to produce more of a good or service than competitors, using the same amount of resources.

Opportunity cost

기회비용

Opportunity cost is the return that a firm's resources could have earned elsewhere in its next most valuable use.

Opportunity cost for a firm is the value of the resources it owns in their next highest valued productive use.

Opportunity cost is the highest-valued foregone alternative when any choice is made.

어떤 행위의 기회비용은 이를 선택함으로 인해 포기해야 하는 여러 행위 중 가장 큰 가치를 갖는 행위의 가치로 측정할 수 있다.

실제로 지출하지 않았다 해도 비용의 성격을 갖고 있으면 모두 포함시키는 포괄적 비용의 개념

Explicit costs

명시적 비용

현금지출을 필요로 하는 요소비용

Explicit costs are observable, measurable expenses such as the dollar cost of production inputs and the interest cost of renting capital.

Implicit costs

암묵적 비용

현금지출을 필요로 하지 않는 요소비용

Implicit costs are not explicitly observable and fall into two categories:

(1) the opportunity cost to a firm of using its own capital and

(2) the opportunity cost of the time and financial resources of the firm's owners.

The implicit rental rate is the term used to describe the opportunity cost to a firm for using its own capital. It represents what the firm could have earned if it had rented its capital to another firm. The implicit rental rate is the sum of

(1) economic depreciation, which is the decrease in the value of a firm's assets over time, and

(2) foregone interest.

Normal profit is the opportunity cost of owners' entrepreneurship expertise. It represents what owners could have earned if they used their organizational, decision making, and other entrepreneurial skills in another activity, such as running another business.

Explicit costs are measurable expenses. Implicit costs include the implicit rental rate (the opportunity cost to a firm from the use of its own capital assets) and normal profit (the opportunity cost associated with the use of the owners' time, resources, and entrepreneurship expertise).

Economic profit is total revenue minus both explicit and implicit costs.

Hedging using Futures

Basis

Basis = spot price of asset to be hedged − futures price of contract used

S_1 : spot price at time t_1

S_2 : spot price at time t_2

F_1 : futures price at time t_1

F_2 : futures price at time t_2

b_1 : basis at time t_1

b_2 : basis at time t_2

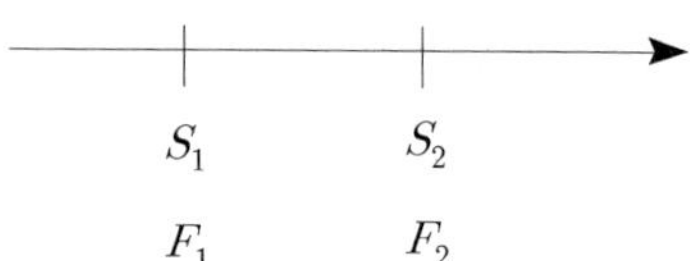

From the definition of the basis,

$b_1 = S_1 - F_1$

$b_2 = S_2 - F_2$

상품선물에서 베이시스는 현물가격과 선물가격의 차이를 일컫는다.

Long hedge

Rational number

A rational number is a number that can be expressed as the quotient or fraction p/q of two integers, a numerator p and a non-zero denominator q.

Irrational number

Irrational numbers cannot be expressed as the ratio of two integers.

An Irrational Number is a real number that cannot be written as a simple fraction.

Irrational number, any real number that cannot be expressed as the quotient of two integers. For example, there is no number among integers and fractions that equals the square root of 2.

Archimedes' constant π

π is commonly defined as the ratio of a circle's circumference C to its diameter d:

$$\pi = \frac{C}{d}$$

The number π is a mathematical constant. It is defined as the ratio of a circle's circumference to its diameter.

e is an irrational number (it cannot be written as a simple fraction).

Euler's number e

Euler's number e, also known as the exponential growth constant, appears in many areas of mathematics, and one possible definition of it is the value of the following expression:

$$e = \lim_{m \to \infty} \left(1 + \frac{1}{m}\right)^m$$

The number e, known as Euler's number, is a mathematical constant approximately equal to 2.71828. It is the base of the natural logarithm. It is the limit of $\left(1+\frac{1}{x}\right)^x$ as x approaches infinity.

Exponential growth

The formula for exponential growth of a variable x at the growth rate r, as time t goes on in discrete intervals (that is, at integer times 0, 1, 2, 3, ...), is

$$x_t = x_0(1+r)^t$$

Compound interest at a constant interest rate provides exponential growth of the capital.

Continuous Compounding

연속복리계산

Consider an amount A invested for n years at an interest rate of R per annum.

If the rate is compounded once per annum, the terminal value of the investment is

$$A(1+R)^n$$

If it is compounded m times per annum, the terminal value of the investment is

$$A\left(1+\frac{R}{m}\right)^{mn}$$

Semiannual compounding refers to the frequency at which interest is calculated and added to the principal balance in a financial instrument, typically a loan or an investment. In semiannual compounding, interest is compounded twice a year, meaning that interest is added to the principal balance every six months.

For example, if you have a loan or an investment with a semiannual compounding frequency and an annual interest rate of 6%, the interest would be calculated and added to the principal balance twice a year, at a rate of 3% each time.

For example, if you have an investment with a 5% annual interest rate compounded semiannually, the interest would be calculated and added to the principal twice a year, at a rate of 2.5% each time.

Quarterly compounding refers to the practice of calculating and adding interest to the principal balance four times a year, at intervals of three months. This compounding frequency is commonly used in various financial instruments such as loans, mortgages, and savings accounts.

For instance, if you have an investment or a loan with a quarterly compounding frequency and an annual interest rate of 8%, the interest would be calculated and added to the principal balance every three months, at a rate of 2% each time.

Example

Suppose that we earn 10% interest per annum.

Solution

Semiannually $(m = 2)$

When we compound twice a year, we earn 5% interest per six months, with the interest being reinvested, and the $100 grows to

$$100\left(1+\frac{0.1}{2}\right)^2 = 110.25$$

Quarterly $(m = 4)$

$$100\left(1+\frac{0.1}{4}\right)^4 = 110.38$$

The interest is compounded quarterly (i.e., 3 months or, 4 times in a year).
Compounding quarterly can be considered as the interest amount which is earned quarterly on an account or an investment where the interest earned will also be reinvested.

Monthly $(m = 12)$

$$100\left(1+\frac{0.1}{12}\right)^{12} = 110.47$$

$100 grows to $110 after one year with a 10% interest rate.
With semiannual compounding, $100 grows to $110.25 after one year with a 10% interest rate.
With quarterly compounding, $100 grows to $110.38 after one year with a 10% interest rate.

자연로그의 밑수 e는 다음과 같이 정의된다.

$$e \equiv \lim_{m\to\infty}\left(1+\frac{1}{m}\right)^{m}$$

e is the mathematical constant for the base of the natural logarithm.

It is the limit of $\left(1+\frac{1}{n}\right)^{n}$ as n approaches infinity.

The number e is an important mathematical constant that is the base of the natural logarithm.

$$\lim_{m\to\infty} A\left(1+\frac{R}{m}\right)^{m} = \lim_{m\to\infty} A\left(1+\frac{R}{m}\right)^{\frac{m}{R}R} = \lim_{k\to\infty} A\left(1+\frac{1}{k}\right)^{kR} = Ae^{R}$$

The limit as m tends to infinity is known as continuous compounding.

$$\lim_{m\to\infty} A\left(1+\frac{R}{m}\right)^{mn} = \lim_{m\to\infty} A\left(1+\frac{R}{m}\right)^{\frac{m}{R}Rn} = \lim_{k\to\infty} A\left(1+\frac{1}{k}\right)^{kRn} = Ae^{Rn}$$

With continuous compounding, it can be shown that an amount A invested for n years at rate R grows to

$$Ae^{Rn}$$

where e is the mathematical constant, 2.71828.

This is the same as the value using daily compounding.

For most practical purposes, continuous compounding can be thought of as being equivalent to daily compounding.

Compounding a sum of money at a continuously compounded rate R for n years involves multiplying it by e^{Rn}.

Discounting it at a continuously compounded rate R for n years involves multiplying by e^{-Rn}.

$$100\left(1+\frac{0.1}{365}\right)^{365} = 110.516$$

$$100e^{0.1} = 110.517$$

$$y=\left(1+\frac{1}{x}\right)^{x}$$

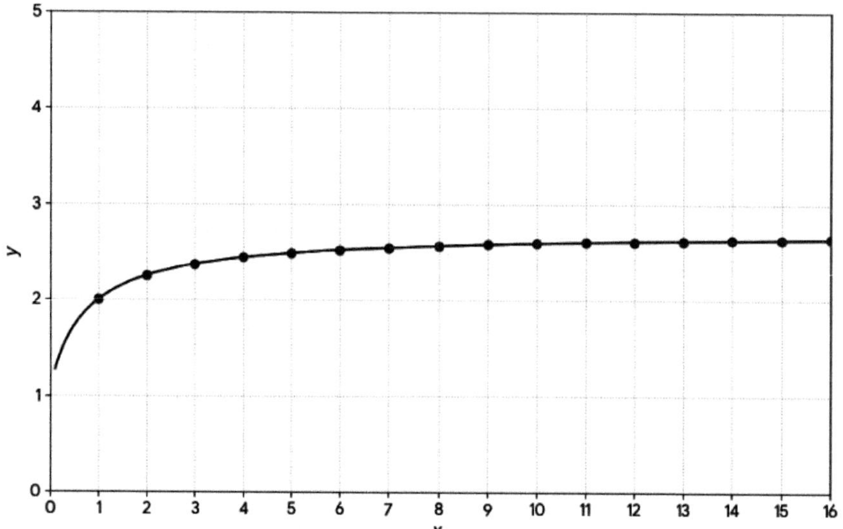

X	$\left(1+\frac{1}{x}\right)^{x}$
2	2.250
10	2.594
100	2.705
200	2.712
300	2.714
365	2.715

Example

Suppose you deposit 100 won in an account. If the account earns 10%, how much will be in the account after one year?

Solution

$100(1+0.1)=110$ won.

Example

Suppose you deposit \$100 in an account. If the account earns 10% with semiannual compounding, how much will be in the account after one year?

Solution

When we compound twice a year, we earn 5% interest per six months, with the interest being reinvested, and the \$100 grows to

$$100\left(1+\frac{0.1}{2}\right)^2=110.25$$

Example

Consider an amount of \$100 invested for one year at an interest rate of 10% per annum. It is compounded 2 times per annum. Calculate the terminal value of the investment.

Solution

$$100\left(1+\frac{0.1}{2}\right)^2=110.25$$

Example

Write T for True and F for False for the following statements. If the statement is false, correct the statement.

Let's say you invest \$100 at an annual interest rate of 10% compounded quarterly for 1 year.

After 1 year, the investment will grow to $100\left(1+\dfrac{0.1}{4}\right)$ with quarterly compounding.

Solution

F,

After 1 year, the investment will grow to $100\left(1+\dfrac{0.1}{4}\right)^4$ with quarterly compounding.

Example

You invest \$100 in a savings account that offers an annual interest rate of 10%, compounded quarterly. How much money will be in the account after 1 year?

Example

Suppose you deposit 100 won in an account. If the account earns 10% with daily compounding, how much will be in the account after one year?

Solution

$$100\left(1+\frac{0.1}{365}\right)^{365} = 110.516$$

Example

Suppose you deposit 100 won in an account. If the account earns 10% with continuous compounding, how much will be in the account after one year?

Solution

$100e^{0.1}$

Example

Consider an amount of 50 won invested for 3 years at an interest rate of 8% per annum. It is compounded 2 times per annum. Calculate the terminal value of the investment.

Solution

$50 \times 1.04^6 = 63.3$

Example

Suppose you deposit 50,000 won in an account. If the account earns 8% with semiannual compounding, how much will be in the account after one year?

Solution

$50{,}000 \times 1.04^2 = 54{,}080$

Example

Suppose you deposit 50,000 won in an account. If the account earns 8% with quarterly compounding, how much will be in the account after one year?

Solution

$50{,}000 \times 1.02^4 = 54{,}122$

Example

Suppose you deposit 50,000 won in an account. If the account earns 8% with continuous compounding, how much will be in the account after one year?

Solution

$50,000e^{0.08}$

Example

Suppose that a lender quotes the interest rate on loans as 8% per annum with daily compounding. How much interest will be paid each day on $3,000,000 loan?

Solution

$3,000,000 \times \frac{0.08}{365} = 658$

Example

은행에서 $3,000,000을 연이율 8%로 매일 이자지급 조건으로 대출받은 경우, 매일마다 지불해야 하는 이자는 얼마인가?

Solution

$3,000,000 \times \frac{0.08}{365} = 658$

Example

Suppose that a lender quotes the interest rate on loans as 8.08% per annum with quarterly compounding.

How much interest will be paid each quarter on $3,000,000 loan?

Solution

$3,000,000 \times \frac{0.0808}{4} = 60,600$

Example

은행에서 3,000,000원을 연이율 8.08%로 3개월마다 이자지급 조건으로 대출받은 경우, 3개월마다 지불해야 하는 이자는 얼마인가?

Solution

$$3,000,000 \times \frac{0.0808}{4} = 60,600\text{원}$$

Example

은행에서 500,000원을 연이율 12%로 매일 이자지급 조건으로 대출받은 경우, 매일마다 지불해야 하는 이자는 얼마인가?

Solution

$$500,000 \times \frac{0.12}{365} = 164\text{원}$$

Example

Suppose that a lender quotes the interest rate on loans as 8% per annum with quarterly compounding.

How much interest will be paid each quarter on $500,000 loan?

Solution

$$500,000 \times \frac{0.08}{4} = 10,000$$

Example

은행에서 500,000원을 연이율 8%로 3개월마다 이자지급 조건으로 대출받은 경우, 3개월마다 지불해야 하는 이자는 얼마인가?

Solution

$$500,000 \times \frac{0.08}{4} = 10,000$$

Example

What rate of interest with annual compounding is equivalent to 5% per annum with quarterly compounding?

Solution

$$\left(1+\frac{0.05}{4}\right)^4=(1+r)$$

$r=5.0945\%$

Example

분기 복리계산 5%와 동등한 연 복리계산 이자율은 얼마인가?

Solution

$$\left(1+\frac{0.05}{4}\right)^4=(1+r)$$

$r=5.0945\%$

Example

What rate of interest with semiannual compounding is equivalent to 5% per annum with quarterly compounding?

Solution

$$\left(1+\frac{0.05}{4}\right)^4=\left(1+\frac{r}{2}\right)^2$$

$r=5.03125\%$

분기 복리계산 5%와 동등한 반기 복리계산 이자율은 얼마인가?

Solution

$$\left(1+\frac{0.05}{4}\right)^4=\left(1+\frac{r}{2}\right)^2$$

$r=5.03125\%$

Put-Call Parity

풋-콜 패리티는 동일한 기초자산에 대해 동일한 행사가격과 동일한 만기를 갖는 풋옵션가격과 콜옵션가격 사이의 균형관계이다. 만기와 행사가격이 동일한 풋옵션과 콜옵션 가격 사이에는 일정한 등가관계가 성립하는 것을 나타낸다.

It shows that the value of a European call can be deduced from the value of a European put, and vice versa.

Suppose we have a portfolio where we purchase one share of stock, one put option, and sell one call option.

The payoffs from the portfolio in either state are listed below.

If $S<X$		If $S\geq X$	
1) You hold the stock	S	1) You hold the stock	S
2) The call option is worthless	0	2) The call option is worth	$-(S-X)$
3) The put option is worth	$X-S$	3) The put option is worthless	0
Your net position is	X	Your net position is	X

No matter what state of the world obtains at maturity, the portfolio will be worth X. Consequently, the payoff from the portfolio is completely risk-free, and we can discount its value at the risk-free rate.

Using discrete discounting, this is

$$S_0 + p - c = \frac{X}{1 + r_f}$$

where S_0: current stock price

p : value of European put option

c : value of European call option

X : strike price of option

The Binomial Option Pricing Model

The stock price can either move up from S_0 to a new level, uS_0, or down from S_0 to a new level, dS_0.

$(u > 1, d < 1)$

If the stock price moves up to uS_0, we suppose that the payoff from the option is c_u.
If the stock price moves down to dS_0, we suppose that the payoff from the option is c_d.

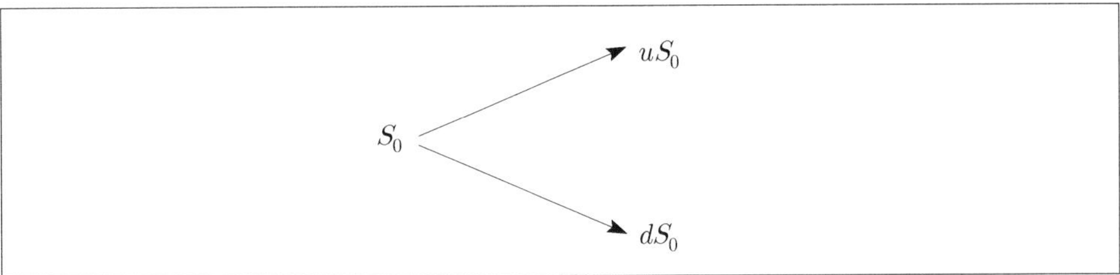

Consider a portfolio consisting of a long position in α shares of the stock and a short position in one call option.

If there is an up movement in the stock price, the value of the portfolio at the end of the life of the option is

$\alpha \times uS_0 - c_u$.

If there is a down movement in the stock price, the value becomes

$\alpha \times dS_0 - c_d$.

$\alpha uS_0 - C_u$

$\alpha S_0 - c$

$\alpha dS_0 - C_d$

$$\alpha \times uS_0 - c_u = \alpha \times dS_0 - c_d$$

The portfolio is risk-less.

The value α which solves this equation, called the hedge ratio, is given by:

$$\alpha = \frac{c_u - c_d}{uS_0 - dS_0}$$

$$\alpha = \frac{c_u - c_d}{(u-d)S_0}$$

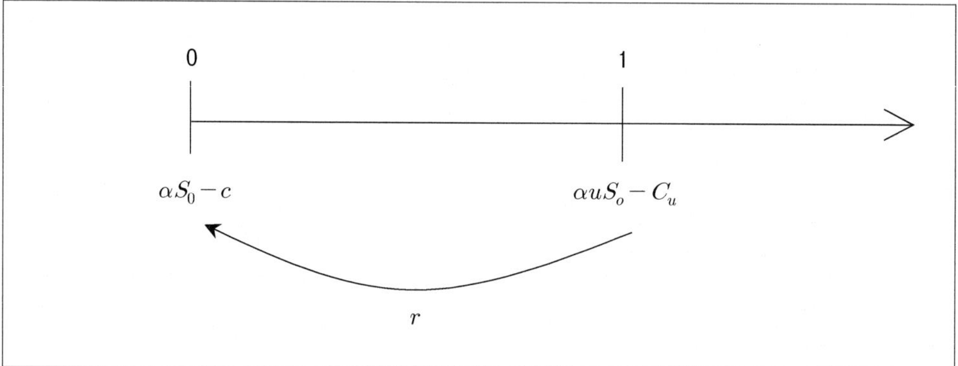

If we denote the risk-free interest rate by r, the present value of the portfolio is

$$\frac{\alpha \times uS_0 - c_u}{1+r}.$$

$$\frac{\alpha \times uS_0 - c_u}{1+r} = \alpha S_0 - c$$

$$c = \frac{\alpha(1+r)S_0 - \alpha \times uS_0 + c_u}{1+r}$$

$$= \frac{\frac{c_u - c_d}{u-d} \times (1+r) - \frac{c_u - c_d}{u-d} \times u + c_u}{1+r}$$

$$c = \frac{Pc_u + (1-P)c_d}{1+r}$$

where, $P = \dfrac{1+r-d}{u-d}$

Value at Risk

VaR is an attempt to provide a single number for senior management summarizing the total risk in a portfolio of financial assets.
The VaR calculation is aimed at making a statement of the following form:
"We are X percent certain that we will not lose more than V dollars in the next N days."

VaR는 특정 목표보유기간(target holding period)과 신뢰수준(confidence level)을 전제로 할 때, 정상적인 시장조건하에서 발생할 수 있는 포트폴리오의 최대손실예상액 추정값이다.
예를 들어, 포트폴리오의 VaR가 1일 동안 신뢰수준 95%에서 10억 원이라면, 이는 이 포트폴리오를 보유함으로써 향후 1일 동안 10억 원 이상의 손실을 보게 될 확률이 5%임을 의미한다.

신뢰수준 95%에서 1주일 동안의 VaR이 5억 원이면, 현재 포지션을 유지하는 경우 1주일 동안 발생가능한 손실이 5억 원보다 클 확률이 5%라는 의미이다.

신뢰수준(confidence level)이란 실제 거래에서 발생하는 손실이 VaR를 넘지 않을 확률을 의미한다.

VaR는 시장이 불리한 방향으로 움직일 경우 보유한 포트폴리오에서 일정기간 동안에 발생하는 최대 손실 가능액을 주어진 신뢰구간하에서 통계적 방법을 이용하여 추정한 수치이다.

Example

"99% 신뢰수준하의 10일 VaR가 5억원이다"가 의미하는 것은 "향후 10일 동안에 손실금액이 5억원 이내일 가능성이 99%이다"라는 것이다.

Delta analysis method

델타분석법은 정규분포를 가정하여 VaR를 계산하는 것으로 95% 신뢰수준하에서의 VaR는 1.65σ, 97.5% 신뢰수준하에서는 1.96σ, 그리고 99% 신뢰수준하에서는 2.33σ를 사용한다.

Continuously compounded rate of return

$$r_t = \ln\left(\frac{S_t}{S_{t-1}}\right)$$

The holding rate of return

$$r_t = \frac{S_t - S_{t-1}}{S_{t-1}}$$

$\ln y$ can be expanded in a series as

$$\ln y = (y-1) + \frac{(y-1)^2}{2} + \cdots$$

Omitting the small terms of second order and higher, we obtain the approximate equality

$$\ln y \approx (y-1)$$

$$\ln\left(\frac{S_t}{S_{t-1}}\right) = \frac{S_t}{S_{t-1}} - 1 = r_t$$

Random Walk

Consider a random walk,

$$y_t = y_{t-1} + \epsilon_t,$$

where $\epsilon_t \sim i.i.d\, N(0,1)$

The standard normal distribution has zero mean and unit variance.

If the process is started with $y_0 = 0$, then

$$y_t = \epsilon_1 + \epsilon_2 + \cdots + \epsilon_t$$

$$y_t \sim N(0,t)$$

$$y_b - y_a = \epsilon_{a+1} + \epsilon_{a+2} + \cdots + \epsilon_b$$

$$(y_b - y_a) \sim N(0,(b-a))$$

$$y_t - y_{t-1} = \varepsilon_t,$$

where $\varepsilon_t \sim i.i.d\; N(0,1)$

We could imagine partitioning the change between $(t-1)$ and t into 2 separate subperiods:

$$y_t - y_{t-1} = \varepsilon_{1t} + \varepsilon_{2t},$$

where $\varepsilon_{1t} \quad i.i.d\; N\left(0, \frac{1}{2}\right)$

$\varepsilon_{2t} \sim i.i.d\; N\left(0, \frac{1}{2}\right)$

We could imagine partitioning the change between $(t-1)$ and t into n separate subperiods:

$$y_t - y_{t-1} = \epsilon_{1t} + \cdots + \epsilon_{nt},$$

where $\epsilon_{1t} \sim i.i.d\, N\left(0, \frac{1}{n}\right)$

$\vdots$

$\epsilon_{nt} \sim i.i.d\, N\left(0, \frac{1}{n}\right)$

The limit as $n \to \infty$ is a continuous-time process known as Brownian motion.

For a general stationary AR(1) process with a constant term:

$y_t = \alpha + \beta y_{t-1} + u_t$

where α is the constant term (drift) and u_t is a white noise error term with E[u_t] = 0.

The standard form for Autoregressive process of order 1 (AR(1)) is:

$y_t = \alpha + \beta y_{t-1} + u_t$

If $y_t = \alpha + \beta y_{t-1} + u_t$, then

$y_1 = \alpha + \beta y_0 + u_1$

$y_2 = \alpha + \beta y_1 + u_2 = \alpha(1+\beta) + (u_2 + \beta u_1) + \beta^2 y_0$

$y_3 = \alpha + \beta y_2 + u_3 = \alpha(1+\beta+\beta^2) + (u_3 + \beta u_2 + \beta^2 u_1) + \beta^3 y_0$

$E(y_t) = \dfrac{\alpha}{1-\beta}$

Example

The equation provided is Autoregressive process of order 1 with a drift term:

$X_t = 3 + \dfrac{1}{2} X_{t-1} + u_t$

What is the expression for x_2 in terms of x_0?

Solution

We can find the expression for x_2 by recursive substitution:

If $y_t = \alpha + \beta y_{t-1} + u_t$, then

$y_1 = \alpha + \beta y_0 + u_1$

$y_2 = \alpha + \beta y_1 + u_2 = \alpha(1+\beta) + (u_2 + \beta u_1) + \beta^2 y_0$

$$X_2 = 3\left(1 + \frac{1}{2}\right) + \left(u_2 + \frac{1}{2} u_1\right) + \left(\frac{1}{2}\right)^2 X_0$$

Example

Consider the time series model:

$X_t = 3 + 0.5X_{t-1} + u_t$

What is the mean of this stationary process?

Solution

$$E(X_t) = \frac{\alpha}{1-\beta} = 6$$

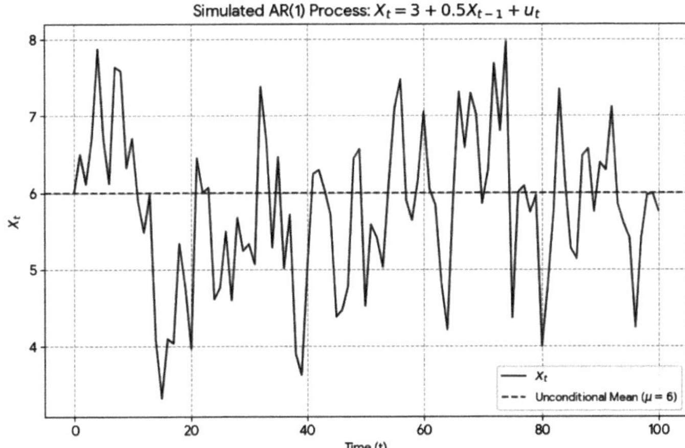

Normal Distribution

The pdf for the univariate normal distribution is

$$f(x)=\frac{1}{\sigma\sqrt{2\pi}}\exp\left[-\frac{1}{2\sigma^2}(x-\mu)^2\right]$$

If $X \sim N(\mu_X, \sigma_X^2)$, $Y \sim N(\mu_Y, \sigma_Y^2)$, and X and Y are independent, then $X+Y \sim N(\mu_X+\mu_Y, \sigma_X^2+\sigma_Y^2)$

When we add two independent normal distributions, the result is a normal distribution where the mean is the sum of the means and the variance is the sum of the variances.

Standard normal distribution

The standard normal distribution, also called the z-distribution, is a special normal distribution where the mean is 0 and the standard deviation is 1.

The probability density function of the standard normal distribution is given by the following equation:

$$f(z)=\frac{1}{\sqrt{2\pi}}e^{-\frac{z^2}{2}}$$

e is the base of the natural logarithm.

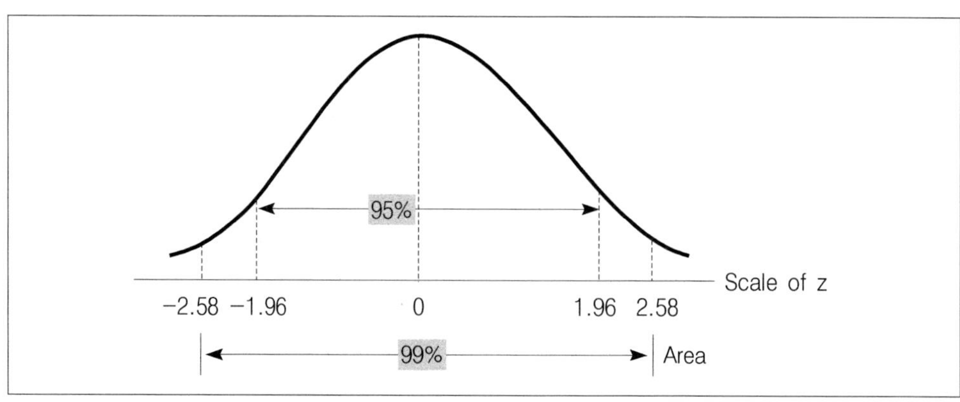

If you have a data point and you calculate its z-score and find it falls within the range of −1.96 to 1.96, you can say that it is within the central 95 percent of the data in a standard normal distribution.

For a 95 percent probability range, you want to find the z-scores for the lower and upper bounds of the range, which correspond to −1.96 and 1.96, respectively.

Any data point with a z-score falling between −1.96 and 1.96 is within the central 95 percent of the distribution, and you can be 95 percent confident that it falls within this range.

For a 95 percent probability, the upper bound z-score is approximately 1.96.

An "upper bound" refers to the maximum value within a specified interval or range for which a certain probability or likelihood is defined.

The upper bound for a probability $P(X \leq U)$ is the maximum value U within the interval for which $P(X \leq U)$ is equal to or less than the desired probability.

The probability that a z-score falls between −1.96 and 1.96 in a standard normal distribution is approximately 0.95.

If you have a data point and you calculate its z-score and find it falls within the range of −2.58 to 2.58, you can say that it is within the central 99 percent of the data in a standard normal distribution.

For a 99 percent probability, the upper bound z-score is approximately 2.58.

The probability that a z-score falls between −2.58 and 2.58 in a standard normal distribution is approximately 0.99.

Cumulative Probabilities and Z-scores

In the case of a z-score of 1.65, it's associated with a cumulative probability of approximately 0.95. This means that about 95 percent of the data falls below a value with a z-score of 1.65 in a standard normal distribution.

A Z-score of 1.65 is associated with a cumulative probability of approximately 0.95.

In the case of a z-score of 2.33, it's associated with a cumulative probability of approximately 0.99. This means that about 99 percent of the data falls below a value with a z-score of 2.33 in a standard normal distribution.

For a normal distribution, 68.26% of the observations are within +/- one standard deviation of the mean, 95.44% are within +/- two standard deviations, and 99.74% are within +/- three standard deviations.

The standard normal distribution is a normal distribution with a mean of zero and standard deviation of 1.

68.26% of data values are within 1 standard deviation of the mean.

95.44% of data values are within 2 standard deviations of the mean.

99.74% of data values are within 3 standard deviations of the mean.

68.26% of the observations will fall within 1 standard deviation of the mean, which is the interval (−1,1) for the standard normal.

95.44% of the observations will fall within 2 standard deviations of the mean, which is the interval (−2,2) for the standard normal.

99.74% of the observations will fall within 3 standard deviations of the mean, which is the interval (−3,3) for the standard normal.

Around 68% of values are within 1 standard deviation from the mean.

Around 95% of values are within 2 standard deviations from the mean.

Around 99.7% of values are within 3 standard deviations from the mean.

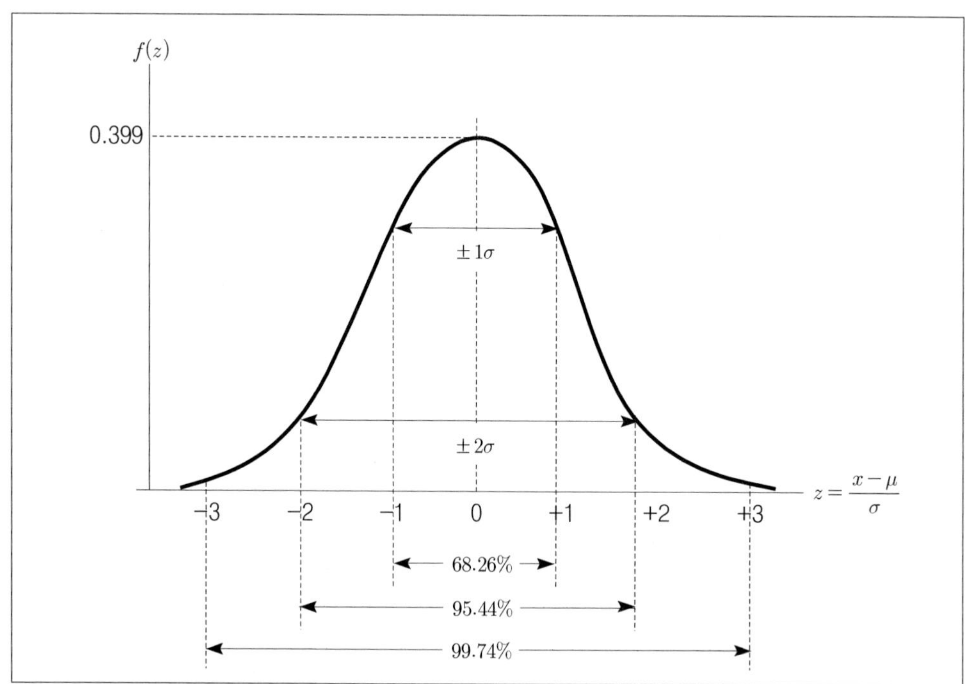

$P(\mu - \sigma \le X \le \mu + \sigma) = 0.6826$

$P(\mu - 2\sigma \le X \le \mu + 2\sigma) = 0.9544$

The z-score formular is:

$$z = \frac{X - \mu}{\sigma}$$

The Z-score formula is used to standardize a given data point within a dataset and express it in terms of standard deviations from the mean.

Example

$X \sim N(80, 16)$ 인 경우, $P(80 \le X \le 84)$를 구하라.

Solution

X를 $Z = \frac{X - \mu}{\sigma}$ 를 이용하여 표준화한다.

$$P(80 \le X \le 84) = P\left(\frac{80 - 80}{4} \le \frac{X - \mu}{\sigma} \le \frac{84 - 80}{4}\right) = P(0 \le Z \le 1) = 0.3413$$

Example

What is the z-score of x, when x = 1 and X ~ N(12,9)?

Solution

$$z = \frac{1 - 12}{3} = -3.67$$

Example

Suppose X has a normal distribution with mean 25 and standard deviation five. Between what values of x do 68.26% of the values lie?

Solution

Between 20 and 30.

Example

The scores on a college entrance exam have an approximate normal distribution with mean 52 and standard deviation 11.

About 68% of the y values lie between what two values?

Solution

About 68% of the values lie between the values 41 and 63. The z-scores are −1 and 1, respectively.

Moderation variable

In statistics and research, a moderation variable, also known as an interaction variable, is one that affects the relationship between two other variables.

In mathematics, moderation variables are commonly associated with regression analysis and modeling.

Moderation variables help us understand how the relationship between two variables changes under different conditions or levels of a third variable.

We can express this relationship using a linear regression model with an interaction term:

$$Y = \beta_0 + \beta_1 X + \beta_2 Z + \beta_3 XZ$$

Example

Let's say you're studying the relationship between two variables, X and Y, and you suspect that a third variable, Z, might influence the strength or direction of this relationship. For instance, suppose X represents the amount of studying time, Y represents exam scores, and Z represents the level of caffeine consumption. You hypothesize that caffeine consumption might moderate the relationship between studying time and exam scores.

In this case, you would include an interaction term between X and Z in your regression model to see if the effect of studying time on exam scores depends on the level of caffeine consumption.

The coefficient β_3 tells us how much the effect of studying time on exam scores changes for different levels of caffeine consumption. If β_3 is significant, it indicates that caffeine consumption moderates the relationship between studying time and exam scores.

Example

The model is:

$Y = \beta_0 + \beta_1 X + \beta_2 Z + \beta_3 XZ$

Where:

X represents the amount of studying time.

Y represents exam scores.

Z represents math scores in high school.

In this model, β_3 represents the moderation effect of high school math scores on the relationship between studying time and exam scores.

If β_3 is significant, it suggests that the effect of studying time on exam scores varies depending on the level of high school math scores. For instance, students with higher math scores in high school might benefit more from additional studying time compared to those with lower math scores, indicating a moderation effect.

표준정규분포표

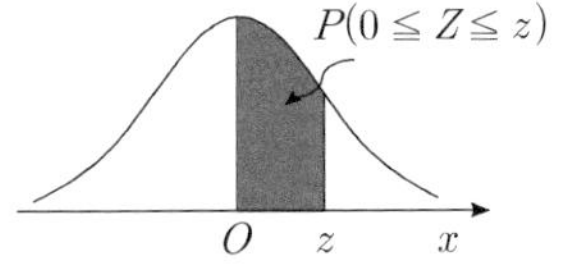

$$P=(0 \leqq Z \leqq z)=\int_0^z \frac{1}{\sqrt{2\pi}} e^{-\frac{x^2}{2}} dx$$

z	0.00	0.01	0.02	0.03	0.04	0.05	0.06	0.07	0.08	0.09
0.0	.0000	.0040	.0080	.0120	.0160	.0199	.0239	.0279	.0319	.0359
0.1	.0398	.0438	.0478	.0517	.0557	.0596	.0636	.0675	.0714	.0753
0.2	.0793	.0832	.0871	.0910	.0948	.0987	.1026	.1064	.1103	.1141
0.3	.1179	.1217	.1255	.1293	.1331	.1368	.1406	.1443	.1480	.1517
0.4	.1554	.1591	.1628	.1664	.1700	.1736	.1772	.1808	.1844	.1879
0.5	.1915	.1950	.1985	.2019	.2054	.2088	.2123	.2157	.2190	.2224
0.6	.2257	.2291	.2324	.2357	.2389	.2422	.2454	.2486	.2518	.2549
0.7	.2580	.2611	.2642	.2673	.2704	.2734	.2764	.2794	.2823	.2852
0.8	.2881	.2910	.2939	.2967	.2995	.3023	.3051	.3678	.3106	.3133
0.9	.3159	.3186	.3212	.3238	.3264	.3289	.3315	.3340	.3365	.3389
1.0	.3413	.3438	.3461	.3485	.3508	.3531	.3554	.3577	.3599	.3621
1.1	.3643	.3665	.3686	.3708	.3729	.3749	.3770	.3790	.3810	.3830
1.2	.3849	.3869	.3888	.3907	.3925	.3944	.3962	.3980	.3997	.4015
1.3	.4032	.4049	.4066	.4082	.4099	.4115	.4131	.4147	.4162	.4117
1.4	.4192	.4207	.4222	.4236	.4251	.4265	.4279	.4292	.4306	.4319
1.5	.4332	.4345	.4357	.4370	.4382	.4394	.4406	.4418	.4429	.4441
1.6	.4452	.4463	.4474	.4484	.4495	.4505	.4515	.4525	.4535	.4545
1.7	.4554	.4564	.4573	.4582	.4591	.4599	.4608	.4616	.4625	.4633
1.8	.4641	.4649	.4656	.4664	.4671	.4678	.4686	.4693	.4699	.4706
1.9	.4713	.4719	.4726	.4732	.4738	.4744	.4750	.4756	.4761	.4767
2.0	.4772	.4778	.4783	.4788	.4793	.4798	.4803	.4808	.4812	.4817
2.1	.4821	.4826	.4830	.4834	.4838	.4842	.4846	.4850	.4854	.4857
2.2	.4861	.4864	.4868	.4871	.4875	.4878	.4881	.4884	.4887	.4890
2.3	.4893	.4896	.4898	.4901	.4904	.4906	.4909	.4911	.4913	.4916
2.4	.4918	.4920	.4922	.4925	.4927	.4929	.4931	.4932	.4934	.4936
2.5	.4938	.4940	.4941	.4943	.4945	.4946	.4948	.4949	.4951	.4952
2.6	.4953	.4955	.4956	.4957	.4959	.4960	.4961	.4962	.4963	.4964
2.7	.4965	.4966	.4967	.4968	.4969	.4970	.4871	.4972	.4973	.4974
2.8	.4974	.4975	.4976	.4977	.4977	.4978	.4979	.4980	.4980	.4981
2.9	.4981	.4982	.4983	.4983	.4984	.4984	.4985	.4985	.4986	.4986
3.0	.4987	.4987	.4987	.4988	.4988	.4989	.4989	.4989	.4990	.4990
3.1	.4990	.4991	.4991	.4991	.4992	.4992	.4992	.4992	.4993	.4993

INDEX

저 / 자 / 소 / 개

❖김남곤

서울대학교 경영학과 졸업

서울대학교 대학원 경영학 석사

서울대학교 대학원 경영학 박사

동덕여자대학교 경영학과 교수

제8판 재무관리 Financial Management

저 자 김 남 곤

발행자 한 헌 주

발행처 도서출판 **경문사**

서울특별시 서대문구 독립문로 21-9

전화 738-7035 FAX. 722-4678

E-mail : kmsp@korea.com

홈페이지 : http://www.kmsp.co.kr

등 록 1995년 11월 9일 제300-1995-138호

2009년 2월 13일 초 판 발행

2026년 2월 10일 제8판 발행

• **정가 36,000원**

ISBN 978 89-420-0086-9 93320